Fund portfolio strategies performance depends on the advisor's or investor's skill in determining the strategic asset class allocations, tactical asset class allocations, the mix of underlying funds, as well as the performance of those underlying funds. Stocks and bonds can decline due to adverse issuer, market, regulatory, or economic developments. International markets may be less liquid and can be more volatile than U.S. markets. The underlying fund's performance may be lower than the performance of the asset class and fund category which they were selected to represent.

A change in one security's valuation may have a more significant impact on a fund's or portfolio's value when a portfolio or fund invests in a limited number of companies. Concentrated portfolio may have greater price volatility.

A word about risk. Global or international and/or emerging market investing involves special risks, such as currency fluctuation, political instability, different methods of accounting, different reporting requirements, interest rates, and economic. These risks may increase share price volatility. Investing in small and emerging growth companies is riskier than investing in more established companies. Investing in mid-sized companies is riskier than investing in more established companies. Government guarantees apply to underlying securities only and not to the prices and yields of a fund. The fund that invests in mortgage-back securities may increase or decrease in value more than other fixed-income funds or securities during times of fluctuating interest rates. High yield bonds or lower rated securities may provide higher returns but are subject to greater-than-average risk. High yield bonds are subject to high levels of credit and default risks. They are not guaranteed to receive back their principal investment. These risks may increase share price volatility. Municipal security funds may subject a small portion of income to state, federal, and/or alternative minimum tax. Capital gains from any type of mutual fund are subject to capital gains tax. If you are not a resident of the state to which a municipal bond fund is targeted, the state tax exemption will not apply. Sector funds invest exclusively in one sector or industry involves additional risks. The lack of diversification subjects the investor to increased industry-specific risk. Non-diversified funds that invest more of their assets in a single issuer involve additional risks such as share price fluctuation due to increased concentration. Small-cap funds invest in stocks of small companies that have greater risk of business failure and are not as well established as larger blue-chip companies. Historically, smaller-company stocks have experienced a greater degree of market volatility than the overall market average. Mid-cap funds invests in companies with market capitalization below $10 billion involve additional risks. The securities of these companies may be more volatile and less liquid than the securities of larger companies. Please see a fund's prospectus for further information regarding risk considerations. Risk is measured by using the standard deviation is a statistical measure of the volatility of the fund's returns.

The experience of the people described in this material may not be representative of the experience of all my clients. Furthermore, the experience obtained by these people is not indicative of the future experiences, which may be obtained by any of my clients.

The following copyright pertains only to Morningstar information. The Morningstar information contained herein: (1) is proprietary to Morningstar; (2) may not be copied; and (3) is not warranted to be accurate, complete or timely. Neither, Morningstar nor its content providers are responsible for any damages or losses arising from any use of this information, ©2004 Morningstar, Inc. All Rights Reserved.

IPM – *Improving Portfolio Management*™: The SECRETS of Building Wealth over Market Cycles

Patrick T. Byrne

Note for Librarians: A cataloguing record for this book is available from Library and Archives
Canada at www.collectionscanada.ca/amicus/index-e.html
ISBN 1-4120-4311-5

*Printed in Victoria, BC, Canada. Printed on paper with minimum 30% recycled fibre.
Trafford's print shop runs on "green energy" from solar, wind and other environmentally-
friendly power sources.*

TRAFFORD
PUBLISHING

Offices in Canada, USA, Ireland and UK
This book was published *on-demand* in cooperation with Trafford Publishing. On-demand
publishing is a unique process and service of making a book available for retail sale to
the public taking advantage of on-demand manufacturing and Internet marketing.
On-demand publishing includes promotions, retail sales, manufacturing, order fulfilment,
accounting and collecting royalties on behalf of the author.

Book sales for North America and international:
Trafford Publishing, 6E–2333 Government St.,
Victoria, BC v8t 4p4 CANADA
phone 250 383 6864 (toll-free 1 888 232 4444)
fax 250 383 6804; email to orders@trafford.com
Book sales in Europe:
Trafford Publishing (uk) Limited, 9 Park End Street, 2nd Floor
Oxford, UK ox1 1hh UNITED KINGDOM
phone 44 (0)1865 722 113 (local rate 0845 230 9601)
facsimile 44 (0)1865 722 868; info.uk@trafford.com
Order online at:
trafford.com/04-2118

10 9 8 7 6 5 4 3 2 1

Foreword

Aristotle understood that those who truly understand a subject have first hand knowledge of it. He believed practitioners are more likely to succeed than those without experience. This book is based on noble prize academic research, empirical evidence, and the collective knowledge of experienced professionals. It applies ground breaking portfolio management work of famous academics and Modern Portfolio Theory with time honored investment principles, investment advisory best business practices, to improve portfolio management. The information has been distilled down to its simplest form and only relevant reliable information is left allowing for a quicker read. Finally a book with sophisticated topics written in plain English! Its use of numerous graphs, bar charts, tables, and illustrations allow the reader to easily grasp pertinent concepts and points and immediately apply them in managing and advising mutual fund portfolios. The book has assembled endless research, statistics, and facts to assist you in making investment management decisions. Furthermore, it provides detailed step-by-step instructions on how to analyze the market, construct a portfolio, actively manage it, and advise clients. Foremost, this body of work has successfully been used advising and managing hundreds of millions of dollars over many market cycles at highly regarded asset management firms. Apply guidelines in the book with only mutual funds; individual securities are subject to different guidelines.

Table of Contents

Chapter Six: IPM Portfolio Construction

Chapter Seven: The Secrets to Fund Selection

Chapter Eight: IPM Portfolio Management Basics

Chapter Nine: IPM Proactive Management

Chapter Ten: IPM Equity & Fixed-income Management

The Secrets to Understanding the Securities Markets

*"Everyone has the brain power to follow the stock market.
If you made it through fifth grade math you can do it."*
-Peter Lynch, legendary portfolio manager

Understanding the Securities Market

Peter Lynch, J.P. Morgan, and Warren Buffet built wealth in all types of markets. You don't have to be best in class in order to build wealth over various market cycles. A basic, fundamental understanding of the financial markets and how they work can provide enough wisdom, investment savvy, and hindsight vision to successfully navigate a portfolio through successive market cycles.

What's the secret to understanding the market?

The first step to take is to divide it into six normal phases. Each phase is distinguishable from the others by its unique policy, fundamentals, psychology, and technical characteristics. By studying the peculiar characteristics of each, a well-informed investor can better gauge where the market is in its cycle. Knowing that much can provide helpful hints as to when it is a good or bad time to buy a particular investment. (See Exhibit 1.1).

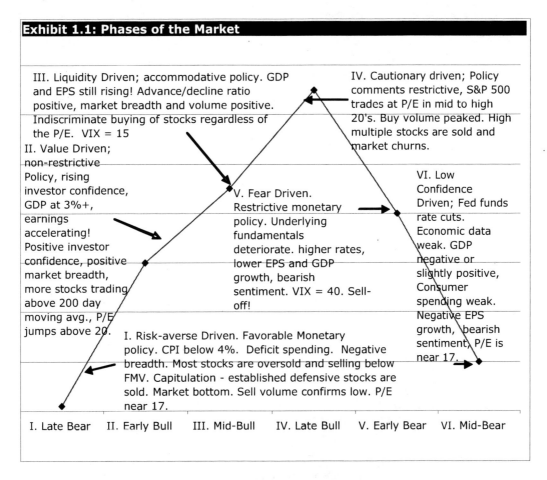

Exhibit 1.1: Phases of the Market

III. Liquidity Driven; accommodative policy. GDP and EPS still rising! Advance/decline ratio positive, market breadth and volume positive. Indiscriminate buying of stocks regardless of the P/E. VIX = 15

II. Value Driven; non-restrictive Policy, rising investor confidence, GDP at 3%+, earnings accelerating! Positive investor confidence, positive market breadth, more stocks trading above 200 day moving avg., P/E jumps above 20.

IV. Cautionary driven; Policy comments restrictive, S&P 500 trades at P/E in mid to high 20's. Buy volume peaked. High multiple stocks are sold and market churns.

V. Fear Driven. Restrictive monetary policy. Underlying fundamentals deteriorate. higher rates, lower EPS and GDP growth, bearish sentiment. VIX = 40. Sell-off!

VI. Low Confidence Driven; Fed funds rate cuts. Economic data weak. GDP negative or slightly positive, Consumer spending weak. Negative EPS growth, bearish sentiment, P/E is near 17.

I. Risk-averse Driven. Favorable Monetary policy. CPI below 4%. Deficit spending. Negative breadth. Most stocks are oversold and selling below FMV. Capitulation - established defensive stocks are sold. Market bottom. Sell volume confirms low. P/E near 17.

I. Late Bear   II. Early Bull   III. Mid-Bull   IV. Late Bull   V. Early Bear   VI. Mid-Bear

It's been said that the market is a market of stocks and not a stock market. The markets, the economy, and all investments do not move in perfectly straight lines. Instead, they veer up and down in a cyclical fashion providing investors with pockets of opportunity.

In any phase of the market's cycle, there are attractive investment opportunities even though the market, as a whole, may not be particularly attractive from a valuation or growth perspective.

Certain categories of mutual funds have historically done better than others, or even better than the overall market, in any given market phase. Knowing this means you can use the market's current phase to determine where the value may be in the market.

Equity Returns: The Recipe for Success

What's the secret of equity returns?

Equity returns, or the returns on stocks, are a function of three key ingredients: current dividend yields, earnings growth, and changes in valuation levels. Individually, the combination of these three components will result in a stock's total return. These same three components, when averaged together for a collection of stocks -- such as those of the S&P 500 Index of stocks -- result in total returns. These total returns, averaged over a set period of years, will produce an average annual return. (See the example in Exhibit 1.2).

Exhibit 1.2: Components of S&P 500 Index Returns

1) Dividend Yield	3.81%
2) Earnings Growth	7.50%
3) Change in Valuation	2.16%
Average Annual Return	**13.47%**

Source: Standard & Poor's; for 1950-2003 period. The S&P 500 Index® is a commonly used broad based index of domestic stocks. The S&P 500 is an unmanaged stock index. S&P 500 is a registered trademark of Standard & Poor's Corporation. Investors cannot invest directly in the S&P 500 Index.

A simple calculation will show that dividends accounted for more than twenty-eight percent of the return of the S&P 500 from 1950 through 2003! According to a study of corporate earnings from 1871 to 2001 done by Dr. Robert D. Arnott, and published in the February 2002 issue of *Financial Analyst Journal,* companies that paid higher dividends inevitably provided higher earnings growth rates.

The most important factor that drives equity prices is corporate earnings. While investors will invest for a variety of reasons, in general investors tend to look for companies that can grow earnings and dividends. A stock cannot justify a higher share price unless its earnings are growing.

Think of the price-to-earnings ratio (PE=P/E). A higher price (P) requires higher earnings (E). Higher growth in earnings justifies a higher stock valuation. A stock's price reflects the expectations about the company's future earnings. It can also reflect irrational and ephemeral market sentiments like optimism or pessimism at times. Generally higher corporate dividend payouts are associated with healthy companies that are growing earnings and can, accordingly, afford to pay increasing dividends.

Economic Conditions Impact Market Dynamics

Stock market valuations are also a function of expectations about economic growth. The market is always mindful about the present and future health of the economy. The stock market is driven by corporate performance. Corporate earnings are dependant on the future strength of the economy. Therefore, the stock market performance is positively correlated to the economy.

Economic growth is dependent upon a laundry list of factors, among them: sound fiscal policy, non-inflationary monetary policy, laws that encourage capitalism, business spending, household income, household spending, productivity growth, low inflation, and low unemployment. Academic studies have concluded that there is a strong relationship between employment, real income, real Gross Domestic Product (GDP), and stock prices. Healthy employment levels, growth in real income and real GDP usually is very supportive of higher stock market valuations.

What's the secret to a higher market?

Historically, global economic growth that paved the way for rising corporate profits has caused the market to advance higher over time. Peter Lynch once said that no one knows whether the next 1,000-point shift in the Dow Jones Industrial Average will be up or down, but that the next 7,000-point shift will definitely be upward because corporations will be making much more money in the future.

History has shown that long-term profits have grown in line with revenues, and revenues, in turn, have grown in line with real GDP growth. Since World War II, large-cap companies' earnings have grown at approximately 7.5% annual rate on average and have produced a an annual return of approximately 12.73%, according to First Call. Annual earnings growth does not have to equal annual GDP growth. In certain years annual earnings growth rate has slipped below the historical average yet the market has advanced based on higher earnings forecast for the next twelve months.

The Influence of Economic Growth

Companies are worth more when their earnings grow. Deregulation, free trade, a balanced Federal budget, lower tax rates, and incentives for capital investments are all conducive to lower inflation, lower real interest rates, higher economic output and fuller employment. When credit becomes cheaper, consumers and corporations borrow and spend more on goods and services. As a result, investment and capital formation increases to satisfy demand. Excess capital allows industry to expand and provide more jobs.

The effect is a self-reinforcing cycle of more work, higher per capita income, and additional investment. These all work together to bolster productivity. Greater demand for goods and services produce higher corporate earnings, which as I have already noted, provide the justification for higher stock valuations.

The economy has a tendency to grow over time pushing stock prices higher. From 1945 through 2002 there were eleven expansionary economic periods lasting, on average, 56 months. There were also eleven recession periods lasting approximately eleven months each time. GDP grew an average rate of 3.5% per quarter for the period. During an expansion GDP grew at rates of 3.5% and greater. In a recession GDP growth rate contracted and grew at a negative rate.

The obvious question is, can the market be counted on to deliver the goods all the time?

Market Gyrations: The Good, the Bad and the Ugly

While many muse that the market works in mysterious ways, in reality the market works in streaks. Consequently, market returns are inherently replete with volatility and dry spells.

The market is quite unlike a bank account which, like clockwork, post interests each day or month. It may have a couple of good days, months, quarters or even years, followed by bad spells and periods of dismal performance. In a given year, one calendar quarter could generate a full year's worth of returns, while the rest of the quarters' produce little in the way of returns. One superior year could even generate three year's worth of average annual returns.

Adding to the mystique is that one never quite knows when the market will rally. The market is very random over short periods. But over the long-term, there is a discernable pattern and identifiable cycle to it.

In the short run, market advances have occurred in erratic spurts. Historically, over longer periods, the market has advanced to higher highs, breaking right through past milestones. Also, in the past such bull markets have tended to last much longer than down, or bear markets, which, on average, have lasted a little over a year. But the descent into bear market territory was often swift and brutal. In general, the bond market's performance has historically been counter cyclical to the stock market.

What would have been the winning bet to make for long-term investors -- equity or fixed-income securities?

Betting against the market was proven to be a loser's game over the long run. In the past, the percentage of positive periods increased over longer investment horizons. In fact, from 1926-2002, the S&P 500 Index posted positive returns approximately seventy-five percent of the time over three-year rolling periods. (See Exhibit 1.3). Granted, betting on a market decline by shorting stocks over the short run can be extremely profitable. However, even the shorts must eventually go long.

The moral is that stocks were a solid long-term investment. But investors tend to ignore the past because they have been drilled to understand that past performance is no guarantee of future performance. Undeniably, present conditions often shape investors' perception of the market, despite the statistical reality.

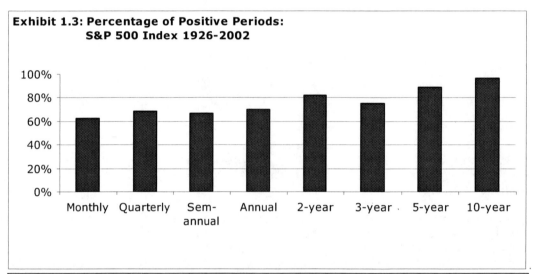

Exhibit 1.3: Percentage of Positive Periods: S&P 500 Index 1926-2002

Source: Standard & Poor's. The S&P 500 Index® is comprised of 500 U.S. stocks and is an indicator of the performance of the overall U.S. stock market. No fees or expenses are reflected in the performance of the index. An investor cannot invest directly in an index, and its results are not indicative of any specific investment. Past performance is no guarantee of future results.

Bad Stuff Happens, But Stay the Course

What other advice should be given to long-term investors?

Peter Lynch said that more money has been lost by trying to protect money from bear markets than lost in bear markets.

My advice is to not fight the long-term trend of the market. It has been more profitable to be a long-term bull. Bear markets and recessions do occur from time to time, but in today's modern day economy the economy has been growing most of the time and the markets have advanced. In the past, long-term, large-cap investors that have held tough through the sometimes dizzying ups and downs of the market have stood a better chance at earning the average market return of twelve percent from 1926-2003.

As noted earlier, since WWII there have been eleven market declines of twenty percent or more. But put into its proper perspective, that is roughly one down year for every five years of advancement! In past down markets, stocks on average lost twenty-nine percent of their value over a 15-month period, according to research from the Leuthold Group. Yet, following each bear market there has been a strong market rally. This cycle of life (and markets) continues over, and over again.

Over the longer term, stock prices have traded around their fair market value. The collective valuation judgment of millions of large and small investors determines the fair market value of a stock. However, irrational emotion rather than rational thought may influence short-term prices. That is why Benjamin Graham said that the prices of stocks are not carefully thought out computations, but rather resultants of a welter of human reactions.

The market likes certainty, just like people do. Demand is higher during times of certainty (prosperity and no wars) and lower during uncertain times (wars and recession). When times are certain it is easier to assess the fundamentals of a stock. Therefore, demand is higher and valuations typically follow.

Markets Change and So Do Risk and Return Levels

One thing is clear. Not all markets are alike. The world changes, and so does the risk affecting the market. Changes from year-to-year can be expected. Sometimes a less risky asset is riskier in a given environment than an asset that has historically been viewed as carrying more risk. The less risky one may be way overbought, and the riskier one oversold.

Short-term market conditions may cause returns and risk to deviate from historical averages. For instance, economic uncertainty often compels investors to rotate from less liquid small-cap stocks to more liquid large-cap equities. Large-cap stock returns tend to exceed their historical averages during periods of uncertainty. The conditions that cause one asset class to outperform, however, may not be present going forward. Moreover, any time an asset class becomes overvalued the expected return tends to regress to its historical mean.

In the 1970s small-cap equities produced double the returns of large-cap stocks. In the 1990s it was the exact opposite. Thus, the problem with relying on historical data is that, over shorter periods, things are less predictable. Therefore, extrapolation can sometimes lead to wrong conclusions. Remember that past performance is not indicative of future performance. That is especially true when underlying fundamentals are no longer supportive.

Wall Street tends to discount Main Street's outlook. The stock market is a forward-looking indicator of both the economy and corporate earnings. Consequently, the stock market typically leads the economic cycle by about six months. Markets rotate from sector to sector in anticipation of future conditions.

How Inflation Levels Effect Market Returns

Strong GDP growth can lead to inflation, which results in a restrictive monetary policy that produces higher rates that slow economic growth. That is why the market corrects even when there is no inflation and the economy is prosperous. The threat of an interest rate hike is enough to stall the market. Likewise, the market can advance even during an economic recession because it is predicting stronger future economic growth and higher corporate earnings.

Generally, the stock market corrects in anticipation of slower future economic growth and lower earnings, and advances before GDP and earnings improve. The market is all about expectations; yesterday is not important.

Which inflation scenario has been beneficial for market returns? The best scenario for stocks has been a period of price stability or moderate inflation. Overall, stocks have outperformed bonds during inflationary periods. The best ten-year period for stocks was 1949-1958. This was a period marked by price stability, and inflation averaged 1.86% per year. (See Exhibit 1.4).

Exhibit 1.4: The Stock Market Prefers Moderate Inflation and Hates Deflation

	S&P 500 Index	Inflation
Avg. annual return for 1926-2002 period	+13.19%	+3.96%
Worst inflationary (1965-1974)	+1.2%	+5.2%
Worst deflationary (1929-1938)	-0.89%	-1.98%
Best 10-year period (1949-1958)	+20.06%	+1.86%

Source: Federal Reserve, Thomson Financial. The S&P 500 Index is comprised of 500 U.S. stocks and is an indicator of the performance of the overall U.S. stock market. No fees or expenses are reflected in the performance of the index. An investor cannot invest directly in an index, and its results are not indicative of any specific investment. Past performance is no guarantee of future results. Inflation is represented by the CPI. CPI data obtained from The Federal Reserve.

During moderate inflationary periods, with the Consumer Price Index (CPI) ranging from 2% to 6%, stocks averaged a positive 12.08% return. Moderate inflation allows companies to raise prices, and that can have the effect of boosting profitability. Stock valuations rise as profitability increases. In contrast, fixed income payments lose value as inflation erodes them. That is why stocks are considered a hedge against inflation.

In the past, when the economy has experienced more rapid inflation, defined as the CPI hitting 6% or greater, stocks recorded a much more modest average annual return of less than 6.8%. In addition, when the CPI fell by more than 2.5%, as occurred in deflationary periods, overall stock returns fell by 6.2% on average. Deflation, the opposite of inflation, is defined as the rate at which prices for goods and services is declining.)

Exhibit 1.5: Average Annual Rates of Return on Various Asset Classes

	CPI	Stocks	Bonds	Cash
Deflation	-3.3%	- 3.3%	+ 5.2%	+4.8%
Price Stability	+1.9%	+20.1%	+ 1.4%	+1.7%
Moderate Inflation	+3.3%	+18.0%	+13.5%	+6.3%
Rapid Inflation	+8.3%	+12.1%	+ 3.1%	+4.7%

Period of study 1926-2002. Source: Morgan Stanley. Stocks are represented by the S&P 500 Index which is comprised of 500 U.S. stocks and is an indicator of the performance of the overall U.S. stock market. No fees or expenses are reflected in the performance of the index. Bonds are represented by the S&P Long-term Government Bonds index. Cash is represented by the Lehman Brothers Three-Month Treasury Bill Index derived from secondary market Treasury bill rates published by the Federal Reserve Bank or the 91-day Treasury bills data. Inflation is represented by the CPI. CPI data obtained from the Federal Reserve. Indices include reinvested income, but not transaction costs or taxes, are unmanaged and cannot be purchased directly by investors. Past performance is no guarantee of future results.

Deflation: The Stock Market's Rare -- But Fierce -- Foe

Deflation is bad news for stocks and non-investment grade bonds. That is because both asset classes rely on earnings growth to support higher price levels. Corporate earnings suffer during deflationary periods because firms have no pricing power - meaning that they cannot raise prices. In addition, although a corporation's fixed expenses remain the same, revenues may drop due to lower sales. Profit margins shrink. Furthermore, during deflationary cycles, consumers tend to hold onto their money. Thus, economic activity slows down. Less consumer purchasing generally results in less manufacturing, which causes per capita income to drop.

The good news is that deflation is a low probability event because The Federal Reserve will generally do whatever it takes to prevent it from occurring. When deflation does rear its ugly head, you can expect the Fed to aggressively lower the Fed Funds rate to flood the market with liquidity. This initiative is aimed at igniting inflation. High quality bonds are one of the better asset classes to own during deflationary bouts. Expect bond yields to drop big time during deflationary times.

It is generally not a good idea to build or solely manage a portfolio based on a deflationary scenario. Deflation is a rare event. During the modern day economy, from 1950-2003, there was only one year of deflation in 1957, according to the National Bureau of Economic Research which compiles economic data and tracks the economy. Deflation occurred during only ten calendar years since 1926, and six of those years were during the Great Depression.

The Bond Market Serves its Own Special Purpose

What about the bond market?

The U.S. Bond market is the largest and most liquid fixed income securities market in the world. The bond market segments by issuer, sector, credit quality, and maturity. There are five investment sectors: U.S. Government, Agency, Corporate, Municipals (State and local), and International (foreign bonds, eurobonds, sovereign debt, global bonds).

Certain sectors have greater risk and potential return than others. A bond is further categorized by using the yield curve to describe it as being short, intermediate, or long. The longer end of the yield curve (which includes long-term bonds) can provide higher return with greater risk than the shorter end of the curve.

Furthermore, the bond market is further segmented into investment grade bonds and non-investment grade bonds - also known as the high yield "junk bond" category.

Generally, investment grade bonds have less risk than non-investment grade bonds. Studies of non-investment grade bonds have shown that the annual dollar default rate of these so-called high yield bonds is approximately four percent. During a recession, however, the default rate can rise into the teens.

Historically, default rates have been higher for debt denominated in foreign currency than local currency. As exchange rate risk increases, the default ratio climbs. U.S. Government bonds carry virtually no credit risk because they are backed by the full faith and credit of the U.S. Government which issues them. Therefore, they are the safest bonds to own from a credit perspective. During times of crisis, investment-grade bond yields drop as prices rise due to demand driven by nervous, risk-averse investors. The opposite is true for non-investment grade bonds whose yields will rise as prices drop due to lack of demand.

Bond prices are largely determined by long-term interest rates. Current market rates determine the value of coupon payments. The present value of a bond's coupon payments determines its price. The credit quality of a company determines the coupon rate that it must offer to attract investors who serve as the lenders. Demand induced by economic activity effects yields of short-term paper. Several factors effect long-term and intermediate bond prices, including monetary policy, the fiscal health of the U.S. Government as well as public corporations, supply and demand, inflation and interest rate levels, the currency market, as well as global political and economic events.

Understanding Market Returns

"The bottom line is that stocks grow your money, bonds provide income and greater price stability, and cash offers liquidity."
-- Anonymous Investment Adviser

What can investors possibly expect to earn from investing in the stock market?

Based on statistical analysis, the expected return of a typical S&P 500 Index investment is close to twelve percent in any given year. Ninety-five percent of all annual returns tend to fall into the approximate range of -6.0% to +34%. Nevertheless, watch out for those tails – tails are the extreme market returns that infrequently occur. The remaining five percent of annual returns can really sock it to you, or put you far ahead. You can look at an investment's two- and three-year standard deviations -- to measure tail risk.

Exhibit 1.6: What Might Investors Expect to Earn From the Stock Market?

-50%	-40%	-30%	-20%	-10%	0%	+10%	+20%	+30%	+40%	+50%	+60%
					2000	1998	2003	1997			
					1990	1986	1999	1995			
					1981	1994	1979	1998	1991		
					1977	1993	1972	1996	1989		
					1969	1992	1971	1983	1985		
					1962	1987	1968	1982	1980		
					1953	1984	1965	1976	1975		
					1946	1978	1964	1967	1955		
				2001	1940	1970	1959	1963	1950		
				1973	1939	1960	1952	1961	1945		
			2002	1966	1934	1956	1949	1951	1938	1958	
		1974	1957	1932	1948	1944	1943	1936	1935	1954	
1931	1937		1930	1941	1929	1947	1926	1942	1927	1928	1933

Range in returns

Source: University of Chicago Center for Security Prices Research, for study period 1926-2003. Stocks are represented by the S&P 500 Index which is comprised of 500 U.S. stocks and is an indicator of the performance of the overall U.S. stock market. No fees or expenses are reflected in the performance of the index. An investor cannot invest directly in an index, and its results are not indicative of any specific investment. Past performance is no guarantee of future results.

Out performance over the Long Haul

Which is a better long-term investment, stocks or bonds?

That depends on many things. But we do know that stocks have outperformed the most often, even though fixed income securities have produced higher long-term returns than stocks a significant number of times.

Treasury bonds and cash have outperformed the overall stock market during periods of war, high inflation and inflated interest rates. You shouldn't be shy about owning fixed income securities during those periods.

As you will see in Figure 1.7, historically, the optimal stock holding period has been five years. Five-year rolling periods have beaten fixed-income securities 93% of the time! Three-years rolling periods have beaten fixed-income securities 72% of the time! Note that a one-year holding period is least reliable at 57%. If the stock market has outperformed fixed income securities over the most recent four consecutive years, you'd be smart to consider an over weighted position in fixed income investments.

Exhibit 1.7: Stocks Have Outperformed Most Often

Number of Times Each Category Has Had Highest Returns

Holding Period	Stocks	Bonds	Cash
15 Years	55	5	3
10 Years	56	5	7
5 Years	**68**	**4**	**1**
3 Years	54	14	7
1 Years	44	18	15

Source: Thomson Financial, Lehman Brothers, The Federal Reserve. For period ending 2002. Stocks are represented by the S&P 500 Index which is comprised of 500 U.S. stocks and is an indicator of the performance of the overall U.S. stock market. No fees or expenses are reflected in the performance of the index. Bonds are represented by the S&P Long-term Government Bonds index. Cash is represented by the Lehman Brothers Three-Month Treasury Bill Index, derived from secondary market Treasury bill rates published by The Federal Reserve Bank or the 91-day Treasury bills data. Indices include reinvested income, but not transaction costs or taxes, are unmanaged and cannot be purchased directly by investors. In addition, its results are not indicative of any specific investment. Past performance is no guarantee of future results.

So What about Risk?

Which investments have been riskier?

Have stock investments overall been riskier investments than fixed income investments?

In the past, stocks have generally had a greater variance in returns than fixed income investments. Winning stocks can definitely make more money for investors. But they can also lose more money than other major asset classes.

Over the short-term stocks are clearly risky investments and can be volatile. However, over the longer term because of the better odds of earning positive after-tax and after-inflation returns, stocks have typically proven to be less risky. Keep in mind that anytime a specific asset class is overbought, whether it is a conservative or aggressive investment type, it becomes more risky.

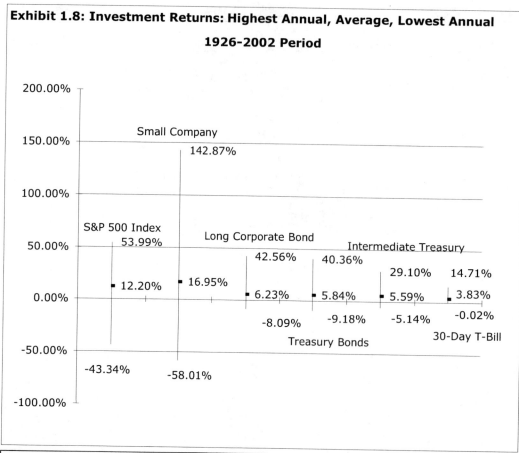

Exhibit 1.8: Investment Returns: Highest Annual, Average, Lowest Annual
1926–2002 Period

Small Company
142.87%

S&P 500 Index
53.99%

Long Corporate Bond

Intermediate Treasury

42.56%   40.36%

29.10%   14.71%

12.20%   16.95%

6.23%   5.84%   5.59%   3.83%

-8.09%   -9.18%   -5.14%   -0.02%

Treasury Bonds   30-Day T-Bill

-43.34%

-58.01%

200.00%
150.00%
100.00%
50.00%
0.00%
-50.00%
-100.00%

Source: Thomson Financial, The Frank Russell Company, Lehman Brothers, Federal Reserve. The S&P 500 Index is a commonly used broad based index of domestic stocks. The S&P 500® is an unmanaged stock index: the S&P 500 is a registered trademark of Standard & Poor's Corporation. Investors cannot invest in the S&P 500 Index directly; Small-cap stocks are represented by the Russell 2000 Index, an index consisting of the smallest 2,000 companies in the Russell 3000 index (composed of 3,000 large U.S. companies as determined by market capitalization, and which represents approximately 98% of the investable U.S. equity market); Treasury bonds are represented by the S&P Long-term Government Bonds index; Intermediate Treasury bonds are represented by the Lehman Long Treasury Bond Index, which is a 10-year Treasury note index. Treasury indices are total return indices held to constant maturities. Cash is represented by the Lehman Brothers Three-Month Treasury Bill Index derived from secondary market Treasury bill rates published by the Federal Reserve Bank or the 91-day Treasury bills data. Corporate bonds are represented by the Lehman Brothers Bond Index. The Lehman Brothers Government/Credit Index measures the performance of all debt obligations of the U.S. Treasury and U.S. Government agencies, and all investment-grade domestic corporate debt. Indices include reinvested income, but not transaction costs or taxes, are unmanaged and cannot be purchased directly by investors. This chart is for illustrative purposes only and the data does not predict or depict the performance of any investment. Past performance is no guarantee of future performance.

The Reliability Factor

Which investment, stocks or bonds, has been more reliable in producing positive returns in the short-run?

As shown in Exhibit 1.9, when you want to increase your chances of a positive return over a three-year investment horizon, stick with short and intermediate bonds and cash (ie: 30-day T-bills). High quality bonds are more reliable because in the past they have produced fewer extreme performance years as measured by the variance in annual returns and range in returns.

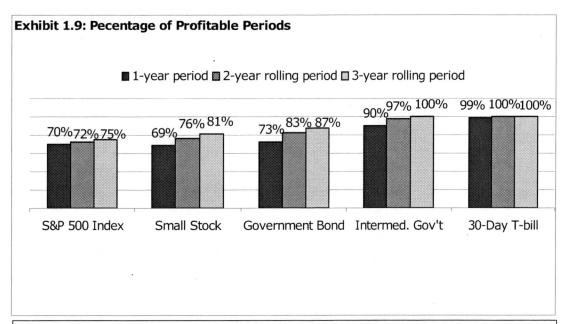

Exhibit 1.9: Pecentage of Profitable Periods

Source: Thomson Financial, The Frank Russell Company, Lehman Brothers, The Federal Reserve. The S&P 500 Index, is a commonly used broad based index of domestic stocks. The S&P 500 is an unmanaged stock index and is a registered trademark of Standard & Poor's Corporation. Investors cannot invest directly in the S&P 500 Index, nor can they invest in any other index mentioned in this book. Small-cap stocks are represented by the Russell 2000 Index, an index consisting of the smallest 2,000 companies in the Russell 3000 index (composed of 3,000 large U.S. companies as determined by market capitalization and which represents approximately 98% of the investable U.S. equity market). Government bonds are represented by the S&P Long-term Government Bonds index. Intermediate Government bonds are represented by the Lehman Long Treasury Bond Index which is a 10-year Treasury note index. Treasury indices are total return indices held constant maturities. Cash is represented by the Lehman Brothers Three-Month Treasury Bill Index derived from secondary market Treasury bill rates published by the Federal Reserve Bank or the 91-day Treasury bills data. Indices include reinvested income, but not transaction costs or taxes, are unmanaged and cannot be purchased directly by investors. This chart is for illustrative purposes only and its data does not predict or depict the performance of any investment. Past performance is no guarantee of future results.

Consider that Stocks Tend to Outperform Over Longer Periods

If we purposefully omit the 1920's and 1930's, a time of gross monetary and fiscal policy blunders, the odds of stocks outperforming other asset classes is clear. Since 1920, stocks have outperformed all other traditional asset classes, were profitable over all 15-year holding periods, and have had only 23 down years.

What's the secret to growing wealth?

In the past, a portfolio invested more heavily in stock investments than fixed income securities grew more over the long term. From 1929 to 2002, although stocks were higher risk and return investments, they tended to double in value over six years.

Exhibit 1.10 indicates that money invested in either bonds or in cash usually grows more slowly, and can take much longer to double in value than money invested in the stock market. Of course, when investing at highs in the cycle it may take twice as much time to double your money. Past performance is no guarantee of future performance.

Exhibit 1.10: Buying Stocks Improved a Portfolio's Return

Investment	Return	Years to Double
Stocks	12.2%	6
Bonds	5.84%	12
Cash	3.83%	19
Inflation*	3.14%	23

*In 23 years $1 loses half its purchasing power

Source: Standard & Poor's, Lehman Brothers, The Federal Reserve. Data for 1926-2002 period. Stocks are represented by the S&P 500 Index which is comprised of 500 U.S. stocks and is an indicator of the performance of the overall U.S. stock market. No fees or expenses are reflected in the performance of the index. Bonds are represented by the S&P Long-term Government Bonds index. Cash is represented by the Lehman Brothers Three-Month Treasury Bill Index derived from secondary market Treasury bill rates published by The Federal Reserve Bank or the 91-day Treasury bills data. Inflation is represented by the CPI. CPI data obtained from The Federal Reserve. Indices include reinvested income, but not transaction costs or taxes, are unmanaged and cannot be purchased directly by investors. Past performance is no guarantee of future results.

Which investment, stocks, bonds, or cash, left the most money in an investors pocket?

Stocks have produced the highest gross returns. Investors' actual return, of course, depends on what investors get to keep after subtracting investment expenses and taxes, and accounting for inflation.

Exhibit 1.11: Investment Returns after Inflation, Taxes and Expenses

Period	Inflation	Stocks	Bonds	Cash
1970-2002	4.92%	4.48%	1.27%	-1.27%

Source: Thornburg Investment Management. Data assumes 1% expenses; 15% Federal tax rate for stocks, 28% Federal tax rate for bonds and cash. Stocks are represented by the S&P 500 Index which is comprised of 500 U.S. stocks and is an indicator of the performance of the overall U.S. stock market. No fees or expenses are reflected in the performance of the index. Bonds are represented by the S&P Long-term Government Bonds index. Cash is represented by the Lehman Brothers Three-Month Treasury Bill Index derived from secondary market Treasury bill rates published by The Federal Reserve Bank or the 91-day Treasury bills data. Inflation is represented by the CPI. CPI data is obtained from The Federal Reserve. Indices include reinvested income, but not transaction costs or taxes, are unmanaged and cannot be purchased directly by investors. Past performance is no guarantee of future results.

Equity, Long-term bonds, intermediate bonds, and municipal bonds are the only investments that have generated an actual positive return over ten-year periods. Other investments have decreased ones wealth.

Sizing Up Bond Investments

What determines a bond portfolio's returns? There is more to the story of bond fund returns than clipping coupons. Nevertheless coupon payments are extremely important to a bond's return.

Factors Effecting Bond Returns Include:

1. Yield = #1 factor.
2. Capital gains/losses.
3. Reinvestment of dividends - earning interest on interest (the compounding effect).
4. Supply and demand.
5. Expected inflation and term structure of interest rates.
6. Sector selection (corporate bonds, Treasuries, agency bonds, etc.).
7. Credit rating (investment grade vs. non-investment grade -- junk bonds).
8. Duration (short-, intermediate-, or long-bonds).
9. Security selection (fundamentals of a company and embedded options impact volatility of the security).
10. Exchange rates (applies to foreign bonds).

In general, coupon payments typically have accounted for the bulk of a bond's return. There are many ways to make money from bonds: interest income, compounding interest, capital gains, and price appreciation from favorable interest rate swings and currency moves.

A 1999 Neuberger Berman study of the global bond market showed that income has consistently contributed over eighty percent of the total return of a bond investment, while capital fluctuation -- due to varying interest rates and currency changes -- have added to and depleted the total return over different periods. The total return of a bond held until maturity will be the coupon payments or yield-to-maturity.

Besides the reliable coupon payments, what else is attractive about bonds compared to stocks? In the past, the bond market has offered greater price stability but less growth than the stock market. You can thank the fixed coupon for the stability and lack of growth.

The average equity mutual fund declined in value in twelve of the past forty years ending in 2002, according to Lipper Inc. By comparison, the average bond fund was down only five years during this period. Bond funds declined 5.2% on average, compared to an 8.9% average decline for equity funds.

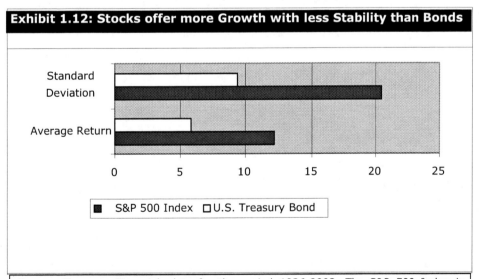

Exhibit 1.12: Stocks offer more Growth with less Stability than Bonds

Legend: ■ S&P 500 Index □ U.S. Treasury Bond

Source: Thomson Financial, data for the period 1926-2003. The S&P 500 Index is comprised of 500 U.S. stocks and is an indicator of the performance of the overall U.S. stock market. No fees or expenses are reflected in the performance of the index. Treasury Bonds are represented by the S&P Long-term Government Bonds index. Indices include reinvested income, but not transaction costs or taxes, are unmanaged and cannot be purchased directly by investors. Past performance is no guarantee of future results. Standard deviation is an indicator of the portfolio's total return volatility. The larger the standard deviation, the greater the volatility.

The Importance of Yield

Why is a bond fund's yield so important to a bond investor?

A bond mutual fund's yield is the focal point because of the current yield's contribution to total return. It is the fund's yield that compensates an investor for default risk, interest rate risk, liquidity risk, reinvestment risk, holding period, etc. Therefore, be mindful of yield differential between categories of bonds.

When yield spreads have widened beyond the historic mean, it may indicate that there is a buying opportunity presenting itself in the higher yielding bond category. But always consider the downside risks as well as the yield opportunity. A 2003 Rochester Investment Management study concluded that bond managers that produced the best total returns were successful at buying higher yielding bonds selected from all sectors, and anticipating credit rating changes.

Are bond investment returns among various categories different from one another over the long haul?

Take a close look at Exhibit 1.13. The returns between short-, intermediate-, and long-bonds of investment grade quality have been roughly the same, but the risks have been significantly greater with long-bonds.

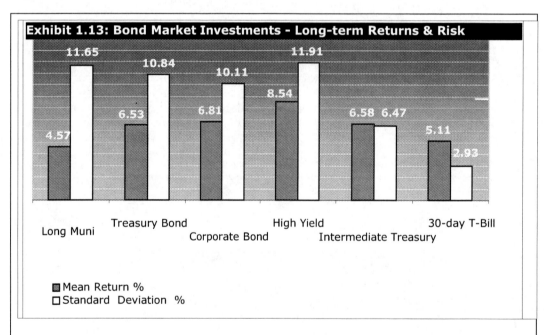

Exhibit 1.13: Bond Market Investments - Long-term Returns & Risk

Source: Lehman Brothers, The Federal Reserve, Moody's Bond Record, Salomon Brothers, Lipper Inc. Data for period 1950-2002. Treasury bonds are represented by the S&P Long-term Government Bonds index; Intermediate Treasury bonds are represented by the Lehman Long Treasury Bond Index which is a 10-year Treasury note index. Treasury indices are total return indices held constant maturities. The Lehman Brothers High Yield Bond Index includes fixed rate, public non-convertible, non-investment grade issues registered with the SEC that are rated BA1 or lower by Moody's Investor Service. Long muni is represented by Lehman Brothers Long-Term Municipal Bond index. Treasury bill is represented by the Lehman Brothers Three-Month Treasury Bill Index derived from secondary market Treasury bill rates published by The Federal Reserve Bank or the 91-day Treasury bills data. Corporate bonds are represented by the Lehman Brothers Bond Index. The Lehman Brothers Government/Credit Index measures the performance of all debt obligations of the U.S. Treasury and U.S. Government agencies, and all investment-grade domestic corporate debt. Standard deviation is an indicator of the portfolio's total return volatility. The larger the portfolio's standard deviation, the greater the portfolio's volatility. Indices include reinvested income, but not transaction costs or taxes, are unmanaged and cannot be purchased directly by investors. This chart is for illustrative purposes only and the data does not predict or depict the performance of any investment. Past performance is no guarantee of future performance.

Understanding Market Volatility

"The market creates the values, you have to recognize them." - Roy Neuberger

Should long-term investors be concerned about the day-to-day ups and downs of their portfolios?

Daily fluctuations in prices have nothing to do with the long-term trend of the market. Wall Street titan J.P. Morgan was asked what would happen to the market over the next year. He wryly replied "fluctuate."

Think of daily price volatility as "random noise." It is best to ignore this noise. It is driven by changing market perceptions that cause investors to trade "emotionally" even though they do not need their money for a long time. Often the perceived problems are not as bad as they seem or do not become a reality.

Exhibit 1.14: S&P 500 Index Average Volatility

Daily volatility: 0.55% +/- moves
Annual volatility: 5% dips occurred 256 times- roughly once every quarter.
Correction: 87 times the market has dropped more than 10% - roughly once a year
                     38 times the market has dropped more than 15% - roughly once every two years.
Bear Market: 23 times the market has dropped more than 20% - roughly once every three and a quarter years

Period of study 1926 – 2004. Source: *Wall Street Journal* period of study 2/20/1928-5/24/2004. Stock market is represented by the Standard & Poor® 500 Index, which is an unmanaged group of securities and considered to be representative of the stock market in general. An investment cannot be made directly in an index. For illustrative purposes only; not indicative of any investment. Past performance is no guarantee of future results.

Market volatility usually increases when investors worry about economic growth and market valuations, and when they become fearful. The market volatility index (VIX) reaches 40 when there is a lot of fear and volatility in the markets. When it drops into the teens, there is low volatility and complacency.

Rising volatility causes a corrective action where investors may typically flee from small-cap stocks and non-investment grade bonds to the safety of liquid investments such as cash, Treasury issues, and large-cap defensive equity issues.

The idea to keep in mind is that higher volatility is not the *cause* of a bear market, nor does it predict the market's direction, but rather it occurs during sell-offs.

Exhibit 1.15: What is the VIX Suggesting?

VIX Index Value	Market Conditions
10-20	Low volatility, market highs, complacency
40+	High volatility, market lows, fear

Source: *Wall Street Journal*

The effects of volatility tend to diminish over time. For instance, if you compare the annual, and three-year rolling period volatility of the market, the annual changes will tend to look like choppy seas in a North Atlantic storm. Over a longer three-years rolling period, you will see smaller waves found in normal seas. A ten-year period might provide a different perspective about the market altogether. It would appear much calmer.

The Anatomy of a Market Correction

If the stock market corrects should investors bail out?

Not necessarily. Corrections are a normal, healthy part of a stable and even bull, market. Moreover, they rid the market of any excess overvaluation.

Corrections are often due to a bout of investor profit taking or unfounded market jitters about growing valuations. They even occur when sound economic fundamentals exist. A major correction usually does not happen because of earnings disappointments. It would take a secondary factor, say a rise in interest rates or persistent inflation, to cause a major stock market correction.

In fact, there were seventeen market corrections of ten percent or greater from 1945 to 1999. All were due to a rise in interest rates. Ned Davis Research points out that once the S&P 500 Index had dropped by ten percent, it had a 50/50 chance of falling by another 15%, and from that point the market had a 60% chance of becoming a bear - exhibiting a decline of 20% or more. In fact, it is normal for the S&P 500 index to continue its descent, approaching the minus 30% mark after crossing the 20% decline threshold.

Typical investor behavior usually dictates that clients will ride out a stock market decline for a year before losing patience. Can the client wait a few more months or so until the market begins to recover? It can be wise to execute a "Buy & Hold" strategy when the market dips, at least until the panic selling is over and liquidity has been restored to the markets. This will help investors ride out the common 10% "V" corrections. A "V" correction is when the market dips by 10% during the year and recovers its losses in about twelve months time or shorter. "V" corrections are part of a healthy normal market if the price decline is temporary.

When the market correction is due to worsening economic fundamentals, and rising interest rates, then it may be time to take enough money off the table to provide liquidity through the current downturn. It is always smart to make any necessary adjustments in a portfolio to ensure that losses do not exceed a client's loss threshold.

Is it a Normal Correction, or a Grizzly Bear?

What are some of the warning signs that suggest that a market decline is more serious than a temporary market correction?

Here are a few common warning signs to determine if a bear market is lurking:

1. **Three steps and stumble rule**. In the past, when the Fed has aggressively raised the Fed Fund's rate, three times the market had seen a healthy correction. The Fed funds rate has to be above the "neutral rate" for this to likely occur. The neutral rate is thought to be somewhere in the range of 3.5% to 5.25%. Historically when the discount rate reached 6%, the market tumbled. In general, an increase in rates of more than 1.5% results in a greater than 20% decline in the market value of stocks from current levels.
2. **A rise in bond yields or yield spreads** is associated with a correction that can turn into a bear market decline. A sell-off in high yield bonds is a bell weather sign.
3. **Economic imbalances or unexpected external factors** can precipitate a bear market. Past examples are: sky rocketing oil prices in 1973, the Asian currency crisis in 1998, and the glut in capacity and inventory levels of 2000.
4. **Investor confidence is irrationally high**, so high that investors are willing to pay higher multiples for new issues of low quality or speculative small stocks. Watch for multiples on NYSE stocks that are trading 20% higher than the high end of the historical trading range for over twelve months, even in a low inflation environment.

5. **Technical indicators turn negative**. Watch for the number of NYSE stocks that are trading above their 200-day moving average to drop toward 50%. Another negative sign is if the VIX, the volatility index, hits 40 (see explanation of VIX above). Trouble may be brewing if the CBOE Put/Call Ratio is rising above 0.5. Other negative metrics include the short interests ratio approaching six, and the specialist's short sale ratio moving towards 50%. If the NYSE upside to downside ratio is less than one, the bear may be around the corner. Narrowing market breadth is also bad sign.

6. **Market sentiment turns negative**. If overall sentiment turns sour, investors typically stop buying on market dips. Keep your eyes on insider selling activity as it usually peaks right before the start of a bear market. Generally, executives know when their company is overvalued and when earnings will slide so they will commonly sell before others do. Also, if mutual fund cash positions increase to higher than 5%, or brokerage account credit balances are high, these can indicate a shift in market sentiment.

7. **Higher market activity in defensive stock groups**. Watch for certain quality defensive stocks to see advances while most other stocks are not moving or are declining in value. Major indexes may hit highs, but fail to advance over months of trying despite trading volume hitting record highs. You may see the market churning. That means the market is trading in a narrow range and is not advancing or declining by much. In this scenario, there's a disconnect, and good economic news does not cause the market to advance. A declining price pattern in the stock market may start to emerge.

Examining Recession Periods

Economic downturns follow bear markets. The average post-WWII recession has lasted eleven months according to the National Bureau of Economic Research. Two consecutive quarters of negative GDP growth and unemployment levels above natural unemployment (5%) do not, by themselves, define a recession. As GDP is often revised, to accurately determine if the economy is in a recession, many economists examine a wider range of indicators of the economy's health than just GDP. The National Bureau of Economic Research defines a recession as a prolonged slump in four "coincident" indicators of a recession. These are:

1. Employment
2. Manufacturing
3. Personal income
4. Business (wholesale) and retail sales

What is believed to have caused most recessions?

The culprit of most past economic recessions has been higher interest rates. Such changes have occurred when The Federal Reserve aggressively raised the federal funds rate in response to an unanticipated change in inflation.

Exhibit 1.16: Rising Interest Rates Pushed the Economy into a Recession

Period	Return on DJIA	Reason
1961-1962	-27.1%	Inflation, Fed increased interest rates
1966	-25.2%	Inflation, Fed increased interest rates
1968-1970	-35.9%	Inflation Fed increased interest rates
1973-1974	-45.1%	Oil Shock, inflation, Fed raised rates
1976-1978	-26.9%	Inflation Fed raised interest rates
1981-1982	-36.1%	Inflation Fed raised interest rates
1987	+ 1.0%	U.S. $ lost value and Fed increased rates
1990	-21.2%	Fed increased interest rates
2001	- 7.10	Technology bubble burst; business spending halted

Source: Dow Jones. 1960-2001 period of study. The Dow Jones Industrial Average® index is an unmanaged group of 30 "blue-chip" U.S. stocks. It is not a diverse index. An investment cannot be made directly in an index. For illustrative purposes only, not indicative of any investment. Past performance is no guarantee of future results.

When should rate hikes cause concern?

The market climbs a wall of worry and worries more as interest rates rise higher and higher. As the stock market's cycle matures, it may be cause for concern about underlying fundamentals. By the mid-bull market phase of the market's life cycle, interest rates may be rising. Higher rates can weaken fundamentals and undermine the case for higher valuations.

Pay attention to the "wicked fours" as I call them. The fours, as defined below, will provide some clues as to where interest rates might be headed. When the fours are deteriorating, then fundamentals will eventually fail to support higher valuations. A correction may then be imminent.

Interest rates tend to RISE when:

1. Higher GDP than historical trend line-GDP growth exceeds 4%.
2. Accelerating Producer Price Index (PPI) . When wholesale price increases can be passed onto the consumer then overall inflation may rise. In response the Fed may raise the Fed Funds rate.
3. CPI - inflation trends towards 4%. Again the Fed is likely to tighten when inflation breaches 4%.
4. Lower unemployment - unemployment approaches 4%.

Interest rates tend to FALL when

1. GDP growth falls below 3.0% for 4 consecutive quarters and continues to trend lower.
2. CPI falls below 4%.
3. Weekly unemployment claims are above 400,000.

Just remember: Don't be too quick to head for the sidelines. Paul Samuelson, the Noble Laureate in Economics, once said, "Stock market declines had anticipated nine of the last five recessions." Of course, what he meant was that a market decline doesn't always point to a concrete recession in the making.

Exhibit 1.17: Average Length of Time and Mean Return of a Bull and Bear Market

	Length	Cumulative Return
Bull Market	30 months	+154.0%
Bear Market	9 months	- 33.0%

Source: Ned Davis Research. Period of study: 1926-2003. Market represented by the Standard & Poor's 500 Index, which is an unmanaged group of securities and considered representative of the U.S. stock market in general. An investment cannot be made directly in an index. For illustrative purposes only; not indicative of any investment. Past performance is no guarantee of future results.

When the Bottom Falls Out

What's there to know about market bottoms?

The secret behind market bottoms is that the market rarely "V" bottoms, meaning that the market doesn't usually hit a low point then clearly start its ascent again. Usually the market will retest its low after hitting bottom. In four of the last eleven bear markets, the market has hit a perceived bottom only to sell off further. Most bottoms look more like a "W" where the bottom is retested.

False bottoms can and do occur when investors become optimistic after deep rate cuts, but where the economy remains weak. Ned Davis Research noted that a market turnaround usually is book ended by 90% days - 90% of dollar and share volume is down in one day and followed by 90% of dollar and share volume being up the next day. An advance of 20% off a market low signifies a new bull market.

Historically, the stock market has bottomed out approximately six months before the economy hit its bottom level, and then started to rally while the economic news was still bad.

The Eight Signs of a Possible Market Bottom are:

1. Lower P/E ratios that are below or closer to the historical average of 15 for large-cap stocks (maybe higher in non-inflationary times).
2. Number of months since the economic downturn began. The average recession since 1950 lasted for about a year according to NBER.
3. An acceleration in money supply growth.
4. An improvement in market breadth.
5. Defensive stock selling has ended.
6. Low inflation.
7. Relatively low interest rates.
8. A marked change in consumer confidence and spending.

The good news is that a bull market has always followed a bear market in the past. Once in the midst of a bear market the best tact to take may be to stay the course given that your portfolio has sufficient liquidity. From February 20, 1928 to May 24, 2004, the average bear market lasted less than a year according to Ned Davis Research. In the past it has taken, on average, two years to recoup losses suffered from the market high. Hard as it might be, when in the clutches of a grizzly bear market, the best medicine is often to wait it out. Only the benefit of hindsight can tell when the bear will resume hibernation and a new bull market will emerge.

After the Bottom: The Bull Market Returns

In the past the reward has been plentiful for investors that weathered the storm. Exhibit 1.18 shows the stock market returns after a market bottom has occurred. In the past, market recoveries did not level off until almost two years after the market bottomed out. Note that most of the best days (highest daily return) have occurred in a bear market or within the first two months of a bull market according to Ned Davis Research.

Exhibit 1.18: It is Always Darkest Before the Dawn

The S&P 500 Index Gains *After* the Market Bottom

Recession	1st 6-months	1st 12-months
1969-70	24.02%	43.73%
1973-75	30.88%	38.01%
1981-82	45.41%	58.33%
1990-91	27.81%	29.10%
2002-03	13.70%	33.09%

Source: Thomson Financial. Past performance is no guarantee of future results. The S&P 500 Index is comprised of 500 U.S. stocks and is an indicator of the performance of the overall U.S. stock market. No fees or expenses are reflected in the performance of the index. An investor cannot invest directly in an index, and its results are not indicative of any specific investment. Past performance is not a guarantee of future performance.

When has historically been a good time to increase stock exposure?

The early bird catches the worm. A bulk of the returns in past bull markets have occurred in the first twelve months of the early phase of a new bull market. A study from The Center for Research in Security Prices concluded that of the markets from 1929-2003, by missing the earliest months of a bull market investors lost as much as 40% of that bull market's total returns. Up to six months of positive trends with key factors should be enough good news to take action.

Exhibit 1.19: Investors that Missed the Bull Market Start Also Missed Out on Returns.

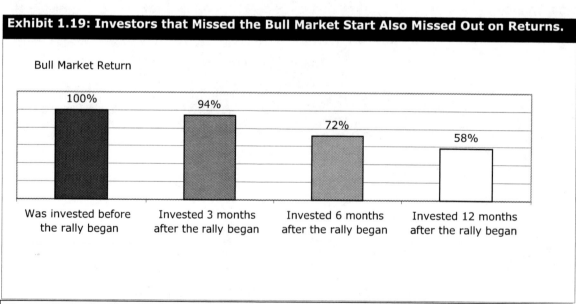

Source: Center for Research in Security Prices; Univ. of Chicago; Used with permission; all rights reserved, 1929-2003 period. Period of study 1926-2003. Market represented by Standard & Poor's 500 Index®, which is an unmanaged group of securities and considered to be representative of the stock market in general. An investment cannot be made directly in an index. For illustrative purposes only and not indicative of any investment. Past performance is no guarantee of future results.

The Secrets to What Drives the Markets

"History does not repeat itself, but it sure rhymes." - Mark Twain.

Market "Noise" vs. Vital Info

You are welcomed to bury yourself in the endless economic and market data available today. But let me let you in on a big secret: Twenty percent of the information available will tell you eighty percent of what you need to know.

There are a few major economic and market factors that affect the securities market's direction over meaningful periods. The rest, especially the weekly reports, are overkill for fund portfolio management purposes and can be considered distracting "noise."

Much of the information found in those reports is rolled up into the major reports that are subsequently released. In my opinion, trading based upon minor "weekly" reports that are frequently revised is quite speculative. I would rather get confirmation from a series of major reports that have clearly established a cyclical trend before making investment decisions.

Keep in mind, fund portfolio management is not like trading or buying individual stocks. Nor does it concentrate into specific industries or a single issuer.

What other secrets should you know about?

Research indicates that the factors that drive the stock market and bond prices are systematic. This is especially true with diversified fund wrap portfolios because specific unsystematic factors that affect individual securities are diversified away.

As a practical guide know what's happening with four top four factors and their underlying reports. P.F.P.T is what drives market valuations. The reports that make-up the P.F.P.T's should tell you eighty percent of what you need to know. These top factors influence the money supply, economic activity, and security prices.

What Determines Market Valuations? *The Top Four Factors are: P.F.P.T's!*

1. **POLICY** - monetary policy and fiscal policy
2. **FUNDAMENTALS** - macro-economic and market fundamentals
3. **PSYCHOLOGY** - investor psychology and consumer psychology
4. **TECHNICALS** - technical indicators

Exhibit 2.1 below shows how it works. Very simply put, "'Policy" drives the "Fundamentals" (inflation, interest rates) that in turn influence the "Psychology" that drives the stock market. The "Technical" indicators reflect "Psychology." In order to identify current trends, one can develop market analysis that summarizes the direction of these top four factors (P.F.P.T)

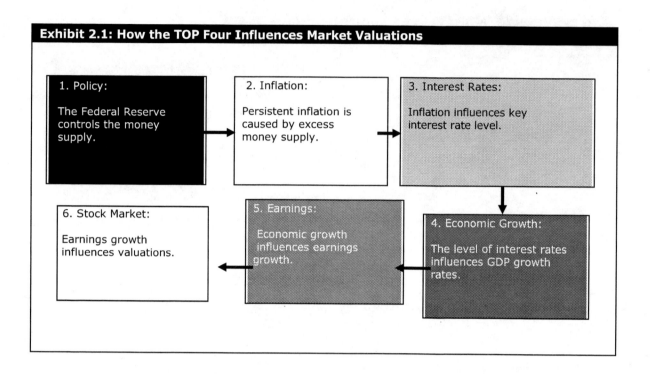

Exhibit 2.1: How the TOP Four Influences Market Valuations

1. Policy:

The Federal Reserve controls the money supply.

2. Inflation:

Persistent inflation is caused by excess money supply.

3. Interest Rates:

Inflation influences key interest rate level.

6. Stock Market:

Earnings growth influences valuations.

5. Earnings:

Economic growth influences earnings growth.

4. Economic Growth:

The level of interest rates influences GDP growth rates.

Geopolitical risk, which is not mentioned here, tends to move markets over the short-term. Nevertheless it must also be considered along with the top four factors.

#1 Policy: Understanding Monetary and Fiscal Policy

Let's begin with monetary policy because the flow of money will ultimately, down the line, determine security prices. Why is monetary policy the leading factor affecting the markets?

The Power of the Federal Reserve Board

The Federal Reserve Board's (Fed) policy decisions influence all other factors either directly or indirectly. The Fed is in charge of monetary policy. It controls the money supply by setting short-term interest rates, but the Fed has no control over long-term interest rates. The market supply, demand for credit, and inflation expectations all factor in to determine long-term interest rates.

What is the objective of Fed policy? The Fed's goal is to establish price stability while fostering the highest level of non-inflationary economic growth. The Fed's goal is to maintain annual GDP growth at moderate levels of about 3.25% while keeping inflation at about three percent. The key to anticipating probable Fed actions lies in understanding what causes inflation and being able to identify threatening trends that can cause persistent inflation.

Why is keeping a lid on inflation so important to the Fed?

Generally moderate price stability -- not disinflation or higher inflation -- results in lower unemployment, greater productivity, and higher per capita income. Low inflation makes it easier for businesses and households to make future plans, it contains cost, forces businesses to become more efficient and productive, and drives interest rates lower, which makes credit more available and cheaper to obtain. These conditions generally allow for overall economic growth.

In the past, expansionary monetary policy that resulted in rapid growth of money supply only produced higher inflation without increasing real output and bolstering employment. Historically, uncontrolled money supply growth tends to end with a recession.

The Inverse Relationship between Interest Rates, and the Market

How does the Fed control the money supply to stem inflation?

The Fed raises or lowers short-term rates as it sees fit. The Fed either assumes a restrictive (higher fed fund's rate) or non-restrictive (lower fed fund's rate) monetary policy to control money supply and economic growth. The Fed uses the fund's rate to implement monetary policy.

The federal fund's rate is the key monetary tool used to control short-term interest rates. The Fed's normal fed fund's rate is usually two percentage points above the inflation rate. When the fed fund's rate is below the inflation rate or approximately equal to it, monetary policy is accommodative. Economists estimate that for every 100 basis points increase in the Federal Funds rate, GDP growth is reduced by six-tenths of a percent. By lowering and raising the federal fund's rate along with Federal Open Market Committee (FOMC) actions of buying and selling U.S. Treasury bonds, the Fed seeks to control the supply of money that effects short-term interest rates, economic activity, and inflation.

When the Fed buys Treasury bonds, banks obtain more reserves. This allows banks to loan more money. Rates fall with greater money supply. When the Fed sells Treasuries, there is less money to lend by the banks and rates rise.

Any time money supply grows short-term rates fall, and when money supply shrinks rates rise. Therefore, money supply influences interest rate levels that in turn affect economic activity. More money in circulation creates the liquidity the economy needs in order to operate and grow. Greater money supply also causes consumer rates to fall. Lower consumer rates produce greater demand for goods and services.

There is an inverse relationship between the level pf interest rates and the markets. Historically, lower interest rates have brought about rising markets and high enough rates often lead to down markets. Falling rates produce greater purchases of goods and services. More sales produce higher corporate earnings growth that supports higher market valuations of corporate stocks. After consumption has been satiated, excess liquidity often finds its way into the stock market driving up stock prices regardless of valuation. This is called a liquidity-driven market.

The Importance of Liquidity

Liquidity is one of the most important factors to watch because it overrides other important factors that normally drive the markets. Monitor the growth rate of MZM - the broadest measure of the money supply. It includes:

- M1 (coins and paper, checking deposits, travelers checks);
- M2 (savings deposits less than $100,000 and money market mutual fund shares);
- M3 (time deposits in excess of $100,000, overnight loans, Eurodollar deposits of U.S. residents).

Other liquidity measures to watch are: fund cash inflows, assets in money market funds, and mutual fund cash positions.

Generally, money supply growth moves stock prices higher and bond prices lower. Studies have shown that there is a high correlation between liquidity and the performance of the NASDAQ Composite and Wilshire 5000 stock indexes.

Interest Rates on the Move

A rise in short-term interest rates rise typically has a domino effect on other economic factors that can eventually cause economic activity to slow down. Fed Fund's rate hikes cause borrowing to become more costly. The higher cost of borrowing slows down the growth in the money supply and economic activity. Usually, an increase in mortgage rates causes a decline in mortgage applications, and a decline in housing construction starts. To throw salt on the wound, adjustable rate mortgages cut away at disposable income as mortgage payment rises. Higher rates dampen consumer spending which results in lower retail sales. This could cause inventory to build up at stores that may force manufacturers to cut back on production. The end result could be lower profits, lower income, and possibly layoffs. That would bring us to higher unemployment but less inflationary pressure (commodity prices fall and labor cost is restrained). (See Exhibit 2.2.)

The opposite (cheerier scenario) typically occurs when interest rates drop.

Exhibit 2.2: How Monetary Policy Interacts with Interest Rates, GDP and Inflation

1. The Federal Reserve's FOMC Operations: Treasury purchases cause rates to fall, while selling increases rates. When Fed Fund's rate is increased short-term interest rates rise; conversely when it is decreased, short-term rates decline.

5. GDP and inflation increases in a lower rate environment. While GDP and inflation declines in a higher rate environment.

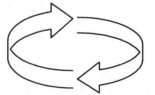

2. When the Fed requires higher **bank reserves**, short-term rates rise. Rates fall when the Fed requires lower bank reserves.

4. Private and public spending and consumption increases with low rates and decreases as rates climb.

3. An increase in **money supply** causes lower consumer rates and when it is decreased, higher rates occur.

The Market's, and Economy's, Reaction to the Fed's Bias

     The market anticipates the Fed's decisions about whether to raise or lower rates. That anticipation will send the market either higher or lower before the Fed takes any action. When the Fed talks about slowing the economy, the market sells off creating higher yields. Stock prices typically follow the direction of bond prices. Security prices discount the anticipated rate hike. The Fed will later affirm the market action by raising the Fed Fund's rate.

     Generally, monetary policy effects the markets immediately because indexes are forward indicators. Price adjustments are based upon expectations of future economic growth. But the overall economy is considerably slower in its reaction time.

     As shown in Exhibit 2.3, looking at data from The Federal Reserve from November 1970 to December 2003, the market has appreciated, on average, 21.6% during the average twenty-six month period it took to ease rates. It took more than a year for monetary policy changes to have an effect on GDP, productivity, employment, and prices. The effect on inflation involved even longer lags.

     The Fed lowered the Fed Fund's rate nine times between 2000 and 2003, from 4.5% to one percent, and it took until 2003 for the economy to respond. A typical restrictive period has run, on average, eighteen months and the market has returned 4.5% on average for the period of study. Historically, once the Fed began raising the Fed Fund's rate, the Fed Fund's rate has climbed 300 basis points, on average, over the last eleven tightening cycles. The range has been one percent to five percent, on average, based on the past eleven tighten cycles.

     Most economists hold that a "neutral" Fed Fund's rate lies somewhere in the 3-3/4 to 5-1/4 percent range or within a percentage point or two to the current inflation rate. Over the past 40 years ending 2004, the federal funds rate has averaged 2.0 percentage points above inflation. That is to say that within this range, money is neither too cheap nor too expensive to borrow, and the economy has ample money to operate and growth at a 3.5 percent rate without inflation becoming an issue.

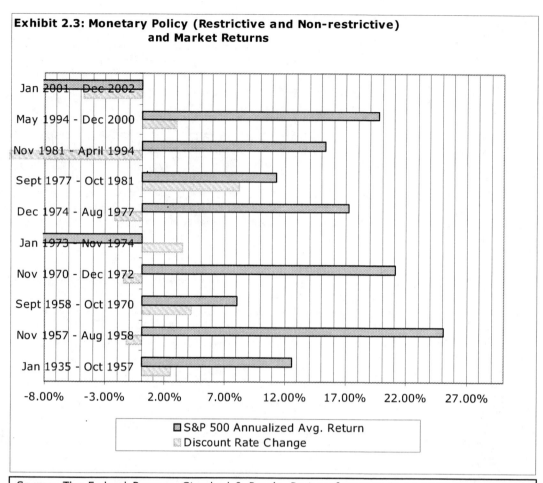

Exhibit 2.3: Monetary Policy (Restrictive and Non-restrictive) and Market Returns

Source: The Federal Reserve, Standard & Poor's. Past performance is no guarantee of future results. The S&P 500 index is comprised of 500 U.S. stocks and is an indicator of the performance of the overall U.S. stock market. No fees or expenses are reflected in the performance of the index. An investor cannot invest directly in an index, and its results are not indicative of any specific investment

How Fiscal Policy Weighs into the Equation

Why is Fiscal policy one of the top factor's that effect the market?

Fiscal policy (spending and taxing by the Federal government) has a great influence on GDP, inflation, and employment. Federal spending creates jobs that could increase employment, income, and economic growth. A Federal policy that lowers tax rates facilitates higher spending that might increase employment, income, and economic activity. A policy that balances the Federal budget lowers interest rates, a factor which is conducive to economic growth.

Fiscal policy is most effective when applied in a counter cyclical fashion. During a recession, the government may spend more and cut taxes. When there is inflationary growth, it may spend less and raise taxes.

But an overall fiscal policy is difficult to execute and there are precise timing problems and lag effect difficulties. Often the medicine is administered too late, or proves to be too much. That is why critics of fiscal policy often caution that fiscal policy changes should not be used to smooth the business cycle. Instead, they argue, the Government should rely on automatic stabilizers such as unemployment compensation, progressive personal income tax, and corporate taxes to create deficit spending (Federal expenditures exceed tax revenues) in recessions, and deficit surpluses (tax revenues that are greater than expenditures) when the economy grows in real terms.

Are Federal budget deficits good or bad?

The answer is a dichotomous yes -- and no.

A Federal budget deficit can potentially drive up interest rates, choking off further economic growth. As the Federal government borrows more to fund expenditures it competes with the private sector for loan money. The law of supply and demand takes hold. Greater demand for funds drives the cost of funds higher. A Federal Reserve study concluded that each percentage point increase in the ratio of deficit to gross domestic product caused long-term interest rates to rise by a quarter percentage point.

However, higher expenditures can also fuel economic growth that increases tax revenues that help pay down the governmental debt and can thrust the budget into the black. Budget deficits are okay to run as long as they produce the intended effect - economic growth. But at some point they can tend to hurt the economy more than help. That is to say, they cause the economy to contract.

What's the bottom line? It is okay to run a deficit in a recession, but once out of that recession, reduce deficit spending to zero as soon as possible. A balanced budget does not promote inflation and higher rates.

#2 Fundamentals: Macro-economic and Market Fundamentals

What major economic and market reports effect the markets?

There are eight key fundamentals to track, as explained in more detail below. As you are tracking normal cyclical trends that have exhibited themselves in past business and market cycles, you can make investment decisions based upon trend analysis.

Remember that monetary policy drives the "**I**"s (inflation and interest rate levels) and that these "**I**"s drive the "**E**"s (economic growth and earnings growth). Therefore, closely watch the trend in inflation and real interest rates because they can have a big impact on GDP, which can consequently effect earnings growth and employment.

The market requires solid fundamentals to justify higher price levels. Generally, economic reports that meet expectation cause no market reaction. The market anticipates news and already discounts news into securities' prices before the release. Be wary of relying on short-term monthly data because of frequent revisions. Jumping the gun often leads to a false start. It usually takes four or more months to establish a real trend.

1. INFLATION

Measuring Inflation

The Consumer Price Index (CPI) measures retail price inflation, and the Producer Price Index (PPI) measures wholesale price changes. The CPI is a market basket of 364 items that includes volatile energy and food prices. The CPI measures overall inflation in the economy, and how fast consumer prices are rising. You can assess inflation by using either the "All Item" CPI (See Exhibit 2.4), or the "Core" CPI rate. But remember that inflation indicators tend to underestimate the true cost-of-living because not all categories of expenses are tracked.

Exhibit 2.4: Components of "All Items" Inflation (CPI)			
* Food and Drinks	*Medical Care	* Apparel	* Energy
* Housing	* Transportation	* Entertainment/other	* Food

The core CPI rate provides a more reliable barometer of the trend. The core rate is better to use from month to month than the "All Item" because it excludes volatile energy and food prices that are seasonal and can spike up for brief periods without turning into long-term trends.

Reacting to a temporary blip in the core CPI may cause someone to make an inaccurate assumption and, consequently, make the wrong investment choice, when energy and food prices are included. However, the more inclusive "All Item" CPI is a better long-term indicator because the more money consumers spend on energy and food the less they have to spend on all other goods and services.

Rising labor cost is a key indicator of inflation. The Employment Cost Index (ECI) measures labor cost. The ECI is the broadest measures of wage, salary, and benefit cost. Labor counts for as much as seventy percent of inflation, while commodity inflation accounts for the rest. When labor costs rise, there is more pressure for firms to raise prices to cover this rising cost. However, productivity gains can offset an employer's need to respond to rising labor costs by increasing prices.

The Influence of Money Supply

Traditionally, excess money supply has been at the root of inflation in the economy. Whenever there has been more money in circulation than is required to operate the economy, the excess money ends up chasing fewer goods or limited services, which drives up prices. This can be a temporary phenomena as production catches up with demand over time, but it is usually tempered by a bout of inflation before this happens.

Whenever, the Fed funds' rate is relatively low or even negative (the Fed funds' rate minus inflation) for a prolong period of time, the potential for inflation builds as the system gets overloaded with money. Everyone borrows more when money is cheap, so remember to keep a sharp eye on the money supply in order to monitor the inflationary threat. MZM or M3 are the key money supply measures to watch. High single or double-digit growth of these measures can be troublesome when conditions do not warrant easy money.

The Inflationary Pressure Cooker

What else has caused inflationary pressure?

When the economy operates at or near capacity, bottlenecks in production generally occur. Bottlenecks can be expected to happen when firms operate at greater than 85% of capacity. In addition, shortages and efficiencies start to develop causing a strain on productivity. In 1994, the capacity utilization rate was at 85%. That was one reason, among many, that led the Fed to raise interest rates an astounding seven times within twelve months -- to slow down consumer demand.

Could a growing current account deficit precipitate inflation?

Current account measures the exchange of goods and services, investment income, and transfers, between the U.S. and foreign countries. A high current account deficit means that there is an excess amount of U.S. dollars. In effect, there is low demand for the U.S. dollar. A current account deficit causes the dollar to weaken, fueling imports to carry higher prices.

World supply capacity has some impact on keeping inflation low. But alone, greater capacity cannot keep it low. A current account deficit is conducive to a lower dollar that may create inflationary pressure. A large portion of what is bought in the U.S. isn't produced abroad (healthcare and housing, for example). Foreign exchange rates can also lower prices.

Predicting Inflation

Inflation is hard to predict. Gold is not a good indicator of inflation because it has historically had a low correlation with inflation since 1985. In 2002-2003 when inflation was approximately two percent, gold prices rose above $375.

The Producer Price Index (PPI) is a good leading indicator of inflation because as it rises, inflation confronts the consumer. Fed policy-makers pay close attention to the personal consumption expenditure (PCE) price index. The PCE is a monthly inflation gauge based upon consumer spending, which excludes volatile food and energy prices. The Fed likes it to be between one and two percent.

The truth is that there is not one single report alone that can consistently forecast inflation. Each measure, PCE, M1, ECI unemployment rate, capacity utilization, has its drawbacks. Therefore, it is prudent to use a variety of measures to assess inflationary trends and the future inflation.

Stocks have performed well during moderate inflationary periods. Moderate inflation tends to be good news for stocks because companies may be able to raise prices, thereby increasing profit margins. Profit growth does not always come from sales growth, cost cutting, or increases in productivity. Raising prices while keeping costs and sales level will increase profit.

Inflation averaged 3.96% a year from 1950-2002 according to the NBER. Historically, CPI levels of more than five percent tend to drive down bond and stock prices.

2. INTEREST RATES

The Impact of Interest Rates

Do interest rates have a big impact on economic growth, company earnings, valuations, and the capital markets?

You bet they do! Generally, there is an inverse relationship between interest rates and economic growth. If interest rates rise high enough economic growth will slow down and vice versa if they fall low enough.

Stocks tend to respond well to lower interest rates because low rates produce greater economic activity. As interest rates drop consumer spending picks up due to cheaper borrowing costs. Capital investment also increases. Greater demand for goods and services boost earnings and, in response, security prices rise. As security prices rise, household wealth increases which stimulates even more household spending.

The dollar generally weakens under non-restrictive monetary policy, and exports typically increase as U.S. goods become cheaper to buy by foreigners. That usually fuels even greater GDP growth. The Fed model suggests that the key factor influencing the market P/E is the level of interest rates.

Moving and Shaking the Rate

What factors determine interest rate levels?

As discussed in greater detail earlier in this chapter, monetary policy determines short-term rates. Inflation expectations and risk premium demands influence the level of long-term rates. Nominal interest rates (inflation plus real interest rates) tend to rise with inflation. Rapid expansion in money supply will eventually increase inflationary pressure that will lead to higher rates. Greater GDP growth coupled with inflationary pressure generally leads to higher market yields and borrowing rates (Federal Funds' rate, prime rate). The 10-year Treasury bond, Mortgage Rates, and Federal Funds' rate all work to determine the credit-sensitive demands for housing and autos. When these rates steadily rise, you can generally expect the economy to eventually slow down and the stock market to see a gradual cooling off. Over the past 40 years ending in 2004, the 10-year Treasury yield has averaged 2.8% points above CPI inflation. If CPI inflation rise by one percentage point then one could expect yields to rise proportionally.

A Brick Wall for the Bull Run?

Will higher interest rates necessarily mean a quick end to a Bull market?

No, if rates rise just enough to keep a lid on inflation without slowing down economic growth and earnings growth.

A Ned Davis Research study of the Dow Jones Industrial Average (DJIA) from 1917 to 2003 shows that after a first interest rate hike, the DJIA closed out, on average, eight percent higher twelve months later. After a second interest rate hike, the DJIA rose three percent, on average. After the third hike, it rose another three percent, on average. It is not until the fourth hike in interest rates, that the DJIA fell, on average, three percentage points over the next twelve months.

However, the answer to this question -- can higher interest rates mean a quick death to a bull market? -- can be yes, if inflation is persistent, and interest rates are increased deeply enough to choke off economic growth.

Exhibit 2.5: Historical Interest Rate Benchmarks

	Average Rate or Yield
Federal funds rate	5.86%
30-day T-bill	0.43%
1-year Treasury	5.93%
Intermediate Government Treasury	6.49%
Long-term Government Treasury	6.88%

Source: National Bureau of Economic Research, Lehman Brothers. Period of study for July 1954-December 2003. Treasury bonds are represented by the S&P Long-term Government Bonds index; Intermediate Treasury bonds are represented by the Lehman Long Treasury Bond Index is a 10-year Treasury note index. Treasury indices are total return indices held constant maturities. Cash is represented by the Lehman Brothers Three month Treasury Bill Index derived from secondary market Treasury bill rates published by the Federal Reserve Bank or the 91-day Treasury bills data. Indices include reinvested income, but not transaction costs or taxes, are unmanaged and cannot be purchased directly by investors. This chart is for illustrative purposes only and does not predict or depict the performance of any investment. Past performance is no guarantee of future performance.

Interest Rates' Pull on the Market

Interest rates lag the business cycle and could precipitate both market rallies and declines. Key rates are raised or lowered after a change in economic conditions. Bull markets tend to begin during recessions. This is when the inflationary threat is low and Fed Funds' rate cuts occur. Generally, before a rate cut the market will rally.

In every cycle since 1950, stocks' overall prices have increased after a series of interest rate cuts. Looking backward through history, the average S&P 500 gain after the first interest rate cut has been about ten percent after three months, and about twenty-three percent after twelve months.

New bull markets usually began with the economy still steeped in recession and with profit growth collapsing or in negative territory. Since WWII, there have been fourteen interest rate cycles according to the Fed. Whenever the Fed lowered rates, which was 91% of the time, the market ended up higher six to twelve months later. Interest rate-driven markets have faded after eighteen months, unless earnings growth improved. In the end, valuation levels achieved through lower interest rates need the extra boost of higher earnings to support higher price levels.

3. ECONOMIC GROWTH

The Solid Foundation

What is the basis for economic growth?

In a nutshell, capital investment, labor, consumption by households, businesses, and sound Government fiscal and monetary policy is a good recipe for economic growth.

How is economic growth measured?

Nominal Gross Domestic Production (GDP measured in current prices) measures the domestic growth of the U.S. economy. It is a broad measure of growth in goods and services. It is the sum total spending by consumers on durable goods, non-durable goods and services, capital spending by businesses (fixed and inventories), purchases of goods and services by the Government, and net exports. (See Exhibit 2.6)

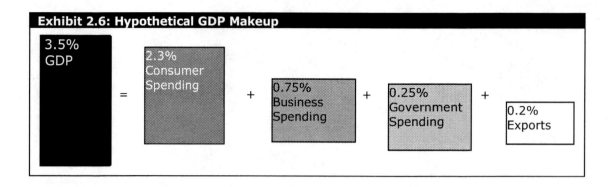

Exhibit 2.6: Hypothetical GDP Makeup

Measuring Economic Growth or Contraction

The Department of Commerce produces the GDP report that is released each quarter and is revised monthly. This is one of the most important reports to watch for. Generally strong GDP numbers tend to push up stock prices and push down bond prices.

Bad domestic and global economic news undermines investor confidence causing the market to see a sell-off. The market discounts future economic activity before the release of the GDP quarterly reports because economists can glean information from other reports.

What rate can the economy grow at without causing inflation?

Most economists believe that rate is approximately four percent. The non-inflationary speed limit may be higher today because of technological productivity gains that allow demand to be met a lot easier. In the past, when demand exceeded supply, prices rose.

Nominal GDP has grown steadily with occasional periods of declines. GDP grew at an average quarterly rate of 3.5% from 1947 to 2002 according to NBER. To determine if the economy is really growing, check out *real* GDP growth. That is the growth in GDP that is a result of higher output and stripped of the effect of inflation.

Other Key Reports to Watch

For a multi-dimensional view of the economy, besides watching the trend in GDP keep a tap on the following reports as well:

- Index of Leading Economic Indicators;
- Federal Reserve Beige book;
- Industrial Production report;
- Institute of Supply Management (ISM);
- Housing starts,
- Trends in the U.S. dollar;
- Global economic growth.

The Index of Leading Economic Indicators attempts to predict future economic activity. This is a closely watched monthly report. The report indicates where the overall U.S. economy may be headed in the next three to six months. Eleven economic series of data make up the indicator: manufacturing hours, initial unemployment claims, building permits, money supply, capital investment contracts, consumer expectations, the S&P 500. Although it does not always predict future economic activity, it does serve to measure current economic activity. This index stood at 100 in 1996, its base year. Generally, when the indicators turn up, stock prices follow and bond prices fall. You can use it along with the Federal Reserve Beige book to confirm a GDP trend.

Investment Advisory Services and Financial Planning Offered Through Aspetuck Financial Management LLC   32

It can also be prudent to follow the trend in industrial production. Industrial production is a gauge for measuring manufacturing activity and can be a proxy for economic growth. Gains in industrial production confirms an economic expansion. Consumer demand, business investment, and foreign demand for U.S. goods all influence industrial production. Rising industrial production is usually good news for stocks and bad news for bonds.

You can use the ISM Index to assess current production levels. Each month, the ISM surveys roughly 400 manufacturers on production, hiring, and new orders. The levels of inventories determine the need for current production. Inventories that are higher in the face of lower demand might mean lower current production and possibly corporate earnings. When the index rises, bond prices may fall and stocks may climb higher. A reading of below 50 indicates shrinking manufacturing activity.

Housing starts directly and indirectly account for ten percent of the economy's output. The housing section is very interest rate sensitive. A robust housing market helps sales growth of many industries such as banking, insurance, furniture, appliances, moving, legal and so on.

The U.S. Dollar: The Strong Man or a 98 Pound Weakling?

Why care about what's happening with the U.S. dollar?

The relative strength or weakness of the dollar can influence the U.S. economic outlook. Historically, a strengthening dollar has had almost the same impact on the economy as a tightening of the monetary policy. A stronger dollar takes away U.S. companies' pricing power because imported goods are cheaper, and affects earnings because corporations cannot raise prices. A strong dollar can produce a trade deficit (whereby imports exceed exports) that may slow down domestic production.

Economists estimate that for every 10% appreciation in the dollar, inflation drops by one percentage point. A strong dollar can subtract as much as 0.5% - 1.0% from GDP growth. A strong dollar that keeps interest rates and inflation low also encourages capital investment from overseas.

In contrast. a weaker dollar makes U.S. goods and services cheaper abroad, thereby stimulating demand and U.S. GDP. It takes about twelve to eighteen months for the effect of a lower dollar to show up in stronger GDP numbers. In general, when demand is greater than supply the U.S. dollar will appreciate.

When U.S. inflation, income growth, and exports are lower, and real interest rates are higher as compared to U.S. trading partners, demand for the dollar will be higher. A restrictive monetary policy can cause the above conditions and create a current account deficit (imports exceed exports) and capital account surplus (the dollar is more in demand than the currency of trading partners). A lower dollar helps to reduce the U.S. trade deficits that helps boost employment, thereby bolstering consumer spending which fuels economic growth.

In addition, keep an eye on broader global economic growth. When foreign economies expand, the demand for U.S. goods and services picks up. Use the Organization for Economic Co-operation and Development's (OECD) composite index to assess global economic growth. It is composed of 23 countries, and is the "Global GDP" measure. If you use it as a leading indicator of global economic growth, it can provide early signals of turning points (peaks and troughs) between expansions and slowdowns of economic activity

4. EARNINGS GROWTH

The Key to Rising Stock Prices

Earnings growth is where the rubber meets the road. At the end of the day what must be concluded from the study of all of the relevant factors that can be evaluated is whether future earnings growth will be high enough to drive the stock market forward.

Stock prices generally reflect future earnings growth, not current earnings. Generally, rising earnings allow stock multiples to rise. The price of a stock is only justified by its earnings growth. Without improving earnings (the "E" in the P/E ratio), stocks will find it difficult to advance higher and justify a higher price ("P"). (See Exhibit 2.7).

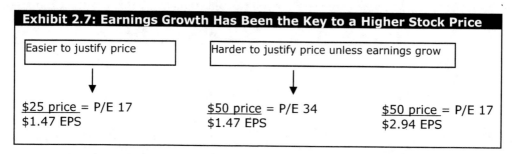

Exhibit 2.7: Earnings Growth Has Been the Key to a Higher Stock Price

Easier to justify price

Harder to justify price unless earnings grow

$25 price = P/E 17
$1.47 EPS

$50 price = P/E 34
$1.47 EPS

$50 price = P/E 17
$2.94 EPS

You can watch the growth in the S&P 500 index's operating earnings to assess the direction of earnings growth. Operating earnings better reflect a company's long-term earnings potential. Corporate earnings have grown at approximately 7.5% annually and stocks responded with 12.02% average annual return.

That earnings growth of 7.5% has allowed the S&P 500 Index to pay an average yield of 3.85%, and appreciate at an average annual rate of 9.08% from 1926-2002. Many economists believe it is very hard to depart from an earnings trend line growth rate of 7.5% over longer periods of time due to fundamental reasons such as productivity.

Even in the recent business cycles, this trend line has been confirmed. The S&P Industrials' earnings grew at an annual average rate of 7.5% from 1971 to 2002. The year with the highest earnings growth rate was 1994, which saw earnings growth spike to 49.7%. Moreover, the lowest year was 2001, which saw negative growth at -63%.

Corporate earnings growth tends to revert to the historical mean. Stock prices rise sharply in advance of bottom in downward earnings revisions and earnings growth. Historically, the stock market bottomed six months in advance of a trough in corporate earnings.

Earnings growth accelerates in the recovery phase of a business cycle. As the business cycle matures earnings growth starts to decelerate indicating that earnings growth may have peaked. If that is the case, then the market is vulnerable to a correction if valuations have overextended themselves.

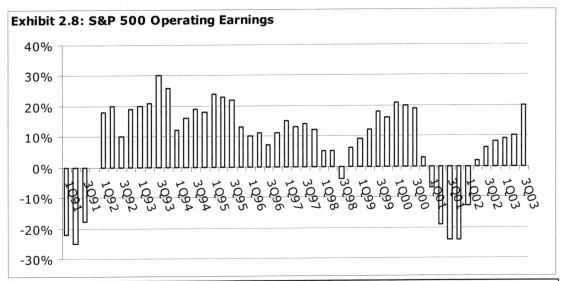

Exhibit 2.8: S&P 500 Operating Earnings

Source: Thomson Financial. S&P 500 Index®, a commonly used broad based index of domestic stocks. The S&P 500 is an unmanaged stock index. S&P 500 is a registered trademark of Standard & Poor's Corporation. Investors cannot directly invest in the S&P 500 Index.

Keep a Watchful Eye on Bell Weather Stocks

It is wise to keep an eye on the earnings growth of bell weather stocks to get additional clues as to the direction of earning growth within an industry. Bell weather stocks are firms within an industry that, because of their business models, tend to be representative of the broader industry. When a bell weather stock does well, then the prospects for that industry look good. Examples of bell weather stocks are Intel (semi-conductors), General Motors (autos), Citigroup (financial services), Wal-mart Department stores (Retail), and General Electric (overall economy).

Remember that the *quality* of earnings is what counts. EPS should be rising because of top line growth and sales growth, and not just because of cost cutting initiatives or a one-time event such as the sale of an asset.

It is important to tune into "earnings season" at the end of each quarter. This is when companies announce whether they have met, exceeded or failed to meet Wall Street's earnings' expectations.

You can get a sense for the direction of earnings surprises (reported earnings are greater than expected). Are more companies surprising on the upside? Positive earnings surprises may lead to persistent positive surprises and result in above average returns.

A 1997 Bernstein and Pigler study found that the best performing stock picking strategy was based on EPS surprises. It provided higher returns and lower risk than seventeen other common strategies. When earnings expectations, taken as a whole, are not met, that may mean the market will have trouble advancing higher and could possibly be in for a correction.

It's not enough to just look at the number of companies beating estimates. Investors must also find out if those companies have provided earnings guidance that states that future earnings are expected to improve on the latest quarter's estimate beating number.

The Retail Reality Check

The Retail Sales report is one of the top monthly reports used to anticipate future economic activity. This report can moves markets both ways! But keep in mind that this report is often subject to significant revisions in subsequent months because of seasonality and cyclical nature of sales.

Profit margins tend to rise when retail sales growth accelerates, and declines when sales growth slows. A firm can meet its earnings estimate and still see its stock price drop when sales growth slows down. With sales growth averaging 6.4% per year from 1971 to 2002, earnings grew at 7.5%.

5. EMPLOYMENT RATE

Employment (and unemployment rates) are Critical Indicators

Lower employment could result in slower wage growth that, in turn, could retard consumer spending. That may consequently hurt overall GDP growth. In general, a rising employment rate leads to increases in consumer spending. Thus, a rising employment rate is a harbinger of economic growth.

Historically, low unemployment has led to faster economic growth and wage inflation that has caused the Fed to raise the Fed Fund's rate in many instances. The unemployment number has been a useful predictor of wage inflation. Although there is no compelling evidence that lower employment directly causes inflation, crummy unemployment numbers cause consumer confidence to wane, and spending may slow thereby threaten earnings.

The normal unemployment rate is about five percent. Most economists believe the economy must grow at its full potential of 3.5% per year to hit five percent unemployment. Historically, low unemployment results in lower bond prices and higher stock prices.

The monthly unemployment rate report is one of the most crucial reports to monitor. It forecasts many other economic indicators such as cyclical trends in personal income, housing starts, industrial production, and GDP. It is the most important report because the Fed make decisions based upon information contained in this report. Furthermore, it contains information that affects data in other reports.

Falling employment and rising unemployment are lagging activity measures. Unemployment can rise even after the economy has begun to recover. The unemployment rate is like a rearview mirror; it tells us where we have been.

Another Employment Indicator

To look forward to where we may be going, be sure to look to the increase in "non-farm payroll employment," which tells us the number of new jobs created in the economy each month. To discern early employment trends, one can watch the weekly jobless claims report produced by the Labor Department. Economists watch the four-week moving average since it smoothes fluctuations in weekly data.

It is believed by many economists that weekly unemployment claims must fall below the 350,000 threshold in order for the economy to be adding jobs and considered to be on a growth track. But be mindful in applying the numbers since unemployment lags.

6. CONSUMER AND BUSINESS SPENDING

Spending is the Link to the Stock Market

Consumer spending is a key link between the stock market and the economy. It has been said that the consumer brings the economy into a recession and also takes it out.

Consumer spending is the main engine that fuels economic growth. Consumer spending represents two-thirds of all economic activity. Consumption is tied to consumer confidence. When confidence is high, consumers feel secure about their job, and are more likely to spend and vice versa.

As a general rule of thumb, as the economy grows, so do corporate profits. Higher profits drive stock prices up. A healthy stock market is very conducive to higher levels of spending. When market indexes rise, investors become wealthier and usually spend more. The Commerce Department's monthly retail sales report is a key indicator of consumer spending.

Debt: The Villain to Spending

What hurts spending?

Historically, high public and private debt levels dampen spending. One measure of high private debt levels is credit card debt. a rising delinquency in accounts indicates high household debt levels and possibly lower future spending ability. in general terms, high debt levels are bad news for stocks and not good news for bonds, especially if private and public default on payments escalates to problematic levels.

Healthy business spending is important too. It confirms the expansion. Generally, businesses will only spend more on technology and make capital expenditures when earnings are expected to improve as a result of improved sustainable consumer spending and economic growth.

7. VALUATION MEASURES

Key Ratios as Measurement Tools

Market valuations attempt to gauge how attractive the market is relative to historical measures. The price-to-earnings ratio (P/E or multiple) is the most commonly used measure because it uses earnings within its calculation and, as we have mentioned, earnings are the primary determinant of a stock's price.

The P/E ratio is the price of the stock divided by its current earnings, or forward earnings projections. It tells analysts, financial advisors and investors how expensive a stock is based upon how much they are paying for a dollar's worth of earnings. The higher the P/E ratio, the more an investor pays for a dollar's worth of earnings.

An investor that buys a higher multiple stock fund, for example, believes that the portfolio's earnings per share will increase. You can use another metric, the "price-to-book" ratio, in conjunction with the price-to-earnings ratio to assess valuation. The price-to-book ratio has a higher correlation with market value and is not subject to earnings manipulation.

Poor valuations suggest limited upside potential until earnings grow at a rate that justifies increased valuations. Empirical research suggests that differences in market P/Es are significantly correlated to differences in long-term market returns. That is to say, that the P/E level of the market at the time you invest can have a big impact on investment returns.

A fairly valued market suggests that it's harder to earn above average returns. While an undervalued market spells a good opportunity to earn above average returns. An overvalued market implies that above average returns will be much harder to achieve especially if EPS growth is decelerating.

Exhibit 2.9 Historical P/E Averages

- S&P 500 is 15.5   (1926-2002 period)
- Russell 2000 is 17.5   (1986-2002 period)
- NASDAQ 100 is 63.0   (inception-2002 period)

Source: Wall Street Journal. The S&P 500 index, a commonly used broad based index of domestic stocks. The S&P 500 is an unmanaged stock index: S&P 500 is a registered trademark of Standard & Poor's Corporation. Investors cannot invest in the S&P 500 Index. Nor can they invest in any other index mentioned in this book; Small-cap stocks are represented by the Russell 2000 Index, an index consisting of the smallest 2,000 companies in the Russell 3000 index (composed of 3,000 large U.S. companies as determined by market capitalization and represents approximately 98% of the investable U.S. equity market); The NASDAQ-100 Index is composed on 100 of the largest non-financial companies listed on the NASDAQ National Market tier of The Nasdaq Stock Market. Indices include reinvested income, but not transaction costs or taxes, are unmanaged and cannot be purchased directly by investors. This chart is for illustrative purposes only and does not predict or depict the performance of any investment. Past performance is no guarantee of future performance.

The Proper Perspective on P/Es

Be careful comparing historical P/E data with current P/E figures. The changes in accounting practices and changes in the components of the benchmark indexes make direct comparisons less reliable. For instance, manufacturing sectors had lower P/Es and dominated the S&P 500 Index in the past. But today, technology sectors that typically grow at higher rates and sport higher P/Es are becoming dominant.

What is known is that valuations tend to regress toward their historical mean, and the mean is slowly getting higher somewhere -- to around seventeen for Large-cap stocks.

Past conventional wisdom held that when inflation wasn't high, stocks thrived. The "Rule of 20" is a valuation measure that maintains that stocks are a good buy when the CPI plus the P/E on the S&P 500 Index is below twenty. Normal inflation is approximately four percent. Earnings have a higher net present value as inflation declines. That is why stocks sport higher P/Es during periods of low inflation.

Just remember not to use the P/E as an indicator of *future* market performance. Valuation measures alone do not determine whether a bull market lives on or ends.

P/E By the Numbers

The greatest bull market of all time began August 12, 1982 and ended on March 10, 2000. Along the way valuations stretched and retreated. In 1998, the stock market's overall P/E hit 28 with inflation at 1.4%, and it still advanced until March 2000 when the stock market's P/E stood above 46!

Historical measures have indicated the stocks are cheap when market P/E approached 11. In the 1974 bear market, the P/E fell as low as 8. In the past, bear markets' P/E ratios have fallen to 14. When the bear market of 2000-2002 bottomed out on October 10, 2002, the P/E ratio was arguably very rich at 23. Yet the market advanced higher in late 2002 and 2003 as earnings rebounded.

In periods of low inflation, like those seen in the 1960s, the S&P 500's P/E has risen above its average. Many market strategists believe the S&P 500's fair value trading range is 17-25. Market strategists believe that the market becomes overvalued when the P/E rises above 25. The market is considered undervalued if its P/E, added to the inflation rate, is less than 20.

Markets have a tendency to become cheap or expensive over its cycle. It is not unusual for the market multiple to stretch to twenty percent over its value before snapping back to its fair market value. There isn't a strong relationship between current valuations and subsequent earnings growth. Investors just tend to over pay for stock earnings which drive valuations higher. Eventually the liquidity dries up and valuations revert to historical mean. In an early bull phase of the market, it is not unusual for P/Es to expand to the mid-twenties as investors anticipate improved earnings.

Higher market valuations may be sustainable if:

1. Higher EPS growth comes about and is sustained;
2. Inflations trends lower (falls below 3%);
3. Interest rates trend downward;
4. Excess money supply finds its way into the market;
5. Investors accept lower future returns;

Is it Time to Buy Stocks?

You can use the S&P 500's earnings yield ratio to assess the attractiveness of stocks. When the 10-year Treasury note's yield is greater than the S&P 500's Earnings/Price ratio (the S&P 500 Earnings/Price ratio is simply the inverse of the S&P 500 P/E ratio), then stocks are overvalued. When the 10-year Treasury note's yield is less than the S&P 500's Earnings/Price ratio, then stocks are undervalued.

If the market P/E is 25, then the Earnings/Price yield is four percent. You can compare the four percent earnings yield to the default free inflation-index (TIPs) yield, then add three percent - which represents the market risk premium. In order for stocks to be attractive to buy, they should offer an earnings yield equal to the TIP's yield plus at least a three percent risk premium.

In practice this is used as a directional indicator rather than a valuation guide because it tends to overstate the bullish case in that it makes stocks seem cheaper than they may actually be. But you can use it as a tool during the early bull to mid-bull phase, just as earnings are accelerating. But use caution as it loses its reliability in the late bull phase as earnings growth decelerates.

Valuation measures provide investors with a yardstick to measure the degree of risk, but they do not help investors with timing. P/E can be both relatively and absolutely high and yet the market can advance for years before a major correction.

Valuation measures may not be as relevant given the strength of non-valuation measures. Mutual fund cash flows, market momentum, and interest rates (given the strong correlation between interest rates and corporate earnings) often determine whether valuations will drift higher.

For instance, if the P/E ratio of the S&P 500 index is above the historical average, but mutual fund cash positions are greater than ten percent, inflation is low, the Fed has injected ample liquidity, and foreign investment in U.S. securities is very strong, then the market could move higher. Moreover, in any given year investor sentiment can play a bigger role in the direction of the market than valuations. Famous investor Warren Buffet once said that, "over the long-term the market is a weighing machine, but over the short-term it's a voting machine."

Just remember that greed and fear can and do drive the market up and down regardless of numerical valuations.

8. THE U.S. DOLLAR

Its Strengths and Weaknesses

The dollar appreciates and depreciates in value based upon supply and demand.

Demand is driven by differentials in actual and expected inflation, interest rates, economic growth, and trade balance between the U.S. and other countries. Empirical evidence shows that overvalued currencies depreciate over time and undervalued currencies appreciate, although the adjustment period may take years.

Lower inflation generally causes the dollar to appreciate. Foreigners tend to accelerate purchases of U.S. securities -- especially Treasuries -- when U.S. inflation falls. The opposite happens when inflation is high in the U.S.

A rise in real interest rates (the real interest rate is equal to the nominal rate minus the rate of inflation), relative to other countries, can result in a higher dollar value. Foreigners are attracted to the higher real interest rates and buy more dollars to earn higher interest on their investments.

Strong economic growth generally results in the dollar strengthening. Economic growth, lower inflation, and moderate-to-high real interest rates are signs of a healthy economy. These conditions tend to attract foreign capital. The foreigners must buy U.S. dollars before buying U.S. securities or U.S. capital assets.

A Give and Take Relationship

A rising or high trade deficit weakens the dollar. Historically a higher trade deficit has been associated with a declining value of a nation's currency. The dollar is sold to buy foreign currency to purchase foreign goods and services. A big trade deficit implies lower demand for the dollar and potentially could prolong its slump. The U.S. economy seems to be less sensitive to high trade deficits than other economies because of its status as a safe haven. The dollar has been one of the safest and most stable currencies to own.

A weaker U.S. dollar could cause higher GDP growth and increase the threat of inflation. A weaker dollar is good for the economy because U.S. goods become cheaper compared to foreign goods. Cheaper goods may result in higher foreign demand. Higher GDP growth typically bodes well for stocks. When the U.S. dollar loses value, the imported goods become more expensive, thereby creating inflationary pressure from both higher imported prices and higher domestic prices. Domestic prices rise because U.S. firms now can raise prices without losing sales to foreign competitors.

Although a weaker dollar could help save jobs and keep consumers spending, it could also cause the Fed to hike interest rates due to inflationary pressure. Therefore, a weak dollar could put pressure on interest rates top rise. Higher U.S. interest rates attract foreign capital creating demand for U.S. dollars, and that drives the value of the dollar higher.

A lower dollar weakens the case for an overweight position in U.S. bonds. Generally, foreign investor demand for U.S. bonds wanes as the U.S. dollar weakens against their home currency. Foreign investors could net a negative return on the U.S. bonds if it takes substantially more U.S. dollars to buy their home currency when converting their investment proceeds. Lack of foreign demand could possibly cause bond prices to drop and yields to rise. Eventually yields may rise high enough to once again attract foreign investors and also make them an attractive alternative to stocks. As the U.S. dollar weakens, U.S. investors in foreign securities benefit from the foreign currency appreciation.

A stronger dollar can slow GDP growth and constrain inflation. In general, a stronger dollar has the opposite impact on U.S. GDP than a weaker dollar. A strong dollar makes imports cheaper for U.S. consumers to buy and exports more expensive for foreigners to buy. A higher dollar is good news for bonds because dollar-denominated assets increase in value due to demand and can cool off the economy because of lower exports.

#3 Psychology: The Psychology of the Investor and Consumer

Understanding Consumer Confidence Metrics

The "herd mentality" is a major part of short-term analysis. Bernard Baruch once said that, "all economic movements, by their very nature, are motivated by crowd psychology." If there is a big enough bullish crowd that believes that economic and market conditions will improve, then even if fundamentals may very well be weak, the market may still advance due to demand, and vice versa. Often it's not the reality, but rather the perception of what is that will determine the direction of the market.

Consumer confidence is important to track because it may provide a glimpse into future consumption. The monthly Consumer Confidence index measures such consumer confidence. The index is a coincidental indicator. A rising trend suggests that consumers are becoming more confident about their future and are likely to buy big-ticket items over the next few months.

One key indicator to watch is the growth in personal disposable income. Consumer confidence will drive consumer demand only when disposable income in healthy. It is prudent to realize that there must be a positive trend in disposable income in order to rely on the Consumer Confidence index. If income and confidence are both positive factors, then expect growing investor demand for stocks.

When consumers lose confidence in the economy, they will usually curtail their spending and increase their savings in the months ahead. Both layoffs and personal debt levels can cause consumers to lose confidence, but consumers will try to maintain their standard of living for as long as possible in a slowdown. That is precisely why consumption levels still hold for a while as unemployment creeps upward.

Positive Sentiment and How it Affects Markets

Consumer confidence/investor sentiment generally leads downturns or upturns in the markets. Consumer confidence has about a five-month lead time on the economy. Some studies show that the stock market has about a six-month lead-time on the economy. That indicates that there is a very close correlation between consumer confidence and overall stock prices.

Typically, investor sentiment has peaked when the market has already peaked, and has hit a low once the market has already hit its bottom. Historically, the stock market has tended to bottom out when pessimism has reached high levels.

A market rally normally develops when there is extreme pessimism. It is interesting to note that at every point of extreme sentiment, the crowd has been wrong!

A savvy watchdog can use the Investor Intelligence survey to gauge sentiment. Generally, a higher confidence level is associated with higher stock valuations and lower bond market valuations. Investor sentiment also captures geopolitical risks. When there is heighten geopolitical risk, such as the Iraq War, investor sentiment typically turns bearish, and markets may move lower. The reverse is true as geopolitical risk abates.

You can confirm investor sentiment surveys by looking at the level of cash inflows and outflows in equity funds and bond funds. Sometimes sentiment is positive, but investors are not buying. Money market assets and equity mutual fund cash positions are generally good indicators of investor sentiment. When mutual fund cash positions rise beyond five percent, money managers tend to come under pressure to raise cash to meet rising liquidations from shareholders. A typical equity mutual fund's cash position runs in the 3% - 4% range. Another sign of negative sentiment is when money market funds' net fund sales are ahead of sales into equity funds.

#4 Technical: Technical Indicators

Detecting Patterns

Technicians believe that markets move in short-term, intermediate and long-term trends and patterns. In contrast, daily price movements are random. Trends are driven by supply and demand as influenced by P.F.P.T. (see more information on this at the beginning of this chapter).

In addition, rational and irrational behavior influences demand. Technicians will look at various indicators and changes in supply and demand to identify reversals or recoveries in price movements. Those patterns can help them decide when to buy or when to sell. They also believe that news is gradually discounted into stock prices so there is opportunity to earn above average returns because a stock can be mis-priced when all the public news isn't reflected in its price.

Whether you believe in technical analysis or not, it can be beneficial to still follow certain technical indicators. Why? The technical indicators mentioned in this section should help you to analyze the current health of the market, its psychology, and its trend. That is the greatest value of technical analysis. It can provide insight as to market psychology - one of the most important factors driving short-term trends. One can utilize the indicators discussed in this section to get a better feel for the short-term direction of the market.

Monitoring the 200-Day Moving Average

Watching the moving 200-day average of the S&P 500 Index can be a useful tool. The number of stocks above or below the trend line is an indicator of market direction as theories suggest that stock prices move in trends. The 200-day moving average of the S&P 500, plotted against the daily movement of the S&P 500, is a common trend line. Using the arithmetic mean of 200 days of S&P 500 Index prices mutes the daily random noise of the market and provides a better view of the immediate trend.

If more than 80% of the stocks that are trading on the NYSE are selling above their 200-day moving average, the market is considered overbought. That is a bearish sign.

When less than 20% of the NYSE stocks are selling above their 200-day moving average, the market is considered oversold, which is a bullish signal.

When the market average breaks through the 200-day average, it could spell correction. More often than not, the 200-day moving average is a better indicator of a resistance point on the upside, and not as good a downside indicator. Often, by the time the daily trend breaks through the 200-day average and turns down 80%, it is too late to use as a bear market signal. On the other hand, when the daily average does break the 200-day average, it often goes back up again! Therefore, it would be premature to sell.

Moving averages do not have an effect on valuations. Instead, analysts, financial advisors and investors use them to identify trends. Technicians believe the "trend is your friend." In order to make money or protect against losses, it can be wise not to fight the trend.

Other Friendly (and Unfriendly) Trends to Watch

The "two tumbles and a jump" rule is used as a buy signal by some. Typically the market does well after two sell-offs followed by a strong broad-based rally.

It can also make sense to pay attention to trading volume as it can indicate bullish or bearish sentiment. Trading volume is the total number of shares bought and sold.

Often market valuations are fostered by perceptions more than anything else is. When perceptions begin to change, volume will increase and markets will moves regardless of the underlying fundamentals. When there is heavy buying in a rally or selling in a correction, it is a confirmation of the direction of the market.

High volume confirms market sentiment. Markets need volume to move higher. When volume is low, a rally can turn into a "fool's rally" and in a sell-off marked by narrow breadth, the sell-off could just be a round of profit taking rather than the beginning of a correction.

Volume spikes generally occur at major market bottoms. In general, the market reaches a bottom when there is record volume. Historical data has shown that the market has typically peaked six months after volume peaked. If monetary policy is still conducive to economic growth, and market fundamentals are relatively healthy, it can be foolish to get too freaked out by low volume. When there is low volume, cash is building up on the sidelines. This is a positive trend because down the road, that very same cash might just fuel a market rally when investor sentiment turns bullish and investors plow that cash back into the stock market.

Watch for Lockstep Market Movements

What else is there to know?

The action of major stock groups has been an indicator of major turning points in the market. For example, a move from interest rate-sensitive stocks (like automobiles or housing) to defensive, non-cyclical consumer growth stock groups (like pharmaceuticals) is a leading indicator that the economy is expected to slow down. That may result in lower corporate profits and a market correction.

In addition, big advances of established large-company stocks, such as the Dow Jones 30 Index component stocks, are often followed by rallies in small-company stocks. The small-stock rally is often due to investor demand as investors shift from higher multiple Dow stocks driven up in price because of demand, to cheaper, undervalued small-company stocks.

A rotation from large-cap stocks to less liquid small-cap companies is a healthy sign that usually means a bull market still has some run left to it. Conversely, a rotation from small- and mid-cap stocks (sometimes referred to as "smid" stocks) to more liquid, defensive large-cap companies indicates that the market may be heading lower or the early bull returns are long gone.

During uncertain economic times, only the best names are bought. In the bond market, it is U.S. Treasury issues, and in the stock market, it is the bluest of blue chips. Generally, stock sector leadership shifts occur during market corrections.

Understanding the Breadth of Changes

It can be smart to evaluate market breadth and investor sentiment to detect signs of a rally or correction. When most stocks -- large-caps, mid-caps, and small-caps -- are participating in a rally, that market has positive breadth. However, when only the S&P 100 stocks are advancing, then there is limited or negative market breadth, which can be a warning sign of a possible correction. Traditionally, market breadth lags and turns negative (evidenced by more declines than advances) at least several months before a market peak.

Market breadth provides insight as to the current health of the market. It measures how many issues are traded. It says nothing about the direction of the market, but positive market breadth is a sign of a healthy bull market, while negative market breadth is a signal of a deteriorating bull market.

It is important to get a feel for market breadth because this will tell you whether a rally or correction is broad based or just confined to a particular area of the market.

The advance/decline ratio (A/D) provides the directional compass. The A/D ratio represents the number of issues that have closed higher than the last close. A bull market is characterized by a trend of increasing the number of stocks hitting their 52-week highs. Usually new highs top out and begin to decline ahead of a market peak. An advance decline ratio above 0.25 is a bullish sign and below -0.25 is bearish. If the A/D line and indexes move together, then the market's breadth is broad and healthy. A divergence between the trend in the index and the A/D line usually signals that a market peak or trough has been reached.

More Ratios That Reflect Bulls and Bears

Upside-to-downside ratio is a broad ratio that focuses on the activity of NYSE market participants. A ratio of 1.5 or higher is a bearish sign indicating that the market is overbought. A ratio of 0.75 implies that the market is oversold which is always bullish.

Upside-to-downside Ratio = Volume of NYSE stocks that increased
Volume of NYSE stocks that decreased

The sell-to-buy ratio looks at how many dollars of shares are sold by insiders for every dollar bought. A ratio of 3:1 is s bearish sign, and 1.25:1 a bullish one. Corporate insiders, such as a CEO, selling his company's stock can be a bearish signal, while buying is often a bullish one. Still, this ratio typically peaks about one month before the market hits a low. A bearish ratio implies that insiders may be betting on earnings disappointments. Keep in mind that transactions due to the personal financial needs of insiders can often be misinterpreted. You may want to think about selling when the sell-to-buy ratio is accelerating.

Sell-to-Buy Ratio = $ amount of shares sold by insiders
$ amount of shares purchased by insiders

The CBOE Put/Call ratio is a trend indicator. The CBOE Put/Call ratio is the daily volume of put options and call options. It is a safe bet to view high pessimism as bullish sign, and high optimism as bearish. A CBOE Put/Call ratio of less than 0.36 is bullish and greater than 0.49 is bearish. Remember the Wall Street adage: when everyone is bullish there is no one left to buy! That is a bad sign. You might want to consider buying stocks when the Put/Call ratio is low.

CBOE Put/Call Ratio = Daily volume of put options
Daily volume of call options

The Short Interest Ratio is an indicator of the level of bearishness in the market. Investors who sell short a stock borrow it and sell it hoping to buy it back at a lower price. Short interest represents the number of shares that have yet to be bought back. The higher the short interest, the greater the bearish sentiment. High short interest is a bullish indicator because eventually the "shorts" must buy back short stocks. A Short Interest Ratio that is above six is a bullish sign, and below four is bearish. Consider buying stocks when short interest is high.

When the Confidence Index (CI) is rising consider buying stocks and high yield bonds. CI is used to determine market sentiment and hence, investing disposition.

Confidence Index = Investment Grade Bond Yields
Average Bond Yields

The CI moves in the opposite direction of yield spreads. As yield spreads widen in down markets and economic contraction, the CI declines. In times of uncertainty and pessimism, investment grade bond yields fall. A flight to quality increases demand for investment grade issues, driving up prices and pushing yields down. In times of optimism, when the economy expands, the CI increases. Investment grade bond yields rise due to declining risk aversion and demand for safe investment grade bonds.

	CI	**Markets**	**Buy**
Good Times	Rises	up	Stocks and non-investment grade (high yield or "junk") bonds
Bad Times	Falls	down	Buy investment grade bonds and Treasuries.

As you will see, in chapter eight these indicators are used in conjunction with your assessment of POLICY, FUNDAMENTALS, and PSYCHOLOGY to determine the appropriate investment action to take.

Investing Principles to Act on Throughout the Market Cycles

"I don't care if a fund is named "The Rock Solid Honestly Safe U.S. Government Guaranty Trust Savings Fund"-- in any market investment you stand a chance of losing your principal."
                    -- Arthur Levitt, former chairman, Securities and Exchange Commission.

The Basic Relationship between Risk & Reward

Congratulations! You have made it through chapters one and two. It may have felt as dry as eating talcum powder. But, hopefully, you've gained an understanding of the dynamics of the markets, and they should not be quite as mysterious anymore.

If you can master the basic investment principles covered in this chapter, you will be better at identifying and measuring risk so you can begin to manage it. After all, investing is all about assessing the risk involved, knowing how much risk to take, and getting compensated for that degree of risk. It can be a smart decision to always focus on risk first, then on return.

If more risk is taken, will the reward be higher? Exhibit 3.1 shows that over longer periods, 1926 thorough 2002, riskier investments such as Small-cap stocks outperformed less risky investments like bonds and cash. True to theory, the higher returns came with greater downside risk.

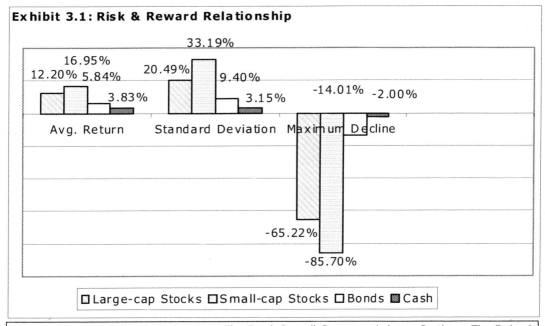

Exhibit 3.1: Risk & Reward Relationship

Source: Standard & Poor's Corporation, The Frank Russell Company, Lehman Brothers, The Federal Reserve. Large-cap stocks are represented by the S&P 500 index®, a commonly used, broad based index of domestic stocks. The S&P 500 is an unmanaged stock index. S&P 500 is a registered trademark of Standard & Poor's Corporation. Investors cannot invest in the S&P 500 Index. Small-cap stocks are represented by the Russell 2000 Index, an index consisting of the smallest 2,000 companies in the Russell 3000 index (composed of 3,000 large U.S. companies as determined by market capitalization, and represents approximately 98% of the investable U.S. equity market). Bonds are represented by the S&P Long-term Government Bonds Index. Treasury indices are total return indices held constant maturities. Cash is represented by the Lehman Brothers Three-month Treasury Bill Index derived from secondary market Treasury bill rates published by the Federal Reserve Bank, or the 91-day Treasury bills data. Standard deviation is an indicator of the portfolio's total return volatility. The larger the portfolio's standard deviation, the greater the portfolio's volatility. Its measured on an annual basis. Maximum decline is based on a calendar year basis. Average return is based on the average investment return using calendar year returns. Indices include reinvested income, but not transaction costs or taxes, are unmanaged and cannot be purchased directly by investors. This chart is for illustrative purposes only and does not predict or depict the performance of any investment. Past performance is no guarantee of future performance. Period of study is from 1926-2002.

Theory has shaped conventional thinking that a riskier investment has a higher expected return than a less risky one. In addition, by that same token the belief is that a riskier investment has a greater potential of loss at any time.

Does the theoretical risk and reward relationship always hold true?

While death and taxes are a sure thing, it is important to understand that there isn't a positive correlation between risk & reward *all* of the time. There are numerous times when bond portfolios, often considered less risky than stock investments, under perform equity portfolios, and even lose more money than equity portfolios.

For example, a supposedly less risky hypothetical portfolio that was invested in the same stocks as the Lehman Brother's U.S. Treasury Securities Long-term Index declined, and returned -6.13% from June 23, 2003 to June 22, 2004. In contrast, a riskier hypothetical equity portfolio that was invested in the stocks of the Russell 2000 Index appreciated, returning 29.43% for the same period.

What happened?

The presumed less risky asset, the Treasuries, actually contained more market risk in the form of higher interest rate risk during the period of study. The presumed riskier Russell 2000-tracked portfolio had less market risk given the P.F.P.T's (see Chapter 2 to review these important factors).

Often a non-diversified portfolio returns less than a diversified equity portfolio. Therefore, investing is all about being compensated for the risk we can't eliminate. The practical value of academic theory is that it helps in understanding and assessing risk.

Is the Potential Return Reward Fair?

How does an investor know if the return fairly compensates for the risk taken?

The concept of being compensated for risk is best illustrated by using the seminal work of William Sharpe's Capital Asset Pricing Model (CAPM). According to that model, market risk (systematic risk) is the most important risk to address when investing through a diversified portfolio. Why? The CAPM theory says that after washing away as much risk as possible using portfolio diversification techniques, the only risk that remains is market risk - systematic risk. One can use beta to measure market risk, which, at the moment, is the best measure of market risk.

The CAPM equation says that the required return in the example below should be 11.4% (see Exhibit 3.2). If the actual return is less than 11.4%, then the investor was not fairly compensated for the amount of risk taken.

Exhibit 3.2: The Required Return Based on CAPM

Required Return = T-bill rate + beta (S&P 500 Index Return minus the T-bill rate)

11.4% = 3% + 1.2 (10% minus 3%)

This table is for illustrative purposes only and does not predict or depict the performance of any investment. Past performance is no guarantee of future performance.

When an investment does not fall on or above the securities market line (SML) then it's not compensating for risk. Plot the Securities Market Line using the results of the CAPM equation (see Exhibit 3.3 below).

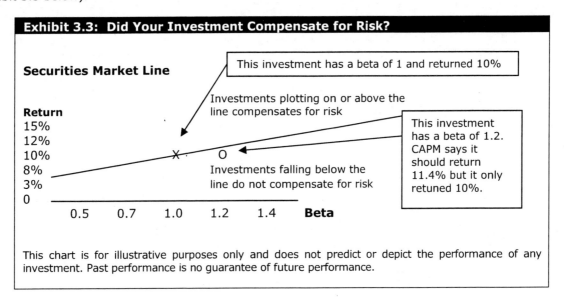

Exhibit 3.3: Did Your Investment Compensate for Risk?

Securities Market Line

This investment has a beta of 1 and returned 10%

Investments plotting on or above the line compensates for risk

This investment has a beta of 1.2. CAPM says it should return 11.4% but it only retuned 10%.

Investments falling below the line do not compensate for risk

Return
15%
12%
10%
8%
3%
0

0.5   0.7   1.0   1.2   1.4   **Beta**

This chart is for illustrative purposes only and does not predict or depict the performance of any investment. Past performance is no guarantee of future performance.

Recognizing Different Risks

What is the first step to investing?

The first step to investing is to assess risk. The truth is, there is no way to escape risk completely. All investments, including cash-equivalent investments such as Certificates of Deposit, have inherent risks.

When investors move money from stocks to cash because of fear of market risk, they unknowingly assume purchasing power risk. Money sitting under a mattress for twenty years will lose more than half of its original value -- a loss of purchasing power (described in more detail below) -- based upon the historical average inflation rate. Usually when the market looks vulnerable to a sell-off, inflation is higher.

Exhibit 3.4: Inflation Risk - Ratio of Remaining Purchasing Power

Inflation Rate	after 5-Yrs.	after 10-Yrs.	after 20-Yrs.
4%	0.82	0.66	0.44
5%	0.77	0.60	0.36

This table is for illustrative purposes only and does not predict or depict the performance of any investment.

When money moves from stocks to bonds, investors expose themselves to interest rate risk and the risk of more modest growth.

Should conservative investors take risk?

As mentioned earlier, risk lurks everywhere, even in seemingly innocuous securities. But keep in mind that without risk, there is no reward. You can manage risk by being able to identify it, by knowing what can break down the positive correlation between risk and return, and by using basic risk management strategies.

Short-term investors should be concerned with liquidity risks while long-term investors should be concerned with earning returns that beat inflation and fairly reward them for the risk taken.

Knowing How Much Risk to Take

How much risk should a client take?

How much investment risk to take depends upon one's psychology, circumstances, financial condition, liabilities, and personal investment needs (liquidity needs, income requirements, investment horizon, return objective, etc.). When an investor can afford to lose money without it causing a financial problem, then it is possible to assume more risk.

If all of an investor's debt payments and financial obligations can be easily met, even with mild portfolio losses, then more market risk can be assumed. An individual can take on more risk if there is an emergency reserve fund that can be tapped to pay for unexpected expenses, or cover fixed expenses for more than a year. Obviously it would be prudent to take less risk when the emergency fund is a paltry sum or all but absent.

Individual investor circumstances determine how aggressive to be. Behavioral research shows that risk attitudes influence how much risk an investor is willing to assume. Optimistic investors usually take more risk than those that do not, and have higher return expectations.

What is the investor's comfort level with investments that fluctuate in value? Did the investor just lose his job or develop serious health problems? When unrealized losses greater than 10% disrupt sleep, it is wise to remain conservative by owning a balanced portfolio.

There are seventeen basic types of risk, see exhibit 3.5, to consider when building a portfolio and managing it.

Exhibit 3.5: Possible Investment and Portfolio Risk

1. Market risk	6. Marketability	11. Purchasing power	16. Selection
2. Interest rate	7. Reinvestment	12. Investment style	17. Timing
3. Liquidity	8. Currency	13. Business/security	
4. Portfolio manager	9. Political	14. Concentration	
5. Credit quality	10. Country	15. Asset class	

Investors can mitigate most of these risks through the IPM portfolio construction, and active risk management strategies.

The Shifting Sands of Risk

Why is risk management necessary when everyone preaches that a buy and hold strategy is the best risk management strategy?

The risk effecting a portfolio is not always the same year in year out. Investment risk is like shifting sands. Risks effecting the markets change each year due to changing economic conditions and investor sentiment. In a given year, the major risk threatening investments may be market risk. The following year it could be interest rate risk, followed by purchasing power risk the next year.

In 1998, liquidity risk threatened the markets. Investors sold less liquid assets such as small-to-mid-cap stocks, and bought liquid blue chip, large-cap stocks and Treasuries. The very next year, in 1999, liquidity concerns faded and one of the safest investments on the globe, U.S. Treasury bonds, lost 15%!

At the start of 2000, the risk of the day was market risk as stock valuations climbed to inconceivable levels. After the market precipitously corrected, purchasing power risk became the major threat as yields fell to levels not seen since the 1960s. The Treasury bond yield fell to 4.36% in May of 2003 - generating negative inflation-adjusted return.

It is therefore important to evaluate a portfolio's risk and the underlying risk of each individual security within a portfolio each year, keeping in mind the current macro-economic and market conditions (see the PFPT factors discussed in Chapter 2). What was safe then, may now be risky because it is has been overbought and therefore is most likely overvalued.

To gain a sense of shifting risks, think of the previous example of two hypothetical portfolios - the one that tracked the Lehman Brother's U.S. Treasury Securities Long-term Index, and the one that matched the Russell 2000 Index.

Is An Asset Allocation Mutual Fund The Magic Bullet?

Should an investor that owns a strategic asset allocation or Lifecycle fund worry about risk?

A mutual fund is only part of an overall portfolio and does not constitute a complete investment plan. Moreover, there are dozens of so-called asset allocation or Lifecycle funds, and each invests according to its own mandate that may, or may not, be a perfect fit for every investor. In addition, there is no guarantee that any mutual fund will meet its investment objective, or for that matter, make money for investors. Furthermore, a mutual fund investment does not have FDIC insurance or government agency backing, nor will it reimburse an investor for any losses should an investor's investment decline in value.

Thus, a single mutual fund cannot always be counted on. Even with single asset allocation funds there is risk buildup that must be managed. It would be smart to use a few low- or non-correlated funds to build a diversified mutual fund portfolio. Properly diversified portfolios will reduce the risk associated with investing in individual securities and the markets in general. However, a even a well-diversified portfolio cannot eliminate all of the risk inherent to investing, nor does diversification ensure a profit or guarantee against a loss in a declining market.

The Essential Types of Risk to Manage

This section covers the essential types of risks that investors encounter and must manage. Total risk is encompasses all the risk covered in section. Know how to identify the following types of risk in investments and the market in order to actively manage a portfolio to reduce total investment risk.

- **_Purchasing Power_** _risk_ is the risk that the cost of living will outpace the return on an investment.

Over time, the value of a non-invested dollar decreases every year. For instance, in 1960 you could mail twenty letters for one dollar, and today only two. (Also see the example in Exhibit 3.6).

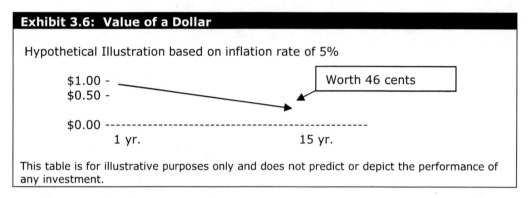

Exhibit 3.6: Value of a Dollar

Hypothetical Illustration based on inflation rate of 5%

$1.00 -
$0.50 -   Worth 46 cents

$0.00 --
        1 yr.   15 yr.

This table is for illustrative purposes only and does not predict or depict the performance of any investment.

Losing purchasing power on your money has the same effect as realizing investment losses in your portfolio. In either case, assets are being eroded. Inflation is real threat to one's standard of living. For example, look at the rising cost of an economy car in Exhibit 3.7:

Exhibit 3.7: Rising Costs Means Your Money Must Work Harder

	1958	**1979**	**2004**	**2029**
Average Cost	$2,200	$16,240	$28,000	$58,629*

Source: U.S. Department of Commerce, Bureau of Economic Analysis, average new vehicle MSRP. * Based on 3% inflation over 25 years from 2004 prices. This table is for illustrative purposes only and does not predict or depict the performance of any investment.

Inflation: The Real Enemy

The increased price of that economy car was due to the effect of an annual average inflation rate of approximately four percent. The rate of inflation for other items, such as college tuition and medical expenses, has been growing at double that inflation rate!

Investors must consider the wealth erosion effect of inflation. Be sure to keep the future cost of living in mind. A $500,000 investment that returns eight percent per year is depleted in thirteen years if the investor withdrew seven percent per year and increased the withdrawal rate by three percent each year to match inflation. That means a sixty-five-year-old retiree would have spent his retirement portfolio by the age of seventy-eight. It is a must to make sure that investments can and will earn a high enough return to outpace the future cost of living. Higher inflation can cause retirees to outlive their life savings.

Purchasing power risk is the number one risk threat to a portfolio's long-term value!

Investors generally don't don't want to lose money. Consequently, they often end up investing in fixed-income investments. Ironically, they may not lose money due to stock market declines, but just the same, they lose money in the form of purchasing power through the erosion of assets. Their money is worth less. They can buy less. Thus, losing money in the market or losing money in the form of lost purchasing power is really the same thing.

It easy to understand stock market loses. The losses are easy to see on your financial institutions' statements. However, investors have a harder time understanding lost purchasing power.

Exhibit 3.8 below shows that $100,000 stuffed into a mattress in 1970 could only buy $40,589 worth of goods and services by 1980! Even U.S. Government bonds lost value! A U.S. Government bond's steady fixed-income stream bought less each year and the principal returned was valued less than the investment!

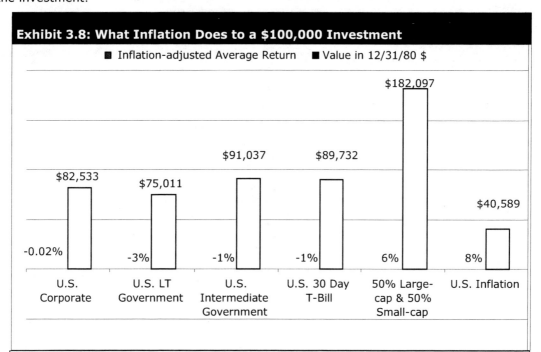

Exhibit 3.8: What Inflation Does to a $100,000 Investment

Source: Standard & Poor's, The Frank Russell Company, Lehman Brothers, Federal Reserve. Data for 1970-1980 period. Source: Ibbotson Associates Inc. ®: All rights reserved. Used with permission; Large-cap stocks are represented by the S&P 500 index®, a commonly used broad based index of domestic stocks. The S&P 500 is an unmanaged stock index: S&P 500 is a registered trademark of Standard & Poor's Corporation. Investors cannot invest in the S&P 500 Index: Small-cap stocks are represented by the Russell 2000 Index, an index consisting of the smallest 2,000 companies in the Russell 3000 index (composed of 3,000 large U.S. companies as determined by market capitalization and represents approximately 98% of the investable U.S. equity market); U.S. Government Long term bonds are represented by the S&P Long-term Government Bonds index; U.S. Intermediate Government bonds are represented by the Lehman Long Treasury Bond Index is a 10-year Treasury note index. Treasury indices are total return indices held constant maturities. U.S. 30-day T-bill is represented by the Lehman Brothers Three month Treasury Bill Index derived from secondary market Treasury bill rates published by the Federal Reserve Bank or the 91-day Treasury bills data. Corporate bonds are represented by the Lehman Brothers Bond Index. The Lehman Brothers Government/Credit Index measures the performance of all debt obligations of the U.S. Treasury and U.S. Government agencies, and all investment- grade domestic corporate debt; Indices include reinvested income, but not transaction costs or taxes, are unmanaged and cannot be purchased directly by investors. Inflation figures obtained from National Bureau of Economic Research. This chart is for illustrative purposes only and does not predict or depict the performance of any investment. Past performance is no guarantee of future performance.

Purchasing Power Risk Applies to Bonds, Too

All fixed-income investments that have a fixed coupon of four percent or less have a high degree of purchasing power risk. Knowing that inflation has averaged four percent, inflation-adjusted yields of four percent are at risk of losing purchasing power.

In fact, Treasury bonds lost purchasing power in more than forty percent of ten-year periods dating back to the 1920s. Treasury bonds, notes, and bills are not viable inflation hedges! (See Exhibit 3.9 below). It is only in low inflationary periods that four percent fixed investments do well by investors in terms of keeping pace with cost of living changes.

Exhibit 3.9: A 4% Yield May Subject Investment to Purchasing Power Risk

Bond Yield's	4%	Overtime the investment lost value given this scenario
Taxes	-1%	
Expenses	-0.20%	
Inflation	-4%	
Actual Return	-1.20%	

This table is for illustrative purposes only and does not predict or depict the performance of any investment. Both principal and yield of investment securities will fluctuate with changes in market conditions. Calculations assume a 25% marginal tax rate.

- *__Credit Quality__ risk* is the risk that the issuer of the security will default on its interest and/or principal payment. Investments that are of investment grade rating are less risky than non-investment grade securities. A high yield bond fund has a high degree of credit quality risk. Moody's Investors Services reported that the 20-year average annual default rate through 2001 for U.S high yield bonds was five percent, and can exceed thirteen percent annually during periods of distress!

- *__Business/security__ risk* is the risk specific to an individual security. It is the risk that a company experiences in operating its day-to-day business. For example, lawsuits, worker strikes, price increases in the commodities used to produce goods, a significant rise in the U.S. dollar hurting exports, all could adversely effects a company's income statement and balance sheet, and even force a company into bankruptcy.

- *__Interest Rate__ risk* is a major risk affecting long-term bond investors. Generally as interest rates rise, bond prices decline and vice versa. In general, long-term bonds are more affected by interest rate changes and are therefore riskier than short- or intermediate-term bonds because the value of outstanding long-term bonds generally declines more than short or intermediate bonds when interest rates rise.

Exhibit 3.10: Long-term Bonds Have Won Big and Lost Big

Fund	Maturity In Years:	Rates Fall 1%; Price Increases:	Rates Rise 1%; Price Decreases:
Short term Bond	1-4	+ 1% to +4%	- 1% to -4%
Intermediate Bond	5-14	+ 4% to +7%	- 4% to -7%
Long-term Bond	15-30	+ 12% plus	- 10% plus

Source: Morningstar. Long-term bond is represented by the by the S&P Long-term Government Bonds index; Intermediate bond is represented by the Lehman Long Treasury Bond Index is a 10-year Treasury note index. Treasury indices are total return indices held constant maturities. Short-term bond is represented by the Lehman Brothers Short-term bond index; Indices include reinvested income, but not transaction costs or taxes, are unmanaged and cannot be purchased directly by investors. This chart is for illustrative purposes only and does not predict or depict the performance of any investment. Past performance is no guarantee of future performance.

- **Reinvestment** *risk* is the risk associated with higher yielding bonds that mature in a declining interest rate environment. When principal is returned, it may only be reinvested in a lower coupon bond. Reinvesting at significantly lower rates could subject investors to purchasing power risk.

- **Market** *risk* is the inherent price fluctuation in the securities market due to changes in market conditions. The market might be down when the investor has to sell. It is also investing when the market is overvalued. That scenario poses the greatest chance for investors to losing money.

- **Marketability** *risk* is the risk that an investor cannot find a buyer for the security he wants to sell. Certain securities do not have an active market in which an investment is readily tradable. In general, mutual funds eliminate this risk since they will redeem shares they underwrite any day that the New York Stock Exchange is open. However, certain mutual funds, such as mirco-cap equity funds, may themselves face greater marketability risk with the underlying securities in the fund. For example, in a down market the market may place a premium on liquidity, and so thinly traded micro-cap stocks may fall in price. Consequently, a portfolio manager may not be able to find a buyer for those stocks.

- **Liquidity** *risk* is the risk of not being able to readily convert an investment into cash and recoup the entire investment. Money market funds, which seek to maintain a stable $1 share price, are an example of a highly liquid investment because their investment objective is to try to maintain a constant share price. Thus, when a shareholder redeems assets from a money market fund, every penny invested (minus expenses) is returned. This may not be the case with a stock fund since the price may fluctuate up or down in value.

- **Currency** *risk* is the monetary exchange risks inherent in international investing when currency is exchanged from one form to another. When the denominating currency of a foreign investment depreciates, the investment losses value in U.S. dollar terms. When the investor sells and repatriates the proceeds back into U.S. dollars, the foreign currency will buy less U.S. dollars resulting in a loss equal to the percentage depreciation of the foreign currency to the home currency (U.S. dollars). Currency risk is a special risk associated only with foreign investing and can be eliminated or reduced through hedging strategies in the futures market, or forward currency market and by investing domestically only.

- **Portfolio manager** *risk* is the risk that a portfolio manager will under perform the market because of too much cash, or poor security and or industry selection. This risk is associated with active management. The way to reduce this risk is to invest a portion of a portfolio's assets in an index fund and build a diversified fund portfolio.

- **Country** *risk* involves the political or economic instability of a particular country that may adversely effect that foreign country's securities markets and consequently foreign securities holdings. Avoiding emerging foreign markets can reduce country risk, as does a more globally diversified portfolio.

- **Concentration** *risk* is when a portfolio is overweight in a particular sector or area of the market. In 2000, investors that were overweight in technology stocks lost as much as 70% of their portfolio value by year-end. A non-diversified mutual fund has greater concentration risk because by design it is allowed to invest more than 5% of fund assets in a particular issuer's security. Since the mutual fund is non-diversified, it may own fewer securities. Many non-diversified funds own, at most, between 20-30 stocks. Business risk and industry risk is greater with these funds, and stock selection and timing becomes even more critical.

- **Investment style** *risk* is the risk assumed when investing in a particular investment style. There are numerous ways money is managed -- some a lot more aggressive than others. Here are just a few:

Equity Investment Styles

-- **Growth equity style:** buys stocks with their P/Es above market multiples;
-- **Aggressive growth equity style:** buys stocks with P/Es greater than 60;
-- **Value equity style:** buys stocks with P/Es less than market multiples;
-- **Deep value equity style:** buys stocks with P/Es less than 11;

Fixed-Income Investment Styles

-- **Limited maturity bond:** buys short-to-intermediate investment grade bonds;
-- **U.S. Government bond:** buys only Treasury and/or agency issues;
-- **High yield bond:** buys non-investment grade ("junk") bonds; and so on.

In any given year, each investment style's success depends, in large part, upon market conditions that favor that particular style. When a manager's style is out-of-favor with the market, expect performance to lag. A smart investor can reduce investment style risk by restricting exposure to each investment style to less than 30% of the portfolio.

- ***Mutual fund selection*** is very critical to proper portfolio construction and performance. Do not let the Brinson study tell you otherwise. That's the study that concluded that asset allocation is responsible for 90% of a portfolio's volatility. You can be right on the choice of asset class but totally miss the reward by not selecting the most appropriate mutual fund. For example, as the economy transitioned out of the 2001-2002 recession, high yield bonds began to outperform investment grade bonds. Out of the 335 high yield bond funds, 148 had a negative 3-year annualized return ending March 31, 2003. The overall category returns ranged from -21.4% to +15.57%, according to Morningstar. If you invested $100,000 in the very worst fund at the beginning of the period (March 31, 2000), it would have been worth only $48,559 by the end of the three-year period. In contrast, the very best performing fund would have been worth a cool $154,360. The goal is to select funds showing overall performance results within the second quartile, not just those funds ranked as five-star funds by Morningstar.

- ***Timing risk*** is very important even though various studies may tell you to bury your head in the sand and ignore timing altogether. It is true that no one can time the market. However, that does not mean that investors should ignore valuations. In March 2000, stocks were overvalued. Moreover, large-cap growth stocks were *extremely* overvalued. CISCO was selling at a multiple of 188! Investors who bought large-cap growth stocks at that time definitely overpaid. As a fund category, large-cap growth funds posted a -23.87% 3-year annualized return ending March 31, 2003. For investors who invested at market highs, it can often take seven to 10 years to break even. Timing risk can be reduced by dollar-cost-averaging purchases into the markets and carefully considering current valuations before investing.

Getting Your Arms around Risk Measurements

"October is one of the peculiarly dangerous months to speculate in stocks.
The other months are November, December, January, February,
March, April, May, June, July, August, and September"
-- Mark Twain

What measures of risk should be considered?

Investor psychology, experience, circumstances, sophistication, age, financial condition, source of information, and needs shape an investor's perception of risk. Below are four ways investors view risk.

1. Loss of principal
This is how most investors view risk. This risk is most associated with equity investments and long-term bond investments.

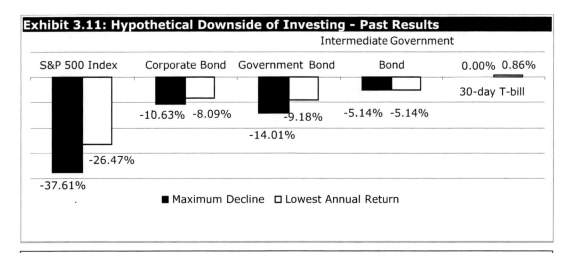

Exhibit 3.11: Hypothetical Downside of Investing - Past Results

This chart is for illustrative purposes only and does not predict or depict the performance of any investment. Past performance is no guarantee of future performance.

2. *Not enough growth*
Investments might not grow enough to meet future goals or expenses. This problem is associated with money market funds and short-term bond funds if they are held over longer periods of time.

Cash-equivalent investments over long periods have generated "actual negative returns" after inflation, taxes, and expenses. Even a preservation of capital objective assumes that capital will be grown at a rate that, at the very least, beats inflation. Otherwise, the objective is not being met in real terms which can compromise retirement goals.

Let's go over a hypothetical example to illustrate the point. How long would it take for a $100,000 30-day Treasury bill portfolio to become a $200,000 portfolio after taxes (assuming a combined federal and state tax rate of 28%), and inflation (the average annualized CPI rate was 3.92% from 12/31/53-12/31/03)? The answer is...never.

If we changed the underlying investment to U.S long Government/corporate bonds, as represented by the Lehman Brothers Aggregate Bond Index, then it would take 92 years, versus 16 years for large-cap equities, as represented by the S&P 500 Index. The example is based upon return data for 30-day Treasury bill from December 31, 1953 to December 31, 2003 and assumes that over the next fifty years that past performance remains constant. The example also assumes reinvestment of capital gains and dividends. (Past performance is not indicative of future results. Investors cannot invests directly in any index.)

3. *Variance in return*

Most investors cannot stomach volatility even though short-term volatility of the markets does not make the average investor rich or poor. The greater the variance in a fund's returns, the greater the risk of losing money.

A mutual fund's standard deviation can provide some insight into the expected positive and negative returns. The range in return is a simple way to get a feel for the potential loss or gain. It provides extreme values and not expected values.

It is also wise to look at a fund's historical *worst* annual return to gauge the extreme downside value that is possible. The idea is to avoid investments that are prone to "blow out" years. Just remember that the worst annual return of any investment is based on past performance that may be the result of poor management at the time.

4. *Liquidity*

Investors who have made it to Easy Street are more concerned with the return *of* their money versus the return *on* their money.

A short-to-intermediate term investment grade bond fund is a good place to park wealth because those investments have provided liquidity and returns that have generally either matched or beaten inflation in the past.

Using Numerical Measures to Quantify Risk

Is it sufficient to use a subjective scale of one to 10 -- with 10 being the riskiest -- to pick an investment that's right for a client's portfolio?

In order to match an investor's risk tolerance with the appropriate portfolio, it's better to use quantitative methods to assess risk and avoid subjective means.

I've known many individuals who rely on a scale of one to 10 to determine a client's risk tolerance. The problem with that method is that it provides ambiguous information that won't allow for an accurate assessment of a client's risk tolerance. A client might say 10 when he can only afford to lose 5%. Another client might say 5 when he can afford to lose 10%.

Below are quantitative measures to use, but be aware that each quantitative method has one or two drawbacks. Therefore, it is necessary to use several methods to gauge the overall portfolio and individual investment risk.

Beta -- Beta measures a portfolio's market risk. It measures the historical price volatility of a fund to a benchmark index. It can be a better way to assess risk than standard deviation since it only measures market risk. In constructing an efficient portfolio, all other forms of risk can be diversified away. Therefore, beta is the appropriate risk measure and not standard deviation.

Typically, an equity portfolio is regressed against the S&P 500 Index. If a portfolio has a beta of one it means that it should go up (or down) with the same magnitude as the market. If an investment has a beta of two, it should increase twice as much as the market up on up side and drop twice as much on the down side. An investment with a beta of 0.5 should decline 50% less than the market.

It is a good idea to use beta with equity mutual funds. Keep in mind that it is more important to assess the beta of the overall portfolio than to worry about the beta of a single investment. Adding a high beta investment to a conservative portfolio may even lower overall portfolio risk. You can build a portfolio first using covariance analysis and then look at the beta to see if the portfolio is too risky. Covariance is a statistical measure of the extent to which two variables move together. Use the covariance to determine the degree to which return on two securities is related. In general, a high covariance indicates similar movements and lack of diversification.

The drawback to beta is that it is often based on past performance. It is also less reliable with non-diversified portfolios and when the measurement period is short. Beta should only be used with investments that are diversified. A diversified portfolio has removed unsystematic risk from the portfolio! Avoid using beta with a non-diversified portfolio such as those that include only gold funds, or only sector funds. Moreover, it's better to use beta calculations for a 3-year period or greater.

Standard Deviation -- The annual standard deviation in return is a statistical measure of the relative price volatility of an investment's annual return. The higher the standard deviation in annual returns, the greater the risk. Standard deviation gives equal weight to upside and downside performance. A low standard deviation investment can be a lousy investment, whereas a high standard deviation investment can be a terrific performer.

Standard deviation also assumes normal distribution of returns when studies have shown that returns are not normally distributed.

One can use a fund's standard deviation to evaluate tail risk. Security returns are not normally distributed but skewed. The shape of return distribution is either more peaked or less peaked. Peaked distributions have a greater amount of outlier returns, making investments with "peaked shaped" return distribution more risky than normal distributions. There is a greater probability of a big loss year and big gain year with a peak return distribution.

It is best to manage investment risk by evaluating distribution of return. When looking at a fund's return based on one standard deviation, investors can expect to earn a return with the one standard deviation two-thirds of the time. Two standard deviation means this is what could happen over longer holding periods.

Exhibit 3.12: Which Portfolio Do You Prefer?

Range in Returns for two Hypothetical Portfolios:

Low Tail Risk Portfolio			High Tail Risk Portfolio		
Mean	1 Standard Deviation	2 Standard Deviation	**Mean**	1 Standard Deviation	2 Standard Deviation
8%	-4% to +20%	-16% to +32%	**12%**	-10% to +34%	-32% to +56%

This table is for illustrative purposes only and does not predict or depict the performance of any investment.

A Matter of Style

Can style analysis help in selecting more conservative or aggressive investments?

Yes. Certain investment styles are more risky than other styles. You can evaluate a style's mean return, standard deviation, number of up to down years, and worst year, over a twenty-year period to assess risk. Small-cap growth and emerging markets are at the top of the higher risk list; large-cap value is at the bottom. The problem with style analysis is that style drift can occur. What was once a conservative investment can morph into an aggressive one.

Risk Metrics for Fixed-Income Investments

Besides beta, what other measures of risk should be used with a bond portfolio?

Duration -- Duration measures the price sensitivity of a bond portfolio's price to a change in interest rates. It indicates the amount of interest rate risk exposure of an investment. The greater the duration of an investment, the higher the interest rate risk and price volatility. The shorter the duration of a portfolio, the lower the interest rate risk and price volatility.

To determine the estimated effect of an interest rate move on the price of a bond fund, for example, you can take the duration of the portfolio and multiply it by the expected point change in interest rates. As a practical matter, a bond fund that has duration of ten will drop in value by ten percent when interest rates move by one point. It is a better measure of interest rate risk than the weighted average maturity because it takes several factors into account including maturity, coupon, call protection, and how long it takes to get a loan paid back.

You can use duration with bond funds and for changes in interest rates of less than one percent. But duration loses its ability to accurately estimate price changes when rates changes are greater than one percent.

Weighted Average Credit Quality -- Weighted average credit quality tells us whether an investment is of grade or non-investment grade quality. When the weighted average credit quality of a portfolio is below BBB, then the overall portfolio has a non-investment grade rating.

The weighted average credit quality of the individual securities in a portfolio is extremely important to know in order to manage risk. When a company (that is not a core holding) goes bankrupt in a diversified stock portfolio, the share price will hardly be affected since there are typically over one hundred stocks, and stock positions rarely exceed 5%. But when a bond defaults, not only will the yield drop but so will the price. Since bond returns are lower than stock returns, it is harder to recoup losses due to defaults.

Therefore, it is wise to maintain an overall investment grade tilt in a portfolio. However, there are times when high quality bonds become overbought -- usually when unfounded pessimism grips the market -- and do not offer the best risk and reward trade off. At these times, when the yield curve between high credits and low credit has substantially widened, it may be better to establish a bigger position in lower credit securities.

Ratios to Capture the Upside and Downside

How can you get a feel for downside risk?

Look at a portfolio's downside capture ratio to get a feel for the downside risk of a particular portfolio's investment approach. The downside capture ratio shows how much of a down market a portfolio has captured. It measures the portfolio's negative return as a percentage of its benchmark's return in quarters with a negative benchmark return. As expected, the upside capture ratio shows the opposite of the downside ratio. It tells investors how much of the upside in the benchmark's positive return was captured by a portfolio.

Exhibit 3.13: Illustration of Downside and Upside Capture Ratios		
Avg. Annualized Return	Growth Objective Model	Benchmark S&P 500 Index
5 years	14%	11%
Downside and Upside Ratios:		
5 years Downside Capture	84%	
5 years Upside Capture	127%	
This table is for illustrative purposes only and does not predict or depict the performance of any investment.		

Risk-adjusted Investing

Legendary investor Warren Buffet once said that the first rule of investing is not to lose money, and the second rule is don't forget the first rule.

Risk-adjusted return investing takes into account the amount of risk taken in order to earn returns. Think about risk, not just past returns, before investing. Unfortunately, most investors focus only on absolute returns. Which portfolio would you choose based on the following annual returns?

Exhibit 3.14: Invests in "Bankable" Portfolio

Fund	Year 1	Year 2	Year 3	Year 4	Year 5
Absolute Portfolio	20%	20%	-25%	20%	20%
Risk Adjusted Portfolio	10%	10%	10%	10%	10%

This table is for illustrative purposes only and does not predict or depict the performance of any investment.

Based on a $100 investment, the results are respectively $159 for the absolute portfolio and $161 for the risk-adjusted portfolio. If the shareholder had sold in the third year or thereafter, the risk-adjusted portfolio would have had a higher return, never had a down year, and generated consistent returns that the shareholder could have banked on.

Absolute Returns Vs. Risk-adjusted Returns

What's so wrong about using absolute returns to evaluate the performance of my portfolio?

Absolute return says nothing about risk-- the probability and potential magnitude of losses. Therefore, return alone is an incomplete measure of performance.

Often a top performing portfolio of the year took more risk by making sector bets, and owning fewer stocks. In 1997, portfolios that were overweight in technology stocks such as Yahoo, Inc. could have found themselves at the top of the rankings. In 1997 Yahoo produced an absolute return of 511%. However, if you bought Boston Chicken, another hot initial public offering (I.P.O.), you were down 82% by year-end.

A Piper Jaffray study showed that the median annual return of I.P.O.s from May 1988 through July 17, 1998 was a paltry 2.4%! T-bills did better!

In 1993, a leading mutual fund group's emerging markets fund returned 81.76%. Assets grew from $15 million to $1.9 billion by year-end. Subsequently, the fund generated a negative return of -17.93%, -3.18%, +10%, -40.77%, in 1994, 1995, 1996, and 1997 respectively. The S&P 500 Index returned 23.79% on average for the same period. That's why it is better to evaluate performance on a risk-adjusted basis.

Is it possible for an investment to have greater risk and produce lower returns?

When comparing mutual fund categories it is clear that during certain periods some categories take on more risk and earn lower returns. Also, certain sub-asset classes provide higher returns per unit of risk. This is also true for individual mutual funds.

Exhibit 3.15: Incremental Return Analysis

	Annualized Returns	Standard Deviation	Return per Unit of Risk
S&P 500 Index	17.68%	13.41%	1.32%
30 Yr. Treasury	10.89%	14.68%	0.74%
5 Yr. Treasury	9.73%	7.37%	1.32%
1 Yr. Treasury	8.25%	3.62%	2.28%

Source: Standard & Poor's, Lehman Brothers, Salomon Brothers, Frank Russell Company. Federal Reserve. Period of study 1980-1998. The S&P 500 index, a commonly used broad based index of domestic stocks. The S&P 500® is an unmanaged stock index: S&P 500 is a registered trademark of Standard & Poor's Corporation. Investors cannot invest in the S&P 500 Index; 30 Year Treasury bonds are represented by the S&P Long-term Government Bonds index; 5 Year Treasury bonds are represented by the Lehman 5 Year Treasury note index. 1 Year Treasury Notes are represented by the Lehman 1 Year Treasury note index. Treasury indices are total return indices held constant maturities. Indices include reinvested income, but not transaction costs or taxes, are unmanaged and cannot be purchased directly by investors. Standard deviation is an indicator of the portfolio's total return volatility. The larger the portfolio's standard deviation, the greater the portfolio's volatility. This table is for illustrative purposes only and does not predict or depict the performance of any investment. Past performance is no guarantee of future performance.

Utilizing Portfolio Management Techniques

Now that you know all of these things what should you do next?

You can apply the risk-adjusted return concept to portfolio construction. In the past, according to modern portfolio theory, an investor would have lowered risk without sacrificing return by combining the right investments together. Two common risk-adjusted portfolio management approaches are value investing, and bullet bond management. Use these approaches with the right combination of investments during supportive market conditions.

Use Roy's Safety Rule to pick the best risk-adjusted return portfolio (based on past performance, which is not indicative of future performance). The rule maximizes the excess return over a threshold return per unit of risk (standard deviation). The idea is to apply the following formula (calculate step 1 then step 2) and pick the portfolio with the highest ratio.

1. **Threshold Return** = (cash outflow + end value required - beginning value)/beginning value
2. **Safety Rule** = (expected return - threshold return)/standard deviation

Which portfolio is better for the client if the client begins with $1,000,000 but needs $1,100,000 by year-end? Answer: portfolio A.

Exhibit 3.16: Roy's Safety Rule Picks the Best Risk-adjusted Return Portfolio

	Expected Return	Stand. Deviation	Threshold Return	Roy's Safety
Portfolio A	14%	15	10%	.27
Portfolio B	11%	9	10%	.11

This table is for illustrative purposes only and does not predict or depict the performance of any investment. Standard deviation is an indicator of the portfolio's total return volatility. The larger the portfolio's standard deviation, the greater the portfolio's volatility.

You can use the Sharpe ratio to compare risk between mutual funds that have different risks to determine which one had a better risk-adjusted return. The drawback once again is that it's based on past results.

Sharpe Ratio = (Expected Return - Risk-free rate)/Standard Deviation

You typically get more "bang for your buck" by choosing the fund with the higher Sharpe ratio. A higher ratio means better risk-adjusted returns. But remember that results of using the Sharpe Ratio are based on past results.

It is smart to ensure that the investment is not currently overvalued. For instance, one would believe that the large-cap value sector would rank higher than small-cap value. As it turns out, for the latest three-year period ending March 31, 2003 (which spans a bear market) small-cap value's ratio was 0.05, while large-cap value's ratio was -0.77, and large-cap growth's ratio was -1.56. What happened? Small-cap value went into the bear market already being oversold and large-cap was way overbought, and therefore overvalued.

Another caveat about the Sharpe Ratio is that the mutual fund with the highest Sharpe Ratio might not be the best fund to add to a portfolio. It is best to pick the highest one when it will be the only mutual fund held by a risk-averse investor. But when adding a fund to a diversified portfolio, you may want to pick a fund that will enhance a portfolio's beta and alpha. The fund with the highest Sharpe Ratio might not be that fund.

Okay you did what I told you to do but are you out-of-the-woods yet?

No. Risk-adjusted investing works better when factoring current valuations into the asset allocation and fund selection process. You can start out by assessing risk and return with past results using Roy's Safety method (see above) and the Sharpe Ratio (also explained above). You can then apply valuation analysis to decide on the tactical weighting. For example, before investing in bonds, determine if bonds are overvalued compared to stocks. Within the bond asset class, decide which areas are overvalued. In late 2002, Treasuries were overvalued compared to undervalued high yield bonds? Therefore, you could underweight Treasuries and overweight high yield bonds in order to improve risk-adjusted returns -- even though past results suggested investing in Treasuries.

The Secrets of Reducing Risk

Pay special attention to the details in this section. By not attempting to reduce risk, investors unconsciously decided to retain risk thereby accepting bigger losses and more volatility then they signed up for.

Unbeknownst to most investors, too often, the "frozen pie" portfolios being sold in the industry are inefficient ones in that have tremendous overlap in investment exposure and are on automatic pilot to invest in areas of the market considered to be overvalued. Over a market cycle risks can build up in a frozen portfolio unless carefully managed. For instance, where a bond portfolio is bought when interest rates are low. As rates increase, interest rate risk builds up.

Logic tells us that slicing a pie up into smaller slices reduces exposure to each investment sector. That's partially correct. But just slicing up the pie into more slices will not necessarily reduce risk if all the slices are highly correlated.

Secret #1: The trick is to slice the pie into about four slices that are not highly correlated.
By investing in four randomly selected asset classes,
most of the risk reducing benefit of asset allocation is accomplished.

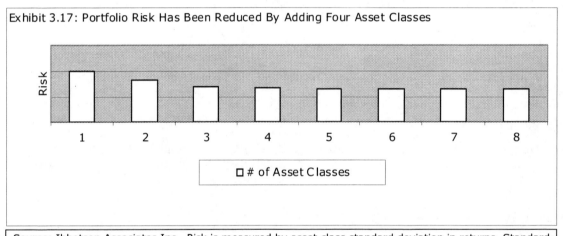

Exhibit 3.17: Portfolio Risk Has Been Reduced By Adding Four Asset Classes

Source: Ibbotson Associates Inc. Risk is measured by asset class standard deviation in returns. Standard deviation is an indicator of the portfolio's total return volatility. The larger the portfolio's standard deviation, the greater the portfolio's volatility. Small company stocks are represented by the fifth capitalization quintile of stocks on the NYSE for 1926-1981 and the performance of the Dimensional Fund Advisors, Inc., U.S. Micro Cap Portfolio, thereafter Large Company stocks - The Standard & Poor's 500® is an unmanaged group of securities and is considered to be representative of the U.S. stock market in general; International stocks are represented by Morgan Stanley Capital International Europe Australasia, and Far east (EAFE®) Index. Long-term Government Bonds-20-year U.S. Government Bond; Business Real Estate-Wilshire Real Estate Securities Index; Long-term Corporate Bonds-Salomon Brothers Long term High Grade Corporate Bond Index; Treasury Bills-30 day U.S. Treasury Bill; International Bonds-Citigroup Non-U.S., 1+ Year Government Bond Index. An investment cannot be made directly in an index. This is for illustrative purposes only and is not indicative of any investment. Past performance is no guarantee of future results.

Asset allocation is very important. Nevertheless, do not let people tell you it is *everything* and that timing and selection does not matter. Even a portfolio evenly divided among four asset classes (large-cap growth, large-cap value, small-cap growth, and corporate bonds) in late 1999 took a big bath over the next three years. Moreover, the losses grew if those assets were in riskier funds.

Diversification is the most common technique used to reduce risk. If done properly, it could reduce total risk down to just market risk. Yet diversification does not ensure a profit or guarantee against a loss in a declining market.

There are two reasons to diversify. First, surprises cannot be predicted and no one can possibly know everything. Secondly, diversification will reduce the variance in portfolio returns. Just adding more funds to a portfolio won't help. In fact, indiscriminately adding funds to a portfolio may increase risk and lower returns!

Secret #2: The number of funds in a portfolio is less important than the correlation of individual fund performance in a portfolio. The greatest payoff to diversification comes when not every fund in a portfolio reacts the same way to market events.

Chances are a portfolio is not diversified if all of the funds increase or decrease in value all in perfect lockstep. Funds that do not invest in similar securities or areas of the market do not have a high correlation with each other. Funds that have a correlation of less than 0.50 are good funds to combine.

Which portfolio do you think would lower overall portfolio risk? Fund A and Fund B are stock funds from top-notch fund companies investing in S&P 500 stocks. The portfolio is re-balanced evenly between Fund A and Fund B annually.

Exhibit 3.18: Hypothetical Improperly Diversified Portfolio

	Annual Returns		
Year	**Fund A**	**Fund B**	**Portfolio A+B**
1990	-10%	-14%	-12%
1991	15%	18%	16.5%
1992	20%	28%	24%
1993	26%	32%	29%
1994	-8%	-5%	-6.5%

This table is for illustrative purposes only and does not predict or depict the performance of any investment.

As you can see, by owning two funds, one cannot assume that a portfolio is diversified. Both funds had similar reactions to market events. When the S&P 500 Index declined, so did both funds. More risk can be "wash out" by diversifying into funds that are not alike. The portfolio below owns a large-cap value fund, and an Intermediate bond fund.

Exhibit 3.19: Hypothetical Properly Diversified Portfolio

	Annual Returns		
Year	**Fund C**	**Fund D**	**Portfolio C+D**
1990	-5.95%	8.72%	1.41%
1991	24.7%	11.85%	18.75%
1992	21.1%	5.18%	13.14%
1993	16.3%	6.8%	11.55%
1994	1%	0%	0.5%

This table is for illustrative purposes only and does not predict or depict the performance of any investment.

The Proper Diversification Wins Out

Which portfolio won?

The Improperly Diversified Portfolio returned 8.9%, whereas the Properly Diversified Portfolio returned 8.8% and did not have a down year! This is quite impressive since 1994 was truly a difficult year; eight out of twelve investment categories were down in 1994 -- intermediate government bonds had their worst year ever! The low correlation between funds reduced the overall portfolio risk without significantly effecting long-term returns.

What's the secret trick to diversification?

Buying a dozens of funds? No! The trick is to diversify across fewer funds that are not highly correlated. Harry Markowitz, Nobel Prize winner in economics, said that "you should consider the portfolio as a whole...diversity means adding things to your portfolio that aren't highly correlated."

> **Secret #3: Owning more than one fund that invests in the same area of the market**
> **has diminished a portfolio's ability to beat the broad market indices.**
> **In fact, the more similar funds are in a portfolio,**
> **the higher the probability of matching the benchmark.**

For instance, a portfolio that owns four growth & income funds will be in almost lockstep performance with the S&P 500 Index because its correlation is 0.97.

Exhibit 3.20: Over-fund-diversification has Increased Risk				
# of Funds	**Fund Objective**			
In the Portfolio:	**Growth**	**Growth & Income**	**Balanced**	**International**
2	.93	.96	.95	.91
4	.95	.97	.96	.92

Source: Morningstar Inc. 2000; Growth funds are represented by Large-cap Growth funds, Growth & Income funds are represented by Large-cap Value funds with a Growth & Income objective, Balanced funds are represented by Balance funds, and International funds are represented by Large-cap International funds. Fund categorization is determined by Morningstar Inc.

Why not just assemble a portfolio of low standard deviation funds to decrease total investment risk?

A fund's correlation with the other investments in the portfolio and not the variance in returns determines its contribution to overall portfolio risk levels. You should combine the right combination of funds to build a portfolio. In choppy seas marked by lower GDP and profit growth, choose defensive investments that have a lower correlation with the S&P 500. When waters are calmer as GDP and profits grow at above historical trend line rates, invests in funds with cyclical stocks and/or have a higher correlation with the S&P 500.

You should build a diversified portfolio by adding funds that have low correlation with the other funds in a portfolio. Correlation analysis can be as simple as getting rid of redundant funds. Just make sure that every portfolio has three investments that invest in different sectors of the market. Those sectors must move in the opposite direction of the rest of the portfolio. When a portfolio is composed entirely of S&P 500 stocks, add funds that have a low covariance to the S&P 500 Index. Big diversifying fund categories include: money markets, commodities, real estate, intermediate bond, precious metals, and currency.

Correlations between world securities markets have significantly increased with the globalization of economies and markets. In addition, correlations increase even more during major market corrections and periods of volatility. Even so, major asset class diversification still works. Spreading your bets among investment categories is still a better way to reduce volatility, downside risk, and streakier returns that can be associated with owning just one asset class or investment category.

The Natural Rotation of Category Kings

Secret #4: You should spread portfolio assets over different types of investment categories and styles because not one category or investment style works all of the time.

Category leadership changes every year or few years, as shown in Exhibit 3:21:

Exhibit 3.21: Investment Performance is a Moving Target

Year	Investment Category	Annual Return
2003	Small-cap Growth	44.36%
2001-2002	Corporate bonds	10.65%, 16.33%
2000	Long-term Gov't bonds	21.5%
1999	Small-company Stocks	29.8%
1995-1998	Large Company Stocks	37.4%, 23.1%, 33.4%, 28.6% respectively
1994	U.S. Treasury Bills	3.9%
1991-1993	Small-company Stocks	44.6%, 23.4%, 21% respectively
1990	Intermediate Gov't Bonds	9.7%

Source: Wall Street Journal. Large-cap stocks are represented by the S&P 500 index®, a commonly used broad based index of domestic stocks. The S&P 500 is an unmanaged stock index: S&P 500 is a registered trademark of Standard & Poor's Corporation. Investors cannot invest in the S&P 500 Index: Small-cap stocks are represented by the Russell 2000 Index, an index consisting of the smallest 2,000 companies in the Russell 3000 index (composed of 3,000 large U.S. companies as determined by market capitalization and represents approximately 98% of the investable U.S. equity market); U.S. Government Long term bonds are represented by the S&P Long-term Government Bonds index; U.S. Intermediate Government bonds are represented by the Lehman Long Treasury Bond Index is a 10-year Treasury note index. Treasury indices are total return indices held constant maturities. U.S. 30-day T-bill is represented by the Lehman Brothers Three month Treasury Bill Index derived from secondary market Treasury bill rates published by the Federal Reserve Bank or the 91-day Treasury bills data. Corporate bonds are represented by the Lehman Brothers Bond Index. The Lehman Brothers Government/Credit Index measures the performance of all debt obligations of the U.S. Treasury and U.S. Government agencies, and all investment- grade domestic corporate debt; Indices include reinvested income, but not transaction costs or taxes, are unmanaged and cannot be purchased directly by investors. This table is for illustrative purposes only and does not predict or depict the performance of any investment. Past performance is no guarantee of future performance.

In addition, leadership changes between growth style and value style have occurred every two to five years from 1975 to 2003. It is best to diversify between both styles to lower risk because their returns are negatively correlated.

Exhibit 3.22: S&P 500 Value versus Growth Leadership Changes		
	Value Style	Growth Style
Period	Avg. Annualized Return	Avg. Annualized Return
1975-1979 Value outperformed	**19.38%**	10.32%
1980-1982 Growth outperformed	14.38%	**15.34%**
1983-1988 Value outperformed	**18.97%**	13.73%
1989-1991 Growth outperformed	12.92%	**23.66%**
1992-1993 Value outperformed	**14.49%**	3.36%
1994-1999 Growth outperformed	18.65%	**27.99%**
2000-2003 Value outperformed	**-0.57%**	-1.09%

Source: BARRA, Inc. Large-cap growth stocks represented by S&P 500 Barra Growth Index. Value stocks represented by the S&P 500 BARRA Value Index. "Growth Stocks" have above average profitability and valuation characteristics. "Value Stocks" have below average profitability and valuation characteristics. Indices include reinvested income, but not transaction costs or taxes, are unmanaged and cannot be purchased directly by investors. This table is for illustrative purposes only and does not predict or depict the performance of any investment.

What more can be done to reduce risk?

Increasing a portfolio's bond position to twenty five percent of assets has lowered downside risk in the past, and did not materially lower past long-term return. A portfolio that invested seventy-five percent in an investment tracking the S&P 500 Index and twenty-five percent in intermediate Government bonds from 1950 to 2002 returned 88% of the S&P 500 index return and its maximum decline was only three-fourths as much.

Short Check List of Ways to Reduce Risk

- Asset Allocation - the workhorse of reducing all types of risk - both unsystematic and systematic - in a portfolio. The *correlation* of sub-asset classes is what's important, not the *number* of sub-asset classes in a portfolio.
- Diversify among investment approaches both active and passive, and among both styles value and growth.
- Add an investment with a negative covariance to the dominant investment category in a portfolio - e.g. commodities, a contrarian fund that shorts the market, etc.
- Add short-to-intermediate bonds and convertible bond funds to an equity portfolio to reduce volatility.
- Periodically rebalance a portfolio to reflect risk preference and to sell overvalued investments.
- Dollar cost averaging or value averaging reduces the risk of buying at overvalued levels.
- Invest only in investment-grade securities to reduce credit quality risk - be tactical with this one.
- Limit the duration of bond component to reduce interest rate risk- be tactical with this one, too.
- Limit the multiple of a portfolio to reduce downside risk.
- Stick with a risk-averse investment approach: value style, bullet bond approach, etc.
- Stick with low beta funds. Avoid funds investing in exotic derivatives, emerging markets, and micro-caps that offer poor incremental returns per unit of risk.
- Minimize exposure to investments with high degree of tail risk such as small-cap growth.
- Have a sell discipline at 11% (sell when an investment drops by 11% from initial investment).

Why not move to the safety of a money market account to reduce risk when the market is experiencing trouble? Market timing is an ineffective way of reducing risk. A market timer's job is to get clients out of the market before it corrects, before days like October 19, 1987, when the DJIA dropped 22%! Nevertheless, it's easier said then done. Market timers have to make two right decisions -- when to get out and when to get in -- which is extremely hard to consistently do over time! Market sell offs tend to catch everyone by surprise and occurs within a few days. The best timers more often capture half the down market and miss most of the market rallies. The rallies that follow a sell-off also are swift in action recovering sometimes up to two-thirds of the previous decline in a few days. For example, Ned Davis research points out that if investors just miss the best 50 days of the market from December 31, 1975 to December 31, 2003, the investor's return dropped from the market return to 5.5% which fell below the average annual return (6.1%) on Treasury Bills for the period. Moreover, timing increases cost and taxes, which lowers returns! Remember what Bernard Baruch said, "Bottoms are bought and tops are sold by liars".

Investing Guidelines to Follow Throughout the Market Cycles

"Success in investing doesn't correlate with IQ...once you have ordinary intelligence, what you need is the temperament to control the urges that get other people into trouble in investing."
- Warren Buffet

Ten Secrets of Sound Advice

You've heard it before but I'll say it again. There is no such thing as a free lunch.

That's no big secret. Investing is not as easy as picking the hottest mutual funds. There isn't a certain formula for riches that works every year. Stock investing requires hundreds of hours of time to evaluate the fundamental value of a company. Even selecting a mutual fund requires numerous hours.

Managing a portfolio is a not a weekend pursuit. For those reasons, hiring an experienced professional is critical to successful investing. A professional can remain rational, understands market behavior, and is trained regarding portfolio management. The secret to improving results lies in removing from the process the emotional behavior and tendencies of investing by using quantitative methods. The same emotional behavior can undermine successful long-term investing.

Empirical research shows that investing is full of irrational behavioral biases that cause bad investment decisions or investor inertia, even where intentions are just the opposite. Forms of irrational investing behavior can include sticking with an investment program that is out dated, staying too long in a mutual fund that once did well but now is a loser, failing to act on professional advice, ignoring what is going on with investments, and not selling a losing investment because it would generate a loss. All these -- and more -- can interfere with successful investing. Try as they might, the reality is that many investors don't know enough to help them avoid common investment mistakes. Moreover, investment mistakes are not discovered until it's too late.

This chapter contains guidelines to prevent investors from being their own worst enemy.

Secret #1: Investing is all About Increasing Purchasing Power

Investing is all about increasing purchasing power and increasing it no matter what you own - cash, bonds, or stocks.

When an investment return does not match the inflation rate, the investment is losing value in purchasing power terms. After all, if you invest one dollar and it grows to $1.04 while inflation increased four percent over the same period, what have you gained? That one dollar is still worth one dollar in purchasing power terms.

You can start evaluating investment performance using inflation-adjusted returns. Inflation-adjusted returns will provide a better measure or your real gain after factoring in the rise in consumer prices. The focus should be not how many dollars are in an account but how much those dollars can buy.

The new fiduciary standards require fiduciaries to balance current income against the need for growth that outpaces inflation. The old standards emphasized protecting against market losses -- not purchasing power loss.

Investors with the goal of preservation of capital often ignore purchasing power risk because they are too worried about stock market losses. Retirees that rely on fixed-income portfolios to pay for the cost of living risk outliving their money, or may face a steady decline in quality of lifestyle. This really applies to retirees that don't have a lot of money. For example, a sixty-two year old retiree owns a $1,000,000 fixed-income portfolio that yields four percent annually. The investment is initially set-up on a systematic withdrawal plan of $40,000 (4%) per year that is increased each year by four percent to allow the income to keep pace with inflation. The portfolio would be depleted by the time the retiree reaches eighty. Moreover, this assumes the impossible -- no extra money for spending! Everyone knows that American's have a propensity to spend until there is nothing left.

Secret #2: If Big Losses Matter, Stay Diversified

It is never a good idea to load up on one mutual fund category or one kind of fund. Concentration can be a double edge sword. It can cut both ways - higher returns and greater losses. In 2000, many investors learned this lesson the hard way by having a 50% plus exposure in the technology sector.

When slicing up the asset allocation pie into seven smaller slices, make sure a few slices have a low correlation to the dominant asset and or sub-asset class. What matters is the *combination* of funds, not the *number* of funds (see the previous chapter, chapter 3, for a more in-depth discussion on this topic). Being too diversified, having too many slices, owning too many redundant funds, can increase risk and lower returns.

Secret #3: Have a Sell Discipline - Both on the Upside and Downside!

Holding onto losers in hope that they will become winners is a common mistake. Some investors take the buy and hold philosophy too far. The number one rule is to protect your portfolio from big losses. Remember, a ten percent loss takes an eleven percent gain to break even. An eleven percent return is easier to earn. A 20% loss takes a 25% gain. That is a lot harder to earn considering market returns, on average, twelve percent a year. You would have to earn more than double the average annual market return to break even. That large a return implies that you may very well be doubling the risk as well. If that big a risk does not pay off, the hole only gets deeper and losses become even harder to recoup.

It is usually better to admit your mistakes and cut your losses short! Conservative investors may consider selling a fund when loses exceed twelve percent. Your upside sell discipline should dictate that you sell 25% of a fund position when its annual return exceeds 40%.

Secret #4: Middle of the Road is the Way to Go for Most Investors

A balanced portfolio of sixty percent stocks and forty percent bonds has, in general, been a simple way to balance out investment risks. A balanced portfolio is an all cycle portfolio. Stocks do well in expansionary times and bonds do well during economic contractions. The heavier weight in stocks increases the portfolio purchasing power and the bonds dampen losses.

Other strategies tend to over expose a portfolio to one type of risk or another. Investors must accept some price volatility in order to offset purchasing power risk. In most cases, even retirees should consider holding at least a 50/50 split among stock and bond investments. A balanced portfolio should not be passively managed since risk will build up in spite of a balanced approach. A savvy investor will want to use tactical economic and market analysis to determine which specific areas of the bond market and stock market to emphasize in a portfolio given the current climate.

Secret #5: Do Waste Time Trying to Time the Market

Bernard Baruch once said, "Nobody buys at the low or sells at the high except liars."

Some investors try to time their investment decisions by predicting market highs and lows. Investors who think they can outsmart the market are in trouble. One thing that has not changed over time is the market's propensity to do the unexpected.

Studies have shown that the risk of missing a big market surge while trying to avoid a tumble is great enough that investors should stay in the market. Investors get big contributions to their long-term returns over very short periods. When investors miss those short periods, they lose all excess returns over the Treasury bill rate!

From 1982 to 1998, the annual rate of return on stocks was 11%. If an investor missed the best twenty days during that period, the return dropped to 3.4%! Unless you are a good short seller, if you do not participate in market rallies you will not reap the benefits of long-term investing.

Secret #6: It's Better to Be Early to the Party and Leave Early

Remember that the market is a forward indicator. It discounts future conditions into prices, so be forward with your investment actions.

History has shown that most of the bull market returns are produced in the early bull phase. To capture those returns investors must be fully invested during the late bear phase. To avoid the full brunt of bear market losses investors must begin to reduce equity exposure during the good times, when the party is roaring as the market crosses over from mid-bull to late bull. At that, point interest rates are rising and it makes sense to increase government bond exposure.

The world renowned money manager, Sir John Templeton, once said that bull markets are born on pessimism, they grow on skepticism, and they mature on optimism, and die on euphoria.

It is a good idea to stay ahead of the curve. Be early to the party and leave early when everyone is whooping it up!

Secret #7: "Rear View Mirror" Investing Can Be Hazardous

Do not be overly reliant on past ratings and performance. Always remember that ratings have a past cycle bias to them!

Highly rated funds have earned their stars in part because their investment approach was favored by market conditions. Of the 41 top quartile funds covered by Morningstar Inc. from 1991-1994, seventy-eight percent fell below the fiftieth percentile over the next four-year period.

When investing, t can be smart to buy what has not done well and avoid what has done extremely well. It often makes more sense to buy a lower rated fund whose investment approach is coming into favor. Based on Morningstar research from 1987 through 1995, investing in unpopular funds -- last year's underperformers -- would beat popular funds -- funds that did exceedingly well over the last twelve months -- 92% of the time. They also beat the average equity fund 79% of the time.

So why do investors buy last years winners? Most are trend investors who believe the trend will continue. Top performance also builds comfort with investors in a fund.

Secret #8: Don't Let Front Page News Drive Decisions

Don't allow emotion to drive investment decisions. The market tends to overreact to both good and bad news. Market volatility due to unfounded bearish market sentiment often creates buying opportunities because panic selling drives stock prices below their fair value. There will always be short-term economic disappointments that cause "V" corrections. Over the longer periods, the market will bounce back because stock earnings increase as a result real economic growth.

Unsuccessful investors may typically fail at seeing the big picture and usually sellout during down turns. When the market is volatile or corrects, investors have three options:

1. Sell
2. Ride it out
3. Manage it

Big losses can be very disturbing for any investor. It is important to always match a portfolio's risk and reward characteristics with the client's investment psychology.

A properly allocated portfolio that does not swing for the fences is a way to keep investors' eyes on the big picture. Managing it means starting out with a diversified portfolio that has a return potential of ten percent and a lot smoother ride, versus one that has a return potential of fifteen percent and a bumpier ride.

It's a good idea to select low P/E, low beta, dividend paying equity funds and high quality short-to-intermediate duration bond funds.

The legendary investor, Ben Graham, said that the market is like a business owner who happens to have a manic personality. There are days when the owner says that the company is worth a lot more than its fundamental value, and other days far less.

The point is that investors tend to overvalue or undervalue assets on a day-to-day basis because of emotion or irrational thinking. This is one reason why the market gets over bought and over sold. Try not to be swayed by the market's emotion.

A great time to invest is when there is bad news, and a resulting fear that drives stock prices lower than fair market value. A sound principle for long-term investors to follow is to buy during price weakness through a dollar-cost-averaging plan.

As I have counseled before, steer clear of weekly or monthly economic numbers to make decisions. Those numbers are frequently subject to revision. Turn off the noise. Using more frequent information leads to counter productive trading that can hurt long- term returns. Extrapolating recent trends is a risky business because one month, or quarter does not make a cyclical trend. Very often these numbers end up being revised next month.

Professor Terrance Odean of the University of California did a six-year study ending in 1996 of investor trading behavior. He found that frequent traders underperformed the market. Another study of 1,607 investors who switched to online trading found their returns dropping from 2% above the market average to 3% below.

Secret #9: Investors Following Popular Trends Run the Risk of Buying Overvalued Investments

Excellent past performance creates a positive "framing effect'" that makes an investment appear to be a good choice even though the security may be overvalued. Investors who get all their news from one source or rely on one source for information are more prone to the herd effect. Their decisions are more susceptible to framing effect --according researchers Mr. Tuersky and Mr. Kahberian. That is, their decision is based on what they see and hear from the news or what they read -- even though the information may be misleading.

Here's an example: Which line is longer?

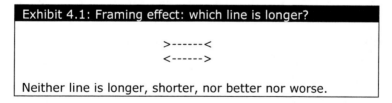

Neither line is longer, shorter, nor better nor worse.

The heard effect occurred with S&P 500 Index funds in the late 1990s. Investors were sold on the premise that an S&P 500 Index mutual fund was the way to invest in stock market. S&P 500 Index funds became extremely popular funds even though their approach to replicating the heavily weighted large-cap growth stock S&P 500 Index was a risky strategy by the end of the 1990s.

Subsequently, those investors took a bear market beating not seen since the Great Depression. The S&P 500 Index lost more than fourteen percent on average each year for the three-year period ending 2002, according to Morningstar. A better strategy, given market conditions, was the Russell 2000 Index which produced positive returns over that period.

In practice, this phenomenon happens a lot with investment timing. Is it a good time to invest or not? That depends on the information you choose to frame your decision.

Are valuations excessive or not? Without factoring in low inflation, productivity gains, and technological innovation, many portfolio managers concluded that stocks were too expensive in 1998 and 1999 and missed two great years of 25% plus returns. Albeit, by the end of 1999 multiples were stratospheric.

By chasing hot funds a portfolio can lose its balance and end up heavily concentrated into one type of investment approach which may, over the short-term, work well, but over the long-term could produce streaky performance or even severe underperformance.

Be careful not to over concentrate assets into any one area of the market at any given time. Conforming to popular trends is a form of herd-like group behavior that can lead to underperformance. It can be smarter to do the opposite when something has been extremely popular for awhile. Chances are that strategy everyone is chasing has been overbought.

Secret #10: Don't Be Blinded By Greed

"I worry about speculating, I worry even more that it will stop." -- anonymous Wall Street saying.

Investors often ignore the basic relationship between risk and reward, especially in bull markets. They become less risk-averse even though they have a low tolerance for loss.

Besides the Internet craze of 1997-1999, the famous Ponzi scheme comes to mind when I think of investor greed entirely driving investment decisions. Charles Ponzi in 1919 invented the pyramid scheme for defrauding investors of their money. Essentially the illegal scheme borrows from one investor to pay the others. Ponzi promised investors a 50% return within 45 days. He conned $10 million from 20,000 investors in six months before being convicted and sentenced to prison.

Investors must not forget that any higher return investment opportunity entails greater risk to principal. And sometimes a promise of greater rewards is simply too good to be true!

In the mid 1980s, investors poured billions of dollars into U.S. Government enhanced funds. These funds marketed yields of 12% when Treasury bonds were yielding 8%. The 4% difference came from less reliable option writing programs designed to enhance the dividend income. Most investors never foresaw the 12% as the option income evaporating when market volatility picked-up and the 8% bonds were called away.

In 2002-2003 when market yields hit 1960 levels, leading insurance companies offered immediate annuities that paid a fixed 8% yield that was 77% tax-exempt. At the time, tax-exempt bonds were yielding approximately 3%. What a terrific deal!

How was the insurance company able to pay 8% when the market yielded 3%? By returning investment principal back to the investor. That is why the fixed payments were tax-exempt. Essentially, investors got their money back and a 2.3% yield.

Investing Strategies

*"There are only two people who know what the stock market is going to do over the next year...
unfortunately both disagree."-- Anonymous*

Understanding the Value of Systematic Investing

What is the most common way of investing?

It's lump sum investing which is simply investing all at once. This method is the most aggressive way to invest since every dollar invests at once and, possibly, precisely when the market is overvalued. The chances of earning a higher return maybe greater, but so is the risk over the short-term.

Generally, lump sum investing is a sound strategy when investing for at least five years. From 1950-2001, lump sum investing in an S&P 500 Index mutual fund at the beginning of each five-year period beat dollar-cost-averaging (DCA) over that same five-year period for every period except two.

Who is systematic investing best suited for?

It is appropriate for a conservative investor. It lowers the "timing" risk of investing. This approach involves investing the same amount at regular intervals -- typically monthly. Systematic investing takes advantage of the ups and downs of the market. When prices are high fewer shares are bought, and when prices drop more shares are bought. The net effect is that the shareholder's average cost per share is less than the average share price.

You can DCA into equity funds during bear markets. Contrary to popular belief, it is wise to DCA into bond funds as interest rates rise. Coupons reinvested at higher interest rates compound at higher rates. The higher compounding is due to higher yields buying bond fund shares at cheaper prices.

What are the kinds of systematic investing?

There are two kinds of systematic investing, one is dollar cost averaging (DCA) which I've just explained. The other is "value averaging" (VA). In all honesty, DCA is the easier way to invest.

Exhibit 4.2: Illustration of "Dollar-Cost-Averaging" Investing

Period	Investment	Bull Market Price	Purchased	Bear Market Price	Purchased
1	$100	$10	10	$10	10
2	$100	$15	6.667	$7.5	13.333
3	$100	$20	5	$5	20
Total	$300		21.667		43.333

Average Price: $45/3 = $15 (Bull Market)
$22.5/3 = $7.5 (Bear Market)
Average Cost: $300/21.667=$13.846 (Bull Market)
$300/43.333=$6.62 (Bear Market)

This table is for illustrative purposes only and does not predict or depict the performance of any investment. Dollar cost averaging cannot eliminate the risk of fluctuating prices and uncertain returns; and cannot assure a profit or protect against loss.

VA is different from DCA in that a goal is set to increase the account value each period by a predetermined amount. When prices drop, the investor is forced to invest more money in order to achieve the predetermined account value goal, whereas, when prices increase, they don't have to invest as much to achieve their goal.

Exhibit 4.3: Illustration of "Value Averaging" Investing

Period	Price	Total Shares	Shares to Buy (Sell)	Amount Invested	Account Value Goal
1	$10	10	10	$100	$100
2	$15	13.333	3.333	$50	$200
3	$20	15	1.667	$33	$300
4	$28	14.286	(0.714)	($20)	$400
Totals		15		$183	

Average Cost per share: $183/15=12.20,   Average Share Price = $15

This table is for illustrative purposes only and does not predict or depict the performance of any investment. Value averaging cannot eliminate the risk of fluctuating prices and uncertain returns; and cannot assure a profit or protect against loss.

If you compare VA to DCA, you will notice that VA results in a lower average cost per share than DCA. The disadvantage of VA is the transaction cost and potential tax liability when selling. It is best to use VA only with no-load funds and qualified retirement plans to avoid transaction costs and reduce potential tax liability.

However, is should be noted that both strategies fail to work with lousy investments. There is no assurance that either one will produce positive results. What really matters is a consistent savings program.

The Secrets Behind Determining When to Invest: Deciphering Investment Patterns and Targeting Decisions

> *"The investor's chief problem -- and even his worst enemy -- is likely to be himself."*
> -- Benjamin Graham

Most investors are constantly concerned about when to invest or when not to invest? On any given day, there are reasons to buy, or not to buy, for that matter. The stock market always seems full of risk or at a high when looking back. On top of that, there are many conflicting statements made about the market every day that make investing so confounding.

For example, here are two statements from *The Wall Street Journal*.

o "Strong economy is good for earnings, which is good for stocks. A weaker economy lowers interest rates, which is good for stocks."
o "A strengthening dollar would encourage foreign investments in the USA, which is good for stocks. A weakening dollar is good because foreigners will buy more US goods and services which are good for stocks."

Which would you believe?

The best advice for long-term investors, given that they own an appropriate portfolio, is not to focus on day-to-day headline news.

When the market is down due to uncertainty, it may be a good time to invest because usually the following year the market is up again. Back-to-back down years do occur, but they have been low probability events followed by big gains.

The S&P 500 Index was down for two consecutive years only three times from 1926 through 2003. It had two three-year down periods and one four-year period of negative returns. The years following the three-year dry spell experienced 20%-plus returns, and the year following the four-year negative period saw a 54% return. Of course, past performance is no guarantee of future performance.

Timing loses some of its importance with long-term investing. Conventional advice is that *time* and not *timing* makes most investors richer! Investing at market highs or lows does not make a substantial difference in your average annual return over twenty years.

A Franklin Resources study showed that $1,000 invested at the high of the Dow Jones Industrial Average, over the last twenty years ending 1998, would have produced an average annual return of 16.3%. In contrast, investing at the low would have generated an average annual return of 18.0%. The investor that had the worst timing still earned eighty percent of the return of the lucky investor who bought at the low. Now most of us will fall in between and earn about 17%. The worst thing to do is to wait for the perfect time to invest. (The Dow Jones Industrial Index®, which is an unmanaged group of 30 "blue-chip" U.S. stocks, is not a diverse index. An investment cannot be made directly in an index. Past performance is no guarantee of future performance.)

Time Diversification

Time diversification underscores the importance of being a long-term investor. Over longer periods, investment returns have not been reliant on short-term market performance, but were derived in part from the long-term trend of the market. Because the market had an upward bias to it, the chance of losing money decreased the longer the holding period. The smartest investors are those who do not try to get in at market bottoms or out at market highs but stay in it for the long run.

In general, a diversified mutual fund investing in a broad market index, such as the Wilshire 5000, is more apt to generate positive returns when held for longer periods than shorter ones. As the market advances, a fund may compound annually at positive returns, thereby building up account value. Even when the market drops in any given year the long-term build up in account value is often enough to prevent losses of the initial investment. (The Wilshire 5000 measures the performance of all U.S. headquartered equity securities with readily available price data. Over 7,000 capitalization weighted security returns are used to calculate the index).

Time Diversification reduces the probability of loss over time. But the magnitude of potential loss increases. For instance, a $10,000 investment compounds at an annual 10% rate of return for four years without a loss. But in the fifth year the stock market corrects 20%. The investor loses $2,928 not $2,000. Even so, the investor still has not lost money, but is still up 17%!

Here is another secret. Timing and selection still maters especially over the short-term. Why? Bad timing and selection could produce negative returns that are so discouraging to an investor, that an investor could quickly change his mind about being long-term and sell.

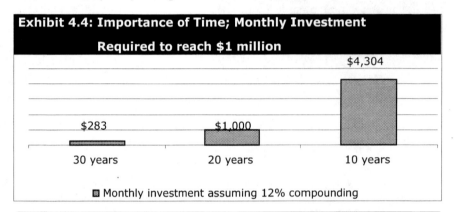

Exhibit 4.4: Importance of Time; Monthly Investment Required to reach $1 million

- $283 — 30 years
- $1,000 — 20 years
- $4,304 — 10 years

■ Monthly investment assuming 12% compounding

This table is for illustrative purposes only and does not predict or depict the performance of any investment.

How does an investor specifically address timing?

Consider seasonal patterns before selling or buying. Seasonal patterns are only a minor factor in overall market analysis. Factor cyclical factor analysis, valuation, inflation trend, etc. to any decision. As always, past performance is not indicative of future results.

Sell in May and Go Away

So, when has been a favorable time to be invested in the market in a given year?

Bears hibernate during the winter months. Typically, the market goes into an uptrend from November through April. Historically, each year the best time to be invested has been from November through April. The S&P 500 Index, on average, has gained approximately 7.2 percent, from 1945-2003 between those months, according to Standard & Poor's. The period from May through November have been less profitable averaging gains of just 1.5 percent.

The best time to start investing has been after September (September has historically had the worst monthly returns) and before the end of October.

You might want to think about selling stocks in August because July has had the best average monthly return. From 1979-2000, the performance of the Russell 2000 over each June-October period was approximately 0.5%, whereas the November-May period returned approximately 14% . NASDQ usually does well from November through June producing an average gain of eight percent. The period of study is 1971 through June 2003. Half of the gain was typically generated in January.

Statistically speaking, in the past, when the month of January had a gain, ninety-seven percent of the time the market ended-up that year. The period of study is from 1950-2003. When the month of January ended down, 52% of the time the year ended down.

According to Stock Trades Almanac, the S&P 500 has been up 70% of the time in December since 1928. The period after December 23rd tends to be bullish compared to the first three weeks of December. It could be that tax loss selling is finished before the Christmas holiday and investors go on vacation until after the New Year.

Don't Fight the Fed

Don't fight the Fed is yet another way to take advantage of another investment pattern. This is not always a sure thing, but in general, when The Federal Reserve cuts the Fed Funds rate, the market rallies. Generally, after one rate cut there is a series of cuts.

From 1921 - 2000, the DJIA went up 1.7% between the first rate cut and the second; from the second to the third there was another 12.2% gain; and twelve months after the third rate cut the DJIA had appreciated 21.1% on average according to NDR.

Keep in mind that timing the market based on past patterns is not a fool proof way to improve results. In addition to relying on high odds patterns, you can use fundamental analysis to determine if the timing and selection makes sense from a valuation perspective. When an investment is overvalued, then do not buy it, but consider selling it. When it's undervalued, then consider buying the investment.

Understanding (and Rejecting) the Herd Mentality When Buying and Selling

It is best not to follow the crowd. An investor caught in the herd mentality buys based on greed at market highs, when financial newspapers are advertising "eye catching" returns, and the economic news cannot get any better. That same investor tends to be a "fear" seller who sells at market lows when the media is broadcasting doom and gloom. Take a look at Exhibit 4.5 to see what I mean.

Exhibit 4.5: 2000-2002 Market Cycle and Investment Patterns

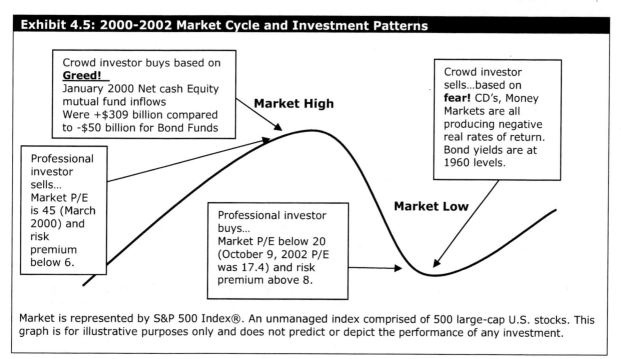

Crowd investor buys based on **Greed!**
January 2000 Net cash Equity mutual fund inflows
Were +$309 billion compared to -$50 billion for Bond Funds

Market High

Crowd investor sells...based on **fear!** CD's, Money Markets are all producing negative real rates of return. Bond yields are at 1960 levels.

Professional investor sells...
Market P/E is 45 (March 2000) and risk premium below 6.

Professional investor buys...
Market P/E below 20 (October 9, 2002 P/E was 17.4) and risk premium above 8.

Market Low

Market is represented by S&P 500 Index®. An unmanaged index comprised of 500 large-cap U.S. stocks. This graph is for illustrative purposes only and does not predict or depict the performance of any investment.

The professional investor does the exact opposite of the crowd-following investor. This investor buys on price weakness when everyone is selling, and sells when everyone else is greedily buying, as the market becomes overvalued.

Why does fear grip the crowd-following investor so firmly?

Investor confidence, and consumer confidence is so low that crowd investors are afraid to invest money they may need to pay bills in case they lose their job!

Investor buying and selling patterns clearly show that the small investor typically buys and sells at the wrong times. ICI 1998 data shows that cash inflows to bond funds usually reach their highest levels after interest rates have bottomed. That happened in 2002 when interest rates hit a fifty-year low and bond cash flows hit record levels. At the market low on October 9, 2002, net bond cash inflows were $140 billion and net equity fund cash flows were negative $28 billion (outflows) according to the ICI. Stocks went on to outperform bonds in 2003.

Hewitt Associates, a consulting firm, reported that investors sold stock funds in their 401(k) plans when the market corrected from August 1998 to its low in October 1998, and switched back in after the market rallied in November 1998. In January of 2000, equity net cash inflows were $309 billion and bond cash inflows were negative $50 billion. Subsequently, the worst bear market since the Great Depression mauled the market.

Crowd investors usually end up buying high and selling low. The average mutual fund posted a 15% average annualized return from 1982 through 1997, yet the typical mutual fund *investor* earned 10% according to research by Greenwich Associates, Charles Ellis.

You should consider trimming down your position in fund categories that have the highest cash inflows over the latest eighteen months. For instance, the science and technology fund category performance peaked in early 2000 as cash flows peaked. Investors pulled money from the large-cap value fund category as it badly underperformed the science and technology category over the three-year period ending 1999. The large-cap value fund category had a $6 billion outflow in January 2000 and went on to trounce the performance of the science and technology sector over the next three years.

When have most investors bought a stock?

Most investors have bought a stock when it looked good -- after it has gone up in price -- and sold after most of the decline in the price had already taken place. Research conducted by Terrence Odean, a professor at the University of California, confirms this pattern. In fact, based on analyzing 10,000 trades at a discount brokerage firm, he found that the stocks that investors sold outperformed the stocks the investors bought by 3.4% over the next year.

What is important to know about individual stock performance?

Stock performance usually begins to improve when investors are ignoring the stocks. Performance slows down when stocks become too popular. Some portfolio managers buy into out-of-favor industries after bad earnings news hits the leader. Often, when the leading company in a sector misses earnings guidance every other company in that sector gets indiscriminately punished, reducing prices and creating investment opportunities.

Higher P/E implies lower future returns and greater downside risk. It just so happens that when economic conditions are good and the market is rallying P/E ratios are rising. It can be wise to take money off the equity table as P/Es inflate.

```
┌─────────────────────────────────────────────────────────────────────┐
│ Exhibit 4.6: Buying at Highs Resulted In Below Average Returns        │
└─────────────────────────────────────────────────────────────────────┘
```

- Bought at a P/E Ratio 20.6 or more produced a 5.3% return
- Bought at a P/E Ratio 14.3 or more produced an 11% return
- Bought at a P/E Ratio below 7.8 or more produced a 17.3% return

Source: Leuthold Group S&P 500 Stocks from 1985-1999. The S&P 500 index® is comprised of 500 U.S. stocks and is an indicator of the performance of the overall U.S. stock market. No fees or expenses are reflected in the performance of the index. An investor cannot invest directly in an index, and its results are not indicative of any specific investment. Past performance is no guarantee of future results

A Contrarian Approach: Buy Early

What do some managers do to avoid buying overvalued stocks that have had their day in the sun?

They use a contrarian approach that "buys chaos and sells euphoria"! That was the famously rich Baron Rothschild's guiding investment principle!

```
┌─────────────────────────────────────────────────────────────────────┐
│ Exhibit 4.7: Baron Rothschild's Formula for Riches                    │
└─────────────────────────────────────────────────────────────────────┘
```

Buy when others sell x **Time** (hold until everyone is buying) = **Wealth**

It is a good idea to use a contrarian approach to improve the timing and selection of securities. It is usually best to buy when investors are pessimistic and definitely not optimistic. You may wish to start buying stocks mid-way through a recession or halfway through a down market -- late bear phase. That is about six month's time into a recession and nine months into a down market. You can start reducing exposure to small- to mid-cap stocks and cyclical large-cap stocks after the mid-bull phase -- about three years into the bull market.

The duration of an up market ranged from two to nine years from 1940-2002. Most upward swings average three-and-a-half years before a down year hit. It is prudent not to wait until the market peaks (which is usually only clearly identified in hindsight).

It is usually the best time to sell when investors are optimistic and not pessimistic. It is prudent to start taking gains even though the market could continue upward. You may want to build up your exposure in large-cap, defensive stocks and Treasury bonds in the late bull market phase. But be mindful to reduce those positions as the economy bottoms after a series of rate cuts.

What is one contrarian approach that can easily be executed?

In a sentence: Buy early when prices are cheap.

The S&P 500 Index average return in the first year of an up market was 24% from 1940-2002. The first year return accounted for approximately 34% of the entire up market's total return. In the first year, small-cap stocks did even better with a 39% return. Small-cap first year's return typically produced approximately 50% of the up market returns for small-cap as a category.

The first year returns are always much higher than the average when the preceding year had double-digit loses. First year returns tend to be lower than the average when the previous year's losses were milder, in the single digits. The returns are also lower -- as a percentage of overall up market returns -- when the up market is long in duration. The last year in an up market for the S&P 500 Indexed averaged 21.77% from 1940-2002.

Investors may ride the market to its peak, and try to squeeze all the juice out of it, but don't try to time the highs. More often than not, investors may be caught in the downswing and could end up giving back last year's return.

	Exhibit 4.8: Past up Market Return Pattern for S&P 500 Index	
Up market	**Up market** Return	**1st Year's Return as %** Up market's total return
1942-45	148%	14%
1947-52	104%	5%
1954-56	91%	58%
1958-61	83%	52%
1963-65	52%	44%
1967-68	35%	68%
1970-72	37%	11%
1975-76	61%	61%
1978-80	57%	11%
1982-89	154%	14%
1991-99	193%	16%

Source: Standard & Poor's. The S&P 500 index® is comprised of 500 U.S. stocks and is an indicator of the performance of the overall U.S. stock market. No fees or expenses are reflected in the performance of the index. An investor cannot invest directly in an index, and its results are not indicative of any specific investment. Past performance is no guarantee of future results.

What could be used as a confirming indicator of when and what to buy or sell?

Following the smart money can confirm timing and selection. Watch insider selling and buying. When corporate insiders begin to sell, it is a good time to consider selling, too. CEOs and CFOs know when profits are expected to drop. In general, corporate insiders tend to buy on weakness and sell on strength. Thus, they tend to be early.

What investments have traditionally done well and when in past business and market cycle?

Generally, the time to overweight these investments is before they enter the business cycle phase that favors the investment. That is when an investment is oversold and undervalued. The time to underweight is at the tail end of the favorable phase. That is when an investment is overbought and overvalued.

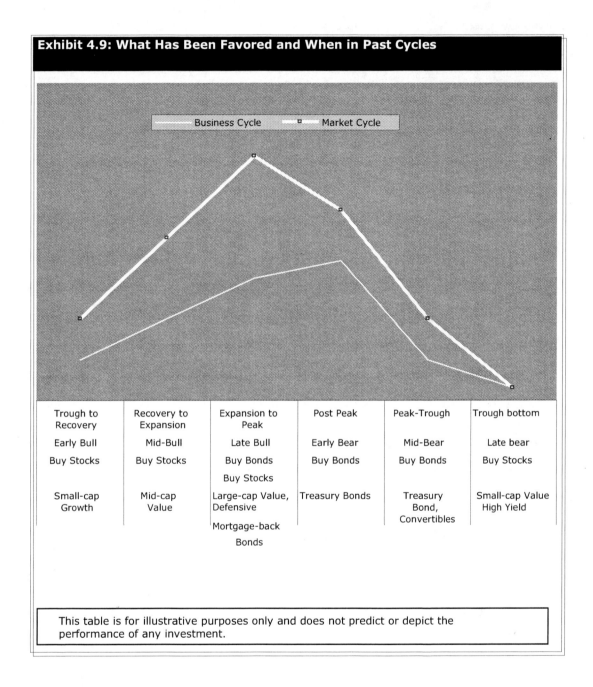

Exhibit 4.9: What Has Been Favored and When in Past Cycles

Business Cycle	Market Cycle				
Trough to Recovery	Recovery to Expansion	Expansion to Peak	Post Peak	Peak-Trough	Trough bottom
Early Bull	Mid-Bull	Late Bull	Early Bear	Mid-Bear	Late bear
Buy Stocks	Buy Stocks	Buy Bonds Buy Stocks	Buy Bonds	Buy Bonds	Buy Stocks
Small-cap Growth	Mid-cap Value	Large-cap Value, Defensive Mortgage-back Bonds	Treasury Bonds	Treasury Bond, Convertibles	Small-cap Value High Yield

This table is for illustrative purposes only and does not predict or depict the performance of any investment.

Guidance on Mutual Fund Selection Patterns

Bernard Baruch, an economic advisor to several Presidents, once said that the way to make money in the stock market is akin to buying straw hats in January. Why? Because straw hats are cheapest in January when demand is at its lowest!

This can be true with a mutual fund. Sometimes it is better to buy a fund when it is cheap (in other words, an out of favor investment) given that emerging trends favor a fund's investment approach. Generally, investment opportunities can be found in areas of the market that are down the most in value, eg. bonds in late 1994 or emerging markets in early 1995, International bonds in 1999, high yield bonds in 2000, small-cap growth stocks in 2002, etc.

Ask yourself these two questions before buying a fund:

1. When I buy a fund, I want to buy a:

    a. Good performing fund
    b. Bad performing fund

2. When I sell a fund, I want to sell a:

    a. Good performing fund
    b. Bad performing fund

The best answers are actually counterintuitive!

It may make more sense to buy an undervalued "bad" performing fund as long as market fundamentals are starting to favor it. Likewise, when a fund becomes overvalued, its past performance is very good! Therefore, sometimes it makes sense to sell good funds or at least take some "profits off the table" especially when changing market fundamentals do not favor it. Also, it can be smart to invest in fund categories that have had two down years or more, as historically, subsequent periods are usually positive.

Exhibit 4.10:	**Top Quintile Managers Under-performed in Subsequent Periods.**	
	Latest Two Year Period	Two Years later
Top	23.62%	**13.89%**
2nd	18.01%	15.18%
3rd	14.81%	15.35%
4th	12.47%	15.72%
Bottom	**6.95%**	**17.71%**

Source: Smith Barney Consulting Group. A study of 72 money managers conducted from January 1, 1987, through December 31, 1996, concluded that top performers do not go on to repeat as top performers.

Should investors buy popular top performing funds or underperforming funds? Unpopular funds went on to beat the average equity fund 78% of the time over the following one-, two-, and three-year periods ending 1997. Morningstar examined the cash flows of mutual funds since 1987 and found that 89% of the funds that experienced negative or low cash inflow beat the funds experiencing heavy cash inflow. The secret to solving this one relies on utilizing a timing and selection process outlined in chapter 7.

The Best Kept Tax Secrets: How to Keep More of What You Have Earned on Your Investments

"You have to tip the waiter...the bigger the meal the larger the tip."
-- Roy Neuberger

It's true. Death and taxes are a certainty!

Taxes cannot be avoided, especially when big gains are realized. The average return for the ten-year period ending June 30, 2002 for U.S diversified equity funds was 10.37%, according to Morningstar Inc. But of that return, taxes gobbled up a huge 2.6%! After taking taxes into consideration (at the 25% Federal tax rate) that net return becomes a more paltry 7.77%.

Since every investor's tax situation is different, tax reduction strategies must be employed at the client's personal level. For example, a large capital gain pay out from a mutual fund does not necessarily mean a taxable event for every shareholder. Some investors may offset that gain with realized losses from other investments. In other cases that fund investment is sheltered under a qualified retirement plan, such as an IRA or 401(k) plan.

1) Do not assume that low turnover funds produce higher after-tax returns. Turnover is not an effective measure of determining the tax efficiency of a fund. A 1995 study by Sanford Bernstein concluded that turnover of greater than 10% loses the benefit of tax deferral from low turnover. For example, a fund that had a 30% turnover ratio lost less than one percent in return. But turnover equal to 50% may lose one percent as well. This means that a fund with a 30% turnover ratio and another with a 100% turnover ratio may actually have the same tax-efficiency.

2) Tax-sensitive funds may reduce realized taxable gains. In many cases, it can depend on whether the fund manager takes a tax managed approach in managing the fund. If a manager is sensitive to taxes, he/she may be savvy in offsetting gains with losses when fund securities are sold.

3) High turnover doesn't necessarily means an entire fund portfolio has turned over. A fund that has a 100% turnover ratio may have turned over ten percent of the portfolio ten times, and could have offsetting gains with losses resulting in little or no distribution.

4) Do not let the tax tail wag the dog. Tax implications shouldn't exclusively determine investment decisions. Even after paying taxes on high turnover funds, the after-tax return can be greater than low turnover funds. A leading dividend growth fund had an average historical turnover rate of 163% as of September 30, 1998. Yet its three years tax adjusted return was 18.96%, which beat every tax-managed fund, save for one. The five-year period return was 18.01%!

5) Savvy fund managers can use their tax tools of the trade. Active managers can use a portfolio's cost accounting method called "higher cost first out" (HCFO) to lower fund shareholders current tax liability.

6) Be mindful of a fund's holding period. The individual holding period of a fund has a greater impact on tax efficiency than a fund's turnover ratio. There are numerous equity fund categories that had comparable tax-efficiency to that of S&P 500 Index funds.

Exhibit 4.11: Not All Equity Funds Were Tax-inefficient

Large-cap Blend   90% of the pre-tax return was kept
Sample of 7 Index Funds   93% of the pre-tax return was kept *

Sample of seven index funds are S&P 500 Index funds. This number does not reflect embedded tax liability. After-tax returns calculated using the highest individual federal marginal income tax rates, and do not reflect the impact of state and local taxes. Actual after-tax returns depend on the investor's tax situation and may differ from those shown. The after-tax returns shown are not relevant to investors who hold their fund shares through tax-deferred arrangements such as 401(k) plans or an IRA. After-tax exclude the effects of either the alternative minimum tax or phase-out of certain tax credits. Any taxes due are as of the time the distributions are made, and the taxable amount and the tax character of each distribution is as specified by the fund on the dividend declaration date. Due to foreign tax credits or realized capital losses, the after-tax returns may be greater then before-tax returns. Data for latest 3-year period ending June 30, 1997.

Source: Morningstar ®. This table is for illustrative purposes only and does not predict or depict the performance of any investment. Investments in mutual funds involve risk. Past performance is no guarantee of future performance. Mutual funds incur fees and expenses (including investment management and administrative fees). Obtain a prospectus for more complete information about the fund, including all fees and expenses, and should be read carefully before you invest. Investment returns and principal value of a mutual fund will fluctuate, so that shares, when redeemed, may be worth more or less than their original cost. Past performance is no guarantee of future performance.

---

7) Passive funds that track an equity index can be a minefield of taxable events. Passive funds that have appreciated and do not pay annual distributions have an embedded unrealized gain. When a shareholder eventually sells his shares, the unrealized gain is realized and the tax-efficiency may be lost. Now there may be a big tax bill to pay!

8) Watch for falling fund assets. Generally, a fund that is experiencing a rapid decline in assets is very likely to lose its tax efficiency. As shareholders sell, fewer shareholders now own more of the realized distributions of the fund. For example, a fund's declares a dollar per share capital gain distribution to 100 shareholders. That is $100 in distributions. But 50 shareholders sell. Now the remaining shareholders will be paid two dollars and not one! Funds that are growing in assets are less prone to losing their tax-efficiency.

In addition, if lots of shareholders sell the fund over a short period of time, the manager may not be able to pay all of those shareholders out of the fund's cash cushion. If the manager is forced to sell securities to realize the cash to pay investors, those sales may produce hefty gains, again inherited by the remaining shareholders.

9) Rebalance to manage risk even though there may be a tax consequence. More money can be lost to the market than to the IRS! It is possible to lose more money in the market by *not* selling rather than what would be paid in taxes as a result of a sale? For instance, $100 investment appreciates to $200 over one year. A rebalance sells half the investment. The tax liability on the gain is $15. What if in the following year the investment fell in value by ten percent? That would be a $20 unrealized loss from the beginning of the year. Remember that no one ever went broke taking a profit.

10) Try to hold winners for one year in order to qualify for the lower long-term capital gains rate. However, do not let a short-term gain turn into a long-term loss because you did not want to incur a taxable event by selling! Shares held for less than twelve months and sold at a gain are taxed as a short-term capital gain. Short-term capital gains are taxed at an individual's ordinary income tax rate. Shares held for twelve months and sold at a gain are long-term capital gains and are taxed at the long-term rate of 15%.

11) Tax-loss selling helps reduce current taxes. Sell a fund that is down at year-end and buy another fund that has the same objective and investment approach. The benefit is that the loss can be used to offset any gains and the portfolio is essentially unchanged. Moving from one fund to another does not trigger the "Wash Sale" rule. You can use tax lot accounting versus average cost to minimize taxes.

12) Use capital losses to offset an unlimited amount of capital gains. First, short-term losses offset short-term gains. If there are still losses left after offsetting short-term losses and short-term gains, then net short-term losses offset long-term gains until short-term losses are gone. The remainder, if any, is a loss carryover. A loss carryover can offset as much as $3,000 of ordinary income. Use the trade date for gains and losses.

13) Do not let the wash sale rule trip you up. Avoid the wash sale rule. An investor is not allowed to buy back shares sold within thirty days at a loss and claim that loss on their tax return. If an investor does, then the loss is not allowed to be claimed on his return.

14) Watch your cost basis. Although a distribution creates an immediate tax burden it also increases the cost basis of an account when reinvested. A higher cost basis helps to lower future tax liability. Adjust the cost basis on an annual basis when on a reinvestment program. Invest after the record date to reduce distributions.

Exhibit 4.12: Cost Basis Calculation

Initial Investment	$10 per share
Sales Charge	$0.30
Reinvested Distributions	$1
Cost basis	$11.30

---

15) Consider tax-exempt bonds to avoid Uncle Sam. To minimize current taxes, consider tax-exempt bond funds. Shareholders got to keep as much as 96% of pre-tax returns from tax-exempt funds over a five-year period ending 1998, according to Morningstar Inc. Government bonds are exempt from state and local taxes, and municipal bonds are exempt from federal taxes. Single state municipal bond funds are exempt of federal, state, and local taxes for denizens of that state. Corporate bond income is subject to federal, state, and local taxes. State income taxes paid on dividends and short-term gains are deductible on the Federal Tax Return. The overall combined rate will be less than the sum of the federal rate and state rate.

16) Weigh tax-exempt against taxable equivalent returns. Use the tax-equivalent yield curve to decide whether taxable or tax-exempt securities would provide a higher after-tax income stream. Sometimes municipals offer a higher tax-equivalent yield then governments and corporate of the same maturity.

Tax-equivalent Yield = tax-exempt yield/ (1- Federal rate - State rate - Local rate)

A client subject to AMT tax may not want a tax-exempt bond fund. Income earned on tax-exempt bond funds derived from private activity bonds is added back to taxable income. To reduce AMT tax, consider investing in a taxable bond fund.

The Secrets of Improving Portfolio Management - IPM

*"If you want to manage your own money, you must become a student of the market.
If you're unable to do that, find someone to manage your money"*
-- Roy Neuberger

Building a "Best Business Practice" Investment Management Process

Would you like to minimize those emotional meetings with clients where you plead with them to maintain a long-term perspective even though their 401(k) has shrunken to a 201(k)?

This section describes how you can do that!

The Recipe for a Sound Investment Management Process

Investment management is like running a day care center. At a day care center, clients drop their children off and expect two things from the center. First, and most importantly, they expect to get their children back in one piece at the end of the day. Secondly, they want their kids to have a fun and rewarding experience.

Clients want exactly the same thing from their money manager. Clients are seeking a fiduciary-like process that embodies a high level of care, caution, skill, loyalty, and impartiality!

The investment management process must be sound enough to withstand the white glove test of even the most discerning investors. It should be chock-full of prudent practices. Although the adviser may not have a fiduciary responsibility, the process should incorporate many "best practices" of the fiduciary investment management process and standards. Fiduciary standards are the highest standards by law used to manage fiduciary assets. It does not get more conservative or cleaner than that! Any marketing statements describing a firm as "a conservative money manager" are undeniably true when a prudent management process follows fiduciary management guidelines. Above all else it places the clients' interests first!

What are the key elements of a prudent disciplined process that resembles fiduciary standards?

First of all the process should easily provide the same level of care and attention to all accounts. Secondly, it should remove potential conflicts of interest. A fee-based account removes many conflicts inherent in a commission-based account.

What other attributes are important?

The process requires an approach that builds a diversified portfolio and incorporates protections from the risk of substantial loss. In addition, it must:

- Include active management that objectively selects (and rejects) fund managers that are appropriate for a given portfolio;
- Incorporate fair dealing with executing investment actions;
- Provide a mechanism for the manager to provide ongoing monitoring of investments and tactically adjust them to satisfy written guidelines that control the management of the account;
- Have a process that allows everyone to supervise the investments owned, the portfolio management, and most importantly, goal achievement.

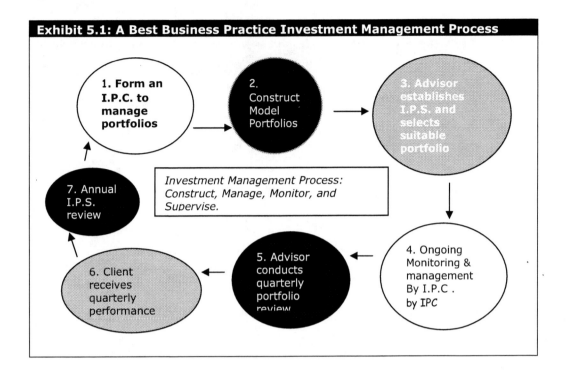

The 7 Step IPM Process

The secret to improving portfolio management is to create structure and organization. The time consuming job of money management shouldn't take more time than there is in a day. Here's a step-by-step roadmap to help you.

Step One: Form an Investment Policy Committee

It can be smart to organize portfolio management activities by creating a formal Investment Policy Committee (I.P.C.).

The I.P.C.:

- Constructs the model portfolios used in a practice and manages them according to written guidelines;
- Defines the strategic asset allocation of model portfolios and the tactical ranges, as well as all other critical portfolio characteristics. (For instance, the I.P.C. decides the primary goal of the portfolio, the capitalization weight, the style orientation, credit quality, foreign security exposure and so on);
- Works 7/24/365 in actively managing clients' portfolios;
- Functions as a "MOM" - that is, a "manager of (fund) managers";
- Takes investment action necessary to ensure that overall portfolio risk is maintained at reasonable levels for each portfolio objective. This active management ensures that a portfolio's investments and characteristics comply with the Investment Policy Statement of clients invested in a model portfolio;
- Will perform ongoing due diligence of the selected suitable funds for each portfolio using an objective prudent fund selection and de-selection process;
- Provides a periodic market overview outlining where the risk is in the global markets. Portfolio management decisions involve top-down, worldwide macro-economic analysis, global market analysis, fund category analysis as well as individual fund analysis. Thorough market and economic analyses determines where the risk is in the world markets, how much risk is prudent to accept, and where to prudently invest. This analysis is used to control risk and make adjustments to keep a portfolio in sync with market conditions.

> **Insider Tip:** Forming an I.P.C.? Turn your firm's ADV Part II into a "gorilla closing" sales brochure by disclosing this. Fiduciary standards require that you disclose the investment management process to prospects and clients. This provides a great opportunity to describe the conservative wealth preserving and building investment management process that's overseen by highly educated, experienced professionals serving on your I.P.C.. It is a superb creditability builder! Moreover, the investment process should be disclosed to clients and prospects. This helps clients determine the appropriateness of the management process for them.

Step Two: Professionally Construct Model Portfolios

What are the major advantages to using a model portfolio approach?

First of all, it creates the structure required to supervise and actively manage an unlimited number of accounts. Secondly, using models easily allows an advisor to consider the appropriateness and suitability of investment recommendations and actions.

Each client is mapped to an appropriate portfolio by completing an investment policy statement (see a more in-depth explanation of the investment policy statement, I.P.S., under Step Three, below). The most critical factor to consider in matching a client with a suitable portfolio is a client's risk tolerance. Each model portfolio is managed according to its own I.P.S. that coincides with the client's I.P.S.

In addition, mutual fund wrap programs that use a model approach allow for easier monitoring of investments and fair dealing in executing investment actions. The advisor will no longer be overwhelmed with managing individual portfolios for hundreds of clients and tracking each and every security in all of those portfolios. Trades made to a model account are automatically executed in all accounts assigned to the model. Now an advisor and clients can travel the globe without worrying about market movements.

How many model portfolios should be offered?

Start with the basic core portfolios that cover the gambit of objectives: tax-exempt income, taxable income, income & growth, growth & income, and growth. Then place clients in suitable portfolios determined by the client's Investment Policy Statement. Since most advisors find it impossible, time wise, to manage hundreds of customized portfolios, the model approach can allow for efficient and cost effective management of a limitless number of accounts. Another benefit is that fewer portfolios allow a more focused, intensive research and management effort with each of the basic core portfolios.

What is the portfolio construction goal?

You should construct model portfolios that have a high probability of achieving inflation-adjusted return goals that will not exceed unrealized loss threshold goals.

Exhibit 5.2: Try To Build Portfolios That Seek To Consistently Beat Inflation

Portfolio Objective	Asset Allocation Stocks/Bonds/Cash	Avg. Inflation Adjusted Return	%Time Beat inflation	% Down Period
Income & Growth	40%/50%/10%	5.2%	92%	4
Growth & Income	60%/35%/5%	6.7%	90%	5

Source: Standard & Poor's, The Frank Russell Company, Lehman Brothers, Federal Reserve. Data is for 5-year rolling periods from 1950-2002: an even weighting among S&P 500 Index represents stocks and Small-cap stocks, Intermediate Government Bonds represent bonds, and Cash is represented by the 30-day Treasury Bills. Past performance is no guarantee of future results. No fees or expenses are reflected in the performance of the index or portfolio. An investor cannot invest directly in an index or portfolio, and its results are not indicative of any specific investment.

What should be expected from the basic building blocks of a portfolio?

In general, cash-equivalents have not lost money over a one-year period. Therefore, cash-equivalents are good investments for clients intending to sell within one year. Intermediate Government bonds have had only two two-year rolling period returns where the returns were barely positive: 1956 - 0.04% and 1959 -0.07%. The rest of the time from 1926-2002, intermediate Government bonds posted positive two-year rolling period returns according to the Federal Reserve. Therefore, intermediate Government bonds are generally good investment alternatives for financial obligations coming due in two years. Equities are generally regarded as good investments for long-term liabilities. Investors had approximately a 92% chance of a positive return when invested for at least three years in an S&P 500 Index portfolio from 1950-2002 according to Standard & Poor's.

Step Three: Investment Policy Statement (I.P.S.)

What is the single most important decision to make?

It is not the asset allocation, but the decision to establish an Investment Policy Statement (I.P.S.). The I.P.S. is actually the first step in the money management process. The strategic asset allocation is the by-product of the I.P.S.. This is one of the best kept secrets in the business!

The I.P.S. is an integral part of the investment management process. It contains vital information about each client's financial, investment, and personal circumstances. Among many other things the I.P.S.:

- Defines the duties of the money manager, the adviser, and the client;
- States who manages the client's assets;
- Notes who supervises the money manager(s);
- Explains how the money will be managed;
- Specifies what the money manager can -- and cannot -- do;
- Indicates how often should a portfolio be rebalanced;
- Notes any investment restrictions;
- Drives portfolio construction and mutual fund selection decisions;
- Determines the investment approach used to achieve a portfolio's objective;
- Ensures that the money is being managed "solely in the client's interest."

Did you know that by establishing a written I.P.S., a top requirement of the fiduciary investment management standards has been met?

That means, in part, that your investment management practice meets the highest standard. You might say, "So what? Who needs one anyway?" I would respond to that by asking, "Would you build a house without a blueprint?"

The I.P.S. is the blueprint that instructs the advisor as to which portfolio to build for each individual client. The I.P.S. matches a client's risk and return preference with a suitable "tailored" portfolio. The client can also control the type of asset classes and investments used in the portfolio by dictating investment restrictions. It guides the portfolio manager on how to manage a portfolio; aggressively or conservatively. It is the plan that clearly defines the client's wishes, goals, and fears.

Now here is the payoff for all of the extra work involved in creating an I.P.S.: There should be less emotion from the investing process, fewer common investment mistakes should be made, and defined goals will allow for easier management, review and tactical adjustments. The advisor uses the I.P.S. to determine a suitable portfolio to recommend that will help achieve a client's· goals and dreams. The advisor monitors the actions of the I.P.C. and model performance.

Did you know that it is harder to be fired when an I.P.S. has been created?

After all, the I.P.S. instructs the advisor and money manager(s) as to what to do and not to do. Clients should not fire an advisor for doing precisely as he/she was told to do! When appropriate, the advisor can release a manager when he or she is not meeting the goal, or where a client's goal has changed.

The 12 Secrets of a Sound Investment Policy Statement (I.P.S.)

The responses from a profiling questionnaire are typically used to establish an Investment Policy Statement. What's the secret to creating a dynamic questionnaire that covers all of the most important bases? Make it as quantitative, and objective as possible, while at the same time capturing an investor's feelings or psychology!

What are the essential components of a high standard Investment Policy Statement?

1) Financial goal(s), dreams, and fears

What are the client's "hot buttons"? Is it retirement, wealth accumulation, or high current income? What are their dreams? What are their worries?

It is the attention to technical details that is what makes dreams and goals come true. A good I.P.S. questionnaire will cover those details, and the management of the account will reflect those particular details.

2) Financial condition

Learn about a client's current financial condition. Is he/she employed? Retired? What is his/her net worth and current disposable income? What is the value of his/her current portfolio holdings? How much is set aside to meet eighteen months of fixed expenses?

Clients that have a high net worth, positive cash flow, relatively large portfolios, and are properly insured can take greater risk if they desire. The opposite is generally true for financially-challenged clients.

3) Portfolio objective

What is the client's return or income objective? What does the client want the portfolio to emphasize? Is the goal preservation of principal and current income, or just growth?

Build a portfolio that supports the individual objective. Meet those objectives otherwise, the client may not be able to achieve financial goals, or satisfy financial liabilities. The chosen objective often depends on where the client is in his/her life cycle. Client's over fifty years of age typically end up in a Growth & Income objective or Income & Growth portfolio. Establish realistic return and income objectives when creating the I.P.S.

What should a client expect?

The reality is that a portfolio must generally own stocks in order to grow over the long-term. Expect a good income portfolio's return to beat inflation. But don't expect it to provide the potential growth of an equity portfolio. Cash-equivalents are relatively non-growth investments, but provide liquidity, modest income, and offset equity risk. The selected and number of asset classes must be consistent with the portfolio objective.

Exhibit 5.3 How Did a Portfolio Grow?

Portfolio	Avg. Return	Yrs. to Double	Actual Return
Treasury-bill	3%	21	Negative
Treasury Bond	6%	12	Break-even
Large-cap	12%	6	Positive

Source: Standard & Poor's, The Frank Russell Company, Lehman Brothers, Federal Reserve. Data based on investment returns for 1950-2002 period. Factors in inflation, taxes, and expenses. Large-cap stocks are represented by the S&P 500 index®, a commonly used broad based index of domestic stocks. The S&P 500® is an unmanaged stock index: Investors cannot invest in the S&P 500 Index; Treasury bonds are represented by the S&P Long-term Government Bonds index; Treasury indices are total return indices held constant maturities. Cash is represented by the Lehman Brothers Three month Treasury Bill Index derived from secondary market Treasury bill rates published by the Federal Reserve Bank or the 91-day Treasury bills data. Indices include reinvested income, but not transaction costs or taxes, are unmanaged and cannot be purchased directly by investors. This table is for illustrative purposes only and do not predict or depict the performance of any investment. Past performance is no guarantee of future performance.

4) Investment approach/philosophy

How will the account be managed? For instance, will this follow an active approach or a "frozen" buy and hold philosophy that ignores valuations? Will it be a diversified or non-diversified portfolio? What is the fund selection process?

You will need to define the process used to manage the account and achieve the portfolio's objective.

5) Risk tolerance

What is the client's "pain threshold" for loss or volatility?

Investments that greatly fluctuate in their value tend to offer a higher potential for gains and losses. A client's financial and psychological ability to accept risk is a major factor in determining the appropriate asset mix and type of funds used to build a portfolio. Investors that are financially healthy, psychologically risk-averse, and retired may want to invest in an Income & Growth portfolio.

Exhibit 5.4: Match Risk Preference and Portfolio

Portfolio	Risk	Asset Mix	Avg. Loss Down Market	Max. Decline	Avg. Return
Growth	Above Avg.	100% Large-cap	-18.19%	64.22%	12.20%
Growth & Income	Avg.	60% Large-cap / 40% Government bonds	-8.6%	-36.2%	9.66%
Income & Growth	Below Avg.	40% Large-cap/ 60% Government bonds	-4.0%	-10.4%	8.38%

Source: Standard & Poor's, Lehman Brothers, Federal Reserve. Data for 1926-2002 period. Large-cap stocks are represented by the S&P 500 index®, a commonly used broad based index of domestic stocks. The S&P 500® is an unmanaged stock index: Investors cannot invest in the S&P 500 Index; Government bonds are represented by the S&P Long-term Government Bonds index; Treasury indices are total return indices held constant maturities. Indices include reinvested income, but not transaction costs or taxes, are unmanaged and cannot be purchased directly by investors. This table is for illustrative purposes only and do not predict or depict the performance of any investment. Past performance is no guarantee of future performance.

What is the most important I.P.S. factor to get right?

Establishing a client's "loss threshold" can be the single most important part of the I.P.S.!

Most investors overstate how much they can afford to lose especially at the tail-end of a bull market. A good method to nail down someone's loss threshold is to show them a table that has the annual expected return and potential loss in a down market of a hypothetical portfolio. Let the prospect pick the one they can sleep well with. Then put them into a portfolio that will probably not exceed that loss threshold in a typical market cycle.

It is important to document client's loss threshold and keep it in their file. It may come in handy during a down market to defend the investment approach of the portfolio. Generally, it is a good idea to allocate more into bonds and cash-equivalents when a client cannot stomach average market volatility. Remember that wealth is built over the long-term by owning equity funds, and not bond funds or money market funds. Some equity exposure is necessary even for the nervous, sleepless, long-term investors.

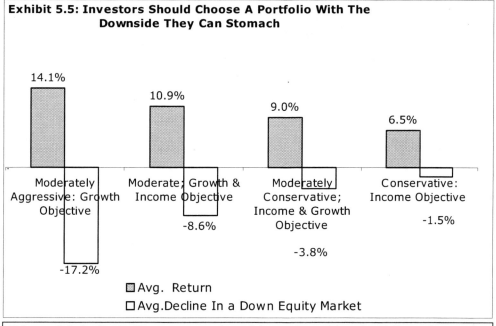

Exhibit 5.5: Investors Should Choose A Portfolio With The Downside They Can Stomach

This graph is for illustrative purposes only and does not predict or depict the performance of any investment. Performance results are hypothetical results.

6) Investment horizon

When does the client need his/her money?

After determining how much risk the client is able to assume, the investment horizon is the second most important factor used in deciding the type of portfolio to own.

Investors often do not match investment time horizon with the appropriate type of portfolio. Many investors end up in growth objective portfolios when they should be in a conservative Income & Growth portfolio. It has been my experience that most clients have been less inclined to panic in a correction when they had sufficient cash reserves and a conservative asset mix that could "weather the storm" and still grow when the storm eventually passes.

Anything can happen in the market in a given year. Generally, clients should not invest in growth objective portfolios when investing for less than three years, or, in general, if they are older than sixty. When investing for five years or more, consider a growth objective portfolio because stocks provide growth of principal that has historically outpaced inflation. Past performance does not guarantee future results. Where a client is in their lifecycle will help decide which portfolio objective is most suitable. Retirees should probably consider a Growth & Income objective or Income & Growth objective, but usually not a Growth objective.

Savers sleep well while investors eat well. The price for eating well is volatility, and streakier returns that are typically associated with Growth objective portfolios. Short-term investors, investing for less than three years, should consider buying high quality, intermediate bonds that provide stability of principal and income given the right market conditions. Investors who need to sell in less than one year should own a money market fund. Remember stock investments attempt to grow your money, bonds provide current income, and cash-equivalents provide liquidity.

A client's investment horizon does not mean they will buy and hold until the horizon is reached. Time horizons constantly shift due to market conditions, and attitudes about the market. Long-term investors become short-term when they suffer intolerable losses. You may be able to prevent them from changing their minds by controlling risk. Based on my past dealings I have learned that my clients do not mind making less on the upside as long as they do not lose as much as the market does on the downside.

7) Income needs

Obviously when a client needs high current income, then you would recommend a larger position in bond funds, given that market conditions are right. However, even income-oriented investors should own equities that can provide growth that outpaces inflation in addition to current income. If a client wants to retire on 60% to 80% of pre-retirement income, and not lose purchasing power, then equities generally must be part of the portfolio.

The exception would be a very wealthy person without money worries.

In the past, building a ten percent equity position in an income portfolio lowered the overall portfolio risk without materially lowering long-term returns. Historically, adding equities has increased portfolio returns over the long run. If a client does not have substantial assets, then they should consider owning bonds and equities in their retirement portfolio. Otherwise, they may risk outliving or depleting their retirement portfolio.

Exhibit 5.6: How Long Might an Investor Live off a Portfolio?				
Withdrawal Rate*	**Rate of Return**			
	6%	**8%**	**10%**	**12%**
6%	22 yrs.	31 yrs.	50+ yrs.	50+ yrs.
8%	31 yrs.	18 yrs.	24 yrs.	26+ yrs.
10%	50+ yrs.	13 yrs.	15 yrs.	19 yrs.
12%	50+ yrs.	10 yrs.	11 yrs.	13 yrs.

This table is for illustrative purposes only and do not predict or depict the performance of any investment. *This assumes an annual withdrawal rate as specified.

8) Liquidity needs

Lower liquidity needs means that the client can assume greater risk. On the other hand, the greater the demand for liquidity, the lower the risk.

What are the client's financial liabilities? The portfolio fund allocation must consider upcoming financial obligations. For example, if a client is planning to make a down payment on a home in a year, the money used to make that payment should not be in equities, but invested in a money market fund.

9) Tax liability

You must consider the tax consequences of investing in order to minimize taxes and maximize the after-tax return to clients. A client in the highest federal income tax bracket who resides in a state that has a high state income tax may consider tax-exempt municipal bonds, given no AMT tax problem.

10) Marketability

What is the client's preference for marketable securities? Does the client need immediate access to his money? If so then stick with mutual funds, and avoid less liquid securities such as direct real estate investments, illiquid securities, deferred annuities, private REIT's, and limited partnerships. You can overweight the money market fund, and intermediate bond fund given the right conditions.

11) Age

The client's age should be considered and factored into the overall decision as to which portfolio to recommend. Older clients, those fifty years and older, should typically start to build a greater fixed income component. The Rule of 100 should not be used to asset allocate. The Rule of 100 says to take an investors age and minus it from 100 to determine how much to invest in equities. For example, if your age is 60, then you should have forty percent in equities. Too many other factors must be considered to determine what is right. If it were as simple as the Rule of 100, everything else I've mentioned in this section would not be considered.

12) Special concerns/considerations

It is a smart move to identify all portfolio restrictions or preferences early on when working with a client. Some clients may want to avoid specific mutual funds they had a bad experience with, such as high yield bond funds or concentrated funds in the technology, financial, or health care sectors. Clients may even have concerns about the characteristics of a particular fund.

It is best to define what asset classes and funds are acceptable to each client. You must also determine if there are regulatory constraints. For example, ERISA assets are subject to the Prudent Investor rule, so make sure assets are managed to protect against losses in real terms.

<u>Step Four: Monitoring the Portfolio</u>

The advisor oversees the management of the portfolios by the I.P.C.. He or she plays the role of the portfolio police!

Above all else, make sure each client perceives that his/her portfolio is being managed to lessen risk and improve returns! If the client feels that the advisor is doing nothing to earn his fee, then you can probably expect to lose the account.

To ensure that a portfolio continuously reflects the investor's I.P.S. and stays in sync with market conditions, a periodic rebalance is necessary to manage risks, return, and income. Market conditions change affecting risk, return, and income levels of a portfolio. For instance, in a declining interest rate environment, funds that pay variable interest in a current portfolio may no longer provide enough income. Therefore, lost income must be replaced.

Step Five: Quarterly Account Review

What are the secrets to providing a thorough account review with your client?

Keep it simple!

When the going is good, some clients might just want the bottom line, such as what their quarter-ending balance is. Others might want more of an explanation.

Here are the key issues and points you will want to discuss with each client:

1) Beginning and ending balances for latest quarter -- Sometimes the ending balance is less than the beginning balance, in spite of a market rally, because of withdrawals. Clients sometimes forget to factor into their evaluation how much money has been withdrawn from the account.

2) Returns for the most recent quarter, year-to-date, latest twelve months, and since account inception -- Be sure to evaluate these returns against the account's return objective first, the appropriate benchmark, on a risk-adjusted basis, and within the context of overall market conditions for the period. Clients are seeking reassurance that they are on target to meet a goal(s). Try to keep emotions in check by providing them with quantitative analysis that shows that the money is being managed appropriately and everything is okay. Of course, everything *must* be okay to take that position. Remember to tell them that past performance is no guarantee of future results.

3) Perform a performance attribution analysis of portfolio returns -- This requires a fund-by-fund evaluation. Again, review the role of each fund in the portfolio, how it has performed against its benchmark, and its contribution to overall portfolio performance -- both its return and its risk. Reinforcement of the investment management process with clients is critical part of any review.

4) Review current asset allocation and fund category allocation compared to the present tactical recommendations that reflect current market dynamics.

5) Review income (dividends and income) versus the objective, and current market rates and yields. Stress total returns in a low yield environment, and explain the importance of total returns.

6) Provide a market update -- Discuss conditions, favored sectors, and the rationale for fund selection.

7) Review each account's I.P.S. -- Make sure each account is being managed according to the established I.P.S.. Check in with the clients to be sure that the I.P.S. is still desirable. For instance, explain that you are managing their portfolio under an aggressive growth approach that has greater volatility, which means that it has the potential to drop as much or more than 23% in a bear market. Then ask, "Do you still want your account managed this way?" Prepare to discuss the development a new I.P.S. if the answer is no, or the client's personal situation has changed dramatically since the I.P.S. was created. (See more about reviewing and amending the I.P.S. under Step Seven below).

8) Discuss tax management strategies -- Early in the fourth quarter, review realized gains and losses for tax planning purposes. Remember to watch out for the Wash Sale rule when selling and buying for tax purposes.

9) Discuss servicing the account – Required minimum distributions from IRAs, gifting, consolidating outside assets, frequency of communications and reviews, etc. to be sure you and the client are on the same page as far as expectations.

Step Six: Quarterly Portfolio Statements

Send a report card each quarter!

Portfolio statements must have personal internal rate of return numbers and portfolio analytics that easily allow clients to assess risk, investment management actions, performance, and goal achievement. The model approach allows composites to be created to report Global Investment Performance Standards -- "GIPS - which is a very powerful prospecting tool! When your performance numbers are "testable" and provable they are vastly more credible! I personally would not invest with an Advisor that can't show any numbers or uses numbers that can not be back-tested and proven.

Step Seven: Annual Review of the I.P.S.

The golden rule is to review the I.P.S. at least once each year. But this can be done more frequently.

The I.P.S. is the understanding between the client and the advisor on how to manage the money. (Review Step Three above for more details). If the client agrees to have his money aggressively managed and the account loses money, the I.P.S. will come to your defense.

Without debate, the hardest job of an advisor is getting the client to stay-the-course and not move to the sidelines when the market corrects. A periodic review makes sure the client has the right portfolio given their circumstances and goals. When done right it will keep the client committed to the current investment program or result in suitable adjustments.

Life circumstances change and so does a person's financial condition. This too may warrant a change in portfolio objective. For instance, when a client's financial condition deteriorates, then a more conservative mix might be a better strategy to follow. When a client experiences a steadily improving financial condition, he/she might decide to become more aggressive by increasing their investment in equity funds. A major rebalance in a portfolio means it is time to update an account's I.P.S.

A Dozen Reasons to Change Portfolio Objectives

Changes to the objectives of a client's portfolio shouldn't be executed haphazardly, but be done as deemed appropriate and with care. These events could trigger a necessary change:

1. Material changes to the I.P.S.
2. Change in a client's portfolio objective
3. Change in one's marital status
4. Birth or adoption of a child(ren)
5. Change of employment status
6. Serious illness
7. Purchase of a new home
8. Caring for an elderly parent
9. Major one time expense (eg; wedding)
10. A "windfall" (eg; inheritance, bonus, sale of business)
11. Business failure or success
12. Major gifting to charity

The Secrets of a Sound Investment Counseling Process

"Above all else, know your client; that's the warning we sport.
Ignore it too often, and we'll see you in court!
It's an ugly way to spend time, when you could be making a dime."
-- Author unknown

The investment counseling process is akin to the way a doctor conducts his health care practice. Doctors do not prescribe medicine until they find out what is ailing the patient and have determined the patient's current state of health, what problems are present, and what treatment plan will be the best for the individual patient. But, the doctor must ask questions and examine the patient first.

It is a best practice to start by using a profiling questionnaire to gather the required information before recommending anything. Make sure you have a good one (remember, the "junk in junk out" philosophy dictates that a poor profile will produce poor results).

The "best interest advice" should involve analysis of the client's investment policies (goals, etc.), circumstances and current holdings. Like a medical doctor, you should have good bedside manners. In other words, be social first.

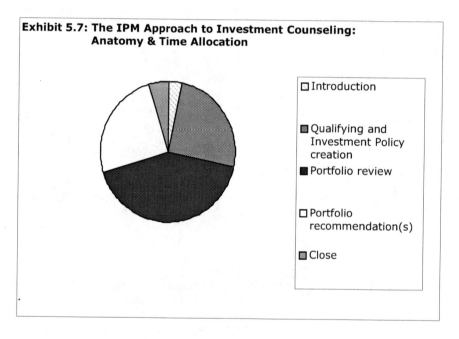

Exhibit 5.7: The IPM Approach to Investment Counseling: Anatomy & Time Allocation

- □ Introduction
- ▦ Qualifying and Investment Policy creation
- ■ Portfolio review
- □ Portfolio recommendation(s)
- ▦ Close

The investment counseling process should help investors avoid common investment management mistakes and reduce portfolio risks. In twenty years of practice I have often come across investors that did not have an asset mix that was right for them. In addition, most portfolios were not in accord with current market conditions, especially at the tail end of a bull market or, alternately, the end of a bear market. I have found that assets are either exposed to unnecessary risk or not working hard enough to beat inflation.

Be sure to provide advice on how to invest in or build suitable portfolios that first meet a client's risk tolerance, then inflation adjusted return needs. It is a good idea to use proposals to assess the suitability of the current portfolio or the investor's investment skills and knowledge.

It can be good to point out past common portfolio construction mistakes and irrational investing behavior (such as always seeking guaranteed returns). You can adjust a client's asset mix by recommending appropriate funds given their circumstances, I.P.S., portfolio needs, and taking into consideration cyclical trends.

Be cautious not to recommend a portfolio cooked up with old market data and frozen strategies. Frozen strategic passive portfolios may increase the chances of investing in overvalued assets, thereby increasing risk!

> **Insider Tip:** According to a 1996 poll by the Securities Industry Association, most broker complaints by investors were with regard to bad advice or recommendations, followed by inappropriate investments, and failure to keep investors informed.

The Backbones of the Investment Counseling Process:

I. Introduction

This is a sales-related topic that naturally falls outside of the scope of this book, so it will not be addressed other than to give it a quick mention. But, suffice it to say -- in a sound bite -- that your introduction should cover your philosophy, specialty, and quickly establish your credentials. People prefer specialists rather than generalists and would certainly prefer a brain surgeon if they needed brain surgery.

II. Qualifying and Establishing the Investment Policy Statement (I.P.S.)

The first step in servicing your client is to have a clear understanding of a client's goals, current financial condition, circumstances, and investment policies. In order to provide sound advice, you would be wise to ask many more questions than what the NASD requires to establish proper suitability. The advisor should understand the client's I.P.S. factors, personal circumstances, and portfolio needs before recommending anything. Qualifying involves assessing:

- ✓ Investment policy factors
- ✓ Investment restrictions
- ✓ Financial Condition
- ✓ Impact of a recommendation on the overall holdings
- ✓ Investment Experience
- ✓ Psychology - emotional ability to withstand unrealized losses and volatility
- ✓ Circumstances

First, find out about their dreams, goals, fears, and feelings. This is just as important as the technical aspects of establishing an I.P.S. and recommending a suitable portfolio.

Qualifying is a casual real conversation that involves skillful probing and questioning to gather suitability information. Never sound mechanical when asking questions. Get the conversation started by using open-ended questions to encourage them to talk. Use the type of questions that cannot simply be answered with a "yes" or "no". Break the ice. Encourage them to tell you about their goal(s) and their investment objectives.

Prefacing your questions can make your customers feel more comfortable with your questions. Tell them why you want to ask questions. Offer a benefit. Explain that you want to be sure the information you give them is appropriate for them and their individualized situation. Then, tell them you would like to ask them some questions.

Use open- and closed-ended questions to gain both value and factual qualifying information. For instance, use value ones to learn about the client's wishes, feelings about risk (the value placed on it), and to get them talking. Nail their responses down by using factual ones. Try it and you will find that it will help you focus on what the client desires and worries most about.

A. "Value" qualifying questions identify concerns that need to be addressed:

*   "What concerns you the most about investing?"
*   "What is most important to you about your portfolio?"
*   "How do you feel about risk?"
*   "How do you feel about managing your own investments?"

B. "Factual" questions identify needs and satisfy NASD suitability requirements:

*   What is your goal?
*   Why are you investing? Is the portfolio meant to provide retirement income, help pay for nursing home care, children's tuition and other goals?
*   What is your investment objective?
*   How much risk are you willing to assume in pursuit of your objective?
*   How much can you afford to lose? This is the most important question to ask. You must a quantify client's "pain threshold for losses."
*   What is your tax bracket?
*   How long can you invest your money without needing to spend it?
*   What is your investment experience?
*   What is your net worth?
*   What is your income?

C. Qualify clients' circumstances and questionnaire answers

*   Ask them, "Is there anything else I should know about your circumstances or financial condition that could affect my recommendation?" Employment status? Retirement date plans? Gifting plans? Health? Past investment results? (Some investors have had horrendous past investment experiences and results; they can't afford to lose more money).
*   Financial condition. Are there adequate resources to achieve goals or meet income needs? What is their net worth and current disposable income?
*   Is the client satisfied with past investment results? How does the client make investment decisions? Why has the client chosen those investments? Does the client just buy top past performers? What has the client done to lower investment risk?
*   Review profiling questionnaire responses. Make sure responses support stated goals and objectives, and question those that seem at odds.
*   Are present policies (portfolio objective, asset mix, income needs, liquidity needs, risk and reward preference, investment horizon, tax situation, etc.) congruent with goals, and personal circumstances?

III. Portfolio Review

Use financial planning, and basic investment and portfolio construction principles as a guide to determine if appropriate methods and principles were used in the past to build the now current portfolio you are reviewing.

Here's a 20-point portfolio review check-up:

1. Does the current portfolio support the client's stated goals and objective?
2. Does the asset mix reflect the I.P.S.? Does the client have a growth objective portfolio when the I.P.S. advocates a growth & income strategy?
3. Is the portfolio over weight in cash-equivalents or in stocks given the client's I.P.S. and market conditions?
4. Is there adequate liquidity given I.P.S. factors, expenses, financial condition, and circumstances?
5. Does the overall portfolio multiple, duration, and credit quality make sense given the portfolio objective and I.P.S.?
6. Is the portfolio overexposed or underexposed to certain asset classes, fund categories, given the portfolio objective, and market conditions? A red flag should pop up when one fund category represents more than 30% of the overall portfolio. When this happens, the total portfolio may not be well diversified. Market conditions must support an overweight decision, otherwise an adjustment is in order. Are equity positions spread out among small, medium, and large-cap sectors and in the right proportion, given portfolio objective and market conditions?
7. Is the portfolio lopsided in market-cap? As a rule, a portfolio starts to become top heavy when more than 50% of the portfolio's assets are concentrated in either large-cap or small-cap sectors. Conditions must support lopsidedness, otherwise, a reallocation would be necessary.
8. Does the portfolio include asset classes that have a low correlation to the dominant asset class?
9. Does the portfolio own any funds that lower overall portfolio volatility and dampen downside risk?
10. Review the combination and number of funds (more than eight can be overkill).
11. Limit each fund position to about 20% of the portfolio.
12. Consider eliminating overlapping and redundant funds.
13. Eliminate "do-it-all" funds such as asset allocation funds, multi-sector bond funds, global equity funds, and global bond funds because they overlap with "pure" category funds. This can create over exposures to asset classes thereby increasing risk.
14. Do they own the right funds given the I.P.S. and portfolio objective?
15. Are the funds way too aggressive (concentrated, high beta, non-investment grade, etc.?) or much too conservative?
16. Is there a fund selection and de-selection criteria? Is the investor indiscriminately buying funds? Do selected funds compliment existing funds?
17. Review current holdings. Identify inefficient investments to weed out. Are there "lazy" investments earning negative real returns?
18. Is the bond portion of the portfolio immunized against interest rate risk and purchasing power risk, or heavily invested in either end of the yield curve? What is being done to manage reinvestment risk?
19. Are bond fund expenses too high?
20. Are bond funds in the portfolio too volatile? Does a bond fund invest heavily is exotic derivatives, illiquid securities, and non-investment grade bonds?

IV. Recommendations

Each recommendation must have a sound basis and be based on the client's individual needs; suitability, investment objective, portfolio needs, facts, research, and not opinions. (See Exhibit 5.8 for a comprehensive list of determining factors to use).

Exhibit 5.8 Investment Policy Factors and Portfolio needs Determine Recommendations

1. Portfolio needs	5. Investment horizon	9. Return Objective	12. Income needs
2. Objective/goal	6. Liquidity needs	10. Tax liability	13. Marketability needs
3. Ability to take risk	7. Investor Psychology	11. Portfolio needs	14. Market conditions
4. Financial condition	8. Affect a portfolio's risk & reward		15. Circumstances

NASD rules require that all material facts be disclosed when recommending an investment. A material fact is something that the investor should know before making a decision. It is a fact that would help assess whether an investment is suitable, given their circumstances and investment policies.

Exhibit 5.9: Specific Material Facts

- Investment objective, approach, philosophy, strategies and policies. What is the management style? Does the portfolio manager use derivatives?
- Portfolio holdings (speculative or conservative). Discuss the P/E, capitalization, beta, credit quality duration, and top ten holdings.
- Cost. Discuss expense ratio (fee table), sales charges and fees management fees), multi-class shares, 12b-1 plans, etc.
- Associated risk: Purchasing power, market, liquidity, marketability, down side, etc.
- Tax features (tax-exempt income, tax-deferred, etc.).
- Insurance or guarantees versus not having it: SPIC, FDIC, AMBAC, contractual fixed rate, stepped-up death benefits, etc.
- Portfolio manager: Bio, etc.
- Return potential and downside risk.
- Other product characteristics or associated services and features.

10 Essential Recommendations to Consider:

It is important to point out any investment program imbalances and make suitable recommendations. Here's a checklist to follow:

1. **Recommend ways to preserve capital**, factoring inflation into the picture.
2. **Recommend diversification strategies** (active, passive, style, capitalization, global, etc.).
3. **Provide suggestions for a risk management program**: manage asset class weights, capitalization orientation, style tilts, industry concentration, multiple, covariance analysis, tactical rebalance, laddered bond component, DCA, reduce dominant fund category risk, and eliminate fund overlap. Be sure to show clients how to protect against reinvestment risk, and beat inflation. Mention ways to offset equity risk, lower volatility, and lower downside risk. Recommend forward looking tactical adjustments to their current portfolio based upon cyclical trends that will mitigate risk in a portfolio. For example, reduce small-cap growth exposure once the early bull phase of the cycle has passed.
4. **Recommend multiple methods** of achieving income, and/or growth.
5. **Explain the process for growing capital** at a higher rate of return to a client.
6. **Explain the process for generating more consistent returns** to a client.
7. **Detail how to build liquidity** without giving up much in terms of yield.
8. **Suggest how a client can achieve higher income** (lower credit, go with longer maturities) given appropriate conditions, and how to get higher tax-exempt income. Use the tax-equivalent yield formula to verify whether tax-exempt or taxable bonds are better. Make sure the client is not subject to the AMT. If he/she is, then a taxable bond fund is better than tax-exempt. Generally, a client knows when he or she is subject to AMT tax because their tax advisor has told them.
9. **Recommend a selection of mutual funds** based upon how each fund will satisfy a portfolio need and impact the current portfolio's volatility, downside risk, P/E multiple, market-cap, industry concentration, credit quality, duration, yield, and its ability to beat inflation. Remember to factor in market conditions. Is the investment approach in favor? Avoid overvalued funds. Assess relative strength. Recommend efficient funds - ones that for the same risk produce higher returns.
10. **Provide suggestions for a tax management program** (tax-exempt funds, tax efficient funds, holding periods, etc.)

Just remember not to drown them with figures. By providing only twenty percent of the information suggested here, and satisfying the necessary suitability requirements, you will have provided more than enough information for the average prospect to make a sound decision. If need be, educate and provide market/sector analysis to those hungry for even more information.

V. Need to Close

The closing subject is a sales topic. Therefore, it too falls outside the scope of the book and will not be covered here.

The Five Biggest Secrets to Understanding Investor Psychology

"Financial markets are an ideal arena to look for irrational behavior."
-- The Harvard Working Group on Behavioral Economics.

Why do some clients have a good investment experience and others a bad one?

Often an investor's investment experience is determined by their psychology. Many clients make irrational investment decisions influenced by greed and fear rather than analytical thought. In fact, investing is a behavioral process for many investors.

So what's the secret to ensuring that more investors have a better investment experience?

You need to understand the psychology of investing (what causes poor decisions), and the psychology of an investor. When an advisor knows how to minimize costly errors driven by irrational behavior, he/she is one step closer to helping investors have a good investment experience.

Here are a few secrets to help you understand and navigate investor psychology:

1. Investors Have a Natural, Risk-averse Tendency

The typical investor has an exaggerated fear of losing money. Here's a quick test to illustrate this point:

Which would you prefer?

1. A 1-in-1,000 chance of losing $5,000

or

2. A sure loss of $5

Based on my own informal 15 years study of prospects and clients I've death with, eighty percent of the people I asked preferred option two. To them, a sure fire, but less significant, financial loss was preferred to even a much more remote *potential* for a greater loss.

Let's try this one. Which investment would you choose in exhibit 5.10?

Exhibit 5.10: Hypothetical Example of Likely Downside

Investment Option Year	Worst Loss Ever	Avg. Loss in a Down
1. Small-cap Fund "A"	-58.01%	-14.5%
2. Intermediate Treasury Bond Fund "B"	-5.14%	-1.4%

This table is for illustrative purposes only and does not predict or depict the performance of any investment. Past performance is no guarantee of future performance.

If you chose investment option one, the Small-cap Fund "A" -- you were not alone. Who wouldn't want to avoid big losses, right?

Yet by seeking to avoid big losses an investor can miss out on growing wealth. While the small-cap category may be more volatile and showed greater losses, it may also show many more gains that could not be captured by that bond fund. That is because small-cap stocks represented by the Russell 2000® Index (which measures the performance of the 2,000 smallest companies in the Russell 3000® Index, which represents approximately 8% of the Russell 3000 total market capitalization) outperformed all types of bonds over any ten-year rolling period from 1950 to 2003, according to The Frank Russell Company.

Investors have a psychological bias of avoiding risk. Studies have shown that investors are four times more motivated to avoid losses then as to pursue gains.

Unfortunately, shortsighted fear of losing money causes many investors to pull out of quality investments when the market is declining and not buy when the market is down. Such a risk attitude often causes investors to make unnecessary mistakes. Many investors stay on the sidelines or invest in low risk investments that do not grow.

As an advisor, you can help clients learn to manage risk instead of avoiding risk. Remember the risk and return relationship -- no risk, no reward! Even so-called "safe" cash-equivalent investments can produce negative real returns once inflation is factored in!

The solution is to establish a personal Investment Policy Statement (see relevant sections above that discuss the I.P.S.) that places the client in a suitable portfolio that matches a client's risk preference. Next, establish an active risk management program. When equity positions exceed and investor's risk preference due to changes in valuations, it would be smart to reallocate into bonds or cash.

It is a good idea to keep the overall portfolio multiple to less than the market multiple. Limit specific industry concentration to less than 30% of a portfolio's assets. Check to see if the portfolio is over concentrated into any area of the market. Carefully manage the maturity, credit, volatility, and sector weights of an income portfolio. Finally, make sure there is sufficient liquidity.

2. Whether Optimist or Pessimist, Risk Attitude Influences Behavior

Investors that have a more optimistic return outlook usually take more risk than those that do not. Optimistic investors buy equity funds even when they need to sell their investment within a year! Pessimistic investors buy fixed-income securities even when their investment horizon is ten years off.

Unfounded pessimism and optimism is rooted in personalities and or circumstances. Take attitudes about risk and reward into consideration along with goals, portfolio objectives, and needs.

Investors' risk attitudes can change as the market changes. In bull markets investors may take unintended risks that they normally would not take, such as invest in areas of the market that can cause their overall portfolio to drop below their loss threshold. The opposite is true in down markets. When the bear is out of hibernation, long-term growth objective investors may get nervous and buy Treasury issues when they should be buying selected stocks at fire sale prices.

Historically, after the market has seen its worst day, it has often produced a positive return one year later. During that time Treasury bill rates dropped.

3. Investors Have a Definite "Pain Threshold"

Don't let clients fool you with their bravado talk about how much risk they can tolerate. Despite reassurances, many will not ride out the occasional correction, let alone a prolonged bear market.

If investors were more prudent in estimating their loss threshold, and were willing to accept less upside potential for lower downside risk, then they possibly could see brighter investment results. They would be less likely to move to the sidelines when the market is at a low. They also wouldn't commit too much to mutual funds that have the potential to lose more money.

In reality, it can be much more important to protect against the downside risk and earn consistently positive real returns than trying to shoot for BIG gains.

An investor's inability to emotionally deal with unrealized losses -- or volatility -- is a major determinant of investment returns. Clients typically start to worry when the market corrects by ten percent. They tend to start heading for the exits when it falls by fifteen percent. They've been known to panic sell at drops of twenty-four percent.

It is vitally important for you to know each of your clients' particular pain threshold and add enough intermediate investment grade bonds and cash-equivalents to avoid stumbling into it in a down market.

A basic investment principle is to let your winners run and cut your losses short. Often investors do just the opposite. Never let losses build up in an account because you hate to admit that you were wrong. Consider booking a loss at twelve percent; still a respectable return. That's roughly the average annual return from the equities market from 1926 to 2003.

Get a feel for when a client will cut losses short. For example, on a $100,000 investment, what unrealized loss would cause him/her to sell? Next, construct a portfolio to balance the return objective with the pain threshold for loss. It is always wise to be conservative in estimating loss threshold. Most clients overstate it and will sell-out during a correction even though they told you that unrealized losses of a certain magnitude would be acceptable.

4. Many Investors Have Unrealistic Expectations

Most non-risk adverse investors prefer absolute returns to risk-adjusted returns. Although there is a low pay-off probability of winning a million dollar Lotto ticket, people still buy them week after week.

Investments that can go up a lot can also go down a lot. Show investors how much they can lose when they aggressively pursue higher returns in a bull market. If they cannot stomach losses of 30% from a market high, then they should temper their return expectations. From my years in practice, I have found that investors tend to overweight the low probability of earning higher returns.

You can use a quarterly bar chart to set return and risk expectations. It is important to manage return expectations. Ask, "What is your return objective?" Then choose a portfolio strategy that has historically averaged the desired return.

You can use the "law of large numbers," ten years or greater, to ensure with greater probability that the return objective is realistic.

In a bull market, clients are more concerned about relative performance. Clients complain when their portfolio underperforms its benchmark, even if absolute returns are stellar. In a bear market its absolute performance that counts. Teach investors to evaluate performance on a risk-adjusted basis. Factor in risk when evaluating performance.

If the low risk portfolio returns 18% while the high risk portfolio returns 24%, then clients should be happy given that the low risk portfolio took, perhaps, half the risk that the high risk portfolio took. If the markets went down instead of up, half the risk the low risk portfolio might post half the losses of the riskier investment portfolio. The low risk portfolio did better on a risk-adjusted basis.

It is smart to always put clients in risk-adjusted portfolios that address the downside.

5. Emotional People Will Overreact and Under React

Investors overreact to market events by buying at tops and selling at lows. Likewise, investors tend to under react by not taking advantage of buying opportunities. Many investors wait until the market reaches its highs again, or invest in a fund that has just had a terrific year! That would be bond investments and money market investments even after the market has bottomed.

When servicing clients, you are most likely dealing with emotions and psyches more so than intellectual capabilities and rational reasoning. Understand each of your client's mental deposition and the emotions that drive actions and behavior.

For example, a client is afraid to invest in equities even though there is nothing but good news about the market and economy emanating from Wall Street, the media, etc. You know that this client will never weather a correction. So take steps to build them a portfolio that takes the client's psyche into consideration.

Understanding your client's disposition is the key to managing the relationship and keeping the account. Know the clients psyche for potential losses, volatility, and both their financial and mental ability to prevent individual behavioral tendencies from undermining and achieving solid long-term results. Consider balanced strategies for emotional clients, and teach clients about common investment pattern mistakes.

Educate clients to recognize that all investments go through cycles. Teach them that there will be periods of time in which their investment objectives are not met or when specific managers fail to meet their expected performance targets. Based on past results, a realistic expectation for growth objective portfolios investing in the S&P 500 Index is to earn about five percent above the rate of T-bills over a 15-year period, but not *each* year.

Expect a down year every few years and maybe two in a row after years posting above average gains. Past performance is no guarantee of future results.

Help them to focus on overall portfolio results, not just one fund. Certain investments such as bonds and cash-equivalents are not growth investments so they will lag in performance in "hot" markets, But when the market corrects they offer liquidity, income, and positive returns.

Likewise, teach them not to expect all equity funds to be a winner each and every year. Leadership in performance will change among them. Help them to understand that it isn't wise to go overboard with tactical fund switching because hyperactive trading increase the likelihood of frequently buying high and selling low. Moreover, it can disrupt the diversification strategy by selling lower correlated funds.

I have found that emotion is a common reason why many investors fail at investing. Use the I.P.S. to reduce the emotion inherent in investing. You should conduct quarterly reviews with emotional clients to keep their emotions from getting the best of them, and be conservative with your advice.

Good luck!

IPM Portfolio Construction

"Good order is the foundation of all good things."
-- Edmund Burke

IPM Portfolio Construction Overview

W.I.I.F.M. is my favorite radio station. W.I.I.F.M stands for "What's in it for me". If you master modern portfolio theory (MPT) and apply it the right way with IPM portfolio construction, then the only thing left for you to do is to manage market risk. All other types of risks are eliminated when a portfolio is efficient according to MPT. Now there is only one ball in the air to focus on -- market risk.

Managing market risk is a formidable task in itself. So, why make it harder on yourself by not reducing other forms of risk that can be controlled. Moreover, any investment selection mistakes will have less of an impact on a portfolio by following the *IPM* guidelines covered in this chapter. That's the what's in it for you!

I believe that the secret to building investment portfolios with a "big sweet spot" is to use mutual funds as the underlying investments. If something goes wrong with a security or even a fund in a fund portfolio, investors shouldn't get hurt as much as if a core stock blows up in a portfolio composed of a dozen stocks. Remember Enron, Tyco, and WorldCom, or what happen to the technology sector from 2000 to 2002? To boot, mutual fund investment opportunities span every kind of investment available to trade. Therefore, you are not limiting returns to one single area of the market or a few highly correlated areas of the market.

The primary objective of *IPM* portfolio construction is to build a portfolio that protects against big losses and produces reliable inflation-adjusted returns.

North by Northwest

The most desirable portfolios are those that fall in the Northwest quadrant of the grid according to Modern Portfolio Theory. Those portfolios produce the highest returns for the least amount of risk. All other quadrants have portfolios that are inferior to the Northwest quadrant, according to MPT. This means that they produce either the same return or produce a lower return for the same risk or higher risk. You can use the portfolio construction guidelines mentioned in this chapter to build a Northwest quadrant portfolio. Back test your portfolio to determine if it was better on a risk-adjusted basis by using the Sharpe ratio.

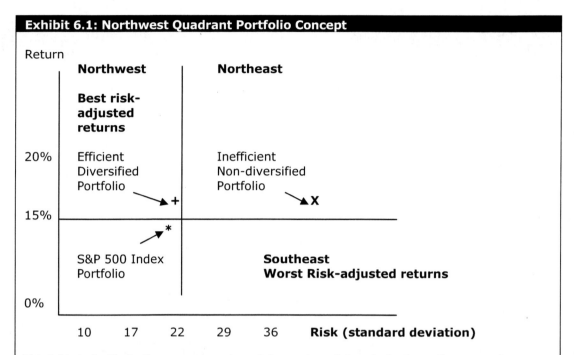

Exhibit 6.1: Northwest Quadrant Portfolio Concept

This table is for illustrative purposes only and does not predict or depict the performance of any investment. Standard deviation is an indicator of the portfolio's total return volatility. The larger the portfolio's standard deviation, the greater the portfolio's volatility.

Must an investor assemble a portfolio of top performers in order to fare well performance-wise and produce top notch returns?

The dream team portfolio of mutual funds does not guarantee better performance. Investors can generate above average returns even with a portfolio of average performing funds. Assembling the right *combination* of fund categories to build a portfolio with, then overweighting those categories favored by market and economic conditions is what counts more than buying top performers.

For example, in the recovery phase of the market cycle, a portfolio can either overweight Morningstar rated five-star large-cap funds or three-star small-to-mid-cap funds. If history does repeat itself, then chances are that a portfolio overweight in small-to-mid-cap funds will outperform the portfolio overweight in large-cap funds in the early bull market stage.

When a portfolio is built using sound diversification strategies, there is more leeway in the investment selection process. That means that a portfolio can do well even with mediocre funds if the portfolio is efficiently allocated. Exhibit 6.2 (see below) shows that by adding even lower return Treasury bills and U.S. Government bonds to a diversified portfolio, the diversified portfolio beat the four asset classes used to build it when evaluating its risk and reward results. As mentioned in previous chapters of this book, by combining funds that have a negative covariance with each other, a portfolio that has some mediocre performing funds could outperform the "dream team."

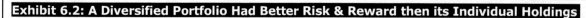

Exhibit 6.2: A Diversified Portfolio Had Better Risk & Reward then its Individual Holdings

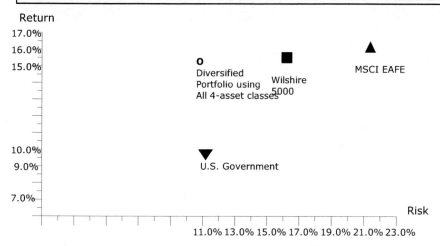

Source: Morningstar: Data for 1971-1999 period. Risk is measured by standard deviation which is an indicator of the portfolio's total return volatility. The larger the portfolio's standard deviation, the greater the portfolio's volatility. The Wilshire 5000 measures the performance of all U.S. headquartered equity securities with readily available price data. Over 7,000 capitalization weighted security returns are used to adjust the index. Morgan Stanley EAFE Index is also known as the Morgan Stanley Capital International Europe, Australia, and Far East Index of over 1,000 foreign stock prices. The index is translated into U.S. dollars. U.S. Long Term Government bonds are represented by the S&P Long-term Government Bonds index; Cash is represented by the Lehman Brothers Three month Treasury Bill Index derived from secondary market Treasury bill rates published by the Federal Reserve Bank or the 91-day Treasury bills data. Diversified portfolio is comprised of a blend of 20% of the MSCI (Morgan Stanley Capital International) EAFE Index, 50% of the Wilshire 5000 Index. 20% of U.S. Long Term Government bonds, 10% Three month Treasury bill Index. Indices include reinvested income, but not transaction costs or taxes, are unmanaged and cannot be purchased directly by investors. This graph is for illustrative purposes only and does not predict or depict the performance of any investment. Risk level is defined as the annualized standard deviation of portfolio returns for the period from 1971 to 1999. Past performance is no guarantee of future performance.

Encapsulating Diversification and Efficiency

What's the secret to building a diversified and efficient portfolio?

As a starting point, you could use MPT as developed by Noble prize laureate Harry Markowitz. MPT uses mean-variance analysis to build a portfolio that has the highest return for each unit of risk (standard deviation). It does this by combining asset classes together in the right proportion to construct the optimal strategic portfolio.

There are three key variables required to perform this analysis:

1. **Historical returns** of each asset class;
2. **Standard deviation** of each asset class;
3. **Correlation coefficients** between each asset class. This is the single most important key to building diversified portfolios. Most investors do not consider the correlation of funds in their portfolio.

Here is the biggest caveat in this book: MPT and any reliable asset allocator tool that relies on mean variance analysis to optimize "past portfolios" is just the *beginning* process of one method of managing money. It is by no means what-so-ever the end all or stand alone solution. There is so much more to managing money than a simple black box. Remember that the efficient frontier is a *theoretical* concept. Therefore, it is best to follow the investment management practices covered throughout this book to manage money in the real world, where almost anything goes and there are no unrealistic assumptions required for the model to work.

The correlation between each fund in a portfolio is critical to maximizing the risk and return trade-off. By combining funds that are not highly correlated with one another, the covariance term of a portfolio moves from +1 to -1, and risk is reduced. Negative one is the maximum risk reduction value -- zero variance. It is smart to focus on correlations of funds and not a fund's beta to reduce overall portfolio volatility.

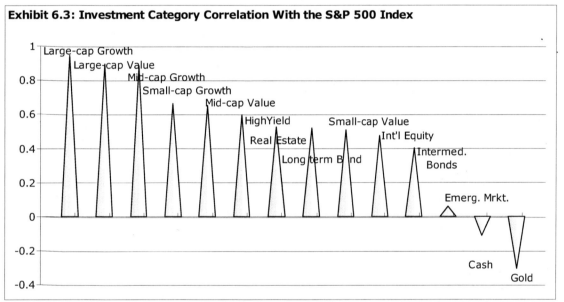

Exhibit 6.3: Investment Category Correlation With the S&P 500 Index

Source: Standard & Poor's, Thomson Financial, Morningstar Inc., The Frank Russell Company, Lehman Brothers, The Federal Reserve, Morgan Stanley Capital International, BGI Barclays Global Investors, Moody's Bond Record, Salomon Brothers, Lipper Inc., World Bank, International Finance Corporation, Wiesenberger™. Gold prices obtained from International Monetary Fund, Federal Reserve, and The Wall Street Journal. Data for 1970-1999 period. Large-cap represented by the S&P 500 Index, a commonly used broad based index of domestic stocks. The S&P 500® is an unmanaged stock index. Large-cap value is represented by the Barra Large-cap Value Index. Mid-cap growth is represented by Barra Mid-cap Growth Index. Mid-cap Value is represented by the Barra Mid-cap Value Index. Small-cap Growth is represented by the Russell 2000 Growth Index. Small-cap Value is represented by the Russell 2000 Value Index. Long term bonds are represented by the S&P Long-term Government Bonds Index. Intermediate term bonds are represented by the Lehman Long Treasury Bond Index, which is a 10-year Treasury note index. Treasury indices are total return indices held constant maturities. Cash is represented by the Lehman Brothers Three-month Treasury Bill Index derived from secondary market Treasury bill rates published by The Federal Reserve Bank or the 91-day Treasury bills data. International equity is represented by the Morgan Stanley EAFE Index, which is also known as the Morgan Stanley Capital International Europe, Australia, Far East Index of over 1,000 foreign stock prices. The index is translated into U.S. dollars. The MSCI EAFE (Europe, Australasia, and Far East) Index is a market-capitalization-weighted index that measures stock performance in 21 countries in Europe, Australasia and the Far East. The MSCI Emerging Markets Free Index represents a market-capitalization-weighted index of emerging market stock markets. Real Estate is represented by the National Association of Real Estate Investment Trusts (NAREIT). Gold is represented by prices obtained from the International Monetary Fund, The Federal Reserve, and The Wall Street Journal. Indices include reinvested income, but not transaction costs or taxes, are unmanaged and cannot be purchased directly by investors. This chart is for illustrative purposes only and does not predict or depict the performance of any investment. Past performance is no guarantee of future performance.

Fine-Tuning Your Process

You must make sure that the covariance analysis is still applicable in the current market. Long-term correlations may not always hold up over the short-term.

For example, precious metal funds usually perform well when the stock market tanks and inflation is high. In addition, they do not do well when the stock market is rallying, and when inflation is low. Yet in 2003, with inflation at a mere two percent, and the S&P 500 Index up over 24% over the last year, the precious metals fund category was up over 26.4% at the end of the third quarter (surprise!) Why? Geopolitical risk caused a disconnection with the past historical relationship.

A savvy advisor will do well to integrate the *IPM* process into MPT. The *IPM* process involves the establishment of an investment policy statement that places investors into suitable portfolios, portfolios built using MPT but also basic investment principles not addressed by MPT. *IPM*™ takes into consideration current market and economic conditions, as well as behavioral tendencies of investors.

Why use *IPM* along with MPT?

In the short-term MPT output may not be reliable because past performance may not repeat each year. MPT states that, based upon seventy-eight years of historical data, this is what might happen next year; that there is a sixty-seven percent chance that this will happen. MPT relies on past performance to repeat itself.

So why does MPT lead us astray in some years and under some circumstances?

MPT does not factor in current cyclical trends, current policy, fundamentals, and investors' psychology. On the other hand, *IPM* does factor these key elements into the investment process.

Furthermore, not all markets are alike. In any given year, an asset class may become overbought and overvalued or oversold and undervalued relative to its mean. Asset class leadership changes almost annually.

Over longer periods, twenty to thirty years, the MPT assumption that the future equals the past is applicable with asset class data because as the period is stretched out, asset class risk and return numbers revert to their mean.

Are there any other draw backs to MPT?

In a word -- Yes. MPT provides the building blocks to structure portfolios by only addressing one type of risk -- standard deviation. MPT measures risk based on what *has* happened and not what *is* happening with an asset class. Now more than ever, changing political, economic, and financial world events can cause asset classes to become mis-priced. In order to reduce risk that is present in today's market it is necessary to overlay tactical asset allocation onto strategic allocation results.

IPM tactical asset allocation relies on assessing current valuation, current market conditions, and forward return analysis to identify those asset classes that have disconnected from fundamentals and rational investment behavior. Sound tactical analysis should have concluded that stocks should be underweighted in February 2000 (S&P 500 selling at a P/E of 32-plus and stock mutual fund cash inflows at record levels) and underweighted bonds in late 2002.

Is there anything else *IPM* takes into consideration that MPT does not?

IPM takes into account behavioral tendencies of investors and circumstances. Investing is very much a psychological process. It has been my experience that many risk-averse investors will not buy and hold a strategic "frozen" portfolio designed for the long-term when losses exceed their loss threshold. Fear infiltrates their psyche and investors lose sleep along with money.

The NASDAQ Index plunged 77.9% from March 10, 2000 through October 9, 2002. Would you have sold if you had lost half your 401k assets, were retired, and were in poor health?

You can correct for MPT shortcomings by factoring individual circumstances such as health, financial condition, marital status, job status, etc. into the investment process and making tactical adjustments to control risk.

Insider Tip: A typical moderate-risk pension fund allocation is 60% stocks and 40% bonds because this mix has generally performed fairly well throughout the ups and down of the entire economic cycle. Bonds tend to perform well when the economy slows down and equities historically do well as the economy picks up. A 60%/40% mix generated about the same return as an 80% stocks/20% bonds mix from 1950-2003, and in down markets declined forty percent *less* than an 80%/20% mix.

Source: Standard & Poor's, Lehman Brothers. Stocks are represented bv the S&P 500 Index which is a total return index widely regarded as the standard for measuring large-cap U.S. stock market performance and includes a representative sample of 500 leading companies based on industry representation, liquidity, and stability. Historically, it includes 400 industrial stocks, 40 financial stocks, 40 public utility stocks, and 20 transportation stocks. Bonds are represented by the Lehman Brothers Aggregate Bond Index which is a market-capitalization weighted index of investment-grade fixed-rate debt issues, including government, corporate, asset-backed, and mortgage-backed securities, with maturities of at least one year. The Lehman Brothers High Yield Bond Index includes fixed rate, public, non-convertible, non-investment grade issues registered with the SEC that are rated BA1 or lower by Moody's Investors Service. Indices include reinvested income, but not transaction costs or taxes, are unmanaged and cannot be purchased directly by investors. This example is for illustrative purposes only and does not predict or depict the performance of any investment. Past performance is no guarantee of future performance.

---

11 Secrets to Improving Portfolio Performance

"Ignorance is bliss"
-- Unknown

1) Asset Allocation

A controversial study by Brinson, Hood, and Beebower for the ten years ended 1991 shows that over ninety percent of the <u>variance</u> in return on a portfolio depended on what type of asset was held -- stock, bond or cash. In other words, your asset allocation has a big impact on the fluctuation in portfolio returns. That is not to say it is what solely determines your returns. Selection and timing greatly impacts return, too. I have work with many advisors that misinterpret the study and misuse it in their financial practice.

The IPM process recognizes that market timing and security selection are extremely important to portfolio performance especially over shorter periods. Roy Neuberger once said that timing isn't everything, but it's a lot.

What if a client invested in an asset allocation fund in 1999 that, in turn, invested in areas of the market that were highly correlated; let's say large-cap growth stocks. On top of that, let's say that the bond portion was invested in bond funds that had, for the most part, invested in low investment grade bonds because the economy was booming but had since slowed. Given this hypothetical example, selection and timing would have had a bigger impact on the portfolio's performance over the next three years due to the ensuing bear market.

Most likely, a risk-averse investor with a low loss threshold would have had a hard time holding on as losses mounted. A 2003 Dalbar study concluded that the typical investor held a fund for two and a half years. Given the typical investor, short investment horizon timing becomes very important.

Even with my advanced education in investment management and twenty years of experience I still cannot figure out how asset allocation based on past data optimizes a portfolio over the coming cycle. How can a portfolio become optimized without taking into consideration the current valuations of the selected asset classes? After all, buying overpriced asset classes is not an optimal solution.

Taking valuation into consideration becomes a timing and selection issue. Let's say an asset allocator tool using mean variance analysis was used in March of 2000. What could have been the likely output? The recommendation could have been to put a big chunk of a growth objective portfolio into large-cap stocks. You know what happened next.

Let's do that again for an income objective portfolio in March 2003. The likely output might have been investing a sizeable amount of money in U.S. Treasuries just months before the Fed started raising interest rates. Ouch!

A 2002 study by Ibbotson Associates found that 60% of the variation in returns is due to security selection, timing, and fee differences between mutual funds. The rest is due to asset allocation.

Many academics and practitioners think that Brinson et al. asked the wrong question in its study. The question should have been "what is the correlation between asset allocation and returns?" One of the central tenets of *IPM* --Improving Portfolio Management -- is factor timing and selection into all investment decisions.

Over longer periods, asset allocation had a bigger impact on performance than timing and selection. If an investor gives an asset allocator tool twenty to thirty years to produce the "optimized" results, then current valuations (timing and selection) won't matter as much.

But keep in mind that rarely does a client give you more then a couple of years to prove yourself. Do not ignore the timing of asset classes and fund selections. Moreover, life events such as retirement, lost jobs, illness, divorce, birth/adoption of children, death of a spouse, need for parental care, etc., affect liquidity needs and investment horizons. Changes to horizon and liquidity needs make selection and timing a central issue in management. Factoring in human nature, real life circumstances, the investors I have worked could not afford to wait for asset allocation to pan out.

What I've experienced and seen is that portfolios that ignored timing and selection and blindly invested in a portfolio of stocks, bonds, and cash investments stood a good chance of underperforming. Portfolios that were built considering timing and selection stood a better chance of producing desired results over the short term. Again, why buy Treasury bonds when interest rates were at a 46-year low in 2003? Everyone in charge of managing money should have known that Treasury bonds would have a tough time when interest rates eventually rose form a 46-year low. The lesson is don't overweight overvalued asset classes.

2) Portfolio construction

Solid correlation analysis and fund category selection is extremely important in constructing portfolios. The mutual fund categories selected and the weighting of each can have a big impact on performance. The types of funds, their weightings, and the combination of investment approaches that are used will greatly affect performance.

Naturally, you will be asking yourself:

- Should you execute your equity asset allocation using large-cap growth or large-cap value?
- Do you choose an aggressive growth style of investing in stocks that have multiples of greater than 50, or a deep value equity approach with a P/E of 10?
- In executing your fixed-income allocation, which sectors do you choose to overweight -- high yield, Treasuries, asset-backed bonds, corporate or foreign bonds?
- On the fixed-income side, do you choose a crossover high yield style fund or corporate bullet approach that heavily overweight in intermediate bonds?
- Which approaches work well together?

Being dead right on the asset class, but dead wrong on the market-cap or investment style, could greatly hinder performance. The best performing asset class was equities in the five-year period ending 1998, according to Morningstar. However, if you were invested in an emerging market equity fund, chances are the return could have been negative, given that the Morningstar fund category average for those funds was about negative 8%.

Therefore, it is no surprise that in order for investors to do well they must identify those investment approaches favored by market conditions and overweight them.

Exhibit 6.4: It Paid to Be Right on Market-cap & Style

Market Indices	Returns Ending 2000	
	1-Yr.	3-Yr.
S&P 500 Growth	-22.08%	12.41%
S&P 500 Value	6.08%	11.10%
Russell Mid-cap Growth	-11.75%	16.32%
Russell Mid-cap Value	19.18%	7.75%
Russell 2000 Growth	-22.43%	3.96%
Russell 2000 Value	22.83%	4.22%
Greatest Difference	**45.26%**	**12.36%**

Source: Russell Investment Group, Standard & Poor's. S&P 500® is an unmanaged stock index: S&P 500 Growth represented by Russell Large-cap Growth index. S&P 500 Value represented by Russell Large-cap Value index Mid-cap growth represented by Russell Mid-cap Growth Index, Mid-cap Value is represented by the Russell Mid-cap Value Index; Small-cap Growth represented by the Russell 2000 Growth Index; Small-cap Value represented by the Russell 2000 Value Index, Indices include reinvested income, but not transaction costs or taxes, are unmanaged and cannot be purchased directly by investors. This chart is for illustrative purposes only and does not predict or depict the performance of any investment. Past performance is no guarantee of future performance.

The weight of each fund category can make a marked difference in performance. For instance, two fund wrap portfolios that own the same funds but have different weightings in each fund will have materially differences in performance.

What's the secret to improving upside and downside performance?

It is wisest to build a portfolio that blends sub-asset classes that have lower correlations. Just slicing up the asset allocation pie into smaller parts will not help if all of the sub-asset classes have a high correlation to each other. Moreover, there is an adverse impact on a portfolio's risk, return, and income performance if it lacks exposure to critical core fund categories. Core fund category selection relies on fund category risk/return/income/valuation characteristics and correlation with the other categories that make up a portfolio.

3. Reigning in Expenses

It is so important to overall performance to keep expenses relatively low. That doesn't mean you must invest only in funds with rock bottom expense levels. That's not the ticket to achieving overwhelmingly better performance. But it is smart to invest in funds with reasonable expense ratios compared to their fund category average. Commissions, management fees, and operating expenses of a fund can all produce a drag on returns.

4. Mind Your Geography

Country or economic zone allocations can have a big impact on returns. Foreign markets, as measured by the Morgan Stanley EAFE Index, outperformed the US market (as measured by the S&P 500 Index) by 5.21% on average per year from 1982 through 1990. Over 10 years, adding compounding at five percent or more, can really snowball account values. However over the next 10 years from 1991 through 1999, the U.S. markets outperformed the foreign markets by a whopping 10.37%! The direction of a country's stock or bond market depends on the health of a country's economy.

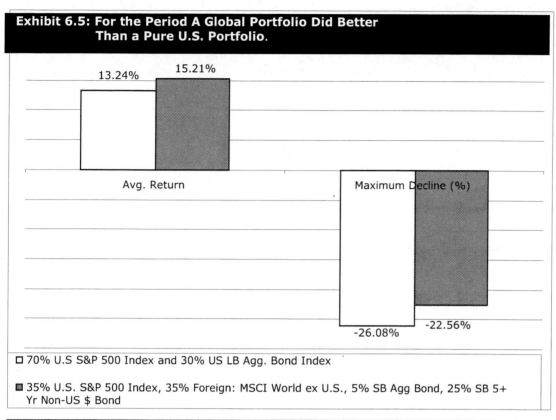

Exhibit 6.5: For the Period A Global Portfolio Did Better Than a Pure U.S. Portfolio.

□ 70% U.S S&P 500 Index and 30% US LB Agg. Bond Index

▨ 35% U.S. S&P 500 Index, 35% Foreign: MSCI World ex U.S., 5% SB Agg Bond, 25% SB 5+ Yr Non-US $ Bond

Source: Standard & Poor's, Lehman Brothers, Morgan Stanley Capital International, BGI Barclays Global Investors. Data for 1970-1999 period. The S&P 500 is a total return index widely regarded as the standard for measuring large-cap U.E. stock market performance and includes a representative sample of 500 leading companies based on industry representation, liquidity, and stability. Historically includes 400 industrial stocks, 40 financial stocks, 40 public utility stocks, and 20 transportation stocks. The Lehman Brothers Aggregate Bond Index is a market-capitalization weighted index of investment-grade fixed-rate debt issues, including government, corporate, asset-backed, and mortgage-backed securities, with maturities of at least one year. The Morgan Stanley All Country World ex-US Index is an unmanaged index comprised of 47 developed and developing market countries and does not include the United States. Index is based in U.S. dollars. The Solomon Brother's SB 5+ Year Non-US dollar index is a foreign bond indexed comprised of sovereign and non-sovereign debt of foreign countries. Indices include reinvested income, but not transaction costs or taxes, are unmanaged and cannot be purchased directly by investors. This chart is for illustrative purposes only and does not predict or depict the performance of any investment. Past performance is no guarantee of future performance.

5. Diversification strategy

Generally, being too diversified or being too concentrated could result in underperformance. Again, the combination of sub-asset classes and funds is what matters most -- not the sheer number of funds in a portfolio. Hence, you should rely on correlation analysis to diversify properly.

A portfolio will have a greater reaction to the same market news when the funds in the portfolio have a more positive correlation. The MSCI EAFE Index had a 0.40 correlation to the S&P 500 Index from 1970 through 1999. Investing 15% of a portfolio's assets in a MSCI EAFE-like foreign fund has, historically, reduced overall portfolio risk during certain time periods. During other time periods it has hurt performance.

That is why mean/variance analysis alone cannot provide the cure all. In addition, valuation analysis and top-down market and macro-economic analysis, which are an integral part of any portfolio construction and management, must be applied. Stock overlap between mutual funds can help or hurt performance, too. A 10% position in a stock is usually adequate. All else being equal, the lower the correlation between various funds in a portfolio, the greater the diversification benefit.

6. Fund selection criteria

Indiscriminately adding funds to a portfolio has the tendency to also hurt performance. Buying only five-star funds, as rated by Morningstar, or chasing returns is not the best way to go.

A 2003 Dalbar study found that the typical U.S. equity fund investor's average annual return was 2.57% from 1989-2002. That is 9% less per year than the S&P 500 Index returned. The study blamed poor fund selection for that gross underperformance.

While common sense dictates that each situation will warrant its own consideration, here are a few tips on fund selection:

*   Limit exposure to funds that have historically had a bad risk and reward trade-off (see some examples below).
*   Use the incremental return analysis per unit of risk method to decide which funds to avoid.
*   The intermediate bond category is one of the most efficient sub-asset classes which is why it is often viewed as a strategic core holding. Again, over the short-term, when conditions do not favor intermediate bonds, it may lose its status as an efficient asset class.

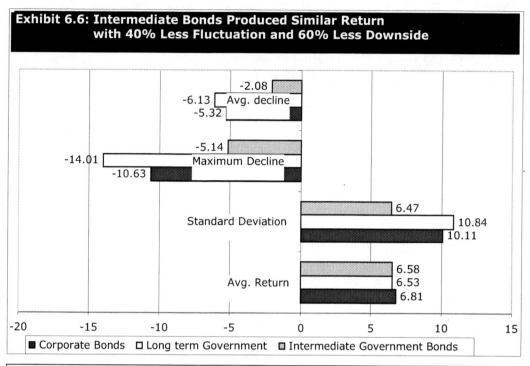

Exhibit 6.6: Intermediate Bonds Produced Similar Return with 40% Less Fluctuation and 60% Less Downside

Source: Lehman Brothers, Salomon Brothers, Federal Reserve. Data for 1950-2003 period. Standard deviation is an indicator of the portfolio's total return volatility. The larger the portfolio's standard deviation, the greater the portfolio's volatility. Long term Government are represented by the S&P Long-term Government Bonds index; Intermediate Government bonds are represented by the Lehman Long Treasury Bond Index is a 10-year Treasury note index. Treasury indices are total return indices held constant maturities. Corporate bonds are represented by the Lehman Brothers Bond Index. The Lehman Brothers Government/Credit Index measures the performance of all debt obligations of the U.S. Treasury and U.S. Government agencies, and all investment- grade domestic corporate debt; Indices include reinvested income, but not transaction costs or taxes, are unmanaged and cannot be purchased directly by investors. This chart is for illustrative purposes only and does not predict or depict the performance of any investment. Past performance is no guarantee of future performance.

Here is a short list of funds that have historically had a poor risk and return trade-off in the past:

- Emerging market funds;
- Micro-cap funds;
- Small-cap aggressive growth funds;
- Zero-coupon bond funds;
- Long-term Government bond funds.

In my opinion, it is best to consider avoiding any bond fund that uses exotic derivatives to enhance performance. I would not buy "hot" performing funds that own overvalued securities that are approaching the end of their performance cycle. In addition, failure to monitor funds and sell losers could have an adverse effect on returns. Studies covered in other chapters of this book show that losers tend to repeat underperformance for years. Past performance is no guarantee of future performance.

7. Dividend income

Do not forget about dividend income when building a portfolio. Studying data from Ibbotson Inc., dividends contributed as much as 35% of the S&P 500 Index return from 1926-2002. Coupon payments represented 90% of the T-bond return from 1926-2002. Furthermore, reinvestment of the income makes a world of difference in terms of the long-term return. One single dollar invested in the S&P 500 from 1926 to 2002 grew to become $2,279! But without any reinvestment of dividends, that same single dollar would have been worth a mere $90 over the same period!

Before the latest tax reform act, dividends were taxed at a rate as high as 38.6%. Now, qualified dividends are taxed at a 15% rate (5% for low income taxpayers). In 2008 those dividend tax rates revert back to the old rates. Consequently, dividend paying funds are more desirable to own than certain other equity funds in flat or down markets because they at least pay dividends.

8. Watch trade execution timing

Fund shares held for more than twelve months qualify for a favorable capital gain rate of 15%. That may produce a higher after-tax return.

It is wise to be aware of funds year-end distribution and try to avoid them by buying *after* the record date with the exception being a strong year-end rally.

9. Minimize Turnover

Frequently shifting assets for market timing reasons may increases taxes and reduce returns. Numerous industry studies have shown that very high turnover funds have produced lower returns than those of lower turnover funds. Of course, past performance is not indicative of future performance.

Even so, in general, keep turnover at a moderate level. Invest for long-term gains. The spread between the highest marginal tax rate and the capital gains rate now stands at twenty percentage points. The tax rate for a qualified five-year gain is 5% for a holding period that began after year 2000. It pays to realize long-term gains versus short-term gains.

10. Rebalancing a portfolio

One interesting study concluded that rebalancing reduced a portfolio's risk by 78% without lowering its return. The study, published by MFS Investments, covered the 1982-2002 period in which a portfolio was rebalanced evenly between the S&P 500 Index and the Lehman Brothers Aggregate Bond Index each quarter. Past performance is no guarantee of future performance.

11. Taxes Matter

Taxes can dramatically reduce real returns. It is smart to match investments with the right account type to increase what you get to keep from account returns. Put interest-paying investments such as bonds and REITs, in qualified plans that grow tax-deferred and would be taxed at ordinary income tax rates if not for the shelter of the qualified account. Also, invest in dividend paying stocks, and equity funds in taxable accounts that are favored by the new lower dividend and long-term capital gain rates. In general, equities have a tax advantage over taxable bonds for high-income bracket investors.

General IPM Portfolio Construction Guidelines

Risk is a Four-lettered Word

You must address risk management in building a portfolio, otherwise you risk losing clients during down markets. It is hard for a client to justify paying an advisory fee when money has been lost. Your friendship may buy you some time, but eventually performance may matter more.

You can use the guidelines listed in this section to build portfolios that seek to reduce risk. These strategies will not prevent all losses, but they may dampen them to tolerable levels.

What is a one of the greatest risks to manage with mutual fund investing?

Security overlap is a big problem with mutual fund investing. Owning a portfolio of funds that each owns the same securities inadvertently builds risk. Reduce this form of risk by mixing funds that have low correlation with each other. For instance, try not to own funds that have an obvious overlapping investment universe. It is not uncommon for a large-cap growth fund to own many of the same stocks a core large-cap fund. The same can be said for large-cap value and core large-cap. In some instances, even large-cap value and large-cap growth funds can own the same stocks. The value manager may justify owning growth stocks by buying them at "value" price levels.

Exhibit 6.7: Overlapping Scenarios

High Overlap Scenario and Less Diversification

	Value	Core	Growth
Large-cap	X	X	X
Mid –cap			
Small-cap			

Low Overlap Scenario and Greater Diversification

	Value	Core	Growth
Large-cap			X
Mid –cap		X	
Small-cap	X		

This chart is for illustrative purposes only and does not predict or depict the performance of any investment.

Mind Your Strategic Asset Allocations

Portfolios that have a primary goal of income should emphasize fixed-income investments, lower variance in returns, and higher liquidity than portfolios that have a primary objective of growth. In contrast, growth-oriented portfolios have less liquidity, higher variance in returns, and are meant for investors with a moderate risk preference and long-term investment horizons. Check-out Exhibit 6.8 for help in deciding the strategic asset allocation for a given portfolio objective.

Exhibit 6.8: Widely Accepted Strategic Asset Allocations

- Growth objective   90% stocks/5% Bonds/Cash 5%
- Growth & Inc. objective   60% stocks/35% Bonds/Cash 5%
- Inc. & Growth objective   40% stocks/55% Bonds/Cash 5%
- Income objective   10% stocks/85% Bonds/Cash 5%

This chart is for illustrative purposes only and does not predict or depict the performance of any investment.

Famed economist Maynard Keynes said that markets remain irrational longer than you can remain solvent. It is wise to make sure there is ample liquidity in conservative objective portfolios such as Income, and Income & Growth objectives.

My experience has taught me that conservative investors are jumpy investors that do not always buy and hold. Be certain to allocate enough assets into liquid investments to meet liquidity needs and address risk tolerance preference. The weighting of each type of fund depends on the portfolio objective, risk preference, liquidity needs, and fund category valuations. It can be smart to overweight liquid large-cap names and Treasury issues, given that they are not overvalued. It is okay to give up some return from less liquid areas of the market.

Exhibit 6.9: The Fund Liquidity Pyramid: Degree of Liquidity

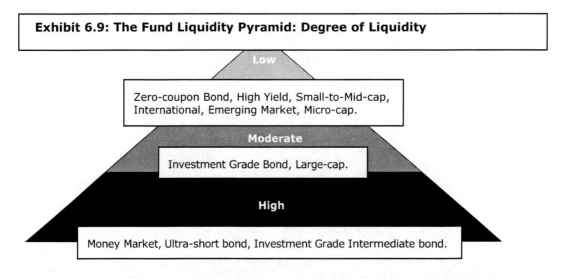

Low
Zero-coupon Bond, High Yield, Small-to-Mid-cap, International, Emerging Market, Micro-cap.

Moderate
Investment Grade Bond, Large-cap.

High
Money Market, Ultra-short bond, Investment Grade Intermediate bond.

Source: Morningstar. Liquidity is measured by standard deviation, investment objective of fund category, and underlying investments of a fund. Standard deviation is an indicator of the portfolio's total return volatility. The larger the portfolio's standard deviation, the greater the portfolio's volatility. This chart is for illustrative purposes only and does not predict or depict the performance of any investment. Investments in mutual funds involve risk. Past performance is no guarantee of future performance. Mutual funds incur fees and expenses (including investment management and administrative fees). Obtain a prospectus for more complete information about the fund, including all fees and expenses, and should be read carefully before you invest. Investment returns and principal value of a mutual fund will fluctuate, so that shares, when redeemed, may be worth more or less than their original cost. Past performance is no guarantee of future performance.

The Multiple Facets of Risk

To minimize the disastrous effect of two standard deviation events, you can build portfolios with tail risk in mind. The desired skyline of past returns of a portfolio should be peaked versus flat.

A flat skyline portfolio has more tail risk. Assuming normal distribution of stock market returns, investors should expect that next year's returns may range from negative 7% to positive 33% about 70% of the time. To protect against the rest of the time, where the range increases to approximately negative 27% to positive 53%, you can combine asset classes that historically will not fall below a stated loss threshold.

In addition, consider underweighting selected asset classes that are cyclically overvalued. Furthermore, minimize exposure to blow-out fund categories-- those where losses have historically been larger -- like emerging markets, small-cap growth, and high yield bonds unless the valuations are too attractive to pass on. Then take a small position of, say, 2.5% to 10% so as to gain exposure but mitigate risk.

Are there certain fund categories that make more sense for a particular portfolio objective than other categories?

Yes, there are essential fund categories that belong in each type of portfolio objective: Income, Income & Growth, Growth & Income, and Growth.

When building a portfolio, it is sensible to use a core holding approach. The core holdings are mutual fund categories that tend to improve a portfolio's risk, return, and income performance and seek to bring about the desired future results.

What makes a fund category a "core" category to own?

Certain asset classes have been more efficient than other ones to use with a given type of portfolio. These are what I call "core asset classes." Be strategic with efficient asset classes and tactical with inefficient ones. Efficient ones provide a higher return for the same level of risk or provide less risk.

You can use efficient asset classes as core asset classes to build strategic portfolios. But do not forget about inefficient ones because there will be times when they offer less risk and higher returns.

Exhibit 6.10: : Asset Class Risk and Return for 1926-2002 Period

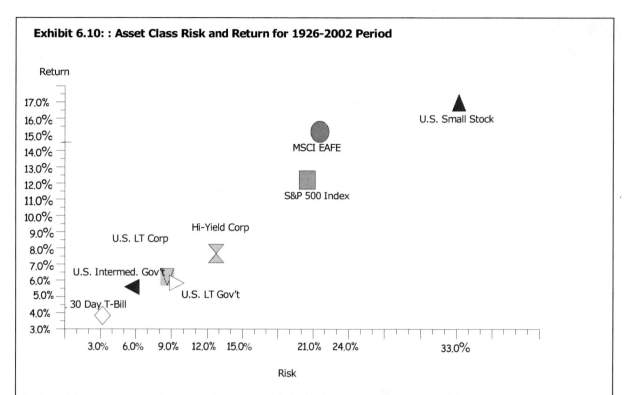

Source: Thomson Financial, Morningstar Inc., The Frank Russell Company, Lehman Brothers, Federal Reserve, Morgan Stanley Capital International, Salomon Brothers, The Federal Reserve. Risk is measured by standard deviation which is an indicator of the portfolio's total return volatility. The larger the portfolio's standard deviation, the greater the portfolio's volatility. The S&P 500 Index is a commonly used broad based index of domestic stocks. The S&P 500® is an unmanaged stock index. S&P 500 is a registered trademark of Standard & Poor's Corporation. Investors cannot invest in the S&P 500 Index. U.S. Small-cap stocks are represented by the Russell 2000 Index, an index consisting of the smallest 2,000 companies in the Russell 3000 index (composed of 3,000 large U.S. companies as determined by market capitalization and represents approximately 98% of the investable U.S. equity market). The MSCI EAFE (Europe, Australasia, and Far East) Index is a market-capitalization-weighted index that measures stock performance in 21 countries in Europe, Australasia and the Far East. U.S. Long-term Government is represented by the S&P Long-term Government Bonds Index. U.S. Intermediate Government is represented by the Lehman Long Treasury Bond Index and is a 10-year Treasury note index. Treasury indices are total return indices held constant maturities. High Yield Corporate is represented by the Lehman Brothers High Yield Bond Index which includes fixed rate, public non-convertible, non-investment grade issues registered with the SEC that are rated BA1 or lower by Moody's Investors Service. U.S. 30-day T-bill is represented by the Lehman Brothers Three-month Treasury Bill Index derived from secondary market Treasury bill rates published by The Federal Reserve Bank or the 91-day Treasury bills data. U.S. Long-term Corporate bonds are represented by the Lehman Brothers Bond Index. The Lehman Brothers Government/Credit Index measures the performance of all debt obligations of the U.S. Treasury and U.S. Government agencies, and all investment- grade domestic corporate debt. Indices include reinvested income, but not transaction costs or taxes, are unmanaged and cannot be purchased directly by investors. This chart is for illustrative purposes only and does not predict or depict the performance of any investment. Past performance is no guarantee of future performance.

The Efficient Portfolio Frontier

What are a few asset classes that have been efficient to use with strategic asset allocation?

The following asset classes produced the highest return for the lowest risk in a given portfolio. I consider them to be the core building blocks for a portfolio:

• U.S. Small-cap
• MSSCI EAFE
• U.S. Intermediate Government Bonds
• Foreign bonds both sovereign and non-sovereign
• 30-day T-Bill

These strategic core asset classes belong in most common portfolios such as a Growth objective portfolio, Growth & Income, Income & Growth objective, etc. Using mean variance analysis tool, the following asset classes improved past returns and risk of the common portfolios mentioned for the entire period from 1970-2003. Without these investments, the hypothetical portfolios had either more risk or lower return, or were more risky and had higher return.

Exhibit 6.11: Long-term Optimizing Asset Classes.

Portfolio Objective	Efficient Asset Classes
Income:	Intermediate Government Bonds, US Small-cap, Foreign bonds, Sovereign Foreign bonds, U.S. 30-day T-bill
Income & Growth:	Intermediate Government Bonds, Foreign bonds, Sovereign Foreign bonds, U.S. 30-day T-bill, U.S. Small-cap, foreign equities.
Growth & Income:	Intermediate Government Bonds, Foreign bonds, Sovereign Foreign bonds, U.S. 30-day T-bill, U.S. Small-cap, foreign equities.
Growth:	U.S. Small-cap, Foreign Equities

This table is for illustrative purposes only and does not predict or depict the performance of any investment. Past performance is no guarantee of future performance. Source: Thomson Financial, Morningstar Inc., The Frank Russell Company, Lehman Brothers, Federal Reserve, Morgan Stanley Capital International, Salomon Brothers, The Federal Reserve. U.S. Small-cap stocks are represented by the Russell 2000 Index, an index consisting of the smallest 2,000 companies in the Russell 3000 index (composed of 3,000 large U.S. companies as determined by market capitalization and represents approximately 98% of the investable U.S. equity market). The MSCI EAFE (Europe, Australasia, and Far East) Index is a market-capitalization-weighted index that measures stock performance in 21 countries in Europe, Australasia and the Far East. U.S. Intermediate Government is represented by the Lehman Long Treasury Bond Index and is a 10-year Treasury note index. Treasury indices are total return indices held constant maturities. U.S. 30-day T-bill is represented by the Lehman Brothers Three-month Treasury Bill Index derived from secondary market Treasury bill rates published by The Federal Reserve Bank or the 91-day Treasury bills data. Sovereign Foreign bonds are represented by the Salomon Non-U.S. World Government Bond Index. Indices include reinvested income, but not transaction costs or taxes, are unmanaged and cannot be purchased directly by investors.

As already discussed, these strategic asset classes can become overvalued and lose their efficiency at a certain point in the cycle. Therefore, you can underweight those that tend to lose efficiency (for example, a Utilities fund in an Income and Income & Growth portfolio when the economy slows down) and tactically use the rest of the asset classes available to attempt to optimize both return and risk going forward.

Getting to the Core of a Portfolio

What else is good about the core holding approach?

A investment strategy that incorporates the use of core holdings actually uses a number of different strategies to generate returns and income to improve the odds of achieving your portfolio objective. A portfolio that bets on one investment approach will never plot close to the theoretical efficient frontier. In other words, a separately managed account using one style or a bunch of similar funds will lower the odds of achieving the portfolio's objective.

Exhibit 6.12, which follows, shows the core holdings of an Income objective portfolio. The bolded font names those sub-asset classes that serve as the risk reducing diversifiers. These had lower correlations to the dominant asset class, which in this scenario is fixed-income.

However, they also support the income objective by providing income and appreciation potential. Other tactical, but not core, asset classes that are not in the table are Utilities, Commodities, and Convertibles. The equity exposure comes from either a Large-cap Value or Real Estate Fund holding. Which one depends on current market conditions and the valuation of a particular fund category.

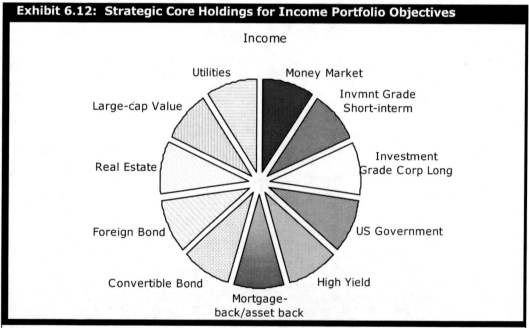

Exhibit 6.12: Strategic Core Holdings for Income Portfolio Objectives

This chart is for illustrative purposes only and does not predict or depict the performance of any investment. Past performance is no guarantee of future performance.

What is another construction method that attempts to reduce risk?

Not having all the slices of a pie (investments in the portfolio) tending to react the same way to cyclical conditions can mitigate risk. Of the nine non-equity pie slices that make up the portfolio, five had a low correlation with bonds. This means that they will have a different performance cycle, react differently to market news, and to a certain extent offset each other's risks. You can attempt to control risk, income, and return by rebalancing the weight of these slices throughout the market cycle.

Exhibit 6.13: Correlation Analysis for Income Objective Portfolio

	S&P 500 Value	LB Gvt	LB Corp	IT Gvt/ Corp	3 Mo T-Bill	Hi-Yld	LB Mrtg.	Non-U.S. Gvt	NAREIT
S&P 500 Value	1.00	0.45	0.52	0.43	-0.08	0.50	0.45	-0.02	0.55
LB Government	0.45	1.00	0.91	0.99	0.26	0.62	0.90	0.44	0.29
LB Corporate	0.52	0.91	1.00	0.92	0.08	0.77	0.96	0.44	0.40
LB IT Gvt/Corp	0.43	0.99	0.92	1.00	0.36	0.65	0.91	0.45	0.32
3 Mo.T-bill	-0.08	0.26	0.08	0.36	1.00	-0.01	0.15	0.17	0.12
Hi-Yield	0.50	0.62	0.77	0.65	-0.01	1.00	0.67	0.31	0.64
LB Mortgage	0.45	0.90	0.96	0.91	0.15	0.67	1.00	0.42	0.21
Non-U.S Gov't	-0.02	0.44	0.44	0.45	0.17	0.31	0.42	1.00	-0.04
NAREIT	0.55	0.29	0.40	0.32	0.12	0.64	0.21	-0.04	1.00

Source: Barra Inc., Morningstar Inc., Lehman Brothers, Federal Reserve, Morgan Stanley Capital International, BGI Barclays Global Investors, Moody's Bond Record, Salomon Brothers, Lipper Inc., Federal Reserve. Data for twenty eight year period ending 1999. The S&P BARRA 500 Value Index; Government bonds are represented by the S&P Long-term Government Bonds index; Intermediate Government bonds are represented by the Lehman Long Treasury Bond Index is a 10-year Treasury note index. Treasury indices are total return indices held constant maturities. Cash is represented by the Lehman Brothers Three month Treasury Bill Index derived from secondary market Treasury bill rates published by the Federal Reserve Bank or the 91-day Treasury bills data. Corporate bonds are represented by the Lehman Brothers Bond Index. The Lehman Brothers Aggregate Bond Index is a market-capitalization weighted index of investment-grade fixed-rate debt issues, including government, corporate, asset-backed, and mortgage-backed securities, with maturities of at least one year. The Lehman Brothers Government/Credit Index measures the performance of all debt obligations of the U.S. Treasury and U.S. government agencies, and all investment- grade domestic corporate debt; High Yield bonds are represented by the Merrill Lynch High Yield Master Index; Foreign bonds are represented by the Salomon Non-U.S. World Government Bond Index; Mortgage-backed bonds are represented by the Merrill Lynch Mortgage-Backed Master Index. Real Estate is represented by the National Association of Real Estate Investment Trusts (NAREIT) Index. Indices include reinvested income, but not transaction costs or taxes, are unmanaged and cannot be purchased directly by investors. This chart is for illustrative purposes only and does not predict or depict the performance of any investment.

Lockstep Performance Can Increase Risk

Exhibit 6.14, below, shows an Income objective portfolio without the core diversifiers. The investment categories tend to react the same way to economic and market news and as a result, performance tends to be in tandem. This parallel performance can add risk to a portfolio.

Exhibit 6.14: Income Portfolio without Core Diversifiers

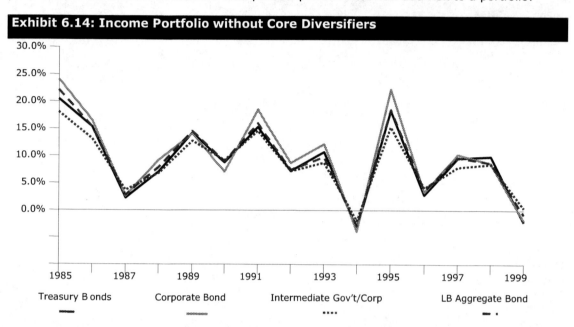

Treasury Bonds   Corporate Bond   Intermediate Gov't/Corp   LB Aggregate Bond

Source: Lehman Brothers, The Federal Reserve, Morningstar. Treasury bonds are represented by the S&P Long-term Government Bonds index. Intermediate Government /corporate bonds are represented by the Lehman Brothers Government/Credit Index which measures the performance of all debt obligations of the U.S. Treasury and U.S. government agencies, and all investment- grade domestic corporate debt. Indices are total return indices held constant maturities. Corporate bonds are represented by the Lehman Brothers Bond Index. The Lehman Brothers Aggregate Bond Index is a market-capitalization weighted index of investment-grade fixed-rate debt issues, including government, corporate, asset-backed, and mortgage-backed securities, with maturities of at least one year. Indices include reinvested income, but not transaction costs or taxes, are unmanaged and cannot be purchased directly by investors. This chart is for illustrative purposes only and does not predict or depict the performance of any investment.

Exhibit 6.15 shows a properly diversified income portfolio that has investments that are matched so as to "zig and zag". When one investment is down another is up. Thereby somewhat offsetting one another to various degrees. The right combination of investments could smooth out the variation in income, returns, and risk.

Portfolio Diversifiers Can Mitigate Risk

Exhibit 6.15: Income Portfolio with Core Diversifiers

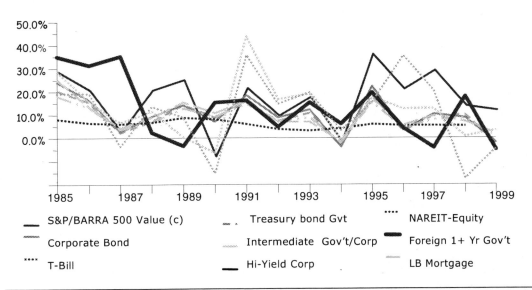

Legend: S&P/BARRA 500 Value (c), Treasury bond Gvt, NAREIT-Equity, Corporate Bond, Intermediate Gov't/Corp, Foreign 1+ Yr Gov't, T-Bill, Hi-Yield Corp, LB Mortgage

Source: Barra Inc., Morningstar Inc., Lehman Brothers, The Federal Reserve, Morgan Stanley Capital International, BGI Barclays Global Investors, Moody's Bond Record, Salomon Brothers, Lipper Inc. Value equities are represented by The S&P BARRA 500 Value Index. Government bonds are represented by the S&P Long-term Government Bonds Index. Intermediate Government bonds are represented by the Lehman Long Treasury Bond Index which is a 10-year Treasury note index. Treasury indices are total return indices held constant maturities. Cash is represented by the Lehman Brothers Three-month Treasury Bill Index derived from secondary market Treasury bill rates published by The Federal Reserve Bank or the 91-day Treasury bills data. Corporate bonds are represented by the Lehman Brothers Bond Index. The Lehman Brothers Aggregate Bond Index is a market-capitalization weighted index of investment-grade fixed-rate debt issues, including government, corporate, asset-backed, and mortgage-backed securities, with maturities of at least one year. The Lehman Brothers Government/Credit Index measures the performance of all debt obligations of the U.S. Treasury and U.S. government agencies, and all investment-grade domestic corporate debt. High yield bonds are represented by the Merrill Lynch High Yield Master Index. Foreign bonds are represented by the Salomon Non-U.S. World Government Bond Index. Mortgage-backed bonds are represented by the Merrill Lynch Mortgage-Backed Master Index. Real Estate is represented by the National Association of Real Estate Investment Trusts (NAREIT) Index. Indices include reinvested income, but not transaction costs or taxes, are unmanaged and cannot be purchased directly by investors. This chart is for illustrative purposes only and does not predict or depict the performance of any investment.

Nailing Down Numbers and Proportions

How many funds are required in a portfolio to diversify?

A portfolio does not generally need to own more than eight funds at a time. Owning the right combination of eight funds should diversify away specific fund risk. You can tactically add specialty funds (such as health sciences, utilities, financial, natural resources, zero-coupon, and TIPs) as conditions warrant, at the expense of underweighting or eliminating other holdings. To determine a fund category weight, you can perform macro-economic and market analysis, fund category and valuation/expected return analysis.

It is important to use only style consistent funds as it will be easier to control desired overall portfolio characteristics. For example, I recommend that you do not use asset allocation funds, a multi-sector bond funds, balanced funds, index bond funds, worldwide bond funds or global equity funds. The portfolio manager's asset allocation decisions can disrupt your desired fund category weights.

For instance, your 20% position in a multi-sector bond fund may invest, say, 25% of its assets in high yield bonds when you already have a 20% position in a high yield bond fund. Now your high yield exposure is excessively high! To control your bond sector diversification strategy stick with pure style funds like high yield fund, a GNMA fund, Government bond fund, corporate bond fund, and foreign bond fund.

Should only funds investing in U.S. securities be owned?

It can be smart to build globally diversified portfolios that typically have up to 25% of their assets invested in foreign markets. Historically, low correlations between worldwide country indexes support global investing as a way to produce better risk-adjusted returns. Country index correlations have been as low as 0.25 according to Morningstar.

What else should be taken into account?

Evaluate the interrelationships between funds to manage risk when building the portfolio. Although a stock fund invests across several different industries and a hundred stocks, each industry and all the stocks may be highly sensitive to the same macroeconomic data, for example, a portfolio diversified among interest rate sensitive industries. Although a portfolio may own ten funds representing different fund categories, the fund categories may all themselves be highly correlated.

To minimize technology risk, choose funds that invest in sectors that have a negative correlation against the Nasdaq such as those in the health care, energy, consumer staples, and basic materials sectors. It's perfectly okay to rely on recent correlations studies to help construct a diversified portfolio. A low correlation fund is one with a correlation of less than 70 to the portfolio's benchmark. You can achieve a greater reduction in portfolio volatility by adding several funds with correlations below 50.

Equity Component Guidelines:

•   **Seek to diminish a single-asset class investment risk**. Over the long run, the chance of a well-balanced portfolio experiencing greater variance in returns is less than a concentrated one. For example, historically, adding a mid-cap value fund to a growth objective portfolio emphasizing large-cap stocks has lowered the standard deviation and increased its return. When building the equity portion of a portfolio, invest among large-cap funds, mid-cap funds, and small-cap funds of various investment styles.

•   **Employ multiple strategies** to build wealth and protect against big losses. It's just plain prudent to mix active, passive, value, growth, large-cap, mid-cap, and small-cap together to build a portfolio that's congruent with the investment policy. Which approaches to mix and emphasize largely depends on the portfolio objective, market conditions and valuations.

•   **Consider the volatility of equity funds**. Certain types of funds have historically been more volatile than other types. Small capitalization equity funds, for example, are generally considered relatively more volatile than large-cap equity funds. Conservative Income & Growth-oriented portfolios should have large-to-mid cap funds as core holdings and a smaller (or even zero) weighting in small-cap funds.

You can build capital appreciation portfolios with higher beta funds. Consider funds that employ concentration strategies and invest in fewer stocks, those heavily concentrated in a few industries, and those that have a large percentage of fund assets in their top ten holdings.

Generally, the aggressive capital appreciation portfolios should have a greater exposure in mid- to small-cap funds and international and emerging market funds, assuming market conditions favor them. When combining funds to create a portfolio, make sure that the overall portfolio beta adheres to the conservative guidelines shown in Exhibit 6.16.

Exhibit 6.16: Overall Portfolio Beta Guidelines	
Portfolio objective	
- Growth	$1 < Beta < 1.2$
- Growth & Income	$Beta < 1$
- Income & Growth	$Beta <= 0.75$
- Income	$Beta <= 0.50$

•   **Consider careful use of sector funds**. Although riskier, sector funds are an excellent way to actively manage a portfolio. Use these funds to build both defensive and opportunistic positions. Use them to concentrate into areas of the market that may out perform the broad market. Technology, biotechnology, healthcare, financial, and even Zero-coupon bond funds are the favorites. Sectors funds are very volatile. Excellent timing is required to do well with them. Be careful of the sector overlap that may be created among the core funds and the sector funds in the fund portfolio.

•   **Consider Active versus passive strategy funds.** In hot markets, and in certain areas of the market, you can use index funds to offset the risk of actively managed funds that are underperforming their benchmarks. You may consider using index funds in the more efficient large-cap area of the market. Actively managed funds are preferable in less efficient areas, such as the small-cap and international stock sectors, where managers have a much better chance of beating their benchmarks. You should consider using index funds in tax-managed portfolios because of lower annual distributions than most actively managed funds.

•   **Invest internationally, including in emerging market funds, to pursue higher returns and diversify**. Mixing U.S. stock funds, foreign stock funds, and both domestic and foreign bond funds has shown to have produced better risk adjusted return than just investing in U.S. stocks and or U.S. bonds during certain time periods. How much to invest in international waters depends on global economic conditions and the direction of the U.S. dollar. When the dollar depreciates against major foreign currencies, chances are U.S. investors invested in an international fund will get a boost in return from the favorable currency move.

In the past it was prudent to limit foreign exposure to 20%-30% of a portfolio. Beyond that, based on past data, risk actually increases. Of course, past performance is no guarantee of future results. I think today its okay to go beyond 30% to as high as 50% for certain non-risk averse investors. The globalization of the world economy and markets has improved the economic management, monetary management, accounting practices, regulations, and so many other things in foreign economies and markets. Overall, the quality of companies found in foreign markets including emerging markets is quite good compared to U.S. companies. There are many foreign companies that are even industry leaders.

You can limit the initial monetary commitment per fund to no more than 20% of a portfolio. Also remember not to over-diversify. Different funds may have very similar exposures to foreign markets and may even own the same stocks within their top holdings. If you are wise, you will pare down your duplicative holdings, stock concentration, and industry concentration. Again, eight different types of funds in a portfolio is plenty.

•   **Limit any specific industry exposure to no more than thirty percent of a portfolio**. Think about what happened to the telecommunications industry from 2000-2002 and you will fully understand the wisdom of this guideline. Hot stocks in this industry lost as much as 80% of their value, and WorldCom filed for bankruptcy.
At the portfolio level, you can manage exposure to cyclical industries by building a portfolio that limits macro sensitivity-- deceases exposure to economically sensitive stock groups.

•   **Limit the portfolio's multiple to 22** based on prudent estimated forward earnings growth. Higher multiples have limited upside potential and significantly increase downside risk. As multiples expand, at some point, value starts to matter more than price momentum. Momentum is inversely correlated with value. When warranted, you should let a Growth objective portfolio's multiple expand a bit, but try to keep it below 25. At 26, the multiple has stretched 20% above the market's historical high-end cyclical trading range.

The Plethora of Tools to Lower Equity Risk

You can add funds that reduce both the impact of volatility and downside risk. Those funds have typically had a low covariance with the dominant asset class or investment approach in a portfolio. A fund has a low covariance with another when the correlation is below 70. The lower a fund's correlation to the rest of the funds, the better it is for reducing volatility.

Here is a short list of potential diversifying funds to consider using: Money market funds, intermediate bond funds, international bond funds, real estate funds, emerging market equity funds, small-cap international, commodities funds, and utility funds. Each of these funds can help to reduce equity risk as well as volatility without shaving too much off long-term returns.

REIT's have a low correlation with both the Nasdaq Index and the S&P 500 Index. The correlation between international bonds and U.S. bonds has been quite low. Emerging market equity funds sport low correlations and offer the greatest degree of diversification among equity fund sub-categories. You may also consider adding funds that employ hedging techniques, such as so-called "bear market" funds. When business conditions start to peak, you may wish to consider high yielding utility stock funds, funds that emphasize dividend paying stocks, REITs funds, and other funds that own predominantly defensive stock groups such as consumer staples, food and beverage, and household products.

Commodities are also an excellent diversification tool. Commodities have a negative correlation to equities and fixed-income investments. They have a negative correlation to the Wilshire 5000 Index (U.S. stocks), the Lehman Brothers Aggregate Bond Index (U.S. bonds), the DJ World Index -- ex. U.S. (foreign stocks), and the Salomon Brothers non-US$ Non-sovereign Bond Index (foreign bonds), according to Oppenheimer Funds. Moreover, commodities have a positive correlation to inflation, and have outperformed the S&P 500 Index and the Lehman Brothers Bond Index over the last thirty years ending 2003, according to Goldman Sachs.

Another way to offset equity risk is to add bonds to a portfolio of common stocks. Certain bonds have protected a portfolio from a "blow out" year. Having one bad year can hurt long-term performance. In years when the S&P 500 Index declined, intermediate investment grade bonds have risen.

Therefore, as part of a sound risk management program, you might wish to add investment grade bonds to an equity portfolio. As illustrated in Exhibit 6.17 below, by allocating 30% to intermediate bonds and only 70% to equities, a portfolio lowered its long-term downside risk and still generated competitive returns for the period of 1950-2002. What's more, the volatility of the portfolio dropped! Owning a portfolio 100% invested in bonds over the long term was actually more risky than owning a portfolio that had as much as 30% invested in equities.

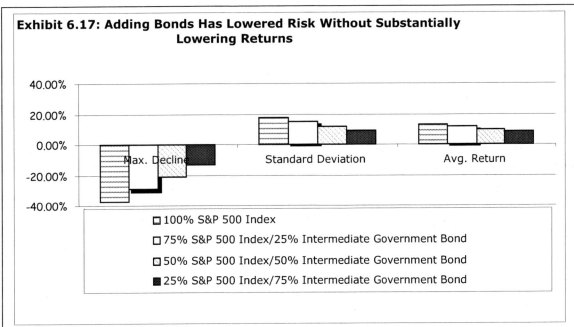

Exhibit 6.17: Adding Bonds Has Lowered Risk Without Substantially Lowering Returns

Source: Thomson Financial, Lehman Brothers. Data for 1950-2002 period. Risk is measured by the standard deviation which is an indicator of the portfolio's total return volatility. The larger the portfolio's standard deviation, the greater the portfolio's volatility. The S&P 500 Index is a commonly used broad based index of domestic stocks. The S&P 500® is an unmanaged stock index. The S&P 500 is a registered trademark of Standard & Poor's Corporation. Investors cannot invest in the S&P 500 Index; Intermediate Government bonds are represented by the Lehman Long Treasury Bond Index is a 10-year Treasury note index. Treasury indices are total return indices held constant maturities. Indices include reinvested income, but not transaction costs or taxes, are unmanaged and cannot be purchased directly by investors. This chart is for illustrative purposes only and does not predict or depict the performance of any investment. Past performance is no guarantee of future performance.

Considering the Choices of Bonds

Which bond fund category was better at reducing risk?

Intermediate bonds, and not long-term bonds, were a better choice for offsetting equity risk. In the past, the long bond had almost as much risk as common stocks. The long-term bond did not significantly reduce the downside risk or reduce volatility from 1980 to 2002. Intermediate bonds provided approximately the same returns as long-term bonds, but with less volatility. Five-year Treasury notes generated approximately 95% of the long-term bond sector's yields with 50% less volatility! (Intermediate Government bonds are represented by the Lehman Long Treasury Bond Index which is a 5-year Treasury note index. Long-term bonds are represented by the S&P Long-term Government Bonds Index. Indices include reinvested income, but not transaction costs or taxes, are unmanaged and cannot be purchased directly by investors. Past performance is no guarantee of future performance.)

Fixed-income Component Guidelines

Fixed income is all about risk control. Fixed income returns are limited, but downside risk is unlimited. Investors should not lose sleep over their fixed income portion of a portfolio. Bond returns among Treasury securities -- T-bills, Treasury notes, Treasury bonds -- are vary minimally, whereas bond risks vary significantly.

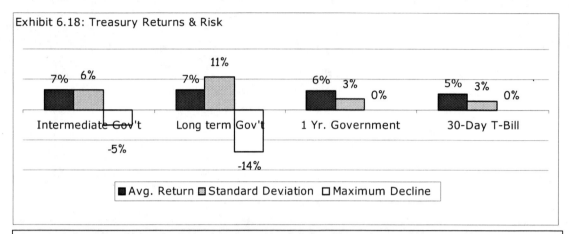

Exhibit 6.18: Treasury Returns & Risk

Source: Lehman Brothers, The Federal Reserve, Moody's Bond Record. Data for 1950-2002 period. Risk is measured by the standard deviation which is an indicator of the portfolio's total return volatility. The larger the portfolio's standard deviation, the greater the portfolio's volatility. Long-term Government bonds are represented by the S&P Long-term Government Bonds Index. Intermediate Government bonds are represented by the Lehman Long Treasury Bond Index, which is a 10-year Treasury note index. Treasury indices are total return indices held constant maturities. Merrill Lynch 1-Year Treasury Index is an unmanaged index tracking U.S. government securities. The index is produced by Merrill Lynch, Pierce, Fenner & Smith, Inc. The 30-day T-bill is represented by the Lehman Brothers Three-month Treasury Bill Index derived from secondary market Treasury bill rates published by The Federal Reserve Bank. Indices include reinvested income, but not transaction costs or taxes, are unmanaged and cannot be purchased directly by investors. This chart is for illustrative purposes only and does not predict or depict the performance of any investment. Past performance is no guarantee of future performance.

Therefore, the key to bond investing is to manage risk. There are four major risks associated with bond investing, *interest rate, reinvestment*, *credit quality,* and *purchasing power*. Income investors must evaluate their portfolio with these risks in mind.

The Six Goals of Fixed-income Investing:

1. **Protect Principal** - the money allocated to bonds is considered "safe money" that investors cannot afford to lose. Equity investors thrive on risk and bond investor's worry about risk. Remember that bond investors are creditors not equity holders. When buying bonds think like a creditor. Above all else creditors want to get their money back! Emphasize quality, and intermediate terms unless conditions strongly suggest not to.
2. **Beat Inflation** - If investment returns do not beat inflation than purchasing power is lost. That is almost the same as losing money. After-tax returns on T-bills don't typically beat inflation, but intermediate bond returns could.
3. **Liquidity** - Since bond money is "safe money" it must be there when needed. Thus, it has to be very liquid. Short-to intermediate-term investment grade bonds are liquid enough for most investors' needs.
4. **Offsets equity risk** - Over the long run, let's say ten years, investing as much as 20% of a portfolio in bonds has reduced the downside risk of a "blowout" year. Of course, past performance is no guarantee of future performance.
5. **Diminish the overall portfolio volatility** of other assets classes.
6. **Balance reinvestment risk and interest rate risk.**

What approaches and principles can be used to reduce bond investment risk and accomplish these six goals?

Here are three strategies that savvy financial advisors could use, in addition to other active management strategies, to reduce risk:

•   **Bullet approach** – investments are heavily overweight in intermediate bonds. Intermediate bonds balance interest rate and purchasing power risk better than long-term or short-term bonds. Over the interest rate cycle, this strategy tends to deliver more consistent performance than the other approaches. This approach doesn't anticipate interest rate changes but follows them to some extent, lengthening the duration as yields fall and shortening duration as yields rise. The bullet approach does well when the yield curve steepens as compared to the Barbell approach and Ladder approach (discussed below). In a rising interest rate environment, higher rates cause long-term bond prices to fall and higher inflation erodes the coupon value of short-term fixed income securities.

•   **Ladder approach** -- has merit because it reduces overall bond risk. This approach spreads the assets evenly among the short-term, intermediate-term, and long-term fixed-income securities. When rates fall, the longer term maturities perform well. But when rates rise, they falter and the short-term bonds' performance pick up the slack. Thus, the ladder approach somewhat immunizes against interest rate risk, and reduces reinvestment risk and purchasing power risk! This is a low risk approach to constructing your bond portfolio and is a lot safer than trying to figure out the direction of interest rates. The aim is to not to beat the market or make any interest rate bets, but attempt to approximate the returns of longer-term bonds, while limiting interest rate risk. This strategy has done well when the economy has experienced moderate growth and moderate inflation.

•   **Barbell approach** -- is designed to balance interest rate risk, reinvestment risk, and purchasing power risk by heavily overweighting long-term bonds, and short-term bonds. This approach always under weight intermediate bonds. The barbell approach offsets interest rate and reinvestment risks. When interest rates drop, prices rise, But at the same time, reinvestment risk also rises. Reinvestment risk is the highest with low yielding funds and lowest with high yielding funds. But low reinvestment risk funds have the highest interest rate risk. This approach has performed well when the Fed has raised short-term rates. When the yield curve flattens, the barbell approach has outperformed the bullet approach.

Getting the Fixed-Income Recipe Right

Should a portfolio just contain Government bonds -- after all, Government bond funds are considered one of the safest investments available?

It can be smarter to utilize multiple strategies to earn income. The multi-sector bond management approach has dampened volatility compared to a single sector emphasis by combining low correlated bond sectors.

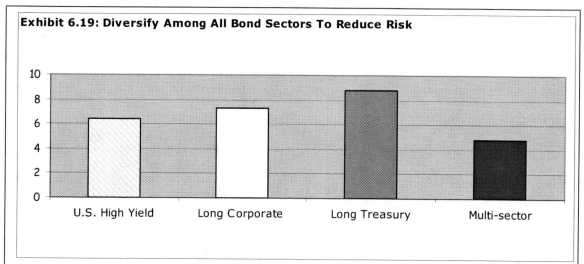

Exhibit 6.19: Diversify Among All Bond Sectors To Reduce Risk

Source: Morningstar Inc. ®. Data is for the three-year period ended September 2002. This table is for illustrative purposes only and does not predict or depict the performance of any investment. Investments in mutual funds involve risk. Past performance is no guarantee of future performance. Mutual funds incur fees and expenses (including investment management and administrative fees). Obtain a prospectus for more complete information about a fund, including all fees and expenses. The fund's prospectus should be read carefully before you invest. Investment returns and principal value of a mutual fund will fluctuate, so that shares, when redeemed, may be worth more or less than their original cost. Past performance is no guarantee of future performance.

You should combine a few low correlated bond funds that invest in different sectors of the bond market, such as Treasuries (T-bills, TIPs, Notes, and Bonds), agency bonds, mortgage-backed securities, asset-backed bonds, corporate bonds (industrial, utility, finance, and bank), high yield bonds, municipal bonds, and international bonds (sovereign debt, multinational, foreign corporate).

Very conservative portfolios should overweight Treasury issues if they want to reduce risk down to its lowest common denominator. Treasuries reduce credit quality risk, political risk, currency risk, reinvestment risk (non-callable), etc. But heed this word of caution -- you should only overweight sectors that are undervalued or at fair value. Overvalued sectors have no probable place to go -- except down.

What if, given the current environment, credit risk is becoming an issue?

You can use investment-grade bond funds to reduce credit risk. The higher the rating, the safer the bond in the eyes of credit-rating agencies.

The income portfolio need not be AAA-rated, but should at least be A- or AA-rated. Generally, the highest rating gives up too much return without a commensurate reduction in risk. You can overweight investment-grade bonds when interest rates rise, when the economy peaks, and throughout most of a recession.

It is prudent to always own Government issues as an "insurance policy" against geopolitical risk and crisis. In good times, you should be underweighted in Government issues, but you probably won't want to entirely withdraw from this asset class.

Remember to Capitalize on Foreign Markets

Should a portfolio invest only in U.S. bond funds?

You can add a 5% to 10% foreign bond exposure to reduce risk and pursue higher returns. The correlation between foreign and U.S. bond indexes has been very low, ranging from 0.14 to 0.33 for the period of 1970-2002. Foreign bonds beat U.S. bonds nine out of eleven times from 1992 through 2002. (Foreign bonds are represented by the Salomon Non-U.S. World Government Bond Index. Corporate bonds are represented by the Lehman Brothers Aggregate Bond Index, which is a market-capitalization weighted index of investment-grade fixed-rate debt issues, including government, corporate, asset-backed, and mortgage-backed securities, with maturities of at least one year. Past performance is no guarantee of future performance.)

Exhibit 6.20: Global Fixed-Income Performance

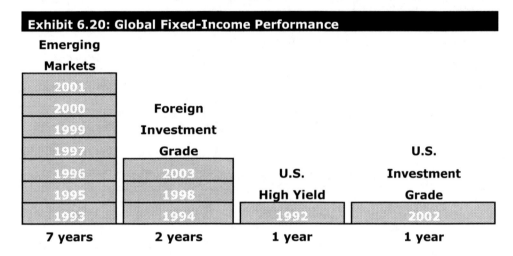

Source: Morningstar ® Inc.; All rights reserved; Used with permission. This table is for illustrative purposes only and does not predict or depict the performance of any investment. Investments in mutual funds involve risk. Past performance is no guarantee of future performance. Mutual funds incur fees and expenses (including investment management and administrative fees). Obtain a prospectus for more complete information about the fund, including all fees and expenses, and should be read carefully before you invest.

It is best to keep foreign exposure low (5% or less when the dollar is strengthening, usually when the US economy is growing and real interest rates are rising). You may wish to overweight foreign bonds when the U.S. dollar is declining against major world currencies. When the U.S. economy is contracting and there is a huge trade deficit this is likely to occur.

The Draw of Convertibles

Why invest in convertible bond funds?

You can invest in convertible bonds to provide higher returns in bull markets and to protect capital in down markets. They react more to GDP news than interest rate movements.

Convertible bonds are a cross between bonds and stocks. Convertible bonds have generally provided the income of bonds, much of the protection of bonds in down markets, as well as capturing some of the upside potential of the stock market.

Throughout the market cycle, convertible bonds have historically provided yields that approximate the yield of a high quality intermediate bond, and they can usually beat the dividend yield of an issuer's common stock. In down markets, convertibles have tended to decline less in value than stocks.

Convertible bond investors' downside risk is limited to its investment value at maturity no matter what happens to its common stock. On the other hand when stocks have rallied, convertible bonds have captured up to eighty percent of the stock market returns while high quality bonds had, in general, fallen on difficult times.

Convertible bonds tend to increase in value when there is volatility with stock prices. Convertibles allow a bondholder to convert the bond into a specified amount of equity shares at a predetermined price -- known as the strike price. When the market price of the company' stock exceeds the bond's strike price, the price of a convertible bond rises above its par value producing gains for the bondholder that sells.

What other risk reducing strategies should be considered in the fixed-income portion of a portfolio?

As with Equities, Diversification in the Fixed-income Domain is Key

Just as every real estate investor knows that the key to real estate is location, location, location, the same strategy holds true for the investment world. Diversification reigns supreme.

It can be a smart investment strategy to diversify municipal bond holdings among both single-state tax-free funds and nationally diversified tax-free funds. This lowers risk without significantly reducing yield.

You can also look to high-yield bonds to diversify the bond-fund portion of your portfolio. To play it very safe limit non-investment grade bond exposure to no more than 15% of a portfolio. Even in good times principal is still exposed to above average risk. In certain markets, the incremental yield from non-investment grade bonds is not worth the risk to principal. Be certain to limit exposure to 5% or less during recessions, given their credit risk.

Diversify existing holdings. For the latest thirty-year period ending 1997, high yield bonds had the lowest correlation to most other basic asset classes used to build a portfolio: large-cap, small-cap, international stocks, long-term bonds, intermediate bonds, etc.

Exhibit 6.22: High Yield Correlation to Core Sub-asset Classes

S&P 500	0.51	**Long Corporate**	0.7
Russell 2000	0.54	**Intermediate Treasury**	0.61
MSCI EAFE	0.27	**30-day T-bill**	-0.05
Treasury Bond	0.62		

Source: Standard & Poor's, The Frank Russell Company, Lehman Brothers, Federal Reserve, Morgan Stanley Capital International. Data for 1950-1999 period The S&P 500 index, a commonly used broad based index of domestic stocks. The S&P 500® is an unmanaged stock index: S&P 500 is a registered trademark of Standard & Poor's Corporation. Investors cannot invest in the S&P 500 Index; the Russell 2000 Index, an index consisting of the smallest 2,000 companies in the Russell 3000 index (composed of 3,000 large U.S. companies as determined by market capitalization and represents approximately 98% of the investable U.S. equity market); The MSCI EAFE (Europe, Australasia, and Far East) Index is a market-capitalization-weighted index that measures stock performance in 21 countries in Europe, Australasia and the Far East. Treasury bonds are represented by the S&P Long-term Government Bonds index; Intermediate Treasury is represented by the Lehman Long Treasury bond Index is a 10-year Treasury note index. Treasury indices are total return indices held constant maturities. H-Yield Corporate is represented by the Lehman Brothers High Yield Bond Index includes fixed rate, public non-convertible, non-investment grade issues registered with the SEC that are rated BA1 or lower by Moody's Investor Service. U.S. 30-day T-bill is represented by the Lehman Brothers Three month Treasury Bill Index derived from secondary market Treasury bill rates published by the Federal Reserve Bank. Long Corporate bonds are represented by the Lehman Brothers Bond Index. The Lehman Brothers Government/Credit Index measures the performance of all debt obligations of the U.S. Treasury and U.S. Government agencies, and all investment- grade domestic corporate debt; Indices include reinvested income, but not transaction costs or taxes, are unmanaged and cannot be purchased directly by investors. This chart is for illustrative purposes only and does not predict or depict the performance of any investment. Past performance is no guarantee of future performance.

High Yield, Beefy Rewards

It can be a good idea to use high yield bonds to increase the income and total return from the bond portion of a portfolio. In the past, the most likely way to make double-digit returns in the fixed-income market was to make a good bet on interest rates and be long in maturity, or buy high yield bonds that manage to cross over into investment grade land. Skilled managers can buy CCC-, B-, and BB-rated credits which may become investment grade. "Cross over bonds" not only reap high income but substantial price appreciation.

High yield bonds have always yielded more than investment grade bonds, and have generated higher total returns. The Merrill Lynch High Yield Master II Index produced an annualized return of 10.62% from 1990 to 2000, substantially outperforming the Lehman U.S. Aggregate Bond Index (7.77%), the Lehman U.S. Corporate Index (8.18%), and 10-year U.S. Treasuries (7.36%). Past performance is no guarantee of future performance.

But tread carefully. Do not commit the investment folly of buying the highest yielding bond funds. Higher yield does not equal better performance. Generally, the highest yielding funds turn into the worst performers. Past performance is no guarantee of future performance.

Exhibit 6.21: High Yield Category Quintile Average Yield and Returns			
	12 mo. Yield	**1 YR.**	**3 YRS.**
1st	10.94%	-3.61%	-4.82%
2nd	10.37%	-2.83%	-2.36%
3rd	9.66%	-2.26%	-4.15%
4th	8.75%	1.81	-0.12%
5th	**7.4%**	**2.34%**	**2.26%**

Source: Lipper. Period ending December 31, 2002. This table is for illustrative purposes only and does not predict or depict the performance of any investment. Investments in mutual funds involve risk. Past performance is no guarantee of future performance. Mutual funds incur fees and expenses (including investment management and administrative fees). Obtain a prospectus for more complete information about the fund, including all fees and expenses, and should be read carefully before you invest.

A smart advisor will practice a total return fixed- income style that invests in all areas of the bond market and abroad in an attempt to pursue yield differentials, and capital appreciation opportunities. The only way to produce double-digit returns in the bond market is by adding capital gains onto market yields.

This can typically be accomplished by managing credit, duration, foreign bond, and bond sector exposure. For instance, crossover non-investment grade bonds, BB-rates bonds that become BBB-rated ones, not only pay high coupons but also kick in a nice single- to double-digit price appreciation. And international bonds pay interest, can rise in price due to improving credit and or declining rates, and toss in gains from foreign currency appreciation.

Cash-equivalent Component Guidelines

How should cash-equivalent be used in the IPM process?

You can use money market funds to offset equity risk, generate modest income, and to provide liquidity. Over the long-term portfolio returns will be about the same, but with greater liquidity and slightly lower volatility.

Conservative growth portfolios, intended for clients with a low pain threshold, could have a cash position as high as 10%. A portfolio with 90% invested in an investment that tracked the S&P 500 and 10% in cash returned 11.2% on average without a down year over the 10-year rolling period from 1950 to 2002. The S&P 500 returned approximately 12% on average for that period. Of course, past performance is no guarantee of future performance.

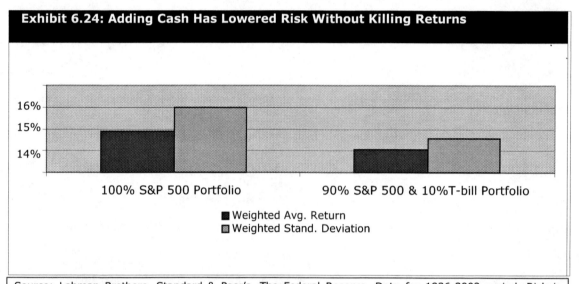

Exhibit 6.24: Adding Cash Has Lowered Risk Without Killing Returns

- 100% S&P 500 Portfolio
- 90% S&P 500 & 10%T-bill Portfolio
- ■ Weighted Avg. Return
- ▧ Weighted Stand. Deviation

Source: Lehman Brothers, Standard & Poor's, The Federal Reserve. Data for 1926-2002 period. Risk is measured by standard deviation which is an indicator of the portfolio's total return volatility. The larger the portfolio's standard deviation, the greater the portfolio's volatility. The S&P 500 Index is a commonly used broad based index of domestic stocks. The S&P 500® is an unmanaged stock index. S&P 500 is a registered trademark of Standard & Poor's Corporation. Investors cannot invest in the S&P 500 Index. T-bill portfolio is represented by the Lehman Brothers Three-month Treasury Bill Index derived from secondary market Treasury bill rates published by The Federal Reserve Bank. Indices include reinvested income, but not transaction costs or taxes, are unmanaged and cannot be purchased directly by investors. This chart is for illustrative purposes only and does not predict or depict the performance of any investment. Past performance is no guarantee of future performance.

Cash Equivalent -- the Great Diversifier

Cash-equivalents have been one of the best diversification tools used with the IPM method because of its low correlation with every major asset class and sub-asset class. You can use it to diversify and not market time. You needn't be too concerned with even using it in an aggressive growth objective portfolio. William Sharpe's Capital Market Line theory suggests that adding a risk-free asset to a universe of risky assets improves the potential risk and reward trade off. The theory says that risk is reduced because a risk-free investment doesn't vary, and thus, it has a zero correlation to risky investments.

Exhibit 6.25: Correlation between Cash-equivalents Core Sub-asset Classes

Large-cap	-0.20
Small-cap	-0.09
Corporate Bond	0.20
Government Bond	0.23

Source: Brothers, Standard & Poor's, Federal Reserve. Data for 1950-1999 period. Large-cap is represented by the S&P 500 index, a commonly used broad based index of domestic stocks. The S&P 500® is an unmanaged stock index: S&P 500 is a registered trademark of Standard & Poor's Corporation. Investors cannot invest in the S&P 500 Index; Small-cap is represented by the Russell 2000 Index, an index consisting of the smallest 2,000 companies in the Russell 3000 index (composed of 3,000 large U.S. companies as determined by market capitalization and represents approximately 98% of the investable U.S. equity market); Government Bond is represented by the S&P Long-term Government Bonds index; Corporate bonds is represented by the Lehman Brothers Bond Index. The Lehman Brothers Government/Credit Index measures the performance of all debt obligations of the U.S. Treasury and U.S. Government agencies, and all investment- grade domestic corporate debt; Indices include reinvested income, but not transaction costs or taxes, are unmanaged and cannot be purchased directly by investors. This chart is for illustrative purposes only and does not predict or depict the performance of any investment. Past performance is no guarantee of future performance.

Obviously, portfolios should probably hold little in cash-equivalents in the late bear and early bull phase of the market, unless there is an imminent need for cash. That's when interest rates have bottomed. At that point any fixed-income investment that has a maturity of less than one year such as money market and or CDs may be producing negative real returns.

Exhibit 6.26: Negative Real Rates of Return after Market Bottoms

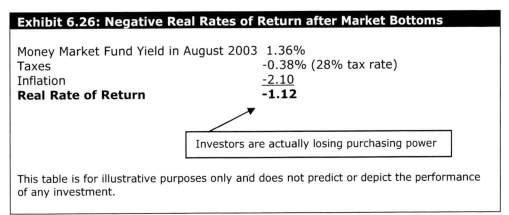

Money Market Fund Yield in August 2003	1.36%
Taxes	-0.38% (28% tax rate)
Inflation	-2.10
Real Rate of Return	**-1.12**

Investors are actually losing purchasing power

This table is for illustrative purposes only and does not predict or depict the performance of any investment.

International Component Guidelines

"International exposure reduces the bad cholesterol and increases the good cholesterol in a domestic portfolio."
-- Anonymous International portfolio manager

Why invest internationally?

You should be investing internationally for strategic portfolio construction reasons. You could invest internationally to potentially lower risk and enhance returns. A global portfolio comprised of U.S. stocks, U.S. bonds, foreign stocks, and foreign bonds during certain periods produced better risk and return characteristics than that of a pure U.S. security portfolio.

Unsystematic risk, which accounts for most of the risk, is eliminated through global diversification. A portfolio of U.S. and foreign stocks has approximately 15% of the risk the typical U.S stock according to a study by Bruno, Solnik and Bernard Noetzlin.

It is smart to invest internationally so as to own leading companies that offer higher returns to shareholders. Forty-seven percent of the world's market capitalization is domiciled outside of the U.S. The world's leaders are not just U.S. companies. Everyone knows them well because we drive their cars, drink their beverages, watch their TVs, and use their cell phones. Philosophically speaking, foreign products have improved the quality of lives and can improve portfolio returns. Furthermore, the globalization of the worlds markets is making foreign markets and even emerging ones a somewhat less risky investment than in the past.

Many foreign companies have a dominant global franchise and dominant brands that translate into higher stock returns for shareholders. Many sell at valuations that are more attractive. Portfolio returns would be limited if the portfolio was only invested in the United States.

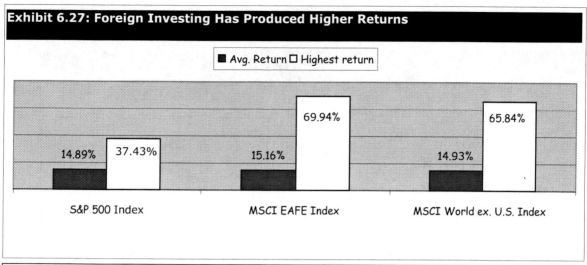

Exhibit 6.27: Foreign Investing Has Produced Higher Returns

Legend: ■ Avg. Return □ Highest return

Index	Avg. Return	Highest return
S&P 500 Index	14.89%	37.43%
MSCI EAFE Index	15.16%	69.94%
MSCI World ex. U.S. Index	14.93%	65.84%

Source: Morgan Stanley Capital International, Standard & Poor's. Data for 1970-1999 period. The S&P 500 is a total return index widely regarded as the standard for measuring large-cap U.E. stock market performance and includes a representative sample of 500 leading companies based on industry representation, liquidity, and stability. Historically includes 400 industrial stocks, 40 financial stocks, 40 public utility stocks, and 20 transportation stocks. The MSCI EAFE (Europe, Australasia, and Far East) Index is a market-capitalization-weighted index that measures stock performance in 21 countries in Europe, Australasia and the Far East. Morgan Stanley All Country World ex US Index. The Morgan Stanley All Country World ex-US Index is an unmanaged index comprised of 47 developed and developing market countries and does not include the United States. Index is based in U.S. dollars. Indices include reinvested income, but not transaction costs or taxes, are unmanaged and cannot be purchased directly by investors. This chart is for illustrative purposes only and does not predict or depict the performance of any investment. Past performance is no guarantee of future performance.

Utilizing Globetrotting Mutual Funds

Mutual funds are a good way to invest internationally because they are typically diversified, professionally managed, and tend to carry lower cost as compared to direct international investments. Mutual funds offer economies of scale that reduce the higher cost of international investing. Moreover, a 2003 study by Goldman Sachs noted that it would take a minimum of 90 foreign stocks (not funds, but individual stocks) to fully diversify a portfolio.

Professional management is very desirable in foreign markets because of the special risks inherent. I wouldn't use an passive "indexed" approach that buys and holds a basket of securities representing an foreign index. Moreover, studies have concluded that a large part of an international fund's performance is tied to investing in the right countries and getting favorable currency movement.

Evidence suggests that actively managed International mutual funds outperformed the MSCI EAFE Index over 3-year rolling periods between January 1985 and May 2003. A study released by Callan Associates used 17 mutual funds that were part of the Lipper International Funds Average that was created in 1985. The Lipper International Funds Average represents a group of diversified international mutual funds with broad investment capabilities. While the MSCI EAFE is an index of developed country stocks, this Lipper index is used as a proxy for international stock market performance. (Of course, past performance is no guarantee of future results. Indexes do not have fees or can be invested in.)

There is also a strong case for investing in foreign bonds at times. Exhibit 6.28 shows that foreign bonds have outperformed U.S Bonds during certain periods.

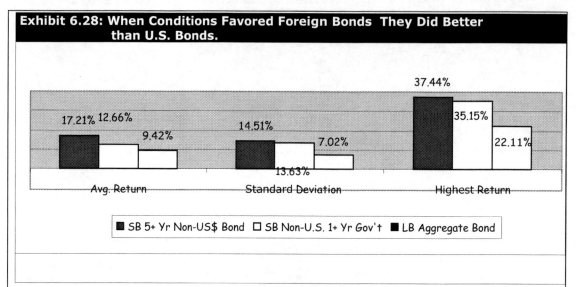

Exhibit 6.28: When Conditions Favored Foreign Bonds They Did Better than U.S. Bonds.

Source: Lehman Brothers, Morgan Stanley Capital International, BGI Barclays Global Investors. Data for 1985-1999 period. Risk is measured by the Standard deviation is an indicator of the portfolio's total return volatility. The larger the portfolio's standard deviation, the greater the portfolio's volatility. U.S. bonds are represented by the Lehman Brothers Aggregate Bond Index is a market-capitalization weighted index of investment-grade fixed-rate debt issues, including government, corporate, asset-backed, and mortgage-backed securities, with maturities of at least one year. The Lehman Brothers Government/Credit Index measures the performance of all debt obligations of the U.S. Treasury and U.S. government agencies, and all investment- grade domestic corporate debt; Foreign Government bonds are represented by the Salomon Non-U.S. World Government Bond Index; Foreign Non-U.S. bonds are represented by the Salomon Non-U.S. World Bond Index Indices include reinvested income, but not transaction costs or taxes, are unmanaged and cannot be purchased directly by investors. This graph is for illustrative purposes only and does not predict or depict the performance of any investment. Past performance is no guarantee of future performance.

Foreign investing, at times, has increased the opportunity to earn more income especially when the U.S. economy is in a low interest rate environment.

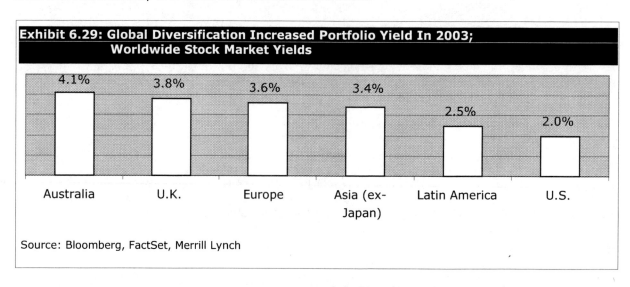

Exhibit 6.29: Global Diversification Increased Portfolio Yield In 2003; Worldwide Stock Market Yields

Source: Bloomberg, FactSet, Merrill Lynch

Foreign investing has the potential to produce higher returns because there is an additional way to profit than by just investing in the U.S. markets.

Exhibit 6.30: Hypothetical Illustration of the Components of Investment Returns		
	Foreign	Domestic
1. Stock Market Yield	4%	4%
2. Capital Appreciation	11%	8%
3. Exchange rate	+/- % change	

This table is for illustrative purposes only and does not predict or depict the performance of any investment. Numbers used in this table are hypothetical.

Understanding Foreign and Domestic Market and Currency Dynamics

Let us take a hypothetical Euro zone country equity fund. If the Euro zone countries experience a market appreciation of 11% and yield 4%, and the Euro currency appreciates 5% against the U.S. dollar, than the total return in U.S. dollars is 20%. In our example, the favorable exchange rate movement allowed for an extra 5% return. In fact, at times the return on the currency can exceed the return from the security itself!

The key to benefiting from exchange rate changes is to identify when the U.S. dollar is cyclically overvalued as compared to the world's major currencies. When the U.S. dollar is overvalued, then there is an opportunity to enhance investment returns by investing abroad. The goal is to pick countries with:

- healthy economies;
- low inflation;
- higher real interest rates;
- low to moderate debt levels;
- no problem with trade deficits and current account balances.

Such countries tend to have a currency that is appreciating and a stock market that is on the rise. But this is not a dart game where countries can be haphazardly chosen. Proper country selection is critical to profiting from exchange rate movements.

U.S. multinational corporations have not always provided international diversification. One would think that conglomerates like 3M, AIG, Coca-Cola, Bristol-Myers Squibb, GE, IBM, Eli Lilly, Pfizer, etc. would provide international exposure since a big percentage of the firm's revenue is derived from foreign market sales. The fact is they don't. U.S. multinational companies are highly correlated to the S&P 500 Index that is tied to the performance of the U.S. economy. When the U.S. economy tanks, so does the S&P 500 Index and these multinationals tend to sink as well.

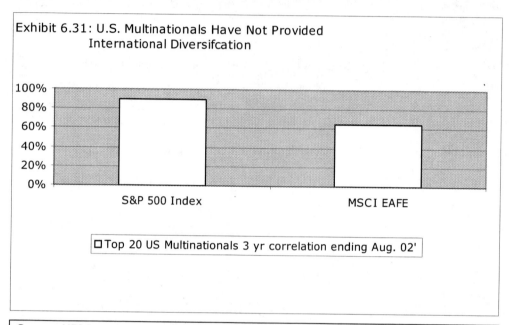

Exhibit 6.31: U.S. Multinationals Have Not Provided International Diversifcation

Top 20 US Multinationals 3 yr correlation ending Aug. 02'

Source: MFS Investment Research. The S&P 500 is a total return index widely regarded as the standard for measuring large-cap U.S. stock market performance and includes a representative sample of 500 leading companies based on industry representation, liquidity, and stability. This historically includes 400 industrial stocks, 40 financial stocks, 40 public utility stocks, and 20 transportation stocks. The MSCI EAFE (Europe, Australasia, and Far East) Index is a market-capitalization-weighted index that measures stock performance in 21 countries in Europe, Australasia and the Far East. This index is based in U.S. dollars. Indices include reinvested income, but not transaction costs or taxes, are unmanaged and cannot be purchased directly by investors. This chart is for illustrative purposes only and does not predict or depict the performance of any investment. Past performance is no guarantee of future performance.

Understanding Foreign Market Diversification

How does foreign investing lower risk?

Foreign markets are not always coordinated with U.S. markets. Somewhat lower correlations between the U.S. market and foreign markets thus allow for further risk reduction. Foreign markets have low correlations with the U.S. market due to the following differences:

1. Foreign economies follow different cycles then the U.S. economy and the ups and downs may occur at different times offsetting each other.
2. Foreign markets have different methods for governing, regulating, and managing economies. For instance, where monetary and fiscal policies are different, a country's economic cycle may well be vastly different from the U.S. economic cycle.
3. Foreign economies are disparate and less diverse than the U.S. economy Issues and events that might affect China's economy may not affect the U.S. economy.
4. Foreign stocks are less sensitive to U.S. monetary and fiscal policy, fundamentals (macro-economic and market), psychology, politics, and technical indicators than U.S. stocks. Consequently, there is a stronger positive correlation between U.S. stocks and the U.S. economy than with foreign stocks.

By adding foreign securities that have a lower correlation to U.S. markets than U.S. stocks, a portfolio's risk can often be reduced through diversification.

Exhibit 6.32: Foreign Markets Are Not Always in Lockstep with U.S.

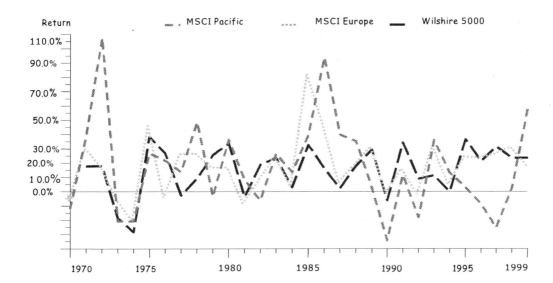

Source: Wilshire Associates, Morgan Stanley Capital International. The Wilshire 5000 measures the performance of all U.S. headquartered equity securities with readily available price data. Over 7,000 capitalization weighted security returns are used to adjust the index. Morgan Stanley EAFE Index is also known as the Morgan Stanley Capital International Europe, Australia, and Far East Index of over 1,000 foreign stock prices. Morgan Stanley Pacific Index comprised of Pacific rim countries of greater Asia. The index is translated into U.S. dollars. Indices include reinvested income, but not transaction costs or taxes, are unmanaged and cannot be purchased directly by investors. This chart is for illustrative purposes only and does not predict or depict the performance of any investment. Past performance is no guarantee of future performance.

In the past, the major U.S. indexes have typically been in lockstep with one another. This situation increases U.S. market risk. U.S. market risk can be reduced by diversifying into foreign markets. See Exhibit 6.33, and notice that there are no "zigs" and "zag" opposite movements among the trip of U.S. equity indexes shown. As one rises or falls, the others move in tandem. That suggests improper diversification.

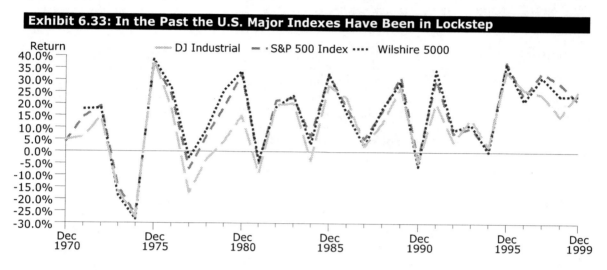

Exhibit 6.33: In the Past the U.S. Major Indexes Have Been in Lockstep

Source: Dow Jones, Thomson Financial, Wilshire Associates. The Dow Jones Industrial Index®, which is an unmanaged group of 30 "blue-chip" U.S. stocks. It is not a diverse index. An investment cannot be made directly in an index. The Wilshire 5000 measures the performance of all U.S. headquartered equity securities with readily available price data. Over 7,000 capitalization weighted security returns are used to adjust the index. Morgan Stanley EAFE Index is also known as the Morgan Stanley Capital International Europe, Australia, and Far East Index of over 1,000 foreign stock prices. The index is translated into U.S. dollars. Indices include reinvested income, but not transaction costs or taxes, are unmanaged and cannot be purchased directly by investors. This chart is for illustrative purposes only and do not predict or depict the performance of any investment. Past performance is no guarantee of future performance.

Has the globalization of world economies reduced the benefits of international diversification? No, the correlations are still low enough to provide some longer-term benefit. Notice the correlations, returns, and standard deviations, as shown in Exhibit 6.34.

Exhibit 6.34: Correlations between U.S. Market and Foreign Markets

	Wilshire 5000 Correlation	Period ending 1999	Average Return	Standard Deviation
Wilshire 5000	1.0	30 yr.	15.29%	6.66%
MSCI EAFE	0.48	30 yr.	15.43%	21.60%
MSCI Pacific	0.26	30 yr.	17.57%	32.84%
IFCG Emerging Market	0.17	15 yr.	16.31%	31.70%

Source: Wilshire Associates, Factset; Morgan Stanley Capital International, International Finance Corporation. Standard deviation is an indicator of the portfolio's total return volatility. The larger the portfolio's standard deviation, the greater the portfolio's volatility. The Wilshire 5000 measures the performance of all U.S. headquartered equity securities with readily available price data. Over 7,000 capitalization weighted security returns are used to adjust the index. Morgan Stanley EAFE Index is also known as the Morgan Stanley Capital International Europe, Australia, and Far East Index of over 1,000 foreign stock prices. Morgan Stanley Pacific Index comprised of Pacific Rim countries of greater Asia. The index is translated into U.S. dollars. IFCG Emerging Index is an unmanaged index comprised of developing market countries and does not include the United States. Index is based in U.S. dollars. Indices include reinvested income, but not transaction costs or taxes, are unmanaged and cannot be purchased directly by investors. This chart is for illustrative purposes only and does not predict or depict the performance of any investment. Past performance is no guarantee of future performance.

Exploring Foreign Bond Market Correlation

The correlation between U.S. and foreign fixed-income securities are still low. A portfolio's risk and reward trade off improves by adding international bonds to an internationally diversified stock portfolio. Moreover, international diversified bond portfolios have produced better performance than pure U.S. bond portfolios.

The correlation between emerging market/foreign developed country bonds, and the U.S. investment grade bonds, U.S. equities, foreign developed countries is -0.02, 0.20, 0.53, and 0.46 respectively according to Factset. The period of study is for January 1, 1994 to March 30, 2003.

Emerging markets offer the lowest correlations to the U.S. market and thus, the highest degree of diversification. Even adding a high risk emerging market fund to a portfolio can lower overall portfolio risk. Emerging markets have also historically been cheaper than developed foreign markets. The P/Es on the IFCI Universe Index from 1988 to 1994 and the MSCI Emerging Markets Index from 1995 to 2003 were lower that the developed foreign markets index represented by the MSCI EAFE Index. Lower historical valuations, higher return potential, and low correlations with global developed markets makes emerging markets a core holding for a growth objective portfolio.

A Holistic Approach to Foreign Markets Investing

How much foreign equity and bond exposure should a portfolio have?

Past results suggests that its wise to limit investment in assets abroad to no more than thirty percent of a portfolio. Normally a growth portfolio has a twenty-five percent position with thirty percent being an overweight position. Given worldwide economic progress, and favorable global financial market changes, I would buck past findings and increase foreign exposure in a portfolio by as much as an additional ten percent over and above the guidelines and just gave you.

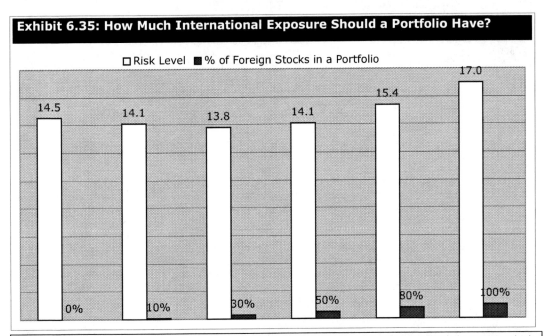

Exhibit 6.35: How Much International Exposure Should a Portfolio Have?

□ Risk Level ■ % of Foreign Stocks in a Portfolio

14.5	14.1	13.8	14.1	15.4	17.0
0%	10%	30%	50%	80%	100%

Source: AllianceBerntsein. Data from 1970-2002: Risk is measured by the standard deviation, which is an indicator of the portfolio's total return volatility. The larger the portfolio's standard deviation, the greater the portfolio's volatility. U.S. Stocks are represented by S&P 500 Index ® which is a total return index measuring large-cap U.S. stock market performance. Foreign stocks are represented by the MSCI EAFE (Europe, Australasia, and Far East) Index is a market-capitalization-weighted index that measures stock performance in 21 countries in Europe, Australasia and the Far East. Indices include reinvested income, but not transaction costs or taxes, are unmanaged and cannot be purchased directly by investors. This chart is for illustrative purposes only and does not predict or depict the performance of any investment. Past performance is no guarantee of future performance.

When Diversifying Internationally, Think Long-term

Are there limitations and risks to international investing?

Yes. The short-term benefits of international diversification are limited because when the U.S. market declines foreign markets usually follow. International diversification does not work as well over the short-term and in highly volatile markets. Actually, correlations tend to increase during volatiles periods like the 2000-2002 bear market and global recession.

When the U.S. experiences a recession, you can expect certain foreign economies to also weaken. Yet, not all G-7 countries and world economies will likely be impacted as much as the U.S. because their economies are less dependent on U.S. economic health. By diversifying internationally in the right regions and countries, a portfolio may drop less in value than one only invested in U.S. equities.

Secondly, it would be a good investment advisor that starts increasing foreign exposure when the U.S. economy enters the recovery phase of the business cycle.

Furthermore, international investing entails additional risks that are associated with the potential to earn higher returns. In the short-term, international stocks may fluctuate in value more than U.S. stocks due to currency fluctuations, as well as political and economic events.

Exhibit 6.36: Foreign Markets Had Higher Standard Deviations

	Standard Deviation
U.S.: S&P 500 Index	16.12
U.S.: Wilshire 5000	16.66
Foreign: MSCI Europe	20.12
Foreign: MSCI World ex. U.S.	20.30
Foreign: MSCI Pacific	32.94

Source: Source: Wilshire Associates, Morgan Stanley Capital International, International Finance Corporation. Data for 1971-1999 period. Standard deviation is an indicator of the portfolio's total return volatility. The larger the portfolio's standard deviation, the greater the portfolio's volatility. The Wilshire 5000 measures the performance of all U.S. headquartered equity securities with readily available price data. Over 7,000 capitalization weighted security returns are used to adjust the index. The S&P 500 is a total return index widely regarded as the standard for measuring large-cap U.E. stock market performance and includes a representative sample of 500 leading companies based on industry representation, liquidity, and stability. Historically includes 400 industrial stocks, 40 financial stocks, 40 public utility stocks, and 20 transportation stocks. Morgan Stanley World ex US Index. The Morgan Stanley All Country World ex-US Index is an unmanaged index comprised of 47 developed and developing market countries and does not include the United States. Index is based in U.S. dollars. The Wilshire 5000 measures the performance of all U.S. headquartered equity securities with readily available price data. Over 7,000 capitalization weighted security returns are used to adjust the index. Morgan Stanley EAFE Index is also known as the Morgan Stanley Capital International Europe, Australia, and Far East Index of over 1,000 foreign stock prices. Morgan Stanley Pacific Index comprised of Pacific Rim countries of greater Asia. The index is translated into U.S. dollars. IFCG Emerging Index is an unmanaged index comprised of developing market countries and does not include the United States. Index is based in U.S. dollars. Indices include reinvested income, but not transaction costs or taxes, are unmanaged and cannot be purchased directly by investors. This chart is for illustrative purposes only and does not predict or depict the performance of any investment. Past performance is no guarantee of future performance.

Special International Investment Risks to Consider

• **Currency risk** -- The potential change in a foreign investment's value due to a given change in the exchange rates is the greatest threat to an international investor. Foreign securities are purchased and traded in the currency of the home country. This means that when investors buy foreign stocks, U.S. dollars must first be converted into the foreign currency. As a result, movements in the foreign currency relative to the U.S. dollar will change the value of the international investment.

When the U.S. dollar appreciates, the foreign investment decreases in value. When the U.S. dollar depreciates, the foreign investment increases in value. For example, if U.K. equities rise ten percent and the U.S. dollar appreciates five percent relative to pound sterling, the net unrealized gain is only five percent.

Nations whose economic policies promote economic growth and stability, and control inflation tend to have currencies that appreciate in value, relative to countries with opposite policies. The currencies of high-inflation economies are weaker than low-inflationary economies, which affects the nation's currency adversely. When the foreign currency that denominates a foreign investment depreciates, so does the investment.

• **Liquidity risk** -- During periods of global economic and political instability, capital has typically flown to more liquid, established markets such as the United States from less liquid foreign markets. Furthermore, less liquid securities of smaller capitalization companies, typical of emerging market securities, are subject to greater price volatility than those of developed markets. In addition, these securities may be less marketable, eg. harder to find a buyer or seller for.

• **Social, economical, and political risk** -- Uncertainty still is great in many developing markets when it comes to individual societal, economic and political issues. In our hemisphere alone most of the countries possess a degree of political risk. Mexico is one country that comes to mind as an example, but I am sure you would be surprised to learn that Canada is another country that is considered politically "at risk."

• **Regulatory risk** -- Foreign markets, in general, may have less stringent regulatory structures, or impose fewer regulations within their securities markets and therefore, may harbor certain regulatory risks. Many emerging market countries do not have an S.E.C.-equivalent regulatory watchdog body or extensive federal statutory securities laws created to maintain order and regulate their markets like the U.S. markets possess. Consequently, in these countries there is greater possibility for market manipulation and/or fraud to occur.

In addition, it may be more difficult or impossible to obtain and/or enforce a claim or judgment. Capital investments could potentially be exposed to nationalization, expropriation, or confiscator taxation.

• **Accounting standards risk** -- Foreign markets may have less reliable accounting standards and securities research may add even more uncertainty and risk. In the Unites States, even in spite of accounting standards and rules and frequently audited financial reports, it is hard to believe everything that is printed in them. Even within the strict U.S. regulatory environment there have been numerous cases of fraud and financial information misstatements associated with firms' closely audited financial reports. Some have eventually led to investor lawsuits, SEC and Federal investigations, and, in some cases, bankruptcy of these firms. Common stock investors have, in some of these cases, sometimes lost every penny they had invested.

• **High costs risk** -- The cost of investing in international mutual funds is typically higher than domestic funds. This may reduce investment returns. The average international fund expense ratio is 1.8% versus 1.08% for the average domestic stock fund, according to Morningstar. An international fund manager knows to expect higher trading costs and to also incur exchange rate fees when converting dollars into a foreign currency to buy or sell securities for the fund portfolio. Investors who invest directly into individual international securities will have to bear these costs directly.

• **Immature markets risk** -- Many international (and especially emerging) markets are in their infancy and have yet to develop proper internal market mechanisms and robust financial systems that are now embedded into the markets of more developed nations. A sound financial base and mechanisms to restore order to markets can prevent periodic market collapses such as the 1997 Asian currency crisis. If not for the $181 billion International Monetary Fund bailout, the 1997 Asian currency crisis could have mushroomed into a broader worldwide economic calamity.

• **Non-hedging risk** -- To diversify and get the full benefit of active management in international waters, you can choose an un-hedged fund. International funds that do not hedge their foreign currency exposure have a lower correlation with both the U.S. bond and U.S. equity markets. A hedged fund has less volatility than an un-hedged one, but gives up the higher return opportunity that investors seek when investing abroad. Un-hedged funds tend to outperform when the U.S. dollar weakens. Total return opportunities are maximized by un-hedged strategies. Another way to mitigate currency risk is to invest in economically sound countries which sport low inflation, budget deficits that don't exceed 3% of the country's GDP, have positive GDP, and Governmental debt that is 60% of GDP or less.

> **Insider Tip**: Investing in emerging markets through an index strategy is a risky approach because certain regions or countries will inevitably experience problems. Investors passively indexed will not be able to avoid those situations which could become major blow-ups. Country allocation is the major determinant of an international portfolio's return. Furthermore, you may want to limit positions in regional or single country emerging market funds because of the unfavorable risk and reward characteristics compared to diversified emerging market funds. Single country funds also have higher currency risk than diversified international funds. My recommendation is to stay away from "world equity funds" as they generally have a poor record of country selection, according to a 2003 Morningstar research report.

The Secrets to Fund Selection

---

*"Investing in a stock before doing your research
is like playing stud poker and not looking at your cards."*
-- Peter Lynch

The IPM Mutual Fund Selection Process

Deciphering Fact from Fiction

Asset allocation studies that claim that security selection is not very important are misleading. Solid mutual fund selection can make a world of difference in affecting a portfolio's performance. By reducing positions in poorly managed funds, the chance of improving portfolio performance is greater.

A Morgan Stanley study of 660 mutual funds over a ten year period ended 1997 showed that there was no repetition of top performers, but losers -- bottom quartile funds -- tended to repeat.

Moreover, selection is more important to portfolio performance than most investors have been led to believe by the easily debatable Brinson, Hood, and Beebower study, "Determinants of Portfolio Performance." William W. Jahnke's 1997 research article "Asset Allocation Hoax" clearly points out how overstated the importance of asset allocation is to a portfolio's returns.

What is a major limitation of most of the mutual fund selection strategies?

Most strategies for creating an ensemble cast of mutual funds are not forward looking. Rather, they are rear view in nature. That is to say that they do not consider the various market and economic factors that can affect future performance.

Reliance on quantitative data that is historical may produce an "out of sync" portfolio that may have been appropriate for *past* economic and market conditions, but may not be appropriate for *future* conditions. That single factor can dramatically increase the risk of underperformance.

A twenty year study of the Standard & Poor's 500® ending year 2000 by The Center for Research in Security Prices of the Graduate School of Business of The University of Chicago, found that the top ten performing stocks over the last three years period did not go on to repeat as top performers. The average 3-year return was 147.5%. The subsequent 3-year return was 4.4%.

Why did performance trail off? Economic and market conditions no longer favored that investment.

What is important when it comes to selecting a fund?

Mutual Fund Selection: Basic Training

It is essential to know precisely what you are buying because each type of mutual fund will affect a portfolio's risk in a different way.

Peter Lynch once said the most important lesson he learned as an investor was to know what you own; because if it goes down you want to understand why so you can decide whether to sell or buy more! I like Mr. Lynch's advice versus Mr. Buffet's buy and hold approach. It recognizes that not every investment should be rated an "eternal buy."

Moreover, certain markets favor specific fund categories. Buying funds that have invested in overvalued areas of the market can prove to be a loser's game.

It is important to understand the relationship of adding a fund to a portfolio. Risk may be inadvertently built up by just adding top performers from highly correlated fund categories.

It is important to evaluate a fund based on its impact on the overall portfolio performance as each fund will contribute to the overall portfolio performance. One fund might provide growth, another income, and others liquidity, diversification or something else.

Odd as it may sound, in some instances adding an aggressive fund might actually lower the overall risk of a portfolio. For example, adding a small-cap growth fund to a conservative bond fund portfolio in late 2002 improved performance in 2003.

It can be wise to add funds that will lower the overall risk characteristics of portfolio, such as low duration bond funds, high quality bond funds, low multiple equity funds, as conditions warrant. You may also want to add funds that will adjust the overall portfolio characteristics such as the market cap orientation, the style tilt, or the credit quality weighting. For example, when the Fed comments imply that inflation is a threat, it can be a good idea to add an intermediate high quality bond fund to shorten the overall duration of a portfolio.

The fund selection process shown in Exhibit 7.1 is designed to pick conservative funds which are favored by market conditions for a portfolio that has been constructed using the guidelines in Chapter six.

Exhibit 7.1: Two Step IPM Fund Selection Process

1. Screen individual funds in desired fund categories based upon:

- Investment approach/style consistency
- Below-to-average expense ratio
- Correlation
- Fund category ranking; relative strength
- P/E
- Market capitalization
- Beta
- Sharpe ratio
- Credit quality
- Duration
- Experienced management
- Asset size
- SEC Yield
- Number of holdings
- Top three industry concentration
- Concentration of top ten holdings
- Derivative/illiquid security exposure

2. Evaluate each fund based on how it interacts with the other investment the portfolio. Ask:

- Will it increase or decrease the beta, multiple, and or industry or fund category concentration?
- Does it help build an overweight position in small-cap as the economy recovers?
- Does it shorten the duration when inflation is mounting in the economy?
- Is the fund highly correlated with the other funds in the portfolio?

It is better to rely on a multi-factor selection process than a single factor. Performance is only one of many things that carry weight in your decision. It is more important to select the fund with the most favorable characteristics for each core fund category in a portfolio. Favorable characteristics affect a portfolio's risk characteristics by lowering cost, and risk measures without sacrificing return.

Even Don Phillips of Morningstar has said that the key to a client's success isn't just performance but understanding the role a fund plays in a portfolio. The appropriateness of a fund depends on how it contributes to the overall risk of a portfolio. Moreover, what is vitally important is how it adjusts the portfolio's characteristics to the desired ones.

The most overlooked characteristic is a fund's correlation figure. Few investors consider the correlation figure in their selection process. Instead they focus on other criteria like performance and expenses ratios. By adding funds that have the desired correlations, a portfolio's risk and reward characteristics can be vastly improved over a selection process that ignores correlations.

As a rule of thumb, it can be the best overall choice to choose the fund that lowers the overall portfolio risk the most. Given two funds as finalists, I recommend that you pick the conservative one that fits the best with the other fund holdings.

Indiscriminately adding hot funds to a portfolio may result in a portfolio of funds that all own the same stocks and may produce inconsistent performance over the long term. Often hot performing funds outperform because their investment approach is in favor.

Imagine if you only bought the hottest, top performing funds each year. In 1993, international funds were top dog. By 1995 they had become the dogs with a serious case of fleas in the wake of a severe worldwide emerging market sell-off.

The point is, do not always base your decision strictly on the ranking of a particular fund. Rather, it may be better to choose a lower rated fund with a proven manager with an approach that is coming into favor.

Finally, be sure to analyze macro-economic and market data to determine whether non-core funds should be tactically added to a portfolio to capitalize on a particular current market opportunity. For example, adding a defensive precious metals fund to a portfolio because geopolitical risk is becoming an issue can be a smart, but sound, investment strategy.

The Baker's Dozen of Almost Fool-Proof Guidelines for Equity Fund Selection

1. Choose funds that bring about desired overall portfolio characteristics

For example, in the early bull phase, a Growth & Income portfolio may favor small-caps over large-caps. As the market enters mid-bull phase, the allocation strategy should favor mid-cap to large-cap. Therefore, you should evaluate funds that have a high correlation to the S&P 500 Index. Large-caps do well as the economy strengthens and big companies tend to regain leadership.

But take care so that all of the funds are not highly correlated. Know the correlation coefficient to a portfolio's benchmark. Little if any risk reduction occurs when adding two funds that have a correlation of 0.70 or higher. Below 0.70 risk reduction starts to occur. The maximum risk reduction happens when two funds have a negative correlation. It is desirable to add a few funds in an eight fund-maximum portfolio that have low correlation to the rest of the funds.

2. Choose style-consistent funds

It can be extremely difficult to manage a portfolio if the underlying mutual funds experience style drift. The portfolio may end up concentrating too heavily in one approach. Style analysis is one of the better ways to assess a fund's risk.

Generally, growth style funds are considered riskier than funds that invest under a value style approach. When there is a portfolio manager change, it is important to determine the style of the new manager. An aggressive growth style manager, who buys high multiple stocks and concentrates holdings, could drastically change the risk levels of a once conservative fund.

You can use the median market capitalization and P/E to determine the fund's style. Generally, funds that sport P/Es of equal to or less than the market P/E are said to be value funds. Ones with P/Es higher than the market P/E are considered growth funds. Deep value funds can sport P/Es as low as 10 and aggressive growth funds' P/Es can stretch to fifty and higher.

3. Assess a fund's median market capitalization to understand which area of the market a fund is invested in --the large-cap, mid-cap, or small-cap arena

It is a smart idea to use the median market capitalization of a fund to best determine where a fund manager is investing. This should be done in order to determine a tactical asset allocation strategy. The median market capitalization represents the size of the companies the fund is investing in, such as larger stocks of the S&P 500, or smaller companies of the Russell 2000. Historically, the market capitalization of a fund has played a big role in what type of long-term returns to expect. However, it can be less reliable over the short term.

Instead, you can analyze current market conditions to determine where market leadership is coming from -- large-caps or small-caps. There is usually a cyclical rotation from low quality small-caps to high quality large-caps as the economy slows down, dragging down earnings growth.

Capitalization also serves to determine risk levels. There are different bankruptcy rates associated with large, medium, and small stocks, with small stocks having the highest rate of failure and thus the greatest *specific business risk*. Consequently, small capitalization funds typically carry more risk than stock funds investing in well-established "blue-chip" companies. Historically, smaller companies' stocks have also experienced a greater degree of market volatility than the average stock. Market capitalization also determines a stock's liquidity. In a down market, mid- to small-cap stocks tend to be less liquid and can therefore be more risky.

But be aware that the lines between the various mutual fund capitalization categories are fuzzy. There are no longer absolutes in market cap definition. Market caps now adjust to the asset valuation effect of rising and falling markets. Lipper Inc. defines large-cap funds as those with greater than $7.6 billion, mid-caps as $1.5 billion to $7.6 billion, small-caps as $300 million to $1.5 billion, and mircro-caps as less than $300 million. In 2003 the average large-cap, mid-cap, and small-cap funds had an approximate weighted market cap of $30 billion, $4 billion, and $800 million, respectively.

Exhibit 7.2: Weighted Market-cap Guidelines

Small-cap: $2 billion or less favorable fund characteristic
Mid-cap: $2 billion to $12 billion favorable fund characteristic
Large-cap: $12 billion and up favorable fund characteristic

---

4. Manage risk by limiting the investment in funds with high Price/Earnings (P/E) ratios

Higher multiples generally limit upside potential and can significantly increase downside risk. The P/E ratio represents the weighted average of the stocks in a fund. As mentioned earlier, the P/E is a good indicator of the management style of the fund. A fund P/E that is higher than the market multiple is typically a growth style fund and a fund with a P/E equal to or lower than the market multiple is generally a value style managed fund. Lower multiple funds tend to have a risk-averse investment style.

Here is another P/E rule of thumb: a fund that has a multiple that is 15% greater than its fund category's P/E has an unfavorable P/E. Of course, the P/Es of international funds tend to be less reliable because of more liberal international accounting practices that can be used to determine earnings per share.

5. Give strong consideration to funds with average to below average expense ratios, but do not rule out a higher expense ratio fund that makes more sense for a portfolio

"If you pit the lowest cost funds against the highest cost funds, the lowest cost funds always win," avers John Bogle, former Chairman of The Vanguard Group.

Bogle may not be correct in every situation. But it is always wisest to compare the loads, fees, and total operating expenses of similar funds. Studies have shown that funds with lower expense ratios will outperform those with higher expense ratios, (assuming they have the same objectives) by the difference in expense ratios! Often, funds with higher overall costs will never outperform that handicap.

In addition, over time compounding at even 1% more, can really add up! How much difference could there be? A $10,000 investment invested for thirty years earning 10% per year could grow to $174,000, while the same $10,000 invested with an 11% annual return would grow to $229,000! Thus, expenses do matter even in up markets! In lean market, return years' expenses could mean the difference between an up or down year.

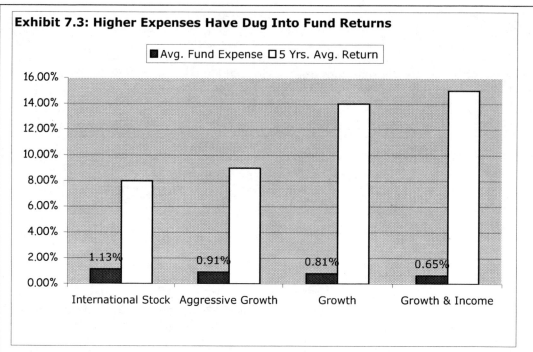

Exhibit 7.3: Higher Expenses Have Dug Into Fund Returns

■ Avg. Fund Expense □ 5 Yrs. Avg. Return

Source: Morningstar Inc. ®. Data is for period ending September 1998. This table is for illustrative purposes only and does not predict or depict the performance of any investment. Investments in mutual funds involve risk. Past performance is no guarantee of future performance. Mutual funds incur fees and expenses (including investment management and administrative fees). Obtain a prospectus for more complete information about the fund, including all fees and expenses, and should be read carefully before you invest. Investment returns and principal value of a mutual fund will fluctuate, so that shares, when redeemed, may be worth more or less than their original cost. Past performance is no guarantee of future performance.

The bottom line is that you should not buy one fund over another just for its lower expense ratio. Investors could end up sacrificing significant returns simply by chasing the lowest cost funds.

While expenses should be considered when evaluating funds, low expense ratio funds don't always beat out higher ones. Look what happened to S&P 500 Index fund investors in the late 1990s. Many were sold on the funds low expense ratio as the way to higher returns when, in fact, many actively managed funds in their peer group did significantly better despite their higher expenses.

A 2004 Lipper mutual fund study concluded that investing exclusively in low expense funds was not a sure way to higher returns. There are other factors that can have an even greater influence on fund performance.

Exhibit 7.4: Higher Expense Large-cap Brethren Beat S&P 500 Index Funds During Certain Years

	Performance (+/- S&P 500 Index Return)				
	1998	1999	2000	2001	2002
Large-cap Growth category	+4.68%	+18.23%	--	--	--
Large-cap Value category	---	---	+7.99%	+7.5%	+3.31%

Source: Morningstar ®. This table is for illustrative purposes only and do not predict or depict the performance of any investment. Investments in mutual funds involve risk. Past performance is no guarantee of future performance. Mutual funds incur fees and expenses (including investment management and administrative fees). Obtain a prospectus for more complete information about the fund, including all fees and expenses, and should be read carefully before you invest. Past performance is no guarantee of future performance.

6. Evaluate funds that have a fund category ranking of the fiftieth percentile or greater for the latest three-year period or life of the fund, whichever is shorter

Even if you are looking for strong, consistent fund performers, you will want to put more emphasis on a fund's recent performance instead of long-term performance and choose funds that have beaten their fund category average by at least one percentage point for the latest quarter, year-to-date, and latest twelve months. The objective is to choose not the top performer nor the bottom dwellers, but funds that are *slightly above average*. The chosen fund can be the one with the best (or closest to best) relative strength among the funds evaluated.

Studies show that it pays to buy funds that exhibit relative strength in leading fund categories. A rising relative strength line means that a fund is outperforming its category average. A fund's "in favor" style, industry weight and stock selection is generally responsible for its out performance.

Leading fund categories initially have better valuation/earnings growth that tends to attract heavy cash flow as they outperform. Heavy cash flows typically create momentum that often lasts even though the fund category becomes overvalued. This trend may last for two to three years before the liquidity-driven phase ends with a big sell-off as valuations become too stretched.

Exhibit 7.5: The Relative Strength Ratio

Fund's Relative Strength = Fund Performance
                                              Average Fund Category Performance
                                              or Benchmark

Why focus on recent performance and long-term performance? Isn't it important to gauge what a fund did ten years ago?

Who *cares* what a fund did ten years ago? Ten years back the fund may have had a different manager(s), was likely operating under different market and/or economic conditions, had different fund metrics, and was possibly run under different prospectus requirements or mandates. What matters is who the portfolio manager is now, and is he or she buying and holding what the market likes going forward?

What other reason is there to focus more on recent history and not the "ancient" five- and 10-year history?

Investing in asset classes that have return momentum early on can produce excellent results. By trading into the asset class that had the best return for the prior year on January 1st of the New Year, you would have invested in the best performing asset class fourteen out of the twenty-eight years and only had three down years. The period of study is from 1970-1997.

The average return for "Trading into Prior Year's Best Performing Asset Classes" was 20.6% versus 12.97% for the S&P 500 Index for the 1970-1997 period. History shows that category leadership continues until an important market event occurs (market correction, discount rate cut, war, oil shocks such as those of the 1970s and 1980s, technology bubble burst of 2000, etc.) and forces investors to focus on the real bargain areas of the market. When this happens, there is generally a change in leadership and a rotation of assets from very overvalued to undervalued areas. Of course, past performance is no guarantee of future performance.

A study by investment manager James O'Shaughnessy showed that the momentum investment strategy outperformed the value strategy and indexed strategy from December 31, 1951 through December 31, 1996. The momentum strategy rebalanced assets into stocks with the best prior year's performance. The value strategy rebalanced assets into the worst performing stocks. And the indexed strategy simply bought and held the S&P 500 Index. The resulting average annual returns for the three strategies had the momentum strategy returning 14.3%, the value strategy returning 3.3%, and the index strategy returning 13.2%. (Remember that past performance is no guarantee of future performance.)

What's the drawback to buying recent performance?

Buying strictly based on relative strength can result in a non-diversified portfolio. For instance, a portfolio may inadvertently become over exposed to technology, growth stocks, interest-sensitive stock groups, or whatever is leading the market. Thus, a portfolio may do very well given that the sector leadership does not change. But is also subject to greater downside risk as the portfolio becomes more concentrated.

What else should investors be aware of when buying top performers?

A five-star rating does not guarantee good performance! A January 2003 study by Dr. Matthew Morey a professor at the Lubin School of Business at Pace University found that top-rated funds do not do any better than average-rated funds, whereas lower rated funds underperformed. The study looked at the five-year performance of 738 funds rated by Morningstar. Don Phillips of Morningstar has said that good funds do not always translate to good portfolios and that is why performance is not the deciding factor in the decision to buy. (Past performance is no guarantee of future performance.)

Exhibit 7.5: Buying Top Quartile Funds Hasn't Ensured Better Performance

241 Funds earned top quartile results for the five-year period ending 1999. Two years later almost 61% of the funds ended up in the bottom quartile in performance!

241 Funds ranked TOP

0.4% - TOP QUARTILE
8.7% - SECOND QUARTILE
30.3% - THIRD QUARTILE
60.67% FELL TO THE BOTTOM

Source: Prudential Securities, Morningstar Inc. Funds evaluated included all funds monitored by Morningstar Inc. This table is for illustrative purposes only and does not predict or depict the performance of any investment. Investments in mutual funds involve risk. Past performance is no guarantee of future performance. Mutual funds incur fees and expenses (including investment management and administrative fees). Obtain a prospectus for more complete information about the fund, including all fees and expenses, and should be read carefully before you invest. Investment returns and principal value of a mutual fund will fluctuate, so that shares, when redeemed, may be worth more or less than their original cost. Past performance is no guarantee of future performance.

How can the odds of improving consistent portfolio performance be improved?

It can be a best to reduce investments in funds that have had blowout years and are inconsistent. Any fund with a standard deviation of greater than 30 falls into this category. The typical U.S. equity fund has a standard deviation of about 20.

A high standard deviation is a good thing when the range of returns is positive. You can evaluate downside performance by studying a fund's worst return over the last ten years and its up-years-to-down-years ratio. A ratio of 4:1 is a good average. Look for funds that pay dividends and have average to below average P/Es. Dividends help boost returns in down markets.

What else can be done to try to improve a portfolio's performance?

Generally, keep expenses low. The market is too efficient to handicap performance with high expenses. The average equity fund's total operating expense was about 1.76% (including commissions) in 2003 while the average index fund's expense ratio was 0.75%.

Furthermore, recent academic studies, including Dr. Matthew Morey's, show that the average load fund underperforms the average no-load fund. A 1996 Journal of Finance study by Mark Carhart concluded that load funds' performance lagged no-loads by sixty basis point per year over the last decade before loads are taken into account. An equity fund that has an expense ratio that is 10% greater than its category average has an unfavorable expense ratio. However, you can relax this rule with single state tax-free funds, emerging market equity funds, emerging market bond funds, and specialty funds.

7. When adding a fund, be sure to assess the change to a portfolio's beta

Beta is a measure of the fund's marginal contribution of risk to a portfolio. High beta funds increase downside risk. The longer the measurement period of the beta the more reliable it will be. You can use the three-year beta, but if you can find a five-year beta, that is even better.

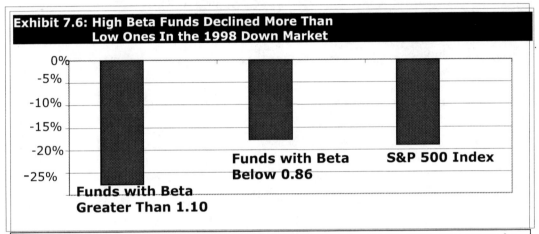

Exhibit 7.6: High Beta Funds Declined More Than Low Ones In the 1998 Down Market

Source: Morningstar Inc. ®. Data is for July 17, 1998 through August 31, 1998. Avg. return for U.S. stock Funds based on beta during the period. This table is for illustrative purposes only and does not predict or depict the performance of any investment. Investments in mutual funds involve risk. Past performance is no guarantee of future performance. Mutual funds incur fees and expenses (including investment management and administrative fees). Obtain a prospectus for more complete information about the fund, including all fees and expenses, and should be read carefully before you invest. Investment returns and principal value of a mutual fund will fluctuate, so that shares, when redeemed, may be worth more or less than their original cost. Past performance is no guarantee of future performance.

Of course, adding a high beta fund to a portfolio might not increase the overall portfolio risk where the new fund has a low correlation with the other fund holdings. For example, adding an emerging market fund to U.S. stock fund portfolio doesn't necessarily increase the overall portfolio's risk. The emerging market fund, if held alone, can be a risky investment. Simply owning one volatile fund may not be a bad strategy, even for conservative portfolios, when it lowers overall risk. The goal is to keep the portfolio beta low in a conservative portfolio.

Beta is relative to a fund category. Generally, growth style funds have a higher beta than value style funds. You can assess a fund's beta instead of its standard deviation. In the selection process, we are more concerned about how a fund's beta will affect the overall portfolio's standard deviation. At the portfolio level, you can manage the standard deviation by controlling the beta through the funds that are added. Riskier categories sport betas of greater than one. Rule of thumb: Funds with a beta that is 20% greater than its category average is generally unfavorable.

Exhibit 7.7: Fund Category Average Beta

Large-cap Growth	1.18	Mid-cap Value	0.7
Large-cap Value	0.76	Small-cap Growth	1.3
Mid-cap Growth	1.30	Small-cap Value	0.7

Source: Morningstar ® 2003 Regressed against S&P 500 Index for the three year period ending December 2003. This table is for illustrative purposes only and do not predict or depict the performance of any investment. Investments in mutual funds involve risk. Past performance is no guarantee of future performance. Mutual funds incur fees and expenses (including investment management and administrative fees). Obtain a prospectus for more complete information about the fund, including all fees and expenses, and should be read carefully before you invest. Past performance is no guarantee of future performance.

---

8. Compare the Sharpe ratio between funds that screen well

Favor funds with higher Sharpe ratios that adjust overall portfolio characteristics to the desired portfolio metrics.

9. Consider a fund that pays dividends because the yield is a big contributor to overall portfolio return

The S&P 500 Index yielded 4.36% and returned 12.20% on average from 1926 to 2002. The dividend yield accounted for 36% of that return. A Credit Suisse First Boston study of S&P 500 stocks from January 1980 to June 2002 found that the highest yielding stocks outperformed the market but were not the top performers. Furthermore, the dividend is taxed at a 15% Federal tax rate! Funds that pay a dividend yield that is equal to or greater than the current market yield have a favorable yield characteristic over those that do not.

10. Have some skepticism about a fund that is very large or very small as compared to other funds in its category

A fund's asset size can be a double-edged sword. The size of a larger fund can lower operating expense ratios thereby increasing a fund's return. But it can also hinder performance.

Exhibit 7.8: Larger Asset Size Funds Had Better Chance of Beating the Market

	Average Return: +/- S&P 500 Index		
	Three-year	Five-year	Ten-years
Avg. for Funds with $1 billion in assets:	+4.12%	+2.62%	+0.12%
Average all Funds:	+1.32%	+0.32%	-1.59%

The average fund under performed the S&P 500 by 1.59%. The typical fund expense ratio is 1.57%

Source: Morningstar Inc. ®. Study is of 6,374 equity funds for period ending March 31, 2003. This table is for illustrative purposes only and does not predict or depict the performance of any investment. Investments in mutual funds involve risk. Past performance is no guarantee of future performance. Mutual funds incur fees and expenses (including investment management and administrative fees). Obtain a prospectus for more complete information about the fund, including all fees and expenses, and should be read carefully before you invest. Investment returns and principal value of a mutual fund will fluctuate, so that shares, when redeemed, may be worth more or less than their original cost. Past performance is no guarantee of future performance.

The asset size of a fund can affect its performance. The larger the fund's asset base relative to the area of the market the fund invests in, the harder it tends to be for the fund to beat its benchmark.

Large funds often affect the stock prices of their holdings when buying or selling them. They can drive up the prices of stocks they are buying due to demand, causing the fund to buy at incrementally higher prices as it builds a position. Likewise, it is difficult for a large size fund to unwind a position without causing downward pressure on the stock's price. This can also be particularly true for micro-cap funds, small-cap funds, and mid-cap funds.

Funds with smaller asset bases do not have this problem. However, if the fund has a very low operating expense ratio, then you may wish to consider overlooking the diminutive asset size, particularly if the fund has a good track record.

Just remember to tread carefully with funds sporting small asset bases. Funds that have less than $100 million in assets may not be as desirable because of the high risk of the fund being merged or dissolved. Also, big producers can easily, and inadvertently, become big shareholders. If you invest $10 million in a $50 million fund, you are a 20% majority owner. That can become problematic if you are still invested should a wave of redemptions occur. In addition, smaller size funds typically have higher expenses than mid- to large-size funds.

Exhibit 7.9: Smaller Size Funds Had Higher Expense Ratios

Fund Assets	Expense ratio
Less than $100 million	1.57%
More than $100 million	1.19%
More than $1 billion	0.93%

Source: Morningstar 2003 6,374 funds. This table is for illustrative purposes only and do not predict or depict the performance of any investment. Investments in mutual funds involve risk. Past performance is no guarantee of future performance. Mutual funds incur fees and expenses (including investment management and administrative fees). Obtain a prospectus for more complete information about the fund, including all fees and expenses, and should be read carefully before you invest. Past performance is no guarantee of future performance.

On the other hand, diminutive funds can offer higher potential returns if they perform well, albeit, with greater risk. The typical mutual fund had $462 million in assets in 2003, according to Morningstar Inc.

Exhibit 7.9: Rule of Thumb for Fund Asset Size

Large-cap:	Assets greater than $7 billion unfavorable fund characteristic.
Mid-cap:	Assets greater than $3 billion unfavorable fund characteristic.
Small-cap:	Assets greater than $2 billion unfavorable fund characteristic.
International:	Assets greater than $2 billion unfavorable fund characteristic.

11. Assess concentration risk and keep diversification in mind

Warren Buffet once admitted that he owns less than ten stocks because it required more right decisions to own more, and a lot more time to monitor.

Research indicates that having a more diversified, less concentrated portfolio is a less risky investment strategy. Look at the number of holdings, industry concentration, and concentration of the top ten holdings. Studies show that when a portfolio owns more than fifteen different stocks from different industries, the unsystematic risk affecting the portfolio is eliminated. Eight stocks from different industries would be enough with blue chip companies. Any further diversification will not "wash" away any more unsystematic risk.

Diversified funds are potentially less risky then non-diversified funds such as sector-specific funds. A fund is not considered a diversified fund if it invests more than five percent of its assets in a security, or it owns more than ten percent of the outstanding shares of a particular issuer.

A diversified fund generally takes positions in stocks that represent one to five percent of a portfolio with the mode being about two percent. A fund that is *too* diversified may under perform because it does not give enough weight to its best stock picks.

As a rule of thumb, as the capitalization gets smaller, the need to own more stocks becomes greater. Holding concentration is relative to the type of fund and universe of stocks. Small-cap funds should have about one hundred stocks because small-caps tend to be much more volatile. In general, small-cap stocks have greater business risk. Investing in one hundred stocks seeks to lower the downside risk. The typical small-cap, mid-cap, and large-cap fund holds approximately 220, 150, and 140 stocks, respectively.

Exhibit 7.10: Rule of Thumb for Concentration

Large-cap: # of holdings less than 50 unfavorable fund characteristic.
Mid-cap: # of holdings less than 75 unfavorable fund characteristic.
Small-cap: # of holdings less than 100 unfavorable fund characteristic.
International: # of holdings less than 100 unfavorable fund characteristic.

Use the percent of assets that the top ten holdings represent and industry concentration to assess a fund's concentration. The more concentrated a fund is, the greater the risk and potential reward. The top ten are core positions of the portfolio; the best stock ideas.

A 2001 Morningstar study found that only 48% of the funds studied could say that their top ten holdings had outperformed the portfolio at large. The average annual return of the top ten fund holdings was 13.2%, as compared to the 13.4% average return for funds in the study. This suggests that greater concentration in the top ten holdings may lower returns and increase risk. The typical equity fund's top ten holdings represent thirty percent of their assets.

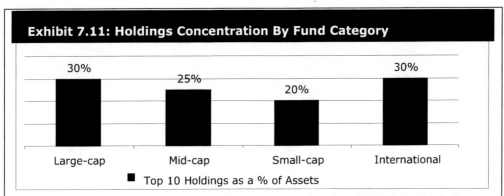

Exhibit 7.11: Holdings Concentration By Fund Category

Source: Morningstar Inc. ®. Data is for three year period ending 2001. This table is for illustrative purposes only and does not predict or depict the performance of any investment. Investments in mutual funds involve risk. Past performance is no guarantee of future performance. Mutual funds incur fees and expenses (including investment management and administrative fees). Obtain a prospectus for more complete information about the fund, including all fees and expenses. The prospectus should be read carefully before you invest. Investment returns and the principal value of a mutual fund will fluctuate, so that shares, when redeemed, may be worth more or less than their original cost. Past performance is no guarantee of future performance.

You can use the following rule of thumb to assess whether a fund has a more aggressive management approach by concentrating assets in its top ten largest holdings. From a conservative view point and based on Morningstar research, it is more desirable to be less concentrated.

Exhibit 7.12: Rule of Thumb for Top Ten Concentration

Large-cap: If greater than 35% = unfavorable fund characteristic
Mid-cap: If greater than 30% = unfavorable fund characteristic
Small-cap: If greater than 25% = unfavorable fund characteristic
International: If greater than 35% = unfavorable fund characteristic

A mutual fund's industry break down shows how the assets are diversified across the economy. This information provides insight into the current investment strategy of the manager.

From this break down, you can determine:

• If the fund is overweight in cyclical companies. If it is, then the manager's expectation is for economic expansion, and/or he believes that is where the values are in the market.

• If the fund concentrates in defensive companies, the manager likely expects an economic slow down or believes that is the most attractive area in the market.

Industry selection is a major determinant of a portfolio's return. When a portfolio manager is not in the right sectors, the portfolio may under perform the market. When a sector becomes out of favor, usually every stock in that sector is penalized. A fund that limits a specific industry exposure to no more than 20% of a portfolio exhibits a favorable industry concentration characteristic. As a risk management tactic, not every industry in the portfolio should be highly correlated -- economic news should not equally affect each industry.

12. Tax-efficiency shouldn't be the top criteria when choosing funds

Should investors be very concerned with the tax-efficiency of a fund?

Tax-efficiency does *not* assure investors of better after-tax returns and has lost much of its importance given the new tax laws.

Many top performing, non-tax managed funds outperform tax-managed funds on an after-tax basis anyway. Turnover of 40-50% is a normal part of active risk management. Tax management should best be accomplished through individual strategies due to every individual's unique circumstances, and not by a one-size-fits-all fund manager. New tax laws tax dividends at a 15% rate and capital gains at a 15% rate (5% for investors in the 15% tax bracket).

You must be careful not to invest in tax-efficient funds that could become tax-*in*efficient. A fund with a huge amount of embedded unrealized gains has a higher potential capital gains exposure. A high capital gains exposure often accompanies a low turnover strategy. These funds are susceptible to realizing large capital gains where there is a manager change or strategy shift.

Morningstar's metric for "Potential Capital Gain Exposure" attempts to determine the percentage of total assets that is represented by unrealized and realized gains that have not been distributed. When a client wants a tax-managed fund, you may wish to choose a fund with a tax-efficiency ratio of 85% or greater. The S&P 500 Index fund has historically had a tax-efficiency ratio of about 92%. Tax-efficiency across all fund categories will improve given new tax laws.

13. Make sure you have experienced managers working for you

Louis Rukeyser once said that *people* are the chief reason some mutual funds do so much better than other ones. Generally, more experienced money managers have a better feel for the markets they deal in, and are more familiar with the companies they own than inexperienced ones.

Roy Neuberger once said that he would not want someone learning how to shave on his face. In that same vein, investors would not want a portfolio manager learning how to manage money at their expense.

There are very talented inexperienced managers in the industry, but to be able to find them they must first post some solid returns. It is generally a best practice to only consider managers with at least five years of experience. The experience of managing money through up and down cycles is quite valuable.

Eight Best Practice Guidelines for Savvy Fixed-income Fund Selection

Why should investors buy fixed-income mutual funds instead of individual bonds?

Bond fund wrap portfolios have an advantage over individual bond portfolios. Small investors can instantly diversify away the specific risk associated with a particular security or bond management approach through risk management strategies that are easier to execute with mutual fund investing.

You will, no doubt, need to be careful with bond fund selection because long-term returns among the various types of bonds funds have not varied by more than the differences in expenses ratios, but the risk has been significantly different. It is a good idea to seek out those bond funds that manage risk.

Exhibit 7.13: Bond Fund Category Returns and Expense Ratios

Category	Avg. Return	Avg. Expense Ratio
Long Government	7.94%	0.94%
Corporate	6.93%	1.02%
High Yield	4.89%	1.33%
Intermediate	6.38%	1.02%
Intermediate Government	6.06%	1.12%
Short Bond	5.45%	0.84%
Short Government	5.45%	0.95%
Multi-Sector	5.62%	1.36%
International	6.17%	1.37%

Source: Morningstar Inc. ®. Data is for 10 years ending June 2003. Used with permission. This table is for illustrative purposes only and does not predict or depict the performance of any investment. Investments in mutual funds involve risk. Past performance is no guarantee of future performance. Mutual funds incur fees and expenses (including investment management and administrative fees). Obtain a prospectus for more complete information about the fund, including all fees and expenses. The prospectus should be read carefully before you invest. Past performance is no guarantee of future performance.

Just like equity funds, bond funds can be actively managed or passively managed. An actively managed bond fund's investment approach can be categorized into one of six taxable approaches. That number of investment approaches will double if tax-exempt is involved.

Each approach has a different risk and return trade off. Basically, a fixed-income fund will assume more interest rate risk by investing in longer term bonds and more credit quality risk by investing in lower credit quality bonds (which could increase yield and return).

Exhibit 7.14:   Basic Bond Management Approaches

Credit Quality/ Duration	Investment Grade	Non-Investment Grade
Duration less than 3 yrs. (Short term bonds)	**Lowest yield and least risky**	**Moderate yield and risk**
Duration greater than 3 < 7 yrs. (Intermediate term bonds)	**Low yield and risk**	**High yield and risk**
Duration greater than 7 yrs. (Long-term bonds)	**Moderate yield and risk**	**Highest yield and risk**

Considering Indexed vs. Active Fixed-income Management

Indexing efficient areas of the bond market can be a sensible strategy particularly in areas of the bond market where it is more difficult to add value. In the period of study from 1989 through 1998, Standard & Poor's Micropal found that actively managed bond funds even had a hard time beating their respective indexes than equity actively managed funds, particularly in the short-to-intermediate duration funds.

You can index investment grade short- and intermediate- areas of the bond market by investing in low operating expense index funds. Active management can add value in other areas from credit analysis (eg; buying bonds that will be upgraded or selling ones that will be downgraded by rating agencies), interest rate management, and sector selection and so on.

Bond indexing does not manage all the risks associated with bond investing. Indexed bond fund do not manage credit quality risk and interest rate risk because there is not a portfolio manager shortening the duration of the fund as interest rates rise. Neither is the credit quality upgraded as the economy contracts or lowered when the economy expands. U.S. bond index funds do not take advantage of the higher return opportunities that foreign bonds may offer.

1. Pick fixed-income funds that are managed utilizing a "total return" approach

Managers typically will have either a total return philosophy to managing bonds or a yield philosophy.

A high yield investment style can be risky because it tends to put principal at greater credit risk. When an investor is risk-averse, then a total return approach is usually a better strategy.

A good bond manager is a risk manager who will seek to protect principal and earn total returns that beat inflation. Remember, it is easy to achieve high income by buying speculative high yield bonds or using derivatives to enhance yield and hoping that you get paid every dime of interest and principal promised. It is much harder to earn consistent annual total returns that beat inflation!

I recommend that you not pick the highest yielding fund. It can be better to look beyond the yield to overall fund performance.

Bond money should not be exposed to downside risk like a client's equity money. It is difficult for bond funds to recoup losses because annual returns from the bond market are not as high as the equity market. Thus, it is smart to avoid strategies that expose client money to downside risk in the bond market.

You can look at the worst year over the last ten years to assess downside risk. Treasury bonds yielded 6.48% for the 1950-2002 period. This means they have a 6.48% income cushion before investors begin to lose principal. The "income cushion" of 6.04% on average yield is less for intermediate Treasury bonds. However, they are also less sensitive to changes in interest rates. Intermediate bond funds generally have a duration that ranges from three to about seven years. If the interest rate increases by one percent, then an intermediate bond fund that has duration of seven years may drop by 7% and long-term bonds may decline approximately 11%.

It just makes sense to hire a good "risk manager" and find out how the manager reduces the risks of fixed-income investing. I recommend that the number of issuers should be greater than 100; bond positions should be limited to no more than 2% of fund's assets. It is also a good idea to limit exposure to derivatives to less than 10% of assets, and cap overall portfolio exposure to low credit quality companies to 20%.

2. Cost is a top consideration but not the only one

Remember that long term returns among fixed-income investments are essentially the same, so cost is a big factor in the decision. Often the difference in yield and return is due to cost differentials. A 2003 Charles Schwab study concluded that every 1% increase in expense ratio is associated with an estimated 0.7 percent decline in annual return.

I personally vote to avoid load and high operating expense bond funds. It can be wise to avoid funds that have operating expenses that exceed 1.11% which is the 2003 industry average expense ratio, with international bond funds weighing in at 1.37%, and indexed bond funds averaging 0.46%. Money market funds' operating expenses should be less than sixty basis points. As a rule of thumb, an expense ratio that is ten percent greater than the category ratio is unfavorable.

3. Seek out consistent fifty percentile or better performance

You should apply the same performance criteria used with equity funds, but with one twist. A long-term bond fund only needs to beat its category average by at least one percentage point for periods evaluated, intermediate bond funds by 0.50%, and short-term funds should at least equal its category average.

4. Over time, the yield is critical to higher return

Although big incremental gains can be made by favorable interest rate swings, over the long run the yield is what you should expect in return. Interest income accounts for 100% of the return of a bond when held to maturity. The yield accounted for 99% of the Lehman Brothers Long-term Government Bond Index return from 1950-2002 and 92% of the Lehman Brothers Ten-year Intermediate Treasury Bond Index, according to Leman Brothers. (Remember that indices include reinvested income, but not transaction costs or taxes, are unmanaged and cannot be purchased directly by investors. Past performance is no guarantee of future performance).

You can shop for yield when buying bond funds but not at great expense to quality. A favorable characteristic is to have a bond fund yield at least what the benchmark is yielding for that particular type of bond fund. Anytime the yield is much higher, then greater risk is being assumed. I believe it is never smart to gamble with exotic derivatives, even if through their use pumped up returns are promised.

5. Consider the duration of a fund in the context of the Fed's current policy and the direction of inflation

You should generally choose higher duration funds when the Fed lowers the key Fed Funds rate. You can pick lower duration funds when the Fed changes its stance to restrictive, especially when inflation is misbehaving. Long-term bond funds generally have a duration that exceeds six, intermediate ranges from three to six, and short-term funds do not exceed three. Choose a fund with the desired duration as a favorable characteristic.

6. Consider the weighted average credit quality in light of the business cycle

Right before the recovery phase of the market begins, it would be wise to screen for funds with lower weighted average credit, and as the expansion peaks, turn to funds with higher weighted average credit.

An average credit quality of less than BBB is an unfavorable fund characteristic for investment grade funds, and average credit quality that is less than BB is unfavorable for a high yield bond fund. It is best not to ever let the overall portfolio average credit quality fall below BBB.

7. Avoid high beta funds as relative to the fund category

Here is a rule of thumb to follow: a long-term bond fund with a beta that is greater than 1.1, an intermediate fund with a beta that is greater than 0.85, and a short-term fund with a beta that is greater than 0.50 are all unfavorable. High beta funds tend to concentrate in a specific bond sector or a few highly correlated bond sectors.

8. Evaluate the bond fund's portfolio composition

What is the fixed-income fund's sector break down? Is the fund investing in more risky sectors of the bond market? Funds that have a significant exposure to risky areas of the bond market, such as emerging markets, exotic derivatives, illiquid securities, and restricted securities, are undesirable.

There is one Government bond fund that actually had a negative 19.08% return in July 2003! It was chockfull of risky derivatives. When a fund has more than a 10% exposure to those areas, it is highly undesirable.

Fund Monitoring and Supervision: A Baker's Dozen of Sell Guidelines That Signal Action is Required

"You can observe a lot by watching" - Yogi Berra

Do not confuse tactical asset allocation with fund de-selection. Each quarter it is a best practice to statistically review the core funds in a portfolio. You will wish to consider selling a core fund if it has sustained third and/or fourth quartile performance results over a meaningful holding period, or is no longer meeting the selection criteria.

It is usually prudent to adhere to the "Cockroach Theory" which acknowledges that when there is bad news there will usually be more to follow.

Practical Sell Guidelines:

1. *Have a "downside" and an "upside" sell discipline*

A "downside" sell discipline should produce better results than aimlessly selling funds to chase performance. A sell discipline must match a client's loss threshold tolerance. A 10% stop loss order is appropriate for the moderate-risk investor. It is best to recognize and admit mistakes early. Remember, a 10% loss only requires an 11% gain to break even, whereas a 20% loss requires a much heftier 25% gain.

Do not let your client fall into a hole they cannot climb out of. To get a 25% return usually means taking on greater risk than normally and risk they shouldn't assume. It is best to compel a client to sell when his/her pain threshold for loss is reached. Empirical studies show that investors tend to hold onto losers in hopes that they will recover. It is best not to get caught in that decision trap.

Have an "upside" sell discipline, too. Bernard Baruch once said that he made most of his money by selling too soon.

Anytime a large-cap, mid-cap, or small-cap fund's return exceeds 40% in a given year, I believe it is time to trim the position down by 25%. You can do the same for foreign stock funds when their annual return exceeds 55%. Historically, large-cap's best annual performance was 52.62%, mid-caps' best annual performance was 50.1%, small-caps' best ever performance was 46.05%, and foreign stocks best performance showing was 65.84% from 1950-2002.

My advice is not to wait around for the record to be broken. Yes, all sub-asset classes have extended those gains in subsequent years for up to three years after a peak return year. Nevertheless, all too often the following years produced lower returns and even negative ones. Take gains when the returns approach 80% of the highest historical return. It is desirable to leave some money on the table. I never met an investor who went broke taking big gains.

2. *Sell when a category outlook dims*

When the outlook for a fund category is unfavorable then sell a fund investing in that sector. In the spring of 2000, Moody's research predicted that high yield bond defaults would reach record levels and they did! Thus, it was smart to reduce the high yield exposure. Over the next three-year period, the fund category lost 3% on average.

3. *Sell when the investment thesis proves just plain wrong*

It is okay to admit misjudgments, sell, and then move on. For example, your top down analysis concludes that you should overweight small-cap value and you are overweighed in large-cap growth as it falters. Admit your mistake and trim down your exposure.

4. *Sell when a fund's relative strength is obviously lacking*

It is a good idea to sell when a fund shows lousy relative strength as compared to the broader market and to its peers over the latest twelve months period, given that nothing has been done to correct the reason for underperformance (such as changing the manager or repositioning of fund assets into the favored area of the market). When a fund is way out of sync with market conditions, it is usually time to either sell or reduce the position.

5. *Sell when valuations get lofty*

It is time to consider selling when valuations become excessive, as in the case of large-cap growth stocks in the first quarter of 2000. That was when the average P/E of the largest 100 growth stocks exceeded 50 while the rest of the market traded at less than 30, and small-cap value stocks traded at less than 20.

By the way, the small-cap value strategy went on to outperform the large-cap sector by over 20%. Remember that momentum is inversely correlated with value. At some point, a fund may have good momentum, but may have lost its value. At that time, it makes sense to sell or reduce exposure to fund.

6. *Have predetermined "trim" positions*

You can reduce a fund position when it exceeds a, say, 30% preset limit in a portfolio. Many portfolio managers set 4% limits for stock positions in a fund. That means a stock may double or even triple to hit the 4% limit before a manager trims the holding.

It is perfectly okay to take some profits while you have them. The same is true for a mutual fund that grows from 20% to 30% of a portfolio. If interest rates are on the rise, the T-bond yield is approaching 7%, quarterly earnings momentum is showing signs of deceleration, the inflationary threat is building, or current valuation levels are extremely high, then it is prudent to reallocate more assets into cash-equivalents to lock into profits and reduce downside risk during a period of weakness.

7. *Sell because there's a better investment elsewhere*

Better investment ideas often offer more promising risk and reward characteristics. Often a fund is sold when it really should be acquired because the fund is coming into favor due to changing market conditions. It proved smart to have bought high yield bonds in early year 2002, when yield spreads between high yield bonds and Treasury bonds were greater then twelve percent!

8. *Sell when a fund has outlives its usefulness in a portfolio*

It can be wise to periodically consider the role a fund plays in a portfolio and assess if it is no longer required. For instance, a utilities fund would not be required when the economy shows signs of a turnaround nor would a long-term Government bond fund.

9. *Consider whether to sell overheated or mega-sized funds*

Sometimes it may make sense to sell a fund that either is growing too fast or has grown too large in asset size for its investment category. Rapid expansion can often negatively affect future performance.

10. Sell when a fund is outperforming

It is often the wisest to sell when the going is good. It makes sense to selectively sell overvalued assets (funds that may still offer growth but no value) throughout the market cycle and buy undervalued funds given improving relative strength. There is a cyclical pattern to investing.

11. Sell if expenses get ahead of performance

It often makes good sense to sell a fund if a fund's expenses have gotten out of whack. A sky rocketing expense ratio as compared to category average is another reason to sell when a replacement fund can be just as good and has a significantly lower expense ratio. An adverse change in an expense ratio may be the result of a new excessive 12b-1 plan, or serious redemption rate.

12. Consider selling if the fund's investment objective or strategy is altered

It can be prudent to sell a fund when there is a change in investment approach that could alter the risk/reward characteristics of the fund and affect its role in the client's overall portfolio.

13. Consider selling if the money manager is changed

A change in portfolio management is another reason to consider selling a fund. After all, you are really hiring the expertise of a specific money manager, and often a specific portfolio manager or team, when buying a fund. You can relax this rule when the new portfolio manager checks out to be a good one based on his/her past track record.

It is worthwhile to conduct a due diligence conference call with each core fund manager at least once each year. Find out if the manager is sticking to his or her knitting. Has the investment approached changed? Has the portfolio become more risky? Reevaluate key fund characteristics. Does the investment approach and holdings still fit with the portfolio investment themes? Make every attempt to get fresh portfolio data. The stale data found on the Internet can easily lead you to the wrong conclusion.

> **Insider Tip:** Based on a study of average market returns of trading days of the month from 1926-1990, the best time to sell a fund is during the first five days of the month and on a Friday, according to *Mutual Fund Magazine*. Best quarters in the market to buy tech stocks (and generally other sectors) are the first and fourth quarters according to Ned Davis research for the 1979-1999 period. Past performance is not a guarantee of future performance.

IPM Portfolio Management

"The problem with the person who thinks he's a long-term investor and impervious to short-term gyrations
is that emotion of fear and pain will eventually make him sell badly."
-- Robert Wibblesman.

Buy and Hold vs. Careful Selection and Proper Timing

Billionaire Warren Buffet's oft quoted advice to investors is to "buy and hold" companies with excellent management. It is so simple that one cannot argue with it. And to boot, Mr. Buffet makes it look so simple and easy to do!

However, when most investors try to do what Mr. Buffet does they are not as successful. Of the thousands of companies available, which ones can be bought at intrinsic value like Mr. Buffet does?

For example, Mr. Buffet bought Coca-Cola and made hundreds of millions of dollars. But that fortune was more a function of his *selection* and *timing* rather than just passively and without conscious thought buying and holding. If you saw that he owned Coca-Cola and followed his lead by buying Coca-Cola in 1998 at a price above $70, would you have made a small fortune as well? By year 2000 the price had dropped close to $30.

Many investors without the financial reserves of Mr. Buffet would think twice about holding for the long haul. Unfortunately your *timing* and *selection* could cost you. Let us say that you did hold on. That begs the question: should a stock never be sold? After all, of the original Blue Chip stocks of the Dow Jones Index, only one is left today -- General Electric -- under its original name.

Okay, so what is my logic behind the reason *not* to always "buy and hold" but instead actively manage money?

If a manager takes care of the short-term, and is successful in stringing up a series of solid one-to-three year numbers, then the long-term results are much more likely to be good. Letting it ride with a steadfast buy and hold conviction, hoping that the client stays the course and praying that bad performance doesn't take a client so far off goal that he can never recoup, can be a loser's game.

It is the short-term market movements that cause investors to abandoned ship. When a portfolio manager takes care of the short-term through active management, then the odds of long-term success tend to improve. The trick to getting clients to truly become long-term investors is to never exceed their loss threshold over the short-term.

Getting to the Core of Portfolio Management

What is portfolio management essentially about?

It is about asset allocation, investment selection, proper timing, and the often overlooked component -- risk management. There is more to portfolio management than a buy and hold strategy of quality companies. You need only look at what happened to all of the quality technology companies from 2000 to 2002 to understand that portfolio management is more than buying quality Treasury bonds, Blue Chips, etc.

The asset allocation principle attempts to directly control portfolio volatility. Indirectly it effects return and investment horizon. Active portfolio management seeks to manage not just volatility but also overall investing risks, return, and income. Practicing a simple asset allocation and buy and hold approach ignores the dynamics of the market.

Passive management is an active decision to disregard political, social, economic, and market events, and the deteriorating or improving business fundamentals of a security. Passive investors are indifferent to overvalued and undervalued investments.

Which are you -- an active or a passive investor?

```
┌─────────────────────────────────────────────────────────────────────────┐
│ Exhibit 8.1: Take the Active Investor versus Passive Investor Test        │
└─────────────────────────────────────────────────────────────────────────┘
```

		Yes	No
1.	Do you believe that there is a market cycle – markets go up and down?	☐	☐
2.	Do you believe there is a business cycle – expansion and contraction?	☐	☐
3.	Do you think that asset classes and sub-asset classes have a performance cycle that's influenced by economic and market conditions?	☐	☐
4.	Do you think that asset classes and sub-asset classes get over bought out perform, and overvalued?	☐	☐
5.	Do you think that asset classes and sub-asset classes get oversold, under perform, and undervalued?	☐	☐
6.	Do you think money can be made or lost in every type of market, up, down, flat, volatile?	☐	☐
7.	Do you think that by not investing in overvalued asset and sub-asset classes your return would improve?	☐	☐
8.	Do you think some investments deserve a "sell" recommendation instead of a buy and hold?	☐	☐

Debunking the Myths of Active versus Passive Management

If most of your answers were no, then you are a passive investor that may be sticking your head in the sand. Without realizing it, you might be taking unnecessary risks by buying overvalued investments. Moreover, you may be missing lay-up returns and income enhancing opportunities. If that is true, then you may be taking more of a financial beating than necessary.

Unlike passive management, active management attempts to lower portfolio volatility and other forms of risk by appropriately responding to the changes in global market conditions.

What is the bottom-line advice even for passive investors?

Be sensitive to valuation levels. Anytime an investor overpays for an asset two things can happen:

1. The investor will lose money;
2. If more fortunate not to lose money, then the investor's return will be greatly diminished

For example, what if you had invested in large-cap growth stocks in January 2000? Would you have bought CISCO, one of the top performing technology stock, at 188 times earnings when, historically, large-cap growth multiples averaged 36? CISCO went on to lose more than 80% of its value within the following two years.

Yeah, I know, buy and hold; be long-term; it is only a paper loss until you sell. But what if your circumstances had changed? What if you had lost your job, your portfolio had lost half its value, you had gotten a divorce, or had become seriously ill? Moreover, what if you simply needed the money. What if you could not wait until CISCO hit that 188 times earnings point again in the next millennium (or ever)?

What is passive management's biggest weakness?

The biggest weakness is that it is blind to valuations when buying and selling. A study published by Professor Edward Tower of Duke University, concluded that Vanguard's actively managed funds beat its index funds from 1977 to 2003. Moreover, it did so with less risk! The main reason why Edward Tower's study had Vanguard's actively managed funds outperforming its passively managed index funds was because passive investment approaches ignored market manias, and securities were bought or sold regardless of market fundamentals.

One of the best selling books in the 1990's, "<u>Stocks for the Long Run</u>", written by Jeremy Siegel, advised investors that stocks are actually less likely to lose money over time, after inflation, than bonds. Even if you bought some of the most expensive stocks at the worst possible time. After the 2000-2002 bear market, he changed his tune somewhat. Now he says that investors shouldn't just buy stocks without any attention to price.

Isn't active management a form of market timing?

In a word, no. There is a *huge* difference between market timing and active management. No one can predict the future. And no one is suggesting that a prudent, active management program include very, very short-term trading of securities or funds.

However, in my opinion and based upon my experience, those who are well trained, experienced, and skilled professionals who are students of the markets and in touch with market conditions, can deftly determine when it is a good time to buy or sell a fund category. The trends in monetary policy, fundamentals, psychology, and technical indicators will provide enough clues to discern buy and sell decisions.

Empirical research shows that macro-economic conditions can be predicted fairly well for six months to twelve months in advance. The goal is to be in sync with cyclical trends and not far behind the curve with decisions.

The Answer to the $64,000 Question

So what is the *real* key to beating the market?

In my opinion, the key to beating the market and/or producing consistently positive returns is to adjust a portfolio accordingly based upon a correct assessment of economic cyclical trends, take advantage of short-term behavioral inefficiencies such as the crowd mentality, capitalize on long-term anomalies, and minimize costs and taxes.

What other special investment strategies attempt to improve performance?

Buying the Dogs of the Dow, or the top fifty S&P stocks with the greatest upward quarterly earnings revision, is a special strategy available to active managers. There is also hedging with derivatives such as S&P 500 Futures.

Remember, in general, active management attempts to profit from behavioral tendencies that can cause stock prices to deviate from their fair market value. Crowd buying and selling behavior may cause stocks to become overvalued and undervalued without a fundamental justification. In addition, extrapolation of news, investor overreaction to past problems and recent good news, are a few more examples of behavioral tendencies that active managers can exploit.

The Building Block Strategies of Active Management

Active managers may leverage their participation in a rally more than passive strategy managers might. For example, active managers can concentrate in certain stock groups that are outperforming. They can buy more of what is in favor: value, growth, defensive, cyclical, small cap, mid-cap, large-cap, international, etc. Here are some active management examples:

• In 1995 active managers were able to beat the broad market by increasing their position in technology stocks.

• In 1998, a leading fund group's large-cap fund returned 79% compared to the 29% return of the S&P 500 Index. The fund's manager did this by concentrating in high multiple, large-cap growth stocks.

• Another $17 billion "focus" type fund that owned only 20 stocks returned 73% in 1998. The fund did this by concentrating into 25-35 stocks, of which 45% of the funds assets was in the technology sector.

Active management can generally follow the market's natural sector rotation better than passive. You may wish to move from cyclical stocks to non-cyclical, brand name, defensive stocks. Stock selection factors in valuations while passive ignores valuations. To limit downside risk, you can buy "value" stocks selling at less extreme multiples when market multiples are stretched beyond fair value.

To further lower downside risk, active managers can increase cash positions in portfolios, although history shows that few ever do. Most stay fully invested out of fear of underperforming the market due to a big cash position. Very few raise enough cash before a downturn to lessen unrealized loses in a bear market. However, they can avoid illiquid areas of the market. Only 30% of listed stocks actively traded are liquid, even in the best of times. In bear markets, however, only 5% are liquid. Illiquid stocks tend to decline further in down markets!

Should passive investment approaches that invest in a broad basket of securities be actively managed for risk?

All portfolios must be risk managed whether they employ active or passive strategies! As a strategy, indexing does not manage risk as well as active management. Passive investors typically do not care about valuations, usually have no buy or sell discipline, and so on. Likewise, passive bond investors tend not to manage credit quality and duration among many aspects. Non-management of those types of risks may result in unnecessary volatility as well as less consistent returns. Active management can limit the duration of a bond portfolio where passive cannot.

The Active Manager's Secrets of Market Inefficiency

Active management relies on two well-known components to add value to portfolio management:

1. **Common cyclical trends will repeat themselves**.

   For instance, inflation will rise and fall. Thus interest rates will go up and will go down. Correspondingly, bond prices will move down and up as interest rates move up and down. Along the way savvy active managers will tactically allocate assets to manage income, return, and risk.

2. **Short-term market efficiency can create value (and opportunity) in the marketplace**.

   Often, the short-term inefficiency is created by investors' buying and selling behavior that professional active management can take advantage of to produce incremental returns.

   For instance, in January of 2001 the spread between the Merrill Lynch High Yield Master Index and the Merrill Lynch Treasury 5-10 Years Index was 8.75%! That yield spread suggested that the high yield bond sector was undervalued as compared to Treasury issues.

   In the previous year 2000, the Investment Company Institute (ICI) had reported that high yield bond funds had experienced net sales of negative $12.3 billion. By adding the two situations together, an active manager might have spotted an oversold condition with high yield bonds.

   By year-end 2001 the ICI had reported that high yield bond fund sales were positive $7.2 billion. That likely meant that there was a short-term opportunity to buy high yields at undervalued price levels. The CSFB High Yield Bond Index went on to produce positive returns throughout a bear market, and in the recovery posted double-digit returns. The index's returns for 2001, 2002, and 2003 were 5.8%, 3.10%, and 27.94%, respectively. (Indices include reinvested income, but not transaction costs or taxes, are unmanaged and cannot be purchased directly by investors. Past performance is no guarantee of future performance.)

Global Markets: The More Inefficient Frontier

There are academic studies and empirical evidence, as well as underlying structural and investor behavioral reasons that suggest that the global market is inefficient over the short run. Moreover, certain market anomalies contradict long-term market efficiency.

- Academic research has shown that the greater the book-to-market value ratio, the better the risk adjusted return tends to be. In addition, low P/E large-cap stock investing has beaten high P/E large-cap stock investing over certain time periods -- such as from 1970 through 2003 -- according to Barra Inc. Furthermore, over the long run small-caps stocks have beaten the broader market (large-cap. stocks) from 1950 to 2003 according to Ibbotson Inc. When investments outperform the broader market, this suggests that the overall market isn't strongly efficient.

- International markets are less efficient. Actively managed International funds have consistently produced better performance than the MSCI EAFE Index. A report issued by Lipper Inc. showed actively managed International funds outperforming the benchmark over most of the three-year rolling periods from January 1982 to March 2003. (The MSCI EAFE is an unmanaged index of equity securities designed to represent the performance of developed stock markets outside of the United States and Canada. The Lipper International Funds average represents the average return of the group of diversified international mutual funds with similar broad investment mandates. There were 17 mutual funds used in the study that had performance going back to 1982. Past performance is no guarantee of future performance. Investors may not invest directly in any index.)

What are the suggested reasons behind the better performance for actively managed International funds?

Active managers can overweight countries with better performing stock markets and stronger economies while the index cannot. In addition, active managers can buy securities that the "market" is not following so they can find mis-priced securities.

- A structural reason why the market is inefficient is due to lack of coverage. Firms that are not adequately covered by research analysts tend to beat ones that have wide coverage because all company information is not always reflected in a stock's price. As a trend, analyst coverage has been dropping since 2002 creating the potential for even more inefficiency. Merrill Lynch, which covers the most companies of any firm on Wall Street, reduced the number of companies it covers from 3,500 in 2002 to 2,469 in 2003.

It gets worse with international securities. Thomson Financial published a report in April 2003 that states that analyst coverage is lower for international companies than for U.S. companies. In the United States only 45% of the public companies have more than five analysts covering the company, while in the United Kingdom and Japan that drops to 25%, and 38%, respectively.

Smaller size companies generally have a better chance of beating the market because of less analyst coverage. Research suggests favoring actively managed small- to mid-cap funds over a passive strategy in less efficient areas of the market.

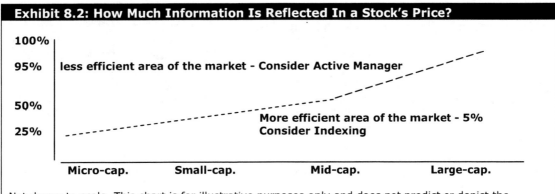

Exhibit 8.2: How Much Information Is Reflected In a Stock's Price?

Not drawn to scale. This chart is for illustrative purposes only and does not predict or depict the performance of any investment. The relationship is an approximation. Past performance is no guarantee of future performance.

The Phenomenon of Pricing Inefficiencies

- **There are times when the market doesn't process information (good or bad) as quickly**. It is hard to interpret the exact impact of certain information on a stock's price. Consequently, investor reaction is often slow. For instance, the seriousness of Oxford Health Care's bill payment delays in 1997 took investors a while to react to.

- **The consensus of equity analysts or market soothsayers are not always right, thus creating price inefficiencies**. In 1994, thirty-two leading economists were polled on expected GDP growth for 1995. Not one forecasted the actual 1995 number. In 2000, S&P 500 operating earnings fell by 21%. Yet among the 8,000 S&P 500 company stock recommendations made by analysts, only 29 were sell recommendations!

- **In the short run, a stock can easily become mis-priced since not everyone involved in the markets will act rationally all of the time**. Human emotion plays a big part in driving a stock's price up and down from fair market value. I do not know anyone who does not get emotional about their money when the market drops. Often investors overreact to real or perceived bad news. Unfounded pessimism may cause a stock, and the broader market, to become oversold. In addition, unwarranted optimism has had the opposite effect. Extreme emotions, greed and fear, can undermine otherwise sound markets. Why else would an investor buy a T-bond yielding five percent in 1998 and not a blue chip stock selling 40% off its 52-week high?

- **Irrational exuberance can impact market efficiency.** In 2004, Eugene Fama, father of the "efficient market hypothesis", conceded that investors could lead the market astray with their irrational investment decisions, causing the market to become less efficient than he had theoretically thought.

- **Over concentrated market segments weigh down efficient markets.** A study of Sweden's effort to privatize its retirement system conducted by Richard Thaler showed Swedish investors over concentrating holdings in domestic technology stocks. Thaler contends that the average investor doesn't make great investment choices. Money pouring into one area of the market can cause the market's efficiency to break down. A good example of this is the asset bubble in NASDAQ technology stocks in 2000. Fed Chairman Alan Greenspan, even referred to the 2000 stock market asset bubble as "irrational exuberance", indirectly confirming that investors can, at times, undermine the efficiency of the market.

- **Investment "fads" can throw market efficiency off-kilter**. Market efficiency assumes that investors make unbiased, independent investment decisions when, in actuality, quite often there is a herd mentality effect on Wall Street. Typically, one source can be responsible for an unwarranted sell-off or flood of buying in a stock. Investment dollars tend to chase the hottest stocks touted by top analysts despite valuations. In February 2000, $39 billion dollars flowed into mutual funds. Almost all of it ended up in small-cap growth and technology funds. Subsequently the NASDQ hit its high on March 10, 2000 and over the next three years, small-cap growth funds lost over fifty percent of their value, on average.

- **Global market time differences can create inefficiencies**. Another structural reason why the market is inefficient over the short-term is due to the way some mutual funds are priced. Foreign stock funds own securities whose prices are set by foreign markets that close hours after the U.S. market shuts down. The closing prices of these mutual fund may not accurately reflect the impact of foreign markets that remain open. This provides a window of opportunity to sell or buy knowing that the share price will react positively or negatively to market events not reflected in the fund closing price.

Active Management and Predictive Cyclical Trends

Is it possible to identify persistent cyclical trends?

I think so, and academic research confirms the short-term trends are fairly well predictable. After all, the Fed's monetary policy decisions are based, in part, on trend analysis.

For the purposes of fund portfolio management, this is accomplished by looking at changes in economic and market fundamentals, changes in technical indicators, changes in investor psychology, changes in supply and demand, and reversals or recoveries in cyclical asset classes and fund category trends.

Although auto correlation and run studies show that stock prices do not move in trends, other studies show that dividend yields, default spreads, quarterly earnings surprises (surprises are not always fully reflected in stock prices) and current bond yields can be used to predict stock and bond returns in the long run. At some point in the cycle conditions change, and the odds of a cyclical economic trend continuing or asset class once again outperforming over the next one to two years diminishes.

You wouldn't want to get into the trading pits at the Chicago Board of Trade and react to each released report with a buy or sell decision. Instead, you would want to take a step back, and take a more macro view, making decisions based upon a select number of discernable macro-economic and market trends (such as those covered in Chapter Two.)

These larger trends influence the trends in fund category performance that produce a reliable cycle of relative out performance and underperformance. Fund categories get overbought, then overvalued, then oversold, and become undervalued. This cycle is driven by attractive fundamentals and investor psychology. Investors tend to place more importance on one thing, or do not value something else. For example, within the backdrop of the bear market, investors became extremely risk averse from 2000 through 2002. Government bonds went from being undervalued in 1999 to being overbought and overvalued by year-end 2002. Six months into year 2003 the Lehman Brothers Long-term Treasury Bond Index was in negative return territory.

Asset and Sub-asset Class Performance Trends

Anecdotally, one can see trends in sub-asset class performance, as shown in Exhibit 8.3. On average, equity investments typically saw four positive years before experiencing a negative year. Bonds showed similar results. Foreign stocks had longer periods of positive returns.

Within any asset class, there are sub-asset classes that exhibited longer consecutive positive years and shorter ones. Here are some historical observations:

- Large-cap value has typically strung up six years of positive results, as did large-cap growth.

- Small-caps produced big returns in short spurts of about three years before correcting with double-digit sell offs.

- Real estate, as a fund sector, had great five-year runs.

- Gold performance was short and streaky at 2.5 years of upside before the downside came.

- Mortgage asset class was the most consistent with very rare down years. Based upon 24 years of data, the mortgages funds sector has been down only once so far. (Past performance is no guarantee of future results.)

Exhibit 8.3: Performance Trends are Driven by Investor Demand Influenced By Fundamentals

	# of Yrs. Studied	Percentage of Positive Years	Most consecutive positive yrs.	Avg. Consecutive positive yrs.	Approximate Total Return for for the Avg. Up Trend
Large-cap	77	70%	9	4	44%
Small-cap	77	69%	9	3	50%
Foreign stock	30	77%	7	4.6	70%
High Yield Bonds	77	73%	11	4	32%
Corporate Bonds	77	78%	15	4	27%
Treasury bonds	77	73%	12	3	19%
Intermediate Treasury Bonds	77	90%	24	6	35%
Gold	32	53%	5	2.5	26%
Real estate	28	80%	12	5	67%
Mortgages	24	96%	18	13	128%

Source: Standard & Poor's, Morningstar Inc., The Frank Russell Company, Lehman Brothers, Federal Reserve, Morgan Stanley Capital International, Moody's Bond Record, Salomon Brothers, World Bank, International Finance Corporation, International Monetary Fund, Federal Reserve, and Wall Street Journal. Data is for period ending 2002. Large-cap represented by the S&P 500 index, a commonly used broad based index of domestic stocks. The S&P 500® is an unmanaged stock index. Small-cap stocks are represented by the Russell 2000 Index, an index consisting of the smallest 2,000 companies in the Russell 3000 index (composed of 3,000 large U.S. companies as determined by market capitalization and represents approximately 98% of the investable U.S. equity market). Corporate Bonds are represented by the Lehman Brothers Aggregate Bond Index is a market-capitalization weighted index of investment-grade fixed-rate debt issues, including government, corporate, asset-backed, and mortgage-backed securities, with maturities of at least one year. The Lehman Brothers High Yield Bond Index includes fixed rate, public non-convertible, non-investment grade issues registered with the SEC that are rated BA1 or lower by Moody's Investor Service. Treasury Bonds are represented by the S&P Long-term Government Bonds index. Intermediate Term Treasury Bonds are represented by the Lehman Long Treasury bond Index is a 10-year Treasury note index. Treasury indices are total return indices held constant maturities. Foreign stock is represented by the Morgan Stanley EAFE Index is also known as the Morgan Stanley Capital International Europe, Australia, Far East Index of over 1,000 foreign stock prices. The index is translated into U.S. dollars. The MSCI EAFE (Europe, Australasia, and Far East) Index is a market-capitalization-weighted index that measures stock performance in 21 countries in Europe, Australasia and the Far East. Real Estate is represented by the National Association of Real Estate Investment Trusts (NAREIT): Gold prices obtained from International Monetary Fund, Federal Reserve, and Wall Street Journal. Indices include reinvested income, but not transaction costs or taxes, are unmanaged and cannot be purchased directly by investors. This chart is for illustrative purposes only and does not predict or depict the performance of any investment. Past performance is no guarantee of future performance.

Catching the Cyclical Waves

What has been the cyclical trend in equity and fixed-income performance?

In the past, positive equity performance has lasted three to five years. Beyond that it becomes a risky proposition to expect a positive trend to continue, although there have been select cycles where the positive trend has lasted much longer than the average. Just the same there have been much shorter positive trends than the average. Typically, fixed-income cyclical performance trends have lasted three years before positive performance started to become a less frequent annual event.

Exhibit 8.4 suggests that investors could go with a trend for a couple of years before trimming down positions. Of course, past performance is no guarantee of future results.

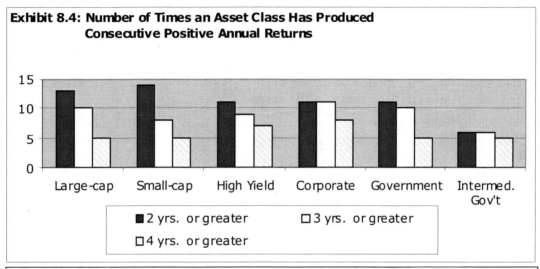

Exhibit 8.4: Number of Times an Asset Class Has Produced Consecutive Positive Annual Returns

Source: Standard & Poor's, Morningstar Inc., The Frank Russell Company, Lehman Brothers, The Federal Reserve, Morgan Stanley Capital International, Moody's Bond Record, Salomon Brothers. Data is for the 1926-2002 period. The S&P 500 Index is a commonly used broad based index of domestic stocks. The S&P 500® is an unmanaged stock index. S&P 500 is a registered trademark of Standard & Poor's Corporation. Investors cannot invest in the S&P 500 Index. Small-cap stocks are represented by the Russell 2000 Index, an index consisting of the smallest 2,000 companies in the Russell 3000 index (composed of 3,000 large U.S. companies as determined by market capitalization and which represents approximately 98% of the investable U.S. equity market). Government bonds are represented by the S&P Long-term Government Bonds Index. Intermediate Government bonds are represented by the Lehman Long Treasury Bond Index which is a 10-year Treasury note index. Treasury indices are total return indices held constant maturities. The Lehman Brothers High Yield Bond Index includes fixed rate, public non-convertible, non-investment grade issues registered with the SEC that are rated BA1 or lower by Moody's Investor Service. Corporate bonds are represented by the Lehman Brothers Bond Index. The Lehman Brothers Government/Credit Index measures the performance of all debt obligations of the U.S. Treasury and U.S. Government agencies, and all investment-grade domestic corporate debt. Indices include reinvested income, but not transaction costs or taxes, are unmanaged and cannot be purchased directly by investors. This chart is for illustrative purposes only and does not predict or depict the performance of any investment. Past performance is no guarantee of future performance.

What about downside cyclical trends?

Take a look at Exhibit 8.5. Generally, negative equity performance lasted one or two years. Fixed-income has typically had one down year usually when the Fed is tightening the money supply or has signaled that it plans to hike interest rates. Consecutive down years in the bond market have occurred, but it has historically been a low probability event. (Of course, past performance is no guarantee of future results).

As I have said in previous chapters, it can be a smart investment decision to get more exposure to an area of the market or asset class when it is at the tail end of its losing streak. In doing this, it is usually possible to catch the acceleration curve early on and potentially maximize returns.

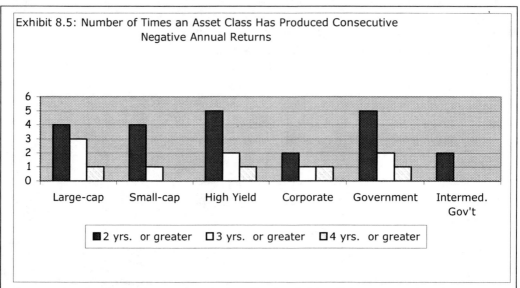

Exhibit 8.5: Number of Times an Asset Class Has Produced Consecutive Negative Annual Returns

Source: Standard & Poor's, Morningstar Inc., The Frank Russell Company, Lehman Brothers, Federal Reserve, Morgan Stanley Capital International, Moody's Bond Record, Salomon Brothers. Data is for 1926-2002 period. The S&P 500 index, a commonly used broad based index of domestic stocks. The S&P 500® is an unmanaged stock index: S&P 500 is a registered trademark of Standard & Poor's Corporation. Investors cannot invest in the S&P 500 Index; Small-cap stocks are represented by the Russell 2000 Index, an index consisting of the smallest 2,000 companies in the Russell 3000 index (composed of 3,000 large U.S. companies as determined by market capitalization and represents approximately 98% of the investable U.S. equity market); Government bonds are represented by the S&P Long-term Government Bonds index; Intermediate Government bonds are represented by the Lehman Long Treasury Bond Index is a 10-year Treasury note index. Treasury indices are total return indices held constant maturities. The Lehman Brothers High Yield Bond Index includes fixed rate, public non-convertible, non-investment grade issues registered with the SEC that are rated BA1 or lower by Moody's Investor Service. Corporate bonds are represented by the Lehman Brothers Bond Index. The Lehman Brothers Government/Credit Index measures the performance of all debt obligations of the U.S. Treasury and U.S. Government agencies, and all investment- grade domestic corporate debt; Indices include reinvested income, but not transaction costs or taxes, are unmanaged and cannot be purchased directly by investors. This chart is for illustrative purposes only and does not predict or depict the performance of any investment. Past performance is no guarantee of future performance.

Cyclical Trend Analysis and the Active Management Process

Why spend so much time on cyclical trend analysis?

The goal of active fund management is to attempt to reduce risk by following cyclical trends that establish themselves and make appropriate adjustments to portfolio characteristics. Trends matter. Short-term fluctuations don't.

If the Fed is raising the Fed Funds' rate, then it is prudent to shorten the bond portfolio maturity. Irving Kahn, business partner of Benjamin Graham, once said, "A serious investor is not likely to believe that the day-to-day or even month-to-month fluctuations of the stock market make him richer or poorer. Nevertheless, the trends do".

The objective is to produce superior risk-adjusted returns by managing risk through a rebalance process that keeps the portfolio in sync with market conditions and shies away from overvalued areas of the market.

Why the emphasis on reducing risk?

In a nutshell, minimizing losses could potentially enhance returns. Everyone knows that by missing market rallies long-term returns fall below the market average. The corollary to not missing rallies is not fully participating in market downturns. By avoiding big losses, the long-term returns have a better chance at rising above the market average.

It is a known fact that no one has consistently and successfully timed each and every gyration of the market -- switching from stocks to cash and from cash to stocks -- anticipating bull and bear markets at precisely the market highs and market lows. However, it is possible to lower downside risk through proven investment management principles and tactical risk management strategies.

Top-Down Approach to Improving Portfolio Management - *IPM*™

> *"Investing is an applied science,*
> *not seat-of-the-pants, anything goes."*
> *-- Zvi Bodie*

The top-down approach to improving portfolio management borrows from the famous "Mosaic Theory" of stock selection. The Mosaic Theory approach to security analysis uses fundamental analysis and qualitative information to develop a picture that is used to determine a course of investment action.

Step one involves analyzing the macro-economic and market fundamentals that affect the equities and fixed-income asset classes. The process involves determining which factors exhibit a positive trend, then overweighting either equities or fixed-income. Likewise, factors that have turned neutral or negative are identified and then underweighted.

The goal is to identify the *turning points* in key economic and market fundamentals that have begun to establish themselves as a cyclical trend. It is not about "if" conditions will change, but understanding *when conditions have changed enough* to determine whether it is a better time to invest in stocks or bonds.

Exhibit 8.6: Cyclical Trend Analysis

Step 1: Monitor Economic and Market Fundamentals to Identify Cyclical Trends

	12 mos. Ago	6 mos. Ago	Latest #	Conclusion	
Economic:				**Equity+**	**Bond -**
Monetary policy	MZM 8% CAGR	MZM 10% CAGR	MZM 15% CAGR	Equity +	Bond -
Fed Funds Rate	6.5	6	5.5	Equity +	Bond +
Inflation	4.6	4.5	4.4	Equity +	Bond +
Interest Rates -10 Yr-T	5.29	5.43	5.56	Eqty. neu	Bond -
Real GDP Dollar	4.1	4.7	5	Equity +	Bond -
Unemployment	5.1	4.9	4.8	Equity +	Bond -
Consumer Confidence	90	96	98	Equity +	Bond -
Consumer Spending	up 2.1%	up 2.3%	up 2.8%	Equity +	Bond -
Fiscal	$10 Billion deficit	$2 billion deficit	$59 billion surplus	Equity +	Bond +
Fundamentals:				**Equity+**	**Bd. neu**
S&P Op Earnings	7% CAGR	10% CAGR	12% CAGR	Equity +	Bd. neu
S&P 500 P/E Valuation	20	23	25	Eqty. neu	Bond +
Yield Curve	Positive	Positive	Positive	Equity -	Bond +
Yield Spread	500 bp	400 bp	350 bp	Equity +	Bond +
Market Sentiment	Neutral	Positive	Positive	Equity +	Bond -
Technical Indicators:				**Equity+**	**Bond -**
NYSE Volume	903,000,000	1,180,000,000	1,500,000,000	Equity +	Bond -
Breadth	Negative	Positive	Positive	Equity +	Bond -
Moving Averages	55% Below	56% Above	68% Above	Equity +	Bond -
A/D	0.19	0.25	0.44	Equity +	Bond -
Put/Call	1.2	1	0.9	Equity +	Bond -
Short Interest	6	5.5	5	Equity +	Bond -

This table is for illustrative purposes only and does not predict or depict the performance of any investment. Past performance is no guarantee of future performance.

The Use (and Misuse) of the Index of Leading Indicators

The Index of Leading Indicators, released at each and every month end, is a compilation of ten forward-looking measures of domestic economic activity. Generally, it leads economic activity by six months. It does provides some insight into what is currently happening, but it is neither foolproof, nor the most reliable predictor of future economic activity. It is always better to wait for three to four changes before making tactical adjustments based upon the Index. Exhibit 8.7 shows what the Index of Leading Indicators is comprised of.

Exhibit 8.7: Leading Indicators

1. Average workweek: positive percentage increase indicates a pick up in economic activity.
2. Consumer orders: positive percentage increase indicates a pick up in economic activity.
3. Equipment orders: positive percentage increase indicates a pick up in economic activity.
4. Stock prices: rising market indicates economic growth to continue.
5. Consumer expectations: Positive increase indicates consumer expectations are high which could lead to higher demand for goods and services.
6. New jobless claims: A negative number indicates weaker economic activity.
7. Vendor performance: positive percentage increase indicates a pick up in economic activity.
8. Building permits: positive percentage increase indicates a pick up in economic activity.
9. Money supply: positive percentage increase indicates a pick up in economic activity.
10. Yield Curve. Positive curve indicates economic growth.

You can confirm the Leading Index's direction with the Federal Reserve Beige Book. If the Leading Index is rising, then it generally means that, at the very least, the economy is not slowing down. This is good news for equities and bad news for fixed-income.

Often bond traders will trade based upon a monthly report that is a component of the Leading Index. For example, where there is a significant drop in the latest new jobless claims, bond traders might sell long-term bonds on fears of inflation.

But tread carefully. It is usually best to wait for the release of the Beige Book to confirm Leading Index readings. The Beige Book is published eight times a year: January, March, April, June, July, September, October, and November. A series of strong reports favors equity investors and weak reports favor bond investors.

What should *not* be done?

It is wise not to use monthly economic numbers to rapidly and tactically allocate assets. The data is frequently subject to revision by the next quarter. Moreover, economic data is inherently volatile. The data is never linear but jumps about, zooming up some months and down others. Sixty-six percent of first reports on GDP from 1985-1999 have been lowered, then revised, according to Paine Webber.

Real time numbers are often distorted by weather-related issues or overreaction by investors. Keep in mind that one month or one quarter does not make a sustainable cyclical trend. Generally, it takes four to six months for an economic trend to be established, so do not be too quick to tactically allocate.

Tactical decisions are some of the most difficult decisions because they involve some speculation about the future. Again, the objective is not to predict the market, but stay in sync with cyclical trends. For example, if the Federal Reserve Board raises the Fed Fund's rate, then a portfolio's duration and credit quality must be evaluated based on where the economy is headed.

Are there any caveats?

Warning! Past relationships, past correlations, past patterns and trends cannot always be relied upon. The present often breaks with the past because of unexpected market and economic news and oversold or overbought conditions. External shocks such as wars, downgrading of a country's debt, energy shocks, overcapacity, asset bubbles, etc. can disrupt past patterns.

Take, for example, fund category performance cyclical patterns and trends. The small-cap is *not* supposed to do well in a bear market, yet the small-cap value fund category produced a positive 7.67% CAGR for the 3-yr. period ending 2002. Why? Because it was so oversold and undervalued going into the bear market of 2000-2002.

Here is another example of a past relationship and pattern not immediately repeating itself. When the market tanked in 2000 the Fed stepped in and lowered the Fed Fund's rate nine times from 4.5% to 1% which was a 45-year low! Typically, when the Fed cuts the Fed Fund's rate, the market moves higher 12 months later, and the economy recovers by 18 months later.

However, this time it took until 2003 for the markets to hold onto its gains and for the economy to get back on track. Terrorism, war, unemployment, corporate scandals, weak corporate earnings, bearish investor sentiment, and weak consumer confidence all weighed down the market and economy and caused the past relationship not to recur as it had done so before.

September happens to be the worst month for stock returns. Yet in any given September, unexpected good economic or markets news can spark a rally that can undermine past patterns. Overall, its is prudent to side with past relationships, but it is important to also check out valuations, the geopolitical environment, as well as the current macro and market environment to determine if the relationship stands a good chance of repeating itself.

Directional Indicators to Help You Find Your Way Through Confusing Markets

You can use directional indicators to get a sense of when to take some money off the table or put more money in the game. Here are some of the ones to watch:

Direction of Monetary Policy   Historically, the stock market advances 3-6 months before the economy recovers. Generally, it is prudent to buy stocks before the first Fed Funds rate cut. Listen to the comments made by the Fed. Are the comments accommodative or restrictive? If accommodative, then most likely a rate cut is on the way.

Fed Stock Valuation Model   When the 10-year T-note yield is greater than the S&P 500 E/P ratio, then stocks are overvalued and a sell could be warranted. When the 10-year T-note is less than the S&P 500 E/P ratio, then stocks are undervalued and a buy should be considered.

Short Sales by Specialists   When the ratio is greater than 50, then Specialists are selling which is a bearish sign; when it is less than 30, they are buying which is a bullish sign

Yield Spreads   When the yield spread between Treasury bonds and High Yield Bonds is widening, then it is a bearish sign. Generally, corporate profitability is improving when spreads narrow, and that is a bullish signal. Normally the yield spread between the T-note and T-bill is about 2%. When the spread widens, the yield curve becomes more positively sloped indicating stronger economic growth ahead. That is a signal to buy stocks.

Mutual Funds' Cash   If it is greater than 10% that is bullish, less than 5% is bearish.

Advisory Polls   When more than 60% of professional advisors are bearish, it is time to be bullish, and when less than 20% are bearish, follow that minority's bearish lead. The Sell-side Indicator is another contrarian indicator. A reading of 70%-plus indicates that most Wall Street Investment strategists are bullish. The market will soon get overbought so you should become bearish and sell. Forty percent of the time this indicator has predicted the variability in the S&P 500 Index return.

CBOE Put:Call Ratio   When the Put:Call ratio is greater than 0.50, the market is bearish, therefore be bullish; and when it is less than 0.35, the market is bullish so be bearish.

Insider Selling/Buying   Buy when corporate insiders buy and sell when they sell.

Fund Category Cash Flow   Begin trimming down fund category positions that have the highest 18 to 24 months' reported net cash flow.

CBOE Volatility Index (VIX)   Traders use VIX, and S&P 100 Index calls and puts to determine the direction of the market. High VIX readings of above 30 usually occur after a sell-off. High readings suggest that investors are bearish and the direction of the market is down. A contrarian views high readings as a buying signal. Typically, high volatility occurs when investors are panic selling. Low readings below 20 suggest the market direction is up. Low readings occur after a big rally when investors are bullish -- a time to sell if you are a contrarian.

Trend Analysis Conclusions

Trend analysis is a quantitative approach that seeks to identify turning points in trends and relies on current "bets" on established trends and not necessarily changing direction. Your cyclical trend analysis conclusions are the basis for determining tactical asset class weights among equities, fixed-income and cash.

Take a look at the summarized cyclical trend analysis in a table shown in Exhibit 8.8. This kind of table allows a market strategist to see the "big picture" and make required tactical asset allocation decisions among the three major asset classes -- equities, fixed-income, and cash/cash equivalents.

For example, the table below concludes that most of the major factors affecting equities are positive. Therefore, that is a signal to tactically overweight equities in every model portfolio.

Exhibit 8.8: Trend Conclusions

	Factors Affecting Equities			Factors Affecting Fixed Income		
	Positive	Negative	Neutral	Positive	Negative	Neutral
Policy	Monetary					Monetary
	Fiscal				Fiscal	
Fundamentals	Inflation			Inflation		
	Interest Rates			Interest Rates		
	GDP					GDP
			Dollar	Dollar		
		Unemployment		Unemployment		
		Consumer Spending		Consumer Spending		
	Earnings					Earnings
			Valuation			Valuation
Psychology	Consumer Confidence				Consumer Confidence	
	Market Sentiment	Geopolitical		Geopolitical	Market Sentiment	
Technical	Volume				Volume	
	Cash flow				Cash flow	
	Positive Yield Curve				Positive Yield Curve	

This table is for illustrative purposes only and does not predict or depict the performance of any investment. Past performance is no guarantee of future performance.

Using Qualitative Analysis to Make Quantitative Decisions

Quantitative approaches are not a certain road to riches. Therefore, it is best to overlay a qualitative assessment of the quantitative conclusions that are reached. A knowledgeable, experienced professional or Investment Policy Committee must make judgments on whether the trend will continue or turn based on investment savvy.

For instance, the trend conclusion in Exhibit 8.8 suggests an overweight position in equities. But a careful review of the "negatives" are also in order. In your opinion are they show stoppers? Is geopolitical risk an issue at the moment? If the negatives are not judged to be show stoppers, then an overweighting of equities makes sense.

As for fixed-income, it is a mixed conclusion. Therefore, you should take a neutral stance. Conclusions cannot be reached by assessing just one factor. The top four factors -- Fed policy, market fundamentals, investor psychology and technical indicators -- must be assessed relative to each other with policy and fundamentals largely carrying more weight in the decision.

You can use the Trend Analysis Conclusion table to give a client a bottom-line, quick, ten-second market update that covers the "four top factors" driving the market. For instance, "Policy is extremely positive, the Fed is on the market's side, the market Fundamentals are positive, investor Psychology is positive, and so are the Technical indicators. Overall, I'm very positive on stocks."

If the client asks for details on why any of the factors is so positive (or conversely, negative) you can use your cyclical analysis to provide further details about earnings' growth and so on. Keep it simple. Characterize each "top four factor" as either being positive, negative, or neutral/mixed.

While two wrongs don't make a right, three rights make for a smooth process toward the goal of improving portfolio management. The goal is to move assets to the:

1) right areas of the market --that means investing in areas of market that are reasonably priced showing improving relative strength.

2) when conditions are right;

3) in the right type of fund -- that is, into funds that are in favor. Based on the top-down analysis choose the fund categories that are most likely to perform the best looking forward based on cyclical trends and current valuation. For instance, in the recovery phase of the business cycle at the beginning of a bull market, the small-cap sector typically gains performance leadership. Therefore, you would overweight small-cap versus large-cap, and overweight growth style funds versus value funds.

Exhibit 8.9 shows a hypothetical situation where small-cap growth gains relative strength as the market enters its early bull phase.

Exhibit 8.9: Hypothetical Illustration of Fund Category Trend Analysis						
	Latest 12 months		**Last Quarter**		**YTD**	
	Growth	**Value**	**Growth**	**Value**	**Growth**	**Value**
Large-cap	**-10.0%**	-12.0%	**2.0%**	4.0%	**8.0%**	**10.0%**
Mid-cap	**-17.0%**	-14.0%	2.0%	1.0%	12.0%	10.0%
Small-cap	**-23.0%**	- 2.0%	**10.0%**	5.0%	**20.0%**	**15.0%**

This table is for illustrative purposes only and does not predict or depict the performance of any investment.

The Art of Closely Watching for Opportunities

It is always a good idea to keep a close tab on fund category trend performance in order to identify opportunities. In the August 2000 issue of *The Journal of Financial Planning*, an article by Thomas Zwirlein contends that the best way to invest is to buy funds with the best quarterly return for the latest ending quarter.

Keep an eye on the various Lipper style indexes to determine short-term cyclical trends. If one style starts to show improving relative strength over several consecutive quarters, then consider tilting assets toward that style. You should confirm fund category performance with economic and market research. If the small-cap sector starts to outperform the defensive large-cap area in a recession, you can check to see if your macro-economic analysis confirms that the economy is in a recovery phase.

Is relative strength in performance the only thing to focus on?

No. The value investor must be aware of price trends, and the trend investor must be cognizant of fundamental value. In other words, investors must not fight the tape, cyclical trends, or fund category momentum. However, at some point valuation will likely matter more than momentum.

In the past, equity cyclical trends were characterized by three phases: P/E expansion, earnings' momentum and surprises, and deceleration of sales growth resulting in firms missing earnings estimates. All good things end. Consider trimming back exposures while a category is still hot as valuations expand, and buying categories that are warming up by showing early signs price momentum.

Be on the look out for three major trend stoppers that can stall price momentum and cause corrections. These show stoppers can be responsible when your cyclical trend analysis conclusions do not to pan out:

1. **External shocks** such as higher energy prices, war, a jump in default rates, the large-scale sell-off of a major currency. A good example of an external shock is record oil prices in 2004. Energy prices skyrocketed due to a disruption in supply as a result of the war in Iraq and record worldwide demand. Even though policy and fundamentals were favorable (corporate earnings topped 20% growth rate over four consecutive quarters which has happened only four times since the 1950s, according to Thomson Financial), the stock market corrected.

2. **Fundamental imbalances** that develop, such as trade, inventories, supply and demand, and extreme valuations compared to historical averages. The 2000 asset bubble in the stock market was partly blamed on overcapacity in many economic sectors especially Telecommunications. On top of that, security valuations hit stratospheric levels based on unrealistic earnings growth projections based on a "new economy".

3. **Policy errors** such as where the monetary policy is too restrictive or too loose or where the trade policy is too protective.

Unexpected shocks to the markets and economy have a greater impact on market valuations than anticipated events. An already anticipated rise in energy prices is less harmful than an unanticipated one and routine business planning will build it into the cost of doing business. Airlines will raise prices to cover costs, and securities markets will reflect higher operating costs and higher or lower profits in the stock price.

IPM Proactive Management

> *I've always been in the right place at the right time.*
> *Of course, I steered myself there.*
> --Bob Hope

Proactive Investment Management

Knowing When to Hold 'Em and When to Fold 'Em

Proactive investment management acknowledges that things do change. Therefore, minor changes to a portfolio are usually in order to keep it on track.

Frozen pie strategic strategies generally ignore changes in the market and assume that in 10 years the world will be a better place at the exact time you need to sell. It embodies the laid back "don't worry if it is left alone, everything will work out" approach.

However, static strategies can cause challenges. Simply put, studies have shown that even strategic portfolios perform better when rebalanced each quarter. Rebalancing seeks to sell appreciated assets that may have become overvalued investments, and buy depreciated assets that perhaps are now undervalued assets. The "net" result could lower portfolio fluctuation, reduce downside movement, and potentially generate more consistent returns.

Professional portfolio construction works to get a client on track. Tactical management aims to keep a portfolio on track and on goal. You can adjust a portfolio throughout the cycle to manage risk by keeping it in sync with changing market conditions, such as making tactical decisions to overweight or underweight the various fund categories. But it is a good idea to never make wholesale changes and completely abandon any core fund category.

The great hockey player Wayne Gretzky once said that you want to be were the puck is going to be - not where it is. The same can be said of portfolio management.

They key is to find where the value is in the market or where the momentum is. Just the same, it is prudent to be counterintuitive with "category tilts." When cash flows have been high for a considerable period of time for stock funds, it would be smart to start to buy bond funds and vice versa. Obviously, you should confirm the "crowd buying effect" with other directional indicators mentioned in previous chapters. You can easily rotate assets from overvalued fund categories to undervalued ones.

The puck was in the Treasury bond space from 2000 through 2002. Treasury yields hit all time lows. That became a space to avoid. Here are some more tactical contrarian moves you might wish to consider:

- Precious metals and utilities funds tend to do well when the S&P 500 Index doesn't.
- When the Confidence index is rising, and yields spreads begin to narrow, you might want to overweight non-investment grade bonds.
- When short sales by Specialists are rising, it can be a signal to reduce equity exposure.

Money moves from stocks to bonds when investors' worries about economic growth and earnings escalate. Money moves from bonds and certain stock groups to cash-equivalents when economic growth surges and the threat of inflation and higher interest rates loom.

Why?

Higher interest rates reduce the present value of a company's future cash flow. Higher rates indirectly cause profits to drop. As I have mentioned before, knowing when to underweight and overweight investments requires a commanding knowledge of economic indicators, investor sentiment, price movements, valuations, and technical aspects of the market.

Keenly Observing Trends and Signals

What key trends, signals and changes should you be watching out for?

A wise advisor will keep a close eye on the direction of inflation and interest rates. Inflation has a big impact on the level of interest rates and on yields. Generally, rising inflation and interest rates are a threat to the market and could cause a market to take a downward turn. The opposite conditions tend to facilitate up markets.

Deflation is just as bad for stocks as inflation. Corporate profit margins shrink in a deflationary economy. Bonds tend to perform well in non-inflationary and low to moderate interest rate environments.

Next, you can focus on the trend of economic growth and earnings. Generally, decelerating economic and earnings growth causes equity valuation corrections.

So when should you increase exposure to stocks?

It can be a good idea to consider increasing equity exposure during a period of economic growth characterized by moderate inflation and declining bond yields. Watch closely the relationship between bond yields and stock prices. Generally, bond yields drop when stock prices rise. Why? A lower discount rate generates a higher P/E multiple. The opposite happens when yields rise.

When inflation and bond yields are moving down, P/E multiples expand and stocks do well. When inflation and bond yields move up, P/E multiples go down, as they did from 1961 to 1975, and in the last bull market ending March 2000.

Earnings downturn, stable inflation, and bond yields will keep multiples from expanding. Historically, double-digit market returns required EPS growth of seven percent plus, lower inflation, and lower bond yields.

You will want to consider an overweight position in stocks when the stock market's P/E is below 20. Exhibit 9.1, which follows, shows that when buying an investment that tracks the S&P 500 Index at a P/E close to 17 or less, the compounded annual return has been greater than nine percent. Other studies have shown that, historically, buying when the P/E is below 17 produced 10-year annualized returns of seventeen percent! Ten-years forwarded return drops to single digits and negative when buying an S&P 500 Indexed investment that is trading at a P/E in the 20s. Consider an underweight position in stocks when the forward P/E is above 22.

Exhibit 9.1: Good Time To Buy Is When There Was a Sale		
P/E Range	**Annualized Return in the Next 10 Yrs.**	**Worst Total Return in the Next 10 Yrs.**
11.7-14.1	10.0%	4.1%
14.1-16.7	9.0%	-19.9
16.7-19.4	5.4%	-23.1%
19.4-32.6	-0.4%	-35.5%

Source: AIMR 1926-2002. Stocks are represented by the S7P 500 Index. The S&P 500 is a total return index widely regarded as the standard for measuring large-cap U.E. stock market performance and includes a representative sample of 500 leading companies based on industry representation, liquidity, and stability. Historically includes 400 industrial stocks, 40 financial stocks, 40 public utility stocks, and 20 transportation stocks. Indices include reinvested income, but not transaction costs or taxes, are unmanaged and cannot be purchased directly by investors. This table is for illustrative purposes only and does not predict or depict the performance of any investment. Past performance is no guarantee of future performance.

A Word about Valuations and Risk Premiums

But be careful applying historical averages. Past markets are never exactly alike. It is better to use relative measures not absolute ones. An asset class can become overvalued by as much as 20% before a correction occurs. This means an investment category can be overvalued and still be attractive on a valuation-momentum-reward basis.

The S&P Barra 500 Growth Index was 15% overvalued in 1997, but it rose 42.16% in 1998, and 43.09% in 1999. In June 1949, just before the 1950-1966 bull market, the S&P 500 Index multiple stood at 9.07. In January of 1966, at the end of the 1950-1966 bull market, the multiple peaked at 24.06. In July 1982, at the bottom of the 1966-1982 bear market, the multiple was 6.64 . By the end of the greatest bull market, the 1982-1999 bull, the multiple had stretched to an astounding 44.20.

In the past, a good time to buy stocks was when the historical equity risk premium was high. The equity risk premium is the excess return investors demand for buying stocks instead of risk-free Treasury bills. It is the difference between the risk free rate and the twelve-month trailing S&P 500 return. A higher risk-premium means investors require a higher return and when it drops, investors require a lower return.

The equity risk premium has an inverse relationship with stock valuations. A higher risk premium means lower valuations -- that is generally a good time to buy. A lower risk premium means higher valuations -- usually signaling it is a bad time to buy. During periods of economic certainty and growth the equity risk premium falls. The opposite happens during periods of uncertainty.

Recent studies by Eugene Fama and Kenneth French suggest that the mean equity risk-premium is 4.5%. While this is not an absolute given, it can be best to consider an over weight in stocks when the equity risk premium is higher then four, and under weight stocks when it is lower then four. Any decision to overweight or underweight must be supported by market research (see the explanation of "PFPT" in Chapter Two. Research indicates that the equity risk premium by itself does not explain the variation in market returns.

Exhibit 9.2: Buy Stocks When Investors Worry About Equity Returns

	Equity Risk Premium	10 Yrs. Avg. Return
1960's	4.7%	8.68%
1970"s	1.22%	7.56%
1980's	8.63%	18.19%
1990's	13.39%	18.98%

Source: Eugene Fama and French; Journal of Investment Management. Source: AIMR 1926-2002. Stocks are represented by the S7P 500 Index. The S&P 500 is a total return index widely regarded as the standard for measuring large-cap U.E. stock market performance and includes a representative sample of 500 leading companies based on industry representation, liquidity, and stability. Historically includes 400 industrial stocks, 40 financial stocks, 40 public utility stocks, and 20 transportation stocks. Indices include reinvested income, but not transaction costs or taxes, are unmanaged and cannot be purchased directly by investors. This table is for illustrative purposes only and does not predict or depict the performance of any investment. Past performance is no guarantee of future performance.

Getting the Timing Right on Equities

When should you consider reducing exposure to stocks?

High inflation has generally been bad news for stocks. Empirical research shows that there is an inverse relationship between inflation and stocks. You can overweight stocks when inflation is between 1% and 4%, and underweight stocks when inflation climbs above 5%.

The market cycle generally leads the economic cycle by six to twelve months. This is why certain industry groups are favored even when business conditions have not yet changed enough to promote strong earnings growth. When earnings growth does materialize, the market has already discounted the earnings growth into the stock prices.

It is good to know which industries are favored by forthcoming economic cycles (see more on the various parts of the cycle which follows) so that you can buy funds focusing in those industries. Non-cyclical defensive stocks outperform right up to the market trough, and under perform up to its peak. Cyclical stocks typically under perform right up to the market trough, and outperform from trough to peak.

Exhibit 9.3: Market Cycle, and Favored Industry		
Market Cycle	Economic Cycle	Favored Industry
- Early Bull	Trough to recovery	Basic industries/materials, Financials
- Middle Bull	Recovery to expansion	Technology, Capital goods
- Late Bull	Expansion to Peak	Basic Industries, Metals, Chemicals, Energy
- Early Bear	Peak	Consumer Non-cyclical, Healthcare
- Middle Bear	Peak to trough	Utilities, Consumer Staples
- Late Bear	Trough bottom	Durable & Non-durable Consumer, Cyclical (Housing, auto, Tech., Financials).

This table is for illustrative purposes only and does not predict or depict the performance of any investment. Past performance is no guarantee of future performance.

When the economy bottoms out, you might consider increasing weightings in funds that have significant exposure to cyclical industries. When a recovery is about to begin, usually marked by low inflation, and after a series of rate cuts, interest rate-sensitive cyclical industries do well. These are typically: technology, housing, autos, transportation, banks, entertainment, and retailers. Cyclical stocks, whose earnings are cyclical just like the economy, depend upon a healthy economy to increase earnings and their stock prices. Cyclical stocks tend to rally during economic recoveries but trail in recessions. When GDP and inflation is trending toward four percent, you will want to build exposure to defensive funds that invest in Utilities, Energy, Consumer Staples, and Real Estate.

The Best Time to Buy Fixed-Income

When has historically been a good time to buy fixed-income investments?

Simply put, when yields rise and prices drop. When T-bond yields exceed the S&P 500's dividend yield by more than 3%, bonds should be on your shopping list.

The dividend yield of the S&P 500 Index has averaged approximately 3.85% from 1926 to 2002. When bond yields approach 6.5%, the risk and reward outlook for stocks generally becomes less favorable. Consequently, bonds become undervalued and tend to become good buys, unless the Fed continues to raise the discount rate further. When the T-bond yield falls towards 5%, then stocks become attractive -- unless a recession is looming on the horizon. On average, T-bond's yielded 6.48% from 1950 to 2002, but the yield range extended broadly from 2.24% to 13.34!

In the past, it has been a good time to buy bonds just at the time that investors are worrying about bond defaults. It can be wise to buy bonds when the bond default premium is high, and sell bonds when it is low.

Historically, the bond default premium averaged 0.37% from 1950 to 2002. The highest default premium was 6.70%.

When the default premium exceeds its historical average and climbs higher, then bonds are said to be cheap to buy. When the premium is at or below the historical average, bonds are considered fairly valued or overvalued. There is an inverse relationship between bond prices and the default premium. Buying bonds on the cheap increases the potential for a higher return. Buying them at expensive levels decreases the return potential and consequently increases the loss potential.

You can overweight intermediate bonds and underweight long-term bonds when there is a persistent inflation trend (inflation breaches 3-1/2%). You can expect the Fed to raise the Fed Funds rate before the breach, and the bond market to sell-off long-term bonds before the Fed's action takes place.

The Time to Take a Shine to Precious Metals

What about the tactical use of precious metals investments?

Precious metals fund performance is driven by inflation, war, global crisis, and geopolitical uncertainty. The worse the news, the more they tend to shine. Commodity inflation is the precious metals' sector's best friend. Inflation expectation is just as important as actual inflation.

In 1993, inflation was trending upward but still not a problem. Even so, the Fed raised the Fed funds' rate two percent killing any chance for inflation to build. The return on the precious metals sector fell from a 1993 return of 17.68% to a 1994 return of negative 2.17%, according to Morningstar Inc.

Exhibit 9.4: Precious Metals Loves Inflation and War!

Year	Inflation	Return	Event
1973	8.8%	72.96%	High inflation
1974	12.2%	66.15%	High inflation
1979	13.31%	126.5%	High inflation
1980	12.4%	15.14%	Low inflation
1993	2.9%	17.68%	High inflation expectation
1994	2.75%	-2.17%	Fed Fund's rate hikes
1997	1.7%	-21.68%	Low inflation
1998	1.61	-0.48%	High inflation
2001	1.55	18.77%	War on terrorism
2002	2.38	62.96%	War on terrorism

Source: Gold prices obtained from the IMF, World Bank and Wall Street Journal. Inflation figures obtained from the Federal Reserve Bank. This table is for illustrative purposes only and does not predict or depict the performance of any investment. Past performance is no guarantee of future performance.

Generally, precious metals do not perform well in a rising market. In the past, this sector has usually dropped in value as the market has risen and as economic and political certainty has been building. Yet the relationship does not *always* hold true. In 2002-2003, the market entered its early bull market phase with small-cap stocks climbing more than 40% in 12 months, as measured by the Russell 2000 index. Yet the Precious Metals sector climbed 60% in 2002 which was followed by another surge of 40% in 2003 due to terrorism and geopolitical uncertainty.

Should a fund investing in commodities ever be considered as a tactical maneuver?

Commodities rise in value when stocks and bonds fall in value. So when you need performance, commodities generally deliver. You can buy commodities when the dollar weakens, inflation pressure builds, as economic growth exceeds three percent, and geopolitical risk heightens.

A Summary of Tactical Asset Allocation Decisions in Rising and Declining Markets.

What are some possible asset allocation guidelines to follow for common portfolio objectives?

Exhibit 9.5 shows recommended tactical asset allocation weights each portfolio could assume during up, somewhat flat, and down markets. The change in weights seeks to minimize downside and improve upside results.

Of course, there is no guarantee that these weights will accomplish the goal set out for each and every client. But, based upon investment history, these tactical weights were favorable for improving portfolio results versus maintaining the strategic weightings shown in exhibit 9.5.

Exhibit 9.5: Summary of Tactical Asset Allocation Decisions

Four Common Portfolio Objectives	Strategic Asset Allocation	Down Mrt. Asset Allocation	Up Mrt. Asset Allocation		Strategic Asset Allocation	Down Mrt. Asset Allocation	Up Mrt. Asset Allocation
1. Growth Objective				**3. Income & Growth Objective**			
S&P 500 Index	35%	50%	20%	S&P 500 Index	20%	20%	20%
Small-cap stock	35%	20%	45%	Small-cap stock	10%	0%	20%
International	25%	10%	30%	International	10%	5%	15%
Intermediate Gov't	0%	15%	0%	Corporate Bond	30%	10%	40%
Treasury Bill	5%	5%	5%	Government Bond	15%	25%	0%
				Intermediate Gov't Bond	10%	30%	0%
				Treasury Bill	5%	10%	5%
2. Growth & Income Objective				**4. Income Objective**			
S&P 500 Index	25%	35%	15%	S&P 500 Index	10%	5%	10%
Small-cap stock	15%	5%	40%	Small-cap stock	0%	0%	5%
International	20%	5%	25%	Corporate Bond	55%	20%	60%
Corporate Bond	25%	10%	20%	Government Bond	10%	30%	0%
Government Bond	5%	10%	0%	Intermediate Gov't Bond	20%	35%	20%
Intermediate Gov't Bond	5%	25%	0%	Treasury Bill	5%	10%	5%
Treasury Bill	5%	10%	5%				

Source: Standard & Poor's. Lehman Brothers, Morgan Stanley Capital International, The Frank Russell Company, Federal Reserve. The S&P 500 index, a commonly used broad based index of domestic stocks. The S&P 500® is an unmanaged stock index: S&P 500 is a registered trademark of Standard & Poor's Corporation. Investors cannot invest in the S&P 500 Index; Small-cap stocks are represented by the Russell 2000 Index, an index consisting of the smallest 2,000 companies in the Russell 3000 index (composed of 3,000 large U.S. companies as determined by market capitalization and represents approximately 98% of the investable U.S. equity market); International is represented by the MSCI EAFE (Europe, Australasia, and Far East) Index is a market-capitalization-weighted index that measures stock performance in 21 countries in Europe, Australasia and the Far East. Government bond is represented by the S&P Long-term Government Bonds index; Intermediate Government bond is represented by the Lehman Long Treasury Bond Index is a 10-year Treasury note index. Treasury indices are total return indices held constant maturities. The Lehman Brothers High Yield Bond Index includes fixed rate, public non-convertible, non-investment grade issues registered with the SEC that are rated BA1 or lower by Moody's Investor Service. Treasury bill is represented by the Lehman Brothers Three month Treasury Bill Index derived from secondary market Treasury bill rates published by the Federal Reserve Bank or the 91-day Treasury bills data. Corporate bonds are represented by the Lehman Brothers Bond Index. The Lehman Brothers Government/Credit Index measures the performance of all debt obligations of the U.S. Treasury and U.S. Government agencies, and all investment- grade domestic corporate debt; Indices include reinvested income, but not transaction costs or taxes, are unmanaged and cannot be purchased directly by investors. This chart is for illustrative purposes only and does not predict or depict the performance of any investment. Past performance is no guarantee of future performance.

How to Use the Business Cycle to Tactically Manage

Understanding the Business Cycle

> *"Forecasting is difficult especially about the future."*
> -- Victor Bogle

The classic business cycle is mark by contraction and expansion activity and is divided into four phases:

I.   Trough to recovery
II. Recovery to expansion
III. Expansion to peak
IV. Peak to trough

Like any model it simplifies matters. The different phases tend to overlap or sometimes skip from one to another and then revert back.

For example, the economy sometimes slips into a recession and then emerges into a brief economic pickup only to recede back into a recession again. This is called a "double dip" recession.

Changes in the level of inflation and employment are a common part of each phase. Eventually, inflationary pressure causes higher rates that slow down in economic activity driving unemployment higher. You can use unemployment rate and inflation rate data to determine where in the the business phase you are.

Is each business cycle the same?

No. As mentioned earlier, no two business cycles are exactly alike. Traditional factors such as employment, consumer demand, and inflation fluctuate and will influence each business cycle. In addition, non-traditional elements, such as currency exchange rates, global competition, and new technologies, have an affect that makes the cycle slightly different from the last one. Moreover, certain characteristics of a cycle may seem out of sync with other characteristics. For instance, there may be strong GDP growth, low unemployment, but yet still low inflation. However, there are more similarities than dissimilarities.

How long is a typical business cycle?

The full business cycle, from start to finish to start again, is roughly a five-year cycle. Typically, the cycle takes 17 months to move from peak to trough and 38 months to move from trough to peak again. The amplitude and duration of each cycle will differ. In addition, a severe recession does not always have to be part of the cycle.

Be cautious and careful when applying these averages. Expansions and contractions just do not die of old age. However, in the modern day economy contractions have been shorter and expansions longer. Exhibit 9.6 shows past business cycles and their duration.

Exhibit 9.6: Business Cycle and Market Cycle				
Peak	Trough	Contraction in Months	Expansion in Months	Cycle In Months
		Peak to Trough	Previous trough to Peak	Trough from previous Trough	Peak from previous Peak
	December 1854	--	--	--	--
June 1857	December 1858	18	30	48	--
October 1860	June 1861	8	22	30	40
April 1865	December 1867	32	46	78	54
June 1869	December 1870	18	18	36	50
October 1873	March 1879	65	34	99	52
March 1882	May 1885	38	36	74	101
March 1887	April 1888	13	22	35	60
July 1890	May 1891	10	27	37	40
January 1893	June 1894	17	20	37	30
December 1895	June 1897	18	18	36	35
June 1899	December 1900	18	24	42	42
September 1902	August 1904	23	21	44	39
May 1907	June 1908	13	33	46	56
January 1910	January 1912	24	19	43	32
January 1913	December 1914	23	12	35	36
August 1918	March 1919	7	44	51	67
January 1920	July 1921	18	10	28	17
May 1923	July 1924	14	22	36	40
October 1926	November 1927	13	27	40	41
August 1929	March 1933	43	21	64	34
May 1937	June 1938	13	50	63	93
February 1945	October 1945	8	80	88	93
November 1948	October 1949	11	37	48	45
July 1953	May 1954	10	45	55	56
August 1957	April 1958	8	39	47	49
April 1960	February 1961	10	24	34	32
December 1969	November 1970	11	106	117	116
November 1973	March 1975	16	36	52	47
January 1980	July 1980	6	58	64	74
July 1981	November 1982	16	12	28	18
July 1990	March 1991	8	92	100	108
March 2001	November 2001	8	120	128	128

Source: NBER

Generally, the market mirrors -- and leads -- the business cycle. A market cycle usually has three to four up years followed by one or two down years.

Exhibit 9.7: The Market Has Hit Bottom Five Months before Recession Troughs		
Recession	**S&P 500 Low**	**Lead Time**
Nov. 1948 – Oct. 1949	June 13, 1949	4.6
July 1953 – May 1954	June 14, 1953	8.4
Aug. 1957 – April 1958	October 22, 1957	6.2
April 1960 – Feb. 1961	October 25, 1960	4.1
Dec. 1969 – Nov. 1970	May 26 1970	6.2
Nov. 1973 – March 1975	October 3, 1974	5.9
July 1981 – Nov. 1982	August 12, 1982	3.6
July 1990 – March 1991	October 11, 1990	5.5

Source: NBER and Standard & Poor's. The S&P 500 is a total return index widely regarded as the standard for measuring large-cap U.E. stock market performance and includes a representative sample of 500 leading companies based on industry representation, liquidity, and stability. Historically includes 400 industrial stocks, 40 financial stocks, 40 public utility stocks, and 20 transportation stocks. Indices include reinvested income, but not transaction costs or taxes, are unmanaged and cannot be purchased directly by investors. This chart is for illustrative purposes only and does not predict or depict the performance of any investment. Past performance is no guarantee of future performance.

Maneuvering Through the Business Cycle

You can use business cycle analysis to make changes to asset allocations and fund category weightings. Each phase of the business cycle favors certain investments. If you study Exhibit 9.8 which follows, you will be able to get a good feel of when an asset class of fund category might do well based upon historical performance.

But be extra careful when applying the results shown in Exhibit 9.8 going forward. Factors such as valuations, currency exchange rates, interest rate differentials between countries, debt levels at the Government/corporate/household levels, defaults rates of corporations and individual households, geopolitical risks, energy prices and supply, overcapacity issues, etc. can impact performance of the business cycle and skew historical results going forward.

It is smart not to overweight overvalued investments. Likewise, even though an asset class or sub-asset class may not be favored within the current phase of the business cycle, it still may be a good investment due to attractive valuations or where other alternative investments are overvalued.

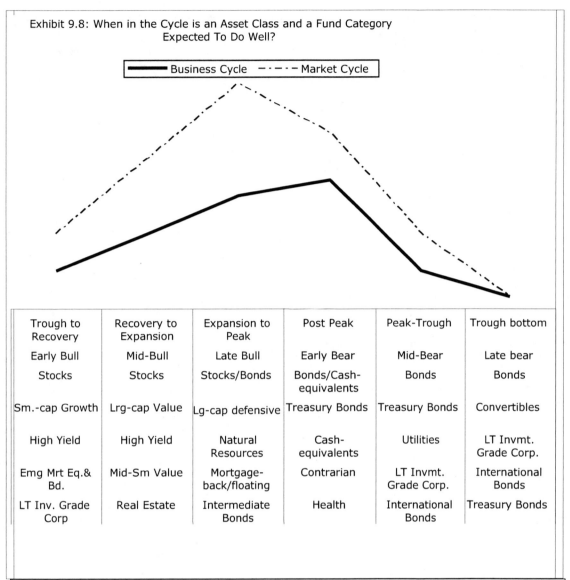

Exhibit 9.8: When in the Cycle is an Asset Class and a Fund Category
Expected To Do Well?

Trough to Recovery	Recovery to Expansion	Expansion to Peak	Post Peak	Peak-Trough	Trough bottom
Early Bull	Mid-Bull	Late Bull	Early Bear	Mid-Bear	Late bear
Stocks	Stocks	Stocks/Bonds	Bonds/Cash-equivalents	Bonds	Bonds
Sm.-cap Growth	Lrg-cap Value	Lg-cap defensive	Treasury Bonds	Treasury Bonds	Convertibles
High Yield	High Yield	Natural Resources	Cash-equivalents	Utilities	LT Invmt. Grade Corp.
Emg Mrt Eq.& Bd.	Mid-Sm Value	Mortgage-back/floating	Contrarian	LT Invmt. Grade Corp.	International Bonds
LT Inv. Grade Corp	Real Estate	Intermediate Bonds	Health	International Bonds	Treasury Bonds

Source: Standard & Poor's, Barra Inc. Lehman Brothers, Morgan Stanley Capital International, The Frank Russell Company, National Association of Real Estate Investment Trusts, Federal Reserve. Study is for 1950-2003 period. Large-cap represented by the S&P 500 index, a commonly used broad based index of domestic stocks. The S&P 500® is an unmanaged stock index: Large-cap Growth represented by S&P 500 Barra Growth Index; Large-cap Value represented by S&P 500 Barra Value Index; Mid-cap Growth represented by S&P MidCap 400/Barra Growth Index; Mid-cap Value represented by S&P MidCap 400/Barra Value Index; Small-cap Growth represented by S&P SmallCap 600/Barra Growth Index; Small-cap Value represented by S&P SmallCap 600/Barra Value Index. Long term bonds represented by the S&P Long-term Government Bonds index; Intermediate Term bonds are represented by the Lehman Long Treasury Bond Index is a 10-year Treasury note index. Treasury indices are total return indices held constant maturities. Cash-equivalents are represented by the Lehman Brothers Three month Treasury Bill Index derived from secondary market Treasury bill rates published by the Federal Reserve Bank or the 91-day Treasury bills data. International Equity represented by the Morgan Stanley EAFE Index is also known as the Morgan Stanley Capital International Europe, Australia, Far East Index of over 1,000 foreign stock prices. The index is translated into U.S. dollars. The MSCI EAFE (Europe, Australasia, and Far East) Index is a market-capitalization-weighted index that measures stock performance in 21 countries in Europe, Australasia and the Far East. The MSCI Emerging Markets Free Index represents a market-capitalization-weighted index of emerging market stock markets. Real Estate is represented by the National Association of Real Estate Investment Trusts (NAREIT): Indices include reinvested income, but not transaction costs or taxes, are unmanaged and cannot be purchased directly by investors. This chart is for illustrative purposes only and does not predict or depict the performance of any investment. Past performance is no guarantee of future performance.

Hypothetical Case Study of Using the Business Cycle to Proactively Manage Assets

The following section shows exactly how tactical allocation could be used with a Growth & Income objective portfolio utilizing a strategic allocation of 60% in equities, 35% in bonds, and 5% in cash-equivalents.

Of course, a hypothetical cast study can begin at any point within the full business cycle. Here is where I have chosen to step into our mock scenario:

Phase I Trough to Recovery

The Backdrop, Phase I:
Investor sentiment is pessimistic. The stock market is approaching a bottom point. Bond prices are nearing/at peak and bond yields have bottomed out (lower bond yields mean good news for stocks).

Facts to Know:
The stock market typically hits bottom 5.4 months before the economy hits its own trough. The average duration of a recession is eleven months.

The Strategy:
Begin to build equity exposure roughly halfway through the recession.

* Lower commodity prices typically signal a recession.
* In the first year of recovery, consumer price inflation tends to fall.
* Small-cap stocks tend to out perform large-cap after a bear market bottoms.
* Historically, value (cyclical stocks) outperform growth consumer stocks. But this trend does not always include growth technology related stocks following a recession.
* High yield usually outperforms Treasuries in the first 12-18 months of recovery as investor confidence is restored along with corporate profitability.
* Generally, the riskier areas of the market outperform the less risky areas.
* When bond yields, short-term rates, inflation, and GDP growth rises, that can signal that it is time to buy cyclical stocks in these sectors: autos, transportation, capital goods, energy, hotels, entertainment, and materials.

	Increasing	Decreasing	Stable	Selected Favored Asset	Asset Mix % Cash/Bonds/Stocks
Inflation		X		Stocks	5 %/35% /60%
Interest Rates		X		Mid-Small-cap	
GDP			X	High Yield Bonds	
Earnings			X	Foreign Bonds	
Employment			X	Corp. Investment Grade	
Consumer Spending			X	REITs	
Consumer Confidence	X				
Yields		X			

Recovery to Expansion - Phase II:

* Commodities bottom out, and interest rates are relatively low.
* Retail sales, housing starts, and consumer credit are all rising.
* Stocks trend upward because the "cost of money" is cheaper.
* Business and consumer borrowing and spending jump sharply higher.
* Consumer spending unleashes production, employment, and income, and creates even more demand. Economists refer to this as the "multiplier effect".
* Corporate earnings rise driving stock prices higher. Typically during the early bull phase companies easily beat the consensus S&P 500 earnings growth forecast by more than three percent. In the mid-bull phase companies beat the consensus earning forecast by 2-3%.

- This may be a good time to buy growth stocks/funds in the technology, telecommunications, media, pharma, biotech, software and services, and hardware and equipment sectors.
- Consumer spending picks up and corporate earnings start to beat estimates.
- Small- to mid-cap stocks are favored.
- Corporate bonds, especially high yield bonds, are favored due to healthy corporate earnings growth.
- Convertible bond investments may do well versus Treasury issues due to a favorable yield spread and appreciation potential.

	Increasing	Decreasing	Stable	Selected Favored Asset	Asset Mix % Cash/Bonds/Stocks
Inflation			X	Stocks	5%/20%/75%
Interest Rates			X	Small-cap	
GDP	X			Mid-cap	
Earnings	X			Convertible Bonds	
Employment	X			Corporate Bonds	
Consumer Spending	X			High Yield	
Consumer Confidence	X				
Yields	X				

Expansion to Peak - Phase III:

- Consumer confidence and spending is at a high!
- Retail sales, housing starts, and consumer credit is very robust.
- Economy is strong.
- Inflationary pressures mount.
- During the expansion phase, the stock market rotates from areas that have grown expensive and performed well to areas that have trailed selling at lower valuations. Small-cap growth, mid-cap growth and large-cap growth assets tend to flow into value sectors (large-cap, mid-cap, and small-cap) to keep the bull running.
- EPS growth supports this rotation, but the Fed Funds' rate hike(s) begins creating worries about future EPS growth.
- Nearing the market peak, large-cap defensive stocks -- such as consumer non-durables, utilities, pharmaceuticals are favored.
- Generally, less risky areas of the market start to come into favor.
- Small-cap stocks are typically cycling out of favor in a rising rate environment.
- Non-investment grade bonds become out of favor as higher rates threaten the expansion.
- Safer short- to intermediate-Treasury issues are in favor.
- Stock prices generally peak eight months before the economy slows down. Thus, it can be wise to begin to take equity profits when stock funds' cash inflows hit peak or record levels.
- A contrarian fund that sells short the market is now a prudent investment.

	Increasing	Decreasing	Stable	Selected Favored Asset	Asset Mix % Cash/Bonds/Stocks
Inflation	X			Stocks	10%/25%/65%
Interest Rates	X			Large-cap	
GDP	X			Foreign Equity	
Earnings	X			Emerging Markets	
Employment	X			Intermediate Bonds	
Consumer Spending	X			Mortgage-back	
Consumer Confidence	X			Commodities	
Yields	X			Contrarian	

Peak to Trough - Phase IV:

- Commodity prices hit highs at the market peak!
- Higher interests rates bring about the market decline, not a decline in corporate earnings as many people think.
- Retail sales, housing starts, and consumer credit all decline from highs. The Fed Funds' rate cuts begin after the market corrects and the economy shows early signs of a slowdown (evidenced by lower spending by both consumers and businesses).
- Interest rates decline, inflation falls, GDP growth weakens, and business and consumer confidence falls.
- Bond yield curve flattens.
- Now would be a good time to buy into defensive areas including growth stocks/funds invested in the food, drug, health care, and utilities sectors.
- Investment grade short- to intermediate-bonds are favored.
- Convertible bond funds do well during volatile periods and recessions.
- Dividend paying stocks, such as utility stocks, are now in favor.
- Foreign bond funds perform well when foreign economies are growing, have higher rates, and sport lower inflation than the U.S. economy.
- This would be an opportune time to consider buying financials, such as diversified financials, insurance companies, banks, as bond yield spreads begin to narrow.

	Increasing	Decreasing	Stable	Selected Favored Asset	Asset Mix % Cash/Bonds/Stocks
Inflation		X		Cash-equivalents	5%/55%/40%
Interest Rates		X		Money market	
GDP		X		LT Gov't Bonds	
Earnings		X		Large Defensive	
Employment		X		Utilities Fund	
Consumer Spending		X		Contrarian	
Consumer Confidence		X			
Yields		X			

Using the Yield Curve to Actively Manage the Bond Component of a Portfolio

Remember: Bad News Is Good News for Bonds

What Affects the Bond Market?

Inflation erodes the purchasing power of fixed income investments. Bond investors often react negatively to reports of economic strength because they fear that rapid economic growth will lead to inflation.

Given inflation of 3%, a 6% coupon bond generates a real rate of return (nominal rate minus the current inflation rate) of 3%. If inflation increases to 4%, the real rate of return drops to 2%! Bond investors look at data on inflation as measured by the CPI and PPI.

How can the Fed reduce inflationary pressure?

The Fed raises the Fed Fund's rate to slow down inflation. Eventually, restrictive monetary policy and higher rates slow economic activity and dampen inflation. Meanwhile, rising interest rates cause bond prices to fall. After inflation rose 2.9% in 1993, the Fed raised the Fed Fund's rate six times in 1994. Intermediate Government bonds, *as* measured by the Lehman Brothers Intermediate Bond Index, posted their worst year ever -- down 3.9%!

Exhibit 9.9: Expect Interest Rates to Rise When
1.   Excessive supply of money.
2.   There is inflationary pressure due to rising labor cost, and commodity prices
3.   Strong private and public sector demand for credit
4.   Restrictive monetary policy
5.   GDP growth is greater than four percent.
Past performance is no guarantee of future performance.

When the economy slows, inflation falls, interest rates decline, and bonds rally. Slower growth is good news for bond investors because it typically means a lower threat of inflation that reduces both interest rate and purchasing power risk. Consequently, the real rate of return on bonds gets better. In 1995, inflation dropped to 2.54% and Intermediate Government bonds, as measured by the Lehman Brothers Intermediate Bond Index, rose 16.69%!

Exhibit 9.10: Expect Interest Rates Fall When
1.   Disinflation.
2.   Weak demand for credit.
3.   GDP growth is less than three percent.
4.   Nonrestrictive monetary policy.
Past performance is no guarantee of future performance.

Understanding the Yield Curve

The yield curve can either be positive, negative or flat. Its slope is determined by credit quality, maturity, market supply and demand, liquidity premiums, fiscal policy, monetary policy, and current economic conditions.

Take, for example, fiscal policy. A Federal budget surplus means that the Government does not have to borrow which has historically driven down interest rates. The opposite is usually true for budget deficits. Monetary policy can influence yields too. In fact, eighty-five percent of the Treasury yield is determined by the Fed Funds' rate. Its shape will tell you which bond sectors to overweight.

A positive yield curve, with its typical shape, has an upward slope to it. That is because as the term to maturity lengthens, the yield increases in order to compensate investors for taking more risk to principal. It also slopes up when long-term bond prices fall due to the threat of faster economic growth, higher inflation, and liquidity premiums. Lower bond prices drive up the yield, while short-term notes and bill yields have dropped in responses to an accommodative monetary policy.

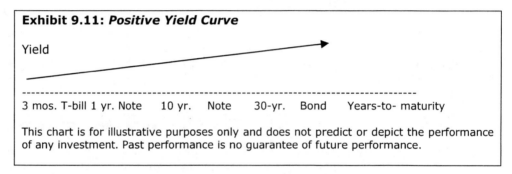

Exhibit 9.11: *Positive Yield Curve*

Yield

3 mos. T-bill 1 yr. Note   10 yr.   Note   30-yr.   Bond   Years-to- maturity

This chart is for illustrative purposes only and does not predict or depict the performance of any investment. Past performance is no guarantee of future performance.

When short-term yields such as those for T-bills are higher than Long-term Treasury bonds, the yield curve is said to be negative. In general, yield curve inversions have been associated with a restrictive monetary policy (Fed Fund rate hikes), economic slowdown, and peaking of yields. Investors tend to be pessimistic about the outlook for the economy. Higher short-term borrowing rates may eventually "choke" the economy, causing a recession.

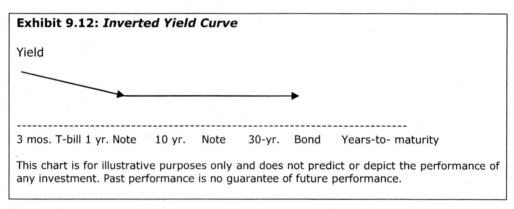

Exhibit 9.12: *Inverted Yield Curve*

Yield

3 mos. T-bill 1 yr. Note   10 yr.   Note   30-yr.   Bond   Years-to- maturity

This chart is for illustrative purposes only and does not predict or depict the performance of any investment. Past performance is no guarantee of future performance.

When short-term bond yields and intermediate-bond yields are approximately equivalent to long-term bond yields, the yield curve is seen as flat. A flat yield curve means that new bond investors will be paid about the same yield no matter what maturity bond they choose. Long-term bond yields are approximately the same as shorter-term maturity yields because long-term bond prices have usually climbed in anticipation of an interest rate cut. Other times, the yield curve flattens because the market is unsure of whether the economy is slowing down or beginning to pick up. At this point in time, the big question is: *when* will the Fed lower the Fed Funds' rate?

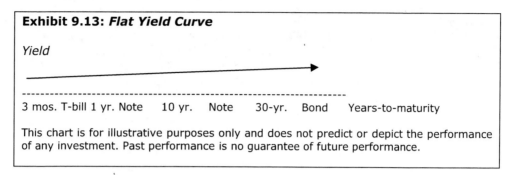

Exhibit 9.13: *Flat Yield Curve*

Yield

3 mos. T-bill 1 yr. Note   10 yr.   Note   30-yr.   Bond   Years-to-maturity

This chart is for illustrative purposes only and does not predict or depict the performance of any investment. Past performance is no guarantee of future performance.

Recognizing Yield Curve Influences and Changes

The bond market typically anticipates the Fed's actions by either buying or selling bonds. Thus, bond prices are driven up or down even before the Fed takes any action. This type of activity causes the yield curve to become either inverted or positive.

For instance, when the yield curve becomes flat the bond market expects that the Fed will lower rates. On the other hand, if the market believes the Fed will increase rates the yield curve will become positive. Long-term bond prices will drop in value due to a lack of demand (future economic activity may produce inflationary pressure increasing the threat of an interest rate increase) and yields will increase. Since 1980, bond yields have declined, on average, four months prior to a Fed Funds' rate cut. Likewise, yields have risen two months, on average, before a hike. The market is very efficient at discounting future Fed policy.

You can use the yield curve as an indicator of future economic activity. Here's how:

- **A positive yield curve** indicates that the market believes that future economic activity will be characterized by higher GDP growth, inflationary pressure, and that the Fed's next move is a rate hike.

- **A positive yield curve** suggests that the market is bullish on the economy and bearish on bond prices.

- **A negative sloping yield curve** usually is a fairly good leading indicator at predicting an upcoming recession. Yet yield curve inversion doesn't always result in a recession. Other fundamentals count, too, such as inflation, productivity growth, the federal fiscal picture, etc. In 2000, the yield curve inverted for technical reasons and not monetary ones. The U.S. Treasury decided to curtail issuance of 30-year Treasury bonds due to the $3 trillion budget surplus. This caused heavy buying of T-bonds driving up prices and driving down yields as the Fed tightened short-term rates.

- **A flat yield curve** implies that the economy may slow down over the next 12 months or that there is economic uncertainty. **A flat yield curve** is a leading indicator of a Fed rate cut.

Using the Yield Curve to Make Appropriate Fixed-Income Adjustments

You can use the yield curve to decide whether it is better to invest in short-term bonds, intermediate bonds, or long-term bonds at the present time. It is best to go long when the yield curve starts to flatten. When it is flat then intermediate and long-term bonds are yielding the same, and it usually does not pay to buy a longer-term bond so buy intermediate bonds.

When there is economic uncertainty, as indicated by a flat yield curve, investors may want to hedge their bet by constructing a laddered bond portfolio. A laddered portfolio would invest money evenly among short-term bonds, intermediate-term bonds, and long-term bonds. The goal of this strategy is to lower reinvestment risk, purchasing power risk, and interest rate risk as compared to the risk of investing under a single maturity strategy.

Moreover, conservative bond investors should not try to guess what the Fed's next move is, but instead buy short-term maturity bonds that provide the closest yield to intermediate maturity bonds. For instance, the six-month T-bill might be yielding more than the one-year T-note. As the spread between Government and corporate bond yields narrows, it is expected that the economy will not dip into a recession, nor rapidly expand causing inflationary pressure.

Bullet, Barbell or Ladder?

o   The Bullet approach does well when the yield curve is steeper compared to a Barbell approach and Laddered approach. In a rising interest rate environment, higher rates cause long-term bond prices to fall as higher inflation erodes the coupon value of short-term fixed income securities.
o   The Laddered approach does well when the economy is experiencing moderate growth and inflation.
o   The Barbell approach performs well when the Fed is raising short-term rates. When the yield curve flattens the Barbell approach should outperform the bullet approach.

The Skinny on Spreads

You should be able to use yield spreads to determine which bond fund categories to overweight and which to underweight.

Yield spreads between fixed-income credit categories tend to narrow in an expansion and widen in an economic slowdown or times of uncertainty. During a recession, yield spreads between lower quality bonds and higher quality bonds become wider. Yield spreads greater than 3% between short-term rates and long-term yields are associated with a slow down. During times of economic uncertainty, T-bonds experience heavy buying because investors' risk-aversion dramatically increases causing a "flight to quality" effect.

When the economy contracts, corporate bonds in cyclical industries experience greater yield spreads between Treasuries. Wider yield spreads reflect investor fear, but can also highlight buying opportunities. When yield spreads between corporate bonds and T-bonds are at peak levels in the cycle, it is then a good idea to overweight corporate and high yield positions. As the economy improves, yield spreads narrow between non-investment grade and investment grade sectors. Yield spreads of less than 3% between short (T-bill) and 10-year Treasury Notes imply that the economy is expected to expand.

Treasury bond spreads are notoriously volatile. They easily overreact to changes in interest rates because they carry virtually no credit risk. Therefore, it is prudent to wait for sustainable yield differentials before making a tactical decision. Again, don't become a Chicago Board of Trade futures trader.

The yield relationship between short-term bonds and 10-year notes is a closely watched economic bell weather. The economy is expected to get weaker if the spread between the current market yields on 10-year Treasury notes and Treasury bills becomes progressively smaller. At this point, it can be wise to buy short-term bonds since the yields are higher than long-term bonds given that the Fed is not expected to lower the Fed Funds' rate in the foreseeable future.

The Secrets of Determining When to Rebalance

"Two old adages on Wall Street; Never tangle with the tape, and never fight the Fed."

How often are adjustments made to a portfolio? The old adage is "Let your winners run." I think this is terrific advice. When the market has strong momentum, then stay invested. When the Fed is lowering rates, stay invested.

However, there comes a point when it makes sense to take profits. After all, the market does not move in a straight line up, and fund performance eventually falters. In general, most adjustments depend on cyclical trends, fund category valuations and relative strength.

Assess the following factors to determine if a rebalance is warranted:

1. **Overall market conditions** -- You can adjust any portfolio throughout the six phases of the market cycle according to the guidelines covered in this book in order to manage risk and maintain portfolio objectives.

2. **Asset class and fund category valuation and reward characteristics** - There is an inverse relationship between valuation and return. In the past buying overvalued investments has generally resulted in lower returns.

3. **Let core fund positions** (usually twenty percent of a portfolio's assets) **appreciate** to thirty percent before trimming back to desired levels.

You can rebalance to control creeping risk levels in a portfolio. Over time every portfolio will lose its strategic alignment because of changes in valuations of asset classes. By not periodically rebalancing, a conservative portfolio can become aggressive. When one asset class approaches a fifteen percentage point variance from target strategic weight, it is generally time to reduce it down to its target weight, and invest the proceeds into underweight asset classes. For instance, a Growth & Income portfolio's normal allocation is 60% in equities, but has grown to become 70%. It is best to rebalance it back in line with its strategic allocation. By sticking close to the strategic allocation -- within the 5%-15% range for each asset class -- the portfolio asset allocation will reflect the client's risk and reward preference.

A rebalanced portfolio will likely see reduced risk but without lowering return. The hypothetical portfolio in Exhibit 9.14 had 50% invested in the S&P 500 Index and 50% in the Lehman Brothers Aggregate Bond Index. Quarterly rebalancing of the portfolio from 1982 through 2001 reduced risk by 78% without lowering the return.

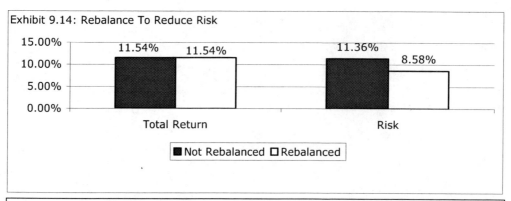

Exhibit 9.14: Rebalance To Reduce Risk

Source: Standard & Poor's, Lehman Brothers. Risk is measured by standard deviation is an indicator of the portfolio's total return volatility. The larger the portfolio's standard deviation, the greater the portfolio's volatility. Data reflects a hypothetical strategy with initial allocations of 50% to stocks as represented by the S&P 500 Index, and 50% to bonds, as represented by the Lehman Brothers 5-Year Treasury bond Index. The rebalanced strategy assumes that allocations were systematically rebalanced when they exceeded rebalancing threshold of 65% S&P 500 Index and Lehman Brothers 5-Year Treasury bond Index. The unrebalanced strategy assumes no rebalancing throughout the time period examined. Both hypothetical strategies assume an initial investment of $100,000. An investor cannot invest directly in an index or average and its performance does not reflect the performance of any mutual fund. The unmanaged S&P 500 Index and 5-Year Treasury Index do not reflect fees and expenses associated with the active management of a portfolio and are broad-based measures of the performance of U.S. stocks and U.S. bonds, respectively. 5-Year Treasury bonds are represented by bonds with the shortest maturity not less than five years. Treasury bonds provide fixed rates of return as well as principal guarantees if held to maturity. Investment returns and principal value of a mutual fund are not guaranteed and will fluctuate so that an investor's shares, when redeemed, may be worth more or less than their original cost. Past performance is not indicative of future results.

A rebalance of 5% had little impact on long-term returns and risk of a portfolio. Tactical changes of fifteen percentage points or greater were required to significantly change past long-term risk and return results. The bar chart in Exhibit 9.15 shows the results of tactical changes made to a portfolio allocated among Treasury-bills and the S&P 500 Index.

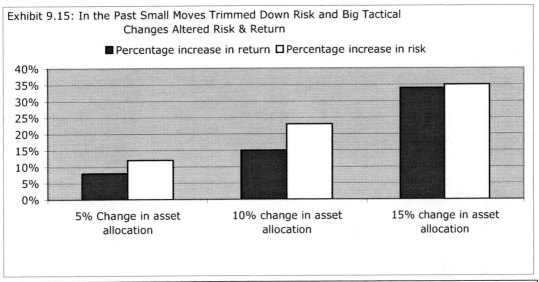

Exhibit 9.15: In the Past Small Moves Trimmed Down Risk and Big Tactical Changes Altered Risk & Return

Source: Thomson Financial, Lehman Brothers. Risk is measured by the Standard deviation which is an indicator of the portfolio's total return volatility. The larger the portfolio's standard deviation, the greater the portfolio's volatility. Data for period of 1926-2002 period. Data reflects a hypothetical strategy with initial allocations of 100%,in stocks as represented by the S&P 500 Index, and reducing stock exposure by 5%, 10%, and 15% by investing in bonds, as represented by the Lehman Brothers 5-Year Treasury Bond Index. The hypothetical strategies assume an initial investment of $100,000. An investor cannot invest directly in an index or average and its performance does not reflect the performance of any mutual fund. The unmanaged S&P 500 Index and 5-Year Treasury Index do not reflect fees and expenses associated with the active management of a portfolio and are broad-based measures of the performance of U.S. stocks and U.S. bonds, respectively. 5-Year Treasury bonds are represented by bonds with the shortest maturity not less than five years. Treasury bonds provide fixed rates of return as well as principal guarantees if held to maturity. Investment returns and principal value of a mutual fund are not guaranteed and will fluctuate so that an investor's shares, when redeemed, may be worth more or less than their original cost. Past performance is not indicative of future results.

Over the short-term minor moves may have a significant impact on risk and reward levels, especially when the market is in a free fall or is sky-rocketing.

You should keep in mind that even if profits are taken when rebalancing a portfolio, rebalancing to manage risk takes priority over saving money on taxes. More money can be lost in the market then to the IRS! Don't forget that long-term gains are taxed at 20%. That means an investor will lose only twenty cents on a dollars worth of gains. If the market takes a turn for the worse, then a dollar's worth of long-term gains could evaporate entirely and an investor would have nothing to pocket and opposed to pocketing eighty cents. If the tax event is significant, then you can reduce the tax bite by offsetting gains with other losses that can be harvested.

It may be necessary to rebalance as much as three times over a market cycle. This means that asset allocation changes may occur every eighteen to twenty-four months. Adjustments should be made when the market favors the proposed asset allocation and usually after an eighteen-month holding period.

General Guideline for Frequency of Tactical Asset Allocation Adjustments

It's hard for a portfolio manager to get up to the plate and not swing at the pitches especially when there are identifiable easy to hit "meat balls" being thrown.

That begs the question of how often should changes be made in a fund portfolio?

Swinging at bad pitches can turn an "at bat" into a strike out. Just the same, making too many changes with a portfolio could result in greater turnover without improved results. Exhibits 9.16, 9.17, and 9.18 offer some conservative guidance on how often to swing that bat. Exhibit 9.16 indicates when to overweight, or underweight, or be neutral in a major asset class.

Exhibit 9.16: Asset Class Changes to Consider

Asset Class	Late Bear/ Early Bull	Mid-Bull	Late Bull	Early Bear/ Mid Bear
Stocks	Overweight	Neutral	Underweight	Underweight
Fixed-Income	Underweight	Neutral	Overweight	Overweight
Cash	Underweight	Neutral	Overweight	Overweight

This table is for illustrative purposes only and does not predict or depict the performance of any investment. Past performance is no guarantee of future performance.

Exhibit 9.17 suggest what changes in asset class weights should be made and when. The principle being applied here is to sell euphoria and buy chaos. That means reduce stocks while the news is still good for stocks and just the same advice for bond investing.

Exhibit 9.17: Percentage in Stocks, Fixed-income, and Cash-equivalents

Portfolio Objective	Late Bear/ Early Bull	Late Bull/ Mid-Bull	Early Bear/ Mid-Bear
Growth	98%/0%/2%	90%/5%/5%	85%/10%/5%
Growth & Income	75%/23%/2%	60%/35%/5%	45%/45%/10%
Income & Growth	55%/43%/2%	40%/55%/5%	25%/65%/10%
Income	15%/83%/2%	10%/85%/5%	5%/85%/10%

This table is for illustrative purposes only and does not predict or depict the performance of any investment. Past performance is no guarantee of future performance.

Selling euphoria and buying chaos applies the greater fool theory. Don't be greedy. Leave some returns on the table to attract the next player. The name of the game is to book long-term profits and not try to sell at highs.

Exhibit 9.18 provides the concept behind selling a bit early while the going is good. This approach seeks to minimize downside risk by reducing exposure to asset classes and fund categories that have had a great run. It also entails not employing new cash into areas of the market that may have gotten pricier.

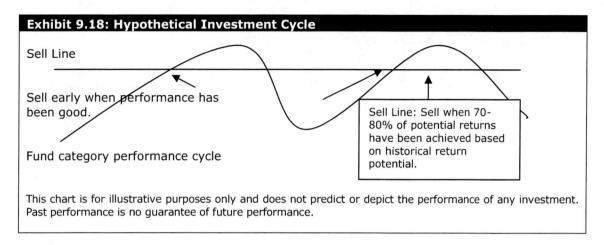

Exhibit 9.18: Hypothetical Investment Cycle

Sell Line

Sell early when performance has been good.

Fund category performance cycle

Sell Line: Sell when 70-80% of potential returns have been achieved based on historical return potential.

This chart is for illustrative purposes only and does not predict or depict the performance of any investment. Past performance is no guarantee of future performance.

Tactical Fund Category Tilts Need Not Cause Vertigo

It is perfectly okay to make fund category tilts throughout the cycle. Changes in fund category weight are made for two reasons. First, to manage overall portfolio characteristics such as capitalization weight, style orientation, P/E weight, foreign market exposure, credit quality weight, and duration. Don't forget that these characteristics have a big impact on a portfolio's performance, risk and return. Secondly, because each fund category will outperform and eventually become overvalued, it makes sense to change the weights accordingly.

You can expect to make fund category weight changes at least once every twenty-four to thirty-six months. Tactical adjustments coincide with the typical duration of a fund category's performance leadership. Try to make changes when asset classes are rebalanced in order to reduce trading activity.

Exhibit 9.19 suggests tactical weight guidelines (Overweight (OW), underweight (UW), and neutral (neu)) for a few fund categories.

Exhibit 9.19: Fund Category Tactical Adjustments

	Large-cap		Mid-cap		Small-cap		Treasury			Corporate Investment Grade	High Yield
	Value	Growth	Value	Growth	Value	Growth	Long	Interm.	short		
Early Bull	UW	UW	Neu	OW	OW	OW	UW	OW	UW	OW	OW
Mid-Bull	OW	Neu	OW	Neu	Neu	UW	Neu	OW	Neu	OW	Neu
Late-Bull	OW	OW	Neu	UW	UW	UW	OW	Neu	OW	UW	UW
Early Bear	Neu	Neu	UW	UW	UW	UW	OW	UW	UW	UW	UW
Mid-Bear	Neu	Neu	UW	UW	UW	UW	OW	UW	UW	UW	UW
Late-Bear	UW	UW	UW	OW	OW	OW	UW	UW	UW	OW	OW

Source: Barra Inc. Morningstar ®, Lehman Brothers: Large-cap Growth represented by S&P 500 Barra Growth Index; Large-cap Value represented by S&P 500 Barra Value Index; Mid-cap Growth represented by S&P MidCap 400/Barra Growth Index; Mid-cap Value represented by S&P MidCap 400/Barra Value Index; Small-cap Growth represented by S&P SmallCap 600/Barra Growth Index; Small-cap Value represented by S&P SmallCap 600/Barra Value Index. "Growth Stocks" have above average profitability and valuation characteristics. "Value Stocks" have below average profitability and valuation characteristics. Indices include reinvested income, but not transaction costs or taxes, are unmanaged and cannot be purchased directly by investors. Corporate bonds represented by the S&P Long-term Government Bonds index; Intermediate Term bonds are represented by the Lehman Long Treasury Bond Index is a 10-year Treasury note index. Treasury indices are total return indices held constant maturities. The Lehman Brothers High Yield Bond Index includes fixed rate, public non-convertible, non-investment grade issues registered with the SEC that are rated BA1 or lower by Moody's Investor Service. Short Treasury is represented by the Lehman Brothers Three month Treasury Bill Index derived from secondary market Treasury bill rates published by the Federal Reserve Bank or the 91-day Treasury bills data. Indices include reinvested income, but not transaction costs or taxes, are unmanaged and cannot be purchased directly by investors. This table is for illustrative purposes only and does not predict or depict the performance of any investment. Investments in mutual funds involve risk. Past performance is no guarantee of future performance. Mutual funds incur fees and expenses (including investment management and administrative fees). Obtain a prospectus for more complete information about the fund, including all fees and expenses, and should be read carefully before you invest. Past performance is no guarantee of future performance.

There will be opportunities to add fund categories not listed above to enhance performance during a particular phase. These opportunities may be special ones like geopolitical instability. For instance, precious metals funds have performed well in the past during periods of heighten geopolitical risk.

A few special opportunity funds to consider are utilities, precious metals, commodities, contrarian, international bond, real estate, pure mortgage-back, Zero-coupon, and convertible securities funds.

You can read on to Chapter Ten to find out when might be a good time to invest in these funds.

IPM Equity and Fixed Income Management

*"It's alright to fall in love with a security-until it gets overvalued.
Then let somebody else fall in love."*
-- Roy Neuberger

The How-to of Equity Management

Now you are ready to learn about the secrets of the **IPM** playbook that seeks to make money throughout market cycles.

The tactics in this playbook have worked for professionals, but cannot be guaranteed. These strategies rely on past investment trends and patterns to repeat themselves as the market moves through its typical cycle. More often than not these trends and patterns do materialize and play themselves out over a normal cycle. For instance, when the Fed lowers rates, bond prices move up. When the economy breaks out of a recession, small-cap stocks outperform large-cap equities. Market cycles and business cycle are expected to repeat themselves over the long-term. Ask around to affirm what I am telling you. Try someone who has been around the block quite a few times.

What exactly is there to manage with equity assets?

Managing equity assets requires attention to details of the **A.C.M.S.M.B.I.** of a portfolio. (See Exhibit 10.1).

Here are the important factors you will need to decide upon:

- **A**sset Allocation (how much to have in equity, fixed-income, and cash-equivalent investments);
- **C**ountry allocation (U.S. versus Foreign markets);
- **M**arket-cap allocation (Small, Mid., Large);
- **S**tyle weight (Value, Growth, Credit quality, duration);
- **M**ultiple of a portfolio (P/E);
- **B**eta; and
- **I**ndustry concentration.

To achieve the desired portfolio metrics, you should actively manage a portfolio's characteristics. The desired portfolio characteristics will depend upon a portfolio's objective and current phase of the business and market cycle. (See more of a discussion on the phases of the market cycle in previous chapters).

Exhibit 10.1: The Elements of Managing Overall Portfolio Characteristics to Control Risk and Improve Return

Growth Objective Portfolio in the Early Bull phase:

Characteristic	Weight %
- Asset Allocation (%Equity/%Fixed-Inc/%Cash)	95/0/5
- Country Allocation: (%US/%foreign)	80/20
- Market Capitalization Allocation (%Large/%Mid-cap/%Small-cap)	30/30/40
- Weighted Market-cap	$6 billion
- Style orientation (%Value/%Growth)	35/65
- P/E	25
- Beta	1.25
- Industry concentration (top three)	Technology 30%
	Financials 25%
	Basic Materials 15%

This table is for illustrative purposes only and does not predict or depict the performance of any investment.

Why are these elements so important?

Investment performance is a moving target. Typically, over a cycle what has done well and ranks at the top in terms of performance often falls to the top by the end of the cycle. Moreover, what has languished in the basement of performance tends to climb toward the top in the new cycle.

Active management of the **A.C.M.S.M.B.I.**'s attempts to reduce risk and provide consistent positive returns. You can bring the overall portfolio's characteristics in line with the desired ones by adjusting the underlying funds in a portfolio. For instance, emphasizing growth style funds over value style funds may produce a higher overall portfolio P/E.

It is also a good idea to overweight parts of the **A.C.M.S.M.B.I.**'s that are favored by the market cycle. The momentum of a particular fund category typically lasts for a few years. For example, large-cap growth outperformed small-cap for the 3-year period ending 1999. Thus, an overweight position was desirable until large-cap became too expensive in 1999.

Over the next 3-year period, however, from 2000 through 2002 an overweight in small-cap value was more desirable. Over that time period small-caps generated a positive return while large-cap's lost 15% on average each year, according to Barra Inc. Exhibit 10.2 shows the potential gains that could be made by managing a portfolio's **A.C.M.S.M.B.I.**'s.

Exhibit 10.2: Get the A.C.M.S.M.B.I.'s Right To Improve Performance

Investment Approach	3-Year Returns*
U.S. Large-cap Growth	240.57%
U.S. Large-cap Value	181.83%
U.S. Mid-cap Growth	208.02%
U.S. Mid-cap Value	168.12%
U.S. Small-cap Growth	133.74%
U.S. Small-cap Value	152.01%
Greatest Difference	106.83%

*Period returns ending 1999. Source: BARRA, Inc., Morgan Stanley Capital International, Lehman Brothers. Large-cap Growth represented by S&P 500 Barra Growth Index. Large-cap Value represented by S&P 500 Barra Value Index. Mid-cap Growth represented by S&P MidCap 400/Barra Growth Index. Mid-cap Value represented by S&P MidCap 400/Barra Value Index. Small-cap Growth represented by S&P SmallCap 600/Barra Growth Index. Small-cap Value represented by S&P SmallCap 600/Barra Value Index. "Growth Stocks" have above average profitability and valuation characteristics. "Value Stocks" have below average profitability and valuation characteristics. Indices include reinvested income, but not transaction costs or taxes, are unmanaged and cannot be purchased directly by investors. This table is for illustrative purposes only and does not predict or depict the performance of any investment.

1) **The Keys to Asset Allocation Management**

Being in the Majors

Everyone knows that by owning just one asset class a portfolio will produce less consistent results over the long-term. Why? Because the single-class portfolio only does well when that asset class does well.

A portfolio can deliver more consistent results by owning the major asset classes -- equities, fixed-income and cash-equivalents -- together. Even more consistent results could be obtained over a market cycle by adjusting the asset allocation of these three major asset classes.

You can decide which asset and sub-asset classes are overvalued using the plethora of indicators that are available. It is usually best to overweight asset classes and sub-asset classes that are in favor with economic and market conditions, and underweight those not in favor.

In an expansion, it is smart to overweight stocks and underweight bonds, whereas in a contraction, you would do the opposite. During the early bull phase of the cycle, it is best to favor small-caps over large-caps. As the bull cycle matures, you can favor large-cap over small-cap. And as the market cycle ages, you can increase the liquidity in a portfolio by increasing exposure to bonds, and cash-equivalents. Two tell tale signs of an aging market cycle are inflation and consumer interest rates.

Use the Index of Leading Economic Indicators (LEI) to judge whether the economy is slowing down or picking up steam. Over the past four decades ending December 2004 when the LEI had a negative reading in it year-over-year change for four consecutive months or more, GDP slowed down almost 90% of the time. Typically GDP slowed by 2.5 percentage points. Of the eight times it had a negative year-over year change for four months or more, the economy had a recession five times. The Lehman Brothers Long term Government Bond Index generated an average total return of 18% for the year after the LEI turned negative for four consecutive months or more and out performed the S&P 500 Index by 380 basis points. Thus over weight bonds when GDP slows down.

When interest rates are rising, favor stocks over bonds, until rates near a cyclical peak. Bond returns are lower than stock returns in a rising interest rate environment (10-year Treasury yield rising from its cyclical low to peak). Over the past 40 years ending 2003, stocks, as measured by the S&P 500 Index, produced an average annualized return of 5.7% in rising rate environment. While bonds, as measured by the Lehman Brothers Aggregate Bond index (1976-2003 period), and the U.S. Intermediate Government Bond Index (1963-1976), produced a 3.2% average annualized return. Source of data is the Federal Reserve and Lehman Brothers.

Alternative Asset Classes

Besides the major asset classes, you can manage alternative asset classes to improve performance. During times of heighten geopolitical risk, higher inflation, and increased demand for real assets, it is a great idea to consider either or both commodities and precious metals investments.

Commodities are a hedge in a risky market and protect against market shocks such as supply shocks (e.g. oil shortages). During periods of increased demand for real assets, such as basic materials, natural gas, petroleum, agriculture, livestock, and precious metals, commodities have performed well.

Real estate, in the form of a liquid real estate or REIT fund, may also makes sense during periods of inflation, and higher demand. It is also a great way to hedge an equity portfolio. Real estate, as represented by the National Association of Real Estate Investment Trusts (NAREIT) Trust, which is an unmanaged portfolio representing thee Equity REIT market, had a low correlation with the S&P 500 index (0.28 correlation), Non-U.S. Equities as measured by the Morgan Stanley EAFE Index (0.27), and bonds as measured by the Salomon Brothers Broad Investment Grade Bond index designed to cover the investment grade universe of bonds issued in the United States (0 correlation). Results are for a ten year period ending March 31, 2004 according to Cohen & Steers Inc. (All indexes are unmanaged, cannot be invested in by investors, and do not have expenses. Past performance is no guarantee of future results).

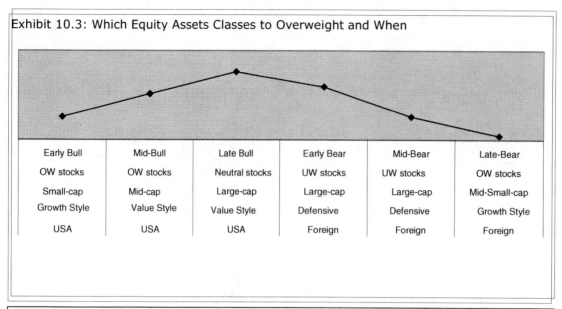

Exhibit 10.3: Which Equity Assets Classes to Overweight and When

Early Bull	Mid-Bull	Late Bull	Early Bear	Mid-Bear	Late-Bear
OW stocks	OW stocks	Neutral stocks	UW stocks	UW stocks	OW stocks
Small-cap	Mid-cap	Large-cap	Large-cap	Large-cap	Mid-Small-cap
Growth Style	Value Style	Value Style	Defensive	Defensive	Growth Style
USA	USA	USA	Foreign	Foreign	Foreign

This table is for illustrative purposes only and does not predict or depict the performance of any investment. Investments in mutual funds involve risk. Past performance is no guarantee of future performance. Mutual funds incur fees and expenses (including investment management and administrative fees). Investment returns and the principal value of a mutual fund will fluctuate, so that shares, when redeemed, may be worth more or less than their original cost. Obtain a mutual fund prospectus for more complete information about the fund, including all fees and expenses, Read it carefully before you invest. Past performance is no guarantee of future performance.

Do not forget to manage the tail risk -- two standard deviation events. No one foresaw the 2000-2002 bear market in the 1990's goldilocks economy. Bear markets tend to catch almost everyone by surprise. Utility funds and precious metal funds also have a low correlation to the S&P 500, with correlations of 0.08 and -0.02, respectively. Then you can add a healthy does of high quality bonds as stock market valuations become frothy.

The Keys to Foreign Market/Country Management

What is the "need to know" scoop on foreign country allocation?

A good time to overweight holdings in foreign markets is when the countries in an International fund comprise countries with strengthening economies, moderate inflation, appreciating or stable currencies, and moderate real interest rates. If the countries in the fund have weak economies, low rates, depreciating currencies, and high inflation, then consider an underweight position. The rule of thumb for U.S. investors is to underweight countries that have a depreciating currency. Let's test this out.

The world's major currencies, particularly the Euro, appreciated against the U.S. dollar over the last three year period ending December 2004. In other words the U.S. dollar declined in value. Which markets outperformed the other over the three year period? The U.S. market or the Global markets excluding the U.S. market? The answer is the global markets. In fact, in eight of the past nine years ending 2004, the direction of the U.S. dollar has predicted which market would out perform the other. When the U.S. dollar fell, the foreign markets, as measured by the DJ Global Market Index excluding U.S., outperformed the DJ U.S. Total Market Index. Thus, when the U.S. dollar drops consider an overweight in foreign stocks and bonds relative to U.S. stocks and bonds. When it goes up consider an underweight in foreign securities.

Exhibit 10.4 shows a common international management approach.

Exhibit 10.4: International Management Process

Step One: Assess regional/country economic prospects before investing. It is most important to pick countries solidly in an expansion mode. Evaluate specific country's fiscal and monetary policy. Determine the direction of interest rates and currency. Minimize exposure to countries with huge budget deficits, high debt levels, lower relative rates, and weakening currencies. Diversify assets among more than 10 countries and at least 100 stocks. Minimize underperformance to benchmark-- keep country allocation weights a minimum of half and maximum of twice the benchmark. Emerging market country exposure should range from 5% to 25% of the portfolio's assets.

Step Two: Assess market conditions. Determine the phase of the market by looking at: Capital Flows-- high in bull phase and low in bear; Volatility -- high at end of bull; Liquidity -- builds at early phase of bull. Stick with a buying discipline. Avoid being caught buying at speculative peaks. Limit P/E to 30% above average historical P/E of stocks in a particular market.

Step Three: Conduct fundamental analysis. Look at upward company earnings revision ratio in a country, corporate earnings to bond yields. Look at free cash flow. Most foreign countries do not yet adhere to stringent Generally Accepted Accounting Principles like the United States, so free cash flow gets around that problem. Use Market Value-to-GDP (Price/Sales) as your tool. Accounting definitions of book values and earnings differ by country. Therefore, it is meaningless to compare P/E and P/B. Industry selection is paramount and ranks up there with country selection in importance. Analyze the sales and earnings prospects for the industry. To minimize the cost of poor stock selection, set maximum individual positions at 5% of assets.

With Foreign Markets, Measure Twice and Cut Once

Look at the valuations in a foreign market before pulling the trigger. That means looking at the multiple of each international fund option.

Historically, from 1970-2003, international stocks have traded at an approximate 26% discount to U.S. stocks according to Oppenheimer Funds. U.S. stocks should sport higher multiples because they operate in an economy that has demonstrated sustainable higher GDP growth. As the U.S. market becomes expensive, you can build exposure to foreign markets that are cheaper.

Secondly, keep an eye on foreign markets' performance trends. Over the last 10-year period ending 2002, the U.S. stock market ranked among the top five performing equity markets only once. Therefore, you can see there is opportunity to enhance returns by an over weight in foreign markets. Exhibit 10.5 has guidelines for two common portfolio strategies.

Exhibit: 10.5 Country Strategic and Tactical Asset Allocation Guide			
Portfolio Strategy	**Strategic %U.S./%Foreign**	**Overweight %U.S./%Foreign**	**Underweight %U.S./%Foreign**
Growth	70%/30%	55%/45%	85%/15%
Growth & Income	85%/15%	75%/25%	90%/10%

This table is for illustrative purposes only and does not predict or depict the performance of any investment. Investments in mutual funds involve risk. Past performance is no guarantee of future performance. Mutual funds incur fees and expenses (including investment management and administrative fees). Investment returns and the principal value of a mutual fund will fluctuate, so that shares, when redeemed, may be worth more or less than their original cost. Obtain a mutual fund prospectus for more complete information about the fund, including all fees and expenses. Read it carefully before you invest. Past performance is no guarantee of future performance.

The Spread between Developed and Emerging Markets

Keep in mind that there is a cycle of out performance and underperformance between developed foreign markets and emerging markets. The difference in quarterly performance between the developed and emerging market was ten percentage points or more for about 40% of the time over the last fifteen years ending 2003, according to Morgan Stanley. You should take into consideration the cycle with tilting decisions. It could make a substantial difference in performance.

It is a good idea to watch out for the boom-bust-boom cycle to emerging markets. In such scenarios, which play out every few years, the market cycle enters a value phase after a severe sell-off and flight of capital. Low valuations are irrelevant when the market is illiquid and the economy is in shambles. As the economy recovers, the market enters a growth phase characterized by big upward earnings revisions that typically attract foreign capital. As foreign capital floods the market amid limited stocks to buy, a liquidity-driven rally occurs and the market enters its momentum phase. How long the momentum will last before an asset bubble burst depends on many factors.

Good judgment, and knowing the warning signs of excess (leverage is one, speculation in all areas of the market and economy is another) can get you to the exit before the stampede occurs.

It is wise to have a strict sell discipline. You should sell when the price target is met, or a change in fundamentals occurs. It is prudent to refrain from practicing a buy and hold strategy when investing abroad. It is best to seek out an active manager in international waters because of past boom and bust cycles. In addition to quantitative measures, many managers use a top down approach that evaluates political, social, and economic environment. Unstable countries are obviously avoided.

Minding Currency Hedges

Some advisors also actively manage currency to capitalize on foreign currency trends, and reduce downside risk and volatility. To manage currency, risk portfolios are hedged. Hedging depends on factors that affect the exchange rates between the dollar and homeland currencies.

Other things to consider are the trade account balance, inflation differentials, central bank policy, and regional economic dynamics. If none of these factors point towards an appreciating foreign currency or stable situation then a hedge is required.

The Keys to Market Cap Management

Why should the market cap of a portfolio be managed?

In a nutshell, smart market cap management could substantially enhance a portfolio's return.

The average difference in return between the large-cap (S&P 500 Index) and the small-cap (Russell 2000 Index) was approximately 15% per year from 1970 through 2003 Russell Inc. Small-cap stocks outperformed large-caps on average by 18% each year for ten consecutive years from 1974 through 1983, according to Ibbotson Inc. That trend reversed itself from 1984 to 1990. For seven consecutive years large-cap outperformed small-cap by 13.02% on average per year.

In the past it has paid to adjust a portfolio's weight among various market cap stock sectors and especially reduce exposure to areas that have seen a terrific run up in prices. (Of course, past performance is no guarantee of future performance).

Small Caps Can Produce Big Returns

Historically, small-cap stock funds performed well after bear market bottoms. Small-caps have outperformed large-caps 12 months after a market bottom by an average of 9% from 1926 to 2003, according Prudential Securities. Over the ensuing 3-year period after a recession, small-caps beat large-caps 22.5% on average. Small-caps tend to have lower profits during a recession than large-caps do. When interest rates bottom, economic growth tends to pick-up and earnings growth accelerates particularly with small-caps.

Other catalysts for out performance by small-caps are: compelling valuations relative to other areas of the market, less need for liquidity of brand name large-cap stocks, and investors being more willing to buy small companies that use leverage to increase profitability.

A study by Prudential Securities found that small-caps gained 14.7% annually versus 11.5% for large-caps during the strongest periods of growth (recovery phase of the cycle) from 1950-1983. To capitalize on this out performance, you can favor small-cap growth category funds that own cyclical stocks. Earnings of the consumer discretionary sector (retailers, autos, etc.), for example, tend to get a big boost from increased consumer spending. Small-cap value funds with lower earnings growth do not tend to benefit as much.

It can be wise to overweight small-caps -- to the tune of as much as 30% -- in the early bull stage of the market for several years. When small-caps outperform large-caps, they tend to do so by double digits. Of course, past performance is no guarantee of future performance).

Mid-Caps Float in Calm, Steady Waters

Mid-cap funds have performed better in periods of relative economic certainty. That is, the economy is growing and the expectation is that it will continue growing at a moderate rate without inflation becoming a problem. This tends to happen after the recovery phase of the business cycle, mark by an end to above average economic growth, and when the early bull phase is complete. In addition, for Mid-cap stocks to outperform Small-cap stocks and Large-cap stocks, there must be a change in investment category leadership from Large-cap and or Small-cap to Mid-cap. Money flows into Mid-caps because they are attractively valued and are considered higher quality stocks than Small-caps at this point.

Mid-cap stocks tend to be less volatile than small-cap stocks and more liquid, but are typically more volatile than large-caps and less liquid in certain markets. *You may want to overweigh mid-caps at the mid-bull stage of the market cycle to a position of 25%.*

Large Caps Love Bull Runs and Uncertain Markets

During a bull market, large-cap stocks tend to participate in the bull market throughout all phases. Large-caps did not have a down year throughout past bull markets from 1926 to 2003. In contrast, small- to mid-cap sectors occasionally sported a down year in a bull phase and have exhibited distinctive times when they have been favored and have outperformed large-caps. (As usual, past performance is no guarantee of future performance).

Based upon past historical results, it is prudent to always have at least 10% to 20% in large-caps. At the later bull stage, you may choose to increase exposure to as high as 40% of a growth objective portfolio.

Although the economy could be very healthy, investors tend to gravitate toward large company stocks when they believe the economy will experience a slowdown over the next 12 months. It is smart to increase large company stock fund positions before the economy begins to slow down, prompted by trend of rising interest rates.

Large-cap funds have historically done well when there is a lot of anxiety about the future of the economy. This nervousness occurs during the late bull market phase. During these times, investors have typically started buying companies with quality earnings and selling those lacking quality earnings.

Quality earnings are defined by G.A.A.P. and not operating earnings. Quality earnings are earnings that use conservative accounting principles that expense stock options, do not use various tricks or shenanigans in speeding up reported revenues or deferring expenses, etc. In addition, companies that leverage earnings growth with debt have lower quality earnings.

It is always a best practice to buy quality large-cap stocks that have sound fundamentals. After the early bull phase of the market cycle is done, the market often shifts from lower quality small-cap stocks (with weaker balance sheets, more debt, less free cash, less liquid assets, and niche players that rely on one product to bring in revenue) to larger cap stocks (sporting stronger balance sheets, better liquidity ratios and operating efficiency ratios, more cash, more free cash flow, higher quality earnings, and broader product lines). This rotation also occurs in times of turmoil.

Moreover, large-cap stocks usually pay dividends whereas it is rarer for smaller cap stocks to pay dividends. In times of turmoil or when the economy slows down and the market dips in response, large-caps could at least pay a dividend until the market gets rolling again. The S&P 500 index has grown dividend payouts by a 17% compounded growth rate from 1978 to 2003, according to Standard & Poor's.

Defending Defensive Large-Caps

You will likely want to choose large-cap funds that hold traditional consumer-oriented defensive stocks. Large defensive stocks' earnings are likely to be less vulnerable to slow downs and are liquid in down markets. That is because even in tough times, people still need to eat, pay electric bills, buy medication, or anything else that is a necessity.

Staple groups like food & beverage, household products, pharmaceuticals, and health care, tend to be relative stable earners, and have historically outperformed when economic activity, and broad market earnings slow. In general defensive large-cap stocks have stable performance across the business cycle compared to small-caps and mid-cap stocks. Historically, increasing volatility favors large-cap dividend-paying stocks, ones that hold defensive stock groups, while declining volatility favors smaller-cap stocks.

Small-cap sectors tend to tanks when short-term interest rates rise due to inflationary pressures in the economy. Higher interest rates usually cause a slow down in corporate earnings. Prudential Securities found that from 1950-1983, large-caps did better than small-caps during weaker period's exhibited by slower economic growth. Large-cap gained 8.6% versus small-cap's lesser 4.9% return. (Past performance is no guarantee of future performance).

Managing Market Caps for International Equities

But it is not just the domestic market that market caps could and should be managed for. Market caps should be managed for international equities, too.

Just as in domestic markets, market cap performance leadership also changes hands between international small-cap (MSCI EAFE Small Cap Index) and international large-cap (MSCI EAFE Index) sectors. International small-cap outperformed International large-cap from 1978 to 1985, 1983 through 1992, and 2001 to 2003 according to Independence International Associates.

The Keys to Style Management

Why is style management so important?

The style (growth versus value) that is favored by current conditions normally outperforms the other style. In fact, studies have shown that 90% of a fund's short- term return can be attributed to style selection. If a style is experiencing strong performance leadership, then it is wise to favor that style. But do not entirely abandon the other. It is simply prudent to diversify with both styles because performance leadership changes over time. Between 1975 and 2004, as a style Value has led 15 times, while Growth has led 15 times. A tie! Furthermore, style leaders sometimes stage repeat winning performances in consecutive years, but not always.

Exhibit 10.6 And The Winner Is...Value Versus Growth Changes In Leadership.				
1975 Value	1982 Growth	1989 Growth	1996 Growth	2003 Growth
1976 Value	1983 Value	1990 Growth	1997 Growth	2004 Value
1977 Value	1984 Value	1991 Growth	1998 Growth	
1978 Growth	1985 Growth	1992 Value	1999 Growth	
1979 Value	1986 Value	1993 Value	2000 Value	
1980 Growth	1987 Growth	1994 Growth	2001 Value	
1981 Value	1988 Value	1995 Growth	2002 Value	

Source: Russell Investment Group, Inc. Growth is represented by the Russell 1000 Growth Index. Value is represented by the Russell 1000 Value Index. "Growth Stocks" have above average profitability and valuation characteristics. "Value Stocks" have below average profitability and valuation characteristics. Indices include reinvested income, but not transaction costs or taxes, are unmanaged and cannot be purchased directly by investors. This table is for illustrative purposes only and does not predict or depict the performance of any investment.

Follow the Leader: Growth vs. Value vs. Momentum Growth

Historically, when The Federal Reserve has lowered interest rates during the trough to recovery phase of the business cycle, Growth style has outperformed Value. Investors tend to become less risk averse at this point and buy juiced up leveraged companies that have low quality earnings with explosive upside potential. Momentum growth style is in favor when earnings growth is accelerating. (Past performance is no guarantee of future performance).

Exhibit 10.7: Growth Performed Well In Early Bull Phase

Easing Period	6 months		12 Months	
	Russell 1000 Growth	Russell 1000 Value	Russell 1000 Growth	Russell 1000 Value
1980	31.1%	18.9%	32.9%	31.5%
1981-1983	-5.2%	-0.7%	12.4%	17.6%
1984-1986	8.9%	13.6%	15.0%	24.0%
1990-92	27.0%	21.2%	28.1%	17.9%
1998-99	34.8%	18.3%	34.9%	18.7%
Average	**19.3%**	**14.3%**	**24.7%**	**21.9%**

Source: Russell Investment Group, Inc. Growth is represented by the Russell 1000 Growth Index. Value is represented by the Russell 1000 Value Index. "Growth Stocks" have above average profitability and valuation characteristics. "Value Stocks" have below average profitability and valuation characteristics. Indices include reinvested income, but not transaction costs or taxes, are unmanaged and cannot be purchased directly by investors. This table is for illustrative purposes only and does not predict or depict the performance of any investment.

Growth has historically performed well during the second half of a recession and for six months after a recession, as shown in Exhibit 10.8. Growth style continues to perform well as companies beat their earnings' estimates. An environment that includes plenty of earnings surprises usually supports Growth investing. Past performance is no guarantee of future performance.

Exhibit 10.8: Growth Has Done Well in Recovery Phase of the Business Cycle

Easing Period	2nd Half of Recessions		6 Months Later	
	Russell 1000 Growth	Russell 1000 Value	Russell 1000 Growth	Russell 1000 Value
1980	18.8%	14.9%	10.0%	7.7%
1980-81	33.3%	25.2%	18.2%	22.7%
1990-91	22.9%	18.2%	0.9%	-2.7%
Average	**24.9%**	**19.4%**	**9.7%**	**9.2%**

Source: Russell Investment Group, Inc. Growth represented by the Russell 1000 Growth Index. Value represented by the Russell 1000 Value Index. "Growth Stocks" have above average profitability and valuation characteristics. "Value Stocks" have below average profitability and valuation characteristics. Indices include reinvested income, but not transaction costs or taxes, are unmanaged and cannot be purchased directly by investors. This table is for illustrative purposes only and does not predict or depict the performance of any investment.

When has the Value style historically done well?

Value funds have tended to perform especially well at the beginning of the recovery phase of the business cycle. This is because typical value companies are cyclical and industrial companies.

Any small increase in corporate earnings, which have been depressed, usually leads to big advances in a stock's price. Value performance also generally picks-up when valuations start to matter with Growth stocks. At this stage the economy is still growing, consumers are confident and are spending.

Large-cap Value has generally performed well during the mid to late bull phase of the market as investors seek cyclical companies that have quality, economically sensitive earnings, and haven't experienced a big run up in price yet. Past performance is no guarantee of future performance.

Generally, Value style tended to lag in performance during hot markets and during the early part of a down market. When the I.P.O. market is bustling, Value tends to lag behind. When the economy starts to cool off, large-cap Growth defensive companies outperform Value because their quality earnings are more reliable than cyclical Large-cap Value. At this stage predictable earnings get rewarded with more investor money. Past performance is no guarantee of future performance.

The Leadership Cycle

The cycle of leadership change among Value and Growth can be traced to the business cycle. Fear of recession, worries concerning earnings, and the threat of reduced liquidity in the market, may all cause a flight to quality and to brand name Growth stocks. Once fear proves to be unfounded, Value tends to recovers leadership. After the economy gets back on a stable growth track Value generally leads the way.

It is during the sell-off of Value stocks when intrinsic value can be bought. Buying stocks at intrinsic value helps Value investors beat the market and outperform Growth over the long periods.

- The "Growth style" oriented S&P 500 Index outperformed the broader market of 1,500 stock universe by 36% from January 1969 to June 1973. The cause of that Growth style leadership was fear of recession. Traditional Value stocks made up of economically-sensitive stocks were shunned. Once the recession hit in 1973-1974, leadership shifted, with Value stocks outperforming by 263% over the next six years.
- In the 16 months leading up to the 1980 recession, Value stocks under performed by 23%. The following eight years Value outperformed Growth by a staggering 271%!
- In the 20 months leading up to the 1990 recession, Growth stocks outperformed Value by 41%. However, in the next 4-1/2 years in the following recovery, Value outperformed by 117%.

Style management with international equities is harder to execute because of the different international accounting standards and practices employed. Those make it harder to calculate the P/E and P/B ratios of foreign stocks.

Data produced by Frank Russell indicates that style cycles have been less pronounced in foreign markets than in the U.S. This may be due to the difficulty in determining a stock style trend across foreign markets. Nevertheless, it is smart to manage the U.S. style allocation based on the market cycle.

The Keys to P/E Management

Why should a portfolio's P/E matter so much and, consequently, never be ignored?

The answer is simple. Higher P/E's suggest poorer valuations and lower future returns. Lower P/E's imply cheaper valuations and higher future returns. Therefore, you would be wise to manage a portfolio's P/E drift.

As the market cycle ages, it is a good idea to decrease a portfolio's overall P/E. You will want to keep it in line with market P/E and always below 25. That is because anytime the market P/E exceeds 24, the threat of a correction and even a bear market becomes looming.

The S&P 500 Index's P/E ranged from 7 to 22 from 1926 until 1990. It did not break out of that range until the 1990s when investors started to pay more for stocks than ever before. In the 2000 asset bubble, the S&P 500's P/E hit an unthinkable forty-five. In a healthy market the market multiple often expands to the high end of its historical trading range of 22 before becoming overvalued.

Investment Advisory Services and Financial Planning Offered Through Aspetuck Financial Management LLC   227

Should equity exposure be reduced when the market P/E hits 22?

The market can stretch 20% to 30% above the high end before correcting, given low inflation, improving earnings growth outlook, and favorable supply and demand. You must also factor in inflation levels, and future earnings growth when evaluating the P/E. Low inflation and low interest rates allow the P/E to expand towards the higher end of the historical trading range without stocks becoming expensive. Its estimated that a one percentage point move in the CPI affects the stock market's fair market value P/E by approximately 20%.

Trailing vs. Forward P/E

The Federal Reserve uses the 12 month forward-looking P/E in it analysis. It is better to focus more on the forward P/E based on future earnings expectations in the early bull to mid bull phases of the cycle. When the economy is recovering earnings' growth that had been suppressed starts to rebound allowing for multiple expansions.

Later in the cycle -- the late bull phase -- you can use both forward and trailing P/E ratios. You should look over your shoulder at the trailing P/E, and rely more on trailing P/E if you believe in regression to the mean. If the trailing P/E is at 22 in the mid to late bull phase, then start taking profits and increasing a cash position or reduce the portfolio's P/E. Allowing the portfolio P/E to expand all the way up to 24, using either forward or trailing P/Es, is far enough even given the most optimistic earnings forecast.

So how do you determine if the market is overvalued?

That depends on how one views earnings -- with an eye toward forward or backward earnings. The S&P 500 Index stood at 1135 on February 3, 2004. Trailing EPS was $50 and forward EPS was estimated to be $60 in 2004. Exhibit 10.9 provides a possible answer to the question, is the market overvalued? Of course, other measures should be considered before reaching a concrete conclusion.

Exhibit 10.9: Is the Market Overvalued?

1. Market P/E = S&P 500 Index/**Trailing EPS**   1135/$50= 22.7 (market is trading expensively; the P/E analysis does not factor in very low inflation and a 45-year low in the Fed Funds' rate).

2. Market P/E = S&P 500 Index/**Forward EPS**   1135/$60= 18.9 (market is not expensive).

This table is for illustrative purposes only and does not predict or depict the performance of any investment.

The P/E of 24 Threshold

When a portfolio's P/E exceeds 24, if you haven't already, it is a good time to begin to bring it in line by replacing higher multiple funds with lower ones and or buying fixed-income investments. Generally, when the market is in its mid bull phase or entering the late-bull phase, it is best to start reducing growth style fund allocation and increase value style orientation. That will serve to keep the overall portfolio multiple at a more reasonable level.

By the time the market reaches its late bull stage, the best of earning acceleration and growth is already behind us and market valuations have almost fully expanded. Understand that the earnings' cycle has a positive relationship with market P/E. When earnings are low the market P/E is generally low, and when earnings are high the market P/E is typically high.

Before earnings crest, it is wise to be counter cyclical with your investment actions. Therefore, it is smart to limit what you pay for stocks by favoring value funds or funds that invest in reasonably priced large-cap defensive stocks because the next move is for earnings to move lower, with P/E being positively correlated to follow. It's a good idea to keep a conservative Growth & Income objective portfolio or Income & Growth objective portfolio's P/E below 22 at the mid to late bull stage.

The Keys to Industry Management

What is one of the most important aspects of a portfolio that is rarely managed?

Industry concentration!

I have reviewed thousands of portfolios over the past twenty years and few investors tracked on their radar screen a portfolio's industry exposure. Even bottom-up portfolio managers generally do not care. Many have admitted to me they backed into an industry exposure. In other words, their stock picking determined the final industry concentration.

It wasn't until after year 2000 that industry concentration suddenly blipped onto many managers' radar screens, and I noticed many professionals starting to limit their industry exposure.

It is very important to know what the overall portfolio's exposure is to various industries. It is always prudent to make sure that a portfolio is heavily invested in industries that are in favor with current business conditions but is not overly concentrated.

Back to the Future

Think back to 2000 when many investors woke up to find that their portfolio had over 70% of their assets invested in the technology sector. A prudent advisor or investor would keep each industry weight at or below 30% of the overall portfolio's assets.

Why is industry exposure important enough to manage, besides the desire to manage risk?

Academic research has shown that a stock's return is explained by the direction of the stock market and the stock's industry. Research by William O'Neil concluded that 37% of a stock's price appreciation is due to industry group strength, and 12% to its sector strength. That means about half (49%) of its return is due to the performance of its industry and sector.

Within leading industry groups the top performing stocks can appreciate as much as 2,000% during the industry's reign at the top, which normally last for a few years. For instance, from October 1990 through March 1994, Cisco Systems, a computer industry stock, appreciated by 2,119%. Many stocks within a favored industry will typically double in value and sometimes quadruple. Therefore, industry selection determines more of a fund's long-term return than securities selection.

Other studies concerning industry performance concluded that performance significantly varies between industries throughout the market cycle. Often the spread between the best and worst performing industry is quite substantial. Exhibit 10.10 shows the performance of various industries from 1992 through 1996, Semi-conductor stocks produced, on average, a 52.3% annual return, whereas the Trucking industry averaged -1.8%.

Exhibit 10.10: Industry Performance Ending 1996

Industry	One-Year	Three-Year	Five-Year
Semi-conductors	+ 69.0%	+ 50.6%	+ 52.3%
Financial Services	+ 36.3%	+ 28.8%	+ 23.2%
Health Care	+ 4.3%	+ 18.4%	+ 21.1%
Media Broadcasting	- 4.5%	- 3.3%	+ 11.0%
Trucking	- 13.2%	- 10.2%	- 1.8%

Source: The Wall Street Journal. This table is for illustrative purposes only and does not predict or depict the performance of any investment. Past performance is not indicative of future performance.

Watching for Sector Rotation

The leadership trend lasted until March 2000 when a sharp reversal of fortune brought the bottom dwellers to the top, a the leaders sank to the murky bottom.

Changes in business conditions cause various industry groups to rotate through periods of out performance and underperformance. Two dozens groups have led the bull market at one time or another over the 10-year period ending 2000.

Supply and demand forces have the biggest impact on industry performance. Macro-economic factors such as interest rates, and the relative strength of the dollar can have a big impact on different sectors and their performance. For example, a strong dollar is positive for most stocks but especially for the diversified financial services sector which includes insurance and bank stocks. Conversely, a strong dollar is *not* good for the retail or household products sectors. Higher interest rates are bad new for banks, brokerages, and technology companies. When consumer demand slips, or over supply cuts prices, corporate earnings usually suffer.

Selecting the Right Securities

If the right industries are selected, then is individual security selection no longer an issue?

Not exactly. Securities selection is important within an industry. The returns among stocks within the very same industry can vary substantially. For example, Intel Corp. had a 5-year average annual return of 61% ending 1996, while Advanced Micro Devices Inc., a technology peer, returned 8% on average. This is an example of being right on the industry, but wrong on the stock.

Securities selection is important but not as important as industry selection because if you pick the wrong industry, generally you will lose money no matter what stocks you buy in that industry. Exhibit 10.11 shows the basic industry breakdown.

Cyclical industries have historically performed well at the end of a bear phase and into the late bull phase of the market cycle. This is when the economy is recovering from a recession and is expanding. Non-cyclical industries take over where cyclical industries leave off. Non-cyclical industries perform well as the expansion peaks and begins its slowdown.

Exhibit 10.11: Basic Industries

Cyclical:
- **Consumer Durable**: Automotive, House ware and Furniture, Manufacturing, Multi-industry, Recreation, Rubber/Plastics, Shoes/Leather, Textiles/Apparel, Homebuilders, etc.
- **Transportation**: Airlines, Railroads, Trucking, etc.
- **Financial Services**: Banks, Brokerages, Insurance Companies, etc.
- **Industrial Cyclical**: Aerospace, Building, Heavy Machinery, etc.
- **Retail**: Department Stores, etc.
- **Services**: Airlines, Broadcasting/Movies/Sports, Business Services, Freight, Hotels/Resorts, Personal Services, Publishing, Recreation/Gaming, etc.
- **Technology**: Aerospace, Computers/Semi-conductors, Data Processing, Electronics, etc.
- **Basic materials**: Chemicals, Metals, Paper, etc.
- **Energy**: Natural Gas and Oil Production and Services, etc.

Non-cyclical:
- **Consumer Staples**: Confections, Cosmetics/Personal Care, Alcohol, Food, Tobacco, etc.
- **Health**: Health Care Providers, Drug Manufacturers, Pharmaceuticals, Medical Supplies, Biotech, etc.
- **Utilities**: Electric, Gas, Telephone, Water, Cable TV, etc.
- **Consumer services**: Internet, etc.

Source: The Wall Street Journal. This table is for illustrative purposes only and does not predict or depict the performance of any investment. Past performance is not indicative of future performance.

The How-to of Fixed-Income Management

*"I'm not so concerned about the return <u>on</u> my money
as I am concerned about the return <u>of</u> my money."*
-- Bernard Baruch

Most advisors prefer to actively manage the fixed-income components of a fund portfolio against the Lehman Brothers Aggregate Bond Index and cyclical trends. Tilting decisions are based upon monetary policy and Fed comments, fiscal policy, cyclical trends (inflation, interest rates, distress ratio, default rates, dollar exchange rates, the Confidence Index), yield curve, valuations, and other factors.

It is best to make "tilts" -- not wholesale moves -- in sectors, maturities, duration, credit quality, and foreign to U.S. exposure allocations. And be certain to take advantage of the price-to-yield curve. Even before the first rate cut, bond yields will typically drop, and prices will rise at an accelerated rate.

What exactly is there to manage with fixed-income assets?

Just as managing the equity component of a portfolio included paying particular attention to the **A.C.M.S.M.B.I.** factors, management of the fixed-income portion of the portfolio means paying attention to the **D.Y.C.V.C.S.S.R.L.** elements.

These stand for:

- **D**uration;
- **Y**ield;
- **C**redit quality;
- **V**olatility;
- **C**urrency risk;
- **S**ector orientation;
- **S**ecurities concentration;
- **R**einvestment risk; and
- **L**iquidity.

That's a lot to worry about! Do not be fooled. Bond investing can be even trickier than equity investing because of what needs to be managed in order to get fairly compensated for the amount of risk. Exhibit 10.12 shows what you will need to properly manage bond investments.

Exhibit 10.12: Manage Overall Portfolio Characteristics to Control

Income Objective Portfolio in the Early Bull phase.

Characteristic	Weight
Asset Allocation (%Equity/%fixed/%Cash)	15%/82%/3%
Country Allocation (%US/%foreign)	80%/20%
Weighted Market Capitalization	$14.3b
Style Orientation (%Value/%Growth)	40%/60%
%Long/%Intermediate/%Short	10%/45%/45%
Duration	5.26
Average Credit Quality	BBB
SEC Yield	6.4%

This table is for illustrative purposes only and does not predict or depict the performance of any investment.

Why even bother messing with the **D.Y.C.V.C.S.S.R.L.**'s?

Fixed-income investing is rife with risk. There are eleven types of risks to manage. As a bond investor, your goal is to protect your safe money from these risks. Even a high quality laddered portfolio does not protect against every type of risk listed in Exhibit 10.13.

Exhibit 10.13: Fixed-Income Portfolio Risks

1. **Interest Rate** -- Longer-term bonds can drop in value when interest rates rise. Treasuries are more sensitive to interest rate risk because they carry virtually no credit risk.
2. **Credit Quality** -- Low rated bonds may default on principal and/or interest payments.
3. **Maturity** -- Determines how much income you will get, or principal you can lose.
4. **Purchasing Power** -- Low fixed coupon bonds buy less goods when inflation rises.
5. **Reinvestment** -- Higher coupon bonds that mature in lower rate environment pay lower income.
6. **Currency** -- Unfavorable exchange rate movements lower the value of foreign bond interests and principal payments. Hence, overall returns drop.
7. **Yield Curve** -- Not all bonds are affected the same way by rising interest rates. Lower yielding bonds drop more in price than high yielding ones as rates rise. (Be sure to manage credit spread risk!)
8. **Liquidity** -- Cannot sell bond fund quickly at a fair price. Investors that buy longer-term maturities demand a liquidity premium.
9. **Price Volatility** -- Certain types of bonds are structured such that they present greater price sensitivity to changes in yields.
10. **Sector concentration** -- Heavy exposure to one sector can produce big losses. For example, there is a higher risk if over concentrated in the transportation sector during a recession, or spiking oil prices.
11. **Security concentration** -- Specific events, such as a merger, industrial accident, earthquakes, or business cycle change affect the ability of an issuer to pay interest and principal.

Risk management is the cornerstone of fixed-income investing. Generally, over a business cycle, returns among bond funds differ by the expense ratio of the funds. But the risk can vary significantly. Look at the results in Exhibit 10.14 for the five-year business cycle ending June 30, 2003, that included a recession and record Fed rate cuts.

Exhibit 10.14: Bond Mutual Fund Category Returns and Risk

	Avg. Return	Standard Deviation
Long-Term Bond	6.59%	5.74
Long Government	7.60%	9.79
Intermediate Bond	6.31%	3.83
Intermediate Government	6.38%	3.72
Short-term Government	5.70%	2.36
Short-term Bond	5.69%	2.15
Greatest difference	**1.91%**	**7.64**

Source: Morningstar June 30, 2003. Risk is measured by the standard deviation, which is an indicator of the portfolio's total return volatility. The larger the portfolio's standard deviation, the greater the portfolio's volatility. This table is for illustrative purposes only and does not predict or depict the performance of any investment. Investments in mutual funds involve risk. Past performance is no guarantee of future performance. Mutual funds incur fees and expenses (including investment management and administrative fees). Obtain a prospectus for more complete information about the fund, including all fees and expenses. Be sure to read carefully the fund prospectus before you invest. Investment returns and the principal value of a mutual fund will fluctuate, so that shares, when redeemed, may be worth more or less than their original cost. Past performance is no guarantee of future performance.

Risk Management Strategies

You will easily see that the greatest difference in return among the fixed-income categories is 1.91%, while the greatest difference in risk was 7.64! Most of the returns were within 1% of one another while there was greater dispersion in risk.

Bond fund risk management attempts to balance price risk, reinvestment risk, and purchasing power risk. When interest rates fall bond prices rise, but lower yields increase reinvestment risk. And when rates rise, falling bond prices cause losses, but reinvestment risk is not an issue.

Sometimes credit risk is an issue and other times it is not. Managers use various strategies such as a bullet, barbell or laddered approach towards managing risks. The appropriate strategy to use depends on the shape of the yield curve, current monetary policy, and the current phase of the business cycle.

Tactical risk management accomplishes two things:

- It maintains proper portfolio construction that balances all of the risks associated with fixed-income investing, and

- It keeps the portfolio in sync with global market conditions in an attempt to produce consistent positive annual total returns.

Without making periodic adjustments in response to changing conditions, you count on the portfolio getting out-of-whack with its stated objective and client's risk preference. In order to control fixed-income investing risks, the nine portfolio characteristics noted above (**D.Y.C.V.C.S.S.R.L.**) must be addressed in the construction and ongoing management.

As I have said numerous times throughout this book, to control risk, it is best to overweight asset classes that are favored by current conditions and are in accord with current Fed Policy actions and comments.

- **High yield bonds** flourish in a growing economy (GDP growth of three percent and greater) and accelerating EPS growth.

- **High quality bonds** -- such as Treasuries, Mortgage-backed (GNMA, FNMA, etc.) and Asset-backed -- thrive in deteriorating business conditions (GDP growth of less than three percent, and rising risk aversion).

- **Treasury issues** are typically hit the hardest when interest rates are on the rise. They are more sensitive to interest rate risk because they have no credit risk.

- **Mortgage-backed bonds** perform well in a rising rate environment because prepayments fall and yields rise, making them more attractive than other fixed-income alternatives.

- **Treasury Zero Coupon Bond** funds typically hit homes runs with double-digit returns when interest rates drop from a cyclical peak. Be sure to use the Confidence Index to determine whether to overweight corporate bonds or Treasuries.

Exhibit 10.15 summarizes the numerous changes a portfolio could experience as the market goes through a normal cycle.

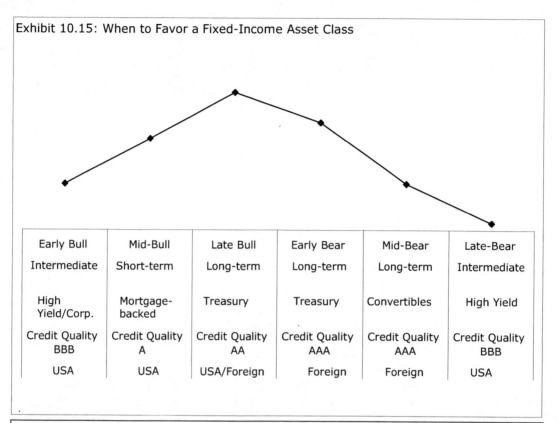

Exhibit 10.15: When to Favor a Fixed-Income Asset Class

Early Bull	Mid-Bull	Late Bull	Early Bear	Mid-Bear	Late-Bear
Intermediate	Short-term	Long-term	Long-term	Long-term	Intermediate
High Yield/Corp.	Mortgage-backed	Treasury	Treasury	Convertibles	High Yield
Credit Quality BBB	Credit Quality A	Credit Quality AA	Credit Quality AAA	Credit Quality AAA	Credit Quality BBB
USA	USA	USA/Foreign	Foreign	Foreign	USA

This table is for illustrative purposes only and does not predict or depict the performance of any investment. Investments in mutual funds involve risk. Past performance is no guarantee of future performance. Mutual funds incur fees and expenses (including investment management and administrative fees). Investment returns and the principal value of a mutual fund will fluctuate, so that shares, when redeemed, may be worth more or less than their original cost. Obtain a prospectus for more complete information about the fund, including all fees and expenses. The fund prospectus should be read carefully before you invest. Past performance is no guarantee of future performance.

Managing the D.Y.C.V.C.S.S.R.L of a Portfolio.

1. Strategies to Duration/Maturity Management

Let us start with the basics.

The average maturity measures the average time that will pass until a bond matures and the investor's principal is returned. Generally, the longer the maturity the greater the yield and price risk due to greater interest rate exposure -- how much price change due to a movement in interest rates. Exhibit 10.16 shows that a bond with longer term-to- maturity has greater potential price fluctuation.

Exhibit 10.16 Bond Maturity and Price Volatility

Type	Avg. Maturity	Price Fluctuation:
Money Market	1-12 mos.	None
Short-term Bond:	1-5 years	Low
Intermediate Bond:	5-12 years	Moderate
Long-term Bond:	12-30 years	High

This table is for illustrative purposes only and does not predict or depict the performance of any investment.

Interest Rate Changes and Duration

Why is managing a portfolio's duration a critical part of bond risk management?

Duration measures the price sensitivity of a bond to changes in interest rates. A 1991 study by Litterman and Scheinkman found that 90% of the variation in the total returns of Treasury securities was explained by changes in interest rate levels. The duration tells you the approximate percentage change in the price of the bond fund due to changes in interest rates. It works well with small changes in interest rates of up to 1%, but loses its accuracy with larger changes of more than 1%.

A fund with a longer average maturity will have a higher duration. Generally, short-term to intermediate-term bonds funds have smaller duration figures ranging from 1 to 7. Long-term bond funds have greater durations of more than 7. The duration of a bond or fund is always a smaller figure than the average maturity figure. Exhibit 10.17 shows which bonds typically sport greater duration numbers.

Exhibit 10.17 How Interest Rates Effect the Value of Bonds

Maturity	Rates Rise By 1%	Rates Decrease by 1%
Short-term	Value Drops 2.7%	Value Rises 2.8%
Intermediate term	Value Drops 5.5%	Value Rises 5.9%
Long-term	Value Drops 11%	Value Rises 13%

Source: T. Rowe Price. Short-term bonds represented by 1-year U.S. Government bonds for 1970-2001 period and Lehman Brothers 1-3 Year Government Bond Index thereafter; Intermediate-Term Government Bonds-5 Year U.S. Government Bond; Long-term Government Bonds-20-year U.S. Government Bond. This information is for illustrative purposes only and is not indicative of any particular investment. The data assumes reinvestment of all income and does not account for taxes or transaction costs. U.S. Government bonds are guaranteed by the full faith and credit of the United States Government as to timely payment of principal and interest. Bonds in a portfolio are typically intended to provide income and/or diversification. U.S. Government bonds may be exempt from state taxes, and income is taxed as ordinary income in the year received. With Government bonds, the investor is a creditor of the government. Past performance is no guarantee of future results.

What determines the price change of a bond due to interest rate changes?

There are three factors which include: maturity, coupon rate, and embedded options.

1. Term structure (**maturity**) of interest rates -- the longer the maturity of a bond, the greater the price change will be due to changes in the level of interest rates.
2. **Coupon rate** -- Low coupon rate bonds are more sensitive to interest rate changes than high coupon rate bonds.
3. **Embedded options** -- Bond features that favor the issuer (such as a call provision) make a bond more sensitive to interest rate changes and tend to increase its price volatility.

Bond Yields Move First, In Advance of Fed Actions

Think back to Chapter one. You may recall my explaining that when the Fed either adopts a restrictive or accommodative policy, the markets will typically anticipate the Fed's move and do the work for the Fed first, with the Fed following up with its particular action. That means that market yields will adjust upward or downward *before* the Fed raises or lowers its key rate -- the Fed Funds' rate.

This usually translates into market yields which can peak way before rate hikes are completed by the Fed. Typically, long-term bond yields peak when tightening is about 70% complete. You can apply the same rule for rate cuts.

It is best not to wait until interest rate cuts are a done deal. Bond prices climb faster than they drop so the first rate cut will produce a big jump in price! If you do not catch the wave of rate cuts early, you may miss the big gains!

It is a smart strategy to buy long-term bonds before the Fed is done with its tightening initiatives and start selling long-term bonds before the Fed completes its cuts. The bond market will have already priced into long-term bond prices any expected rate hikes and cuts. Therefore, it is better not to wait for the Fed to get the job done.

You can look to the yield curve to determine interest rate risk and, hence, which bond fund categories to underweight and overweight. If the yield curve is positive then rates are expected to rise. This means you should consider staying short in corporate bonds.

When the yield curve is negative rates are expected to fall. An overweight position in Treasury bonds is desirable. A flat yield curve suggests that market rates are expected to not change.

Strategies for a Rising Rate Environment

What is an appropriate tactic if rates are expected to rise?

When rates are trending upwards, it is prudent to stick with an overweight position in high yield bonds. High yield bonds are more defensive in an economy growing at three percent-plus and given that the Fed is not changing to a restrictive policy.

High quality bonds, such as Government bonds and investment grade bonds, are more sensitive to interest rate risk. It is a good idea to hold off on increasing exposure to these bond categories until rates have begun their ascent in the mid bull phase, or when rate hikes have already been factored into prices.

When yield spreads between Treasuries and high yield bonds narrow enough to wipe out the incentive to take greater credit risk, then it is smart to favor Treasuries over corporate bonds. Normally the yield spread between the short-end of the yield curve and long-end is 90 basis points according to Merrill Lynch. If the spread widens they stay short in your portfolio. Widen yield spreads imply faster economic growth. Not good news for Long term bonds.

It can also be a good idea to consider high quality floating rate securities. Floating rate bond mutual fund yields should rise as interest rates rise. Although these securities are considered speculative because they are non-investment grade, the floating rate securities market, as represented by the CSFB Leveraged Loan Index, has produced positive returns in every credit tightening cycle since 1990. The Fed Fund's rate was increased six times in 1994, one time in 1997, three times in 1999, three times in 2000, and the floating rate securities market's returns were 10.32%, 8.30%, 4.69%, and 4.94%, respectively in those specific years. (Source of information is Credit Suisse First Boston LLC. Floating Rate Loans are represented by the CSFB Leveraged Loan Index, a representative index of tradable, senior secured, U.S. dollar-denominated non-investment-grade loans. It is not possible for retail investors to invest directly in a floating rate loan index. Past performance is no guarantee of future results).

Floating rate bonds are attractive because they have less sensitivity to interest rate changes, have a low correlation with investment grade bonds, and may offer higher income than fixed-income bonds during periods of rising rates.

Strategies for a Declining Rate Environment

What tactic is appropriate if interest rates fall?

When rates are falling, resist the urge to invest your money in a mattress. Investing or reinvesting in low yield securities lowers income. When higher yields are hard to find, then it can be a good strategic decision to buy high yield bond funds. As rates drop default rates decline.

It is a good idea to decrease the weight held in mortgage-backed securities (MBS) when rates are falling. Mortgage-backed securities (MBS) do not benefit as much from a drop in interest rates as do long-term corporate or Treasury bonds.

MBS have limited upside potential compared to long-term bonds due to prepayment risk. Also be sure not to overweight MBS when rates are spiraling upward. When rates rise, prepayments associated with MBS slow down, leaving investor capital invested at lower rates than current higher market rates.

Instead, look for mortgage-backed funds that use collateralized mortgage obligations (CMOs) to manage the risk of MBS investing. There are CMOs that perform better when rates rise and ones that do well when rates fall. For instance, principal only (PO) CMOs perform well when interest rates drop because a borrower will prepay loans and the cash flow to PO bond holders increases thereby increasing the return on a PO.

The opposite is true with interest only (IO) CMOs. As interest rates fall they under perform, and when rates rise they outperform as the income stream increases.

Why change the duration of a portfolio?

In addition to managing the duration of a fixed-income portfolio to accommodate changes in the interest rate, it is important to manage a portfolio's duration because there are times when it does not always pay to go long on the yield curve. If yield spreads narrow, it implies slower economic growth. Good news for Long term bonds. The tactical trade is to extend your portfolio's duration when the yield spread between the short and long end of the yield curve is less than 90 basis points and shrinking.

From 1950 until 2002, U.S. Government intermediate bonds returned 6.58% with a standard deviation of 6.47, while the riskier Treasury bond sector returned on average 6.53% with a standard deviation of 10.84! No great reward for going longer (a measly 5 basis points of return), and look how much more risk was taken on (the standard deviation spread was 4.37).

Historical data show that the T-bonds sector's worst decline was -14.01%, compared to U.S. Government intermediate bonds -5.14% return. Thus, intermediate bonds are a core holding at all times, while long bond funds are tactical bets placed when the fed is easing rates.

The cost of Holding a Bond Until Maturity

Why not hold a bond until maturity? Doesn't that eliminate all the risk of bond investing?

Bond portfolio managers rarely hold bonds until maturity. Rather they actively manage the portfolio to manage investment risks and capitalize on investment opportunities created by changing bond market conditions. The **D.C.V.C.S.S.R.L.** factors of bond investing are constantly changing and effecting the value of a bond. It might actually be more profitable to sell a given bond then hold it to maturity. Sure, you get your money back, but that money could be worth far less given the inflation rate.

There is an opportunity cost to holding some bonds until maturity. Holding a low yielding bond when market rates rise could cost an investor a lot of income. The investor could earn more by selling low yielding bonds and investing the proceeds in newly issued higher yielding bonds.

Likewise, a premium bond that yields more than the market yield will lose its premiums when the bond matures. Therefore, it may be better to sell while the premium still exists and reinvest it a little latter on when interest rates go up again.

Conservative active portfolio management advocates following interest rate trends versus making anticipatory moves. For instance when rates trend upward, it is wise to shorten the average maturity of the fund and when rates decrease lengthen the maturity. Zero coupon bonds are very sensitive to interest rate changes and are a way to profit on changes in interest rates.

2. Strategies to Yield Management

Why do yields differ?

Yields differ among these fixed-income sectors because of credit quality differences and risk premiums due to the specific risks associated with each sector. For example, Industrials' (energy companies, manufacturers, etc.) yields are higher than Utilities (telephone, gas and electric companies) because they are sensitive to consumer demand, but Utilities are less impacted by business cycles.

Municipal yields are lower than corporate bond yields because their income is exempt from federal, state, and local taxation. Typically, Municipal bond yields are 10% to 30% lower than Treasury yields, and 30-70% lower than corporate bond yields. At certain times, on a tax-equivalent basis, municipals may yield more than Treasuries or certain investment grade corporate bonds.

You would be wise to investigate yield differentials of bond funds that have about the same credit ratings across bond fund categories -- Treasuries, mortgage-back, corporate within various industries -- to obtain the best yield. For example, historically, high quality mortgage-back securities yielded more than Treasury securities. Treasury securities usually yield less than high quality corporate bonds which yield less than high yield bonds.

Within each sector, there are categories of bonds where there exist yield differentials of 50 basis points between bonds of equivalent credit qualities.

Tactics for Widening or Narrowing Yield Spreads

You will want to overweight investment grade corporate bonds and Treasury issues when yield spreads begin to widen. You can also underweight Treasury issues and investment grade issues when yield spreads peak and overweight non-investment grade bonds.

You will also wish to consider an over weight of high quality mortgage-backed securities when interest rates are rising. The Merrill Lynch Mortgage Master Index posted positive returns in the 1994 and 1999 calendar years in spite of a series of Fed rate hikes. (The index, which consist of coupon bearing pools of mortgage pass-through securities that have various maturities, has no expenses, and investors cannot invested in it.)

It is a wise strategy to invest in international bonds when rates are higher abroad given that the U.S. dollar is weakening against major world currencies or is not expected to rise. When Treasury yields have hit cyclical lows, then you may want to overweight high yield bonds to increase income.

3. Strategies to Credit Quality Management

How is a bond's credit rating assessed?

Bond ratings are a way to assess the credit worthiness of an issuer's fixed-income securities. Higher ratings provide greater assurance that the loan will be paid back to bondholders. According to Standard & Poor's, the top four categories are investment grade ratings: AAA, AA, A, and BBB, and suitable for bank investments. Any rating lower than BBB is said to be speculative and non-investment grade, such as: BB, B, CCC ratings. Bonds rated CC, or C may be in default, and those rates DDD, DD, D are defaulted bonds.

The overall credit rating of a portfolio can be assessed by calculating a portfolio's weighted average credit rating. Generally, when a portfolio downgrades the average credit quality of the portfolio, the portfolio's yield will rise. An upgrade in average credit quality will result in a lower portfolio yield.

A higher credit rating doesn't guarantee that a fund will perform well, nor does insurance by a bond insurance agency like MBIA or AMBAC. Prices of bonds, not matter what the credit quality, will fluctuate due to changing market and economic conditions. Again, typically after a recession, high yield bonds have outperformed Government bonds. (Past performance is no guarantee of future performance).

Why manage a portfolio's credit quality?

As you know by now, the yield of a bond is the biggest contributor to its total return. The credit rating and maturity are major determinants of a bond's yield. Therefore, you can and should manage the credit quality of a portfolio to maximize income and total return.

Since U.S. Government has the highest credit rating in the world, the bonds it issues yield less than other issuers' yield and are safer. Investment grade corporate bonds pay higher yields than Treasuries, followed by lower rated investment grade bonds with BBB rated bonds paying the highest yields among corporate investment grade bonds. Non-investment grade bonds pay the highest yields, however, they are speculative investments.

There are times in the market cycle where low credits (non-investment grade) securities outperform high credits (investment grade). By tilting more into non-investment grade issues, a portfolio can enhance its yield and total return.

You can manage the credit quality of a portfolio to protect against losses. In general, according to a 2002 Sanford Bernstein study, you can expect 25% of the issuers to be downgraded. Default rates skyrocket higher as credit quality sinks lower in the non-investment grade credits. Annual default rates on high yield bonds have averaged 5% and ranged from 1.70% to 13% per year (Moody's study 2002). Default rates average 1.2% for Ba-rated bonds, 6.5% for B-rated bonds, and over 24.7% for Caa-rated bonds according to a 1970-2001 Moody's study.

Exhibit 10.17 shows the impact of a downgrade on a bond.

Exhibit 10.18: Estimated Price Change of A Downgrade

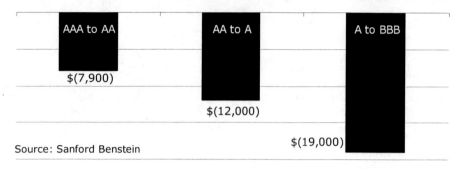

Source: Sanford Benstein

Managing with an Eye toward the Business Cycle

When just one single issue defaults on principal or interest in a bond fund, it will immediately lower the yield and the share price will also take a hit. When a bond defaults, the lender typically only recovers 38%, on average, of the loan amount (Moody's, 1995). Correlation analysis indicates that the high yield spread-versus-Treasuries leads shifts in the default rate by about six months.

You should manage a portfolio's credit quality with the business cycle in mind. In a recession downgrades spike upward and decline in an expansion. Empirical research indicates that year-over-year shifts of 5.0 percentage points or more in the distress ratio have consistently predicted changes in the direction of the default rate.

It is best to avoid lower credits when the distress ratios -- a leading indicator of default -- rise, and instead favor investment grade issuers. When the distress ratio declines by 5% or more, you would be well served to increase non-investment grade exposure, and vice versa. Therefore, late in the market cycle, specifically the late bull phase, a portfolio should emphasize high credit quality. In the early bull phase, it would be smart to favor low credit quality companies.

Bonds have a tough time overcoming "bad" return years because historically they have been low return investments. The equity market can overcome bad years more quickly than the bond market can because equities typically produce higher annual returns. Therefore, it is critical not to incur a down year due to losses resulting from defaults.

The most widely used credit risk management strategy is to broadly diversify among various bond sectors and own over 200 different bonds of numerous issuers.

In a rising rate environment, it is best to favor higher yielding bonds so long as Fed rate increases do not kill the economic expansion. You can stick with this strategy into the late stages of a bull market. High yield bond have both stock and bond characteristics. They appreciate in value with good news on EPS growth, while generating high yields. High yield bond prices respond more to equity market news than monetary policy. Thus, you would be wise to overweight high yield bond fund positions after rates have dropped and based upon improving earnings expectations.

4. Strategies for Volatility Management

Why must fixed-income volatility be managed even if the approach is a "hold-to-maturity" approach?

Simply put, bond money is usually safe money or the "insurance" part of a portfolio, so why subject it to unnecessary volatility?

How is volatility measured?

Both duration and convexity are measures of a bond's volatility. They are calculated by figuring in the bond's term to maturity, coupon, market price, and call provision. Think of duration and convexity as a rubber band: Duration measures how far the rubber band will stretch (price will go up); convexity determines how fast it will snap back (price will go down). Long-term bonds have greater duration and convexity than short-to-intermediate bonds, and thus, are more volatile.

Interest rates fluctuate over time effecting bond prices. Market volatility can wipe out any yield differentials among long-term bonds and short-term bonds. Price volatility is higher than when yields are low. Any small change in yields has a big effect on price. In a declining interest rate environment, bonds reap big price gains. When yields are high, the price curve is flatter.

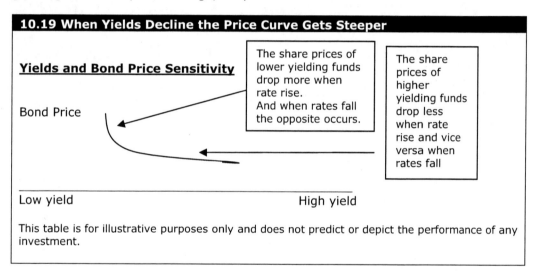

10.19 When Yields Decline the Price Curve Gets Steeper

Yields and Bond Price Sensitivity

Bond Price

The share prices of lower yielding funds drop more when rate rise.
And when rates fall the opposite occurs.

The share prices of higher yielding funds drop less when rate rise and vice versa when rates fall

Low yield   High yield

This table is for illustrative purposes only and does not predict or depict the performance of any investment.

Bond prices rise a lot faster than they fall because they have positive convexity. Bond prices are less sensitive to changes in interest rates when yields are high, and very sensitive to changes in interest rates when yields are low. That is why it makes sense to overweight high yield bonds up until the late bull phase.

After rates have risen and low yielding Treasuries have been beaten up in price, at this point in the cycle (late bull) you can overweight long Treasuries.

Courting Convertibles

You will want to consider buying convertible bonds and Treasury bonds when stock market volatility picks up, usually in the late bull phase. Convertibles tend to increase in value when there is more volatility. Moreover, if heightened volatility due to bearish fundamentals turns into a market decline, convertibles tend to outperform stocks.

Convertibles also can do better than stocks where the market is trading in a tight trading range that it appears it cannot break out of -- such as with flat, or low return years in stock market performance.

You can do just the opposite during the early bull phase of the market cycle, when volatility diminishes and the market rallies. That is generally the perfect time to underweight convertibles which tend to under perform stocks on the upside.

In addition, you can minimize exposure to derivatives that leverage the assets of the fund, such as interest only (I.O.s), and principal only (P.O.s), structured notes, inverse floaters, and callable bonds because they tend to create more volatility. Bonds that have embedded options also have greater price variability. Manage volatility by buying Intermediate bonds that are two-thirds less volatile than long-term bonds, are shorter in duration, and lower in convexity.

5. Strategies for Currency Management

What is the easiest way to manage currency risk?

Currency risk can be managed by keeping fixed-income investments limited to domestic markets, although avoiding international markets could hurt total returns, income potential, and growth in purchasing power. You may wish to favor U.S. markets when U.S. inflation is falling, the economy is growing normally, trade deficit is not disruptive, and real interest rates are relatively high.

You may be wise to increase foreign bond exposure as the U.S. dollar weakens due to a slowing U.S economy, where the U.S. has a relatively big trade deficit and account deficit, and where there are lower real U.S rates.

Overall, it is a good idea to favor domestic bonds to lower the currency risk of international bonds, and any geopolitical risk. You can own international bonds to reduce total investment risk, and enhance returns. In the best case scenario, you would earn higher returns from the international bonds portion of a portfolio rising in value, and get a foreign currency kicker, too.

6. Strategies for Purchasing Power Management

Good bond investments protect the principal in a portfolio against the effects of inflation. As mentioned earlier in this book, higher inflation erodes the purchasing power of fixed coupon payments. The 30-day T-bill averaged an inflation-adjusted return of 1.14% from 1950 to 2002. After taxes and expenses, T-bills produced negative returns.

Therefore, it is important to make sure a significant part of a bond portfolio is invested in intermediate bonds with maturity of greater than two years. Government intermediate bonds produced a 2.6% inflation adjusted average annual return from 1950 to 2002. That return, after taking inflation and taxes into account, was high enough to maintain purchasing power.

Holding a fixed-income investment until maturity could result in a loss in purchasing power. By buying and holding until maturity, a 30-year Government bond from 1950 up to the mid-1980s would have produced a negative inflation adjusted return. From the mid-1980s on, inflation was low and the inflation-adjusted returns were positive.

Anytime a fixed-income investment yielding 4% or less is bought, the risk of losing purchasing power is greater. Historically, inflation has averaged 4% per year from 1950 to 2002. After inflation, taxes, and expenses the actual return is negative.

If inflation trends above 4%, then the loss in purchasing power is even greater. Long-term Government bonds yielded 6.48% from 1950-2002. Buying them around 4% and holding them until maturity can become a risky investment. Sure, the principal is returned when it matures, but it could be worth less in terms of purchasing power.

7. Strategies for Sector Concentration/Selection

Sector selection and rotation attempts to identify attractive sectors based upon yield spreads and risk/reward characteristics. You can impose constraints because if a mistake is made in sector picks the bond portfolio will not deviate wildly from its benchmark -- hopefully only by one standard deviation.

Suppose the combined exposure to companies within the financial services sector (banks, brokerage houses, and insurance companies) was greater than 50% in a rising interest rate environment. Your bond portfolio would certainly under perform your benchmark. Generally, as rates rise to levels that curb consumer borrowing and decrease the amount of discretionary income to invest, financial service firms earnings growth slows down. Fifty percent of your portfolio would be in a sector not favored by business conditions. It is a prudent step to limit sector concentration to 50% less or 50% more than the Lehman Brothers Aggregate Bond sector weight. Overvalued sectors -- such as U.S. Treasuries in 2002 and high yield finance bonds in 2000 -- should have an under weight, and so on.

Bond sector selection depends on the phase of the business cycle. Here are some guidelines as to what to favor when:

-- In the trough to recovery phase, it is best to favor high yield investments.
-- In the recovery to expansion phase, it is smart to incorporate a mix of high yield and corporate bonds.
-- In the expansion to peak phases, you would want to overweight mortgage-backed, high quality asset-backed (adjustable rate bank loans), and Treasuries.
-- In the post-peak phase, you will likely desire to stick with Treasury bonds.
-- During the peak to trough decline, a mix of convertible bonds and Treasuries will serve you well.
-- And, from trough to the bottom, high yield bonds should be favored once again.

8. Strategies for Security Concentration/Selection

Security concentration is a big bet that can really hurt a portfolio if things go wrong with a firm.

Typically, bond managers will limit each position to 3% to 5% of the portfolio's assets. In addition, credit-sensitive issuers will rarely exceed 5%. Government issues can represent as much as 10% to 20% positions.

Managers would be best served by performing security analysis, with particular emphasis on credit analysis. Buy only companies with sound balance sheets and that generate free cash flow, and steer clear of companies that look too good to be true (because they usually are!)

9. Strategies for Managing Reinvestment Risk

When a higher coupon bond matures in a lower coupon environment, the proceeds can only be invested in lower yielding bonds. The net effect is lower future income and return.

Reinvestment risk is greater with long-term bond funds than shorter-term, and can be minimized by investing in short-to-intermediate bond funds and zero coupon bond funds. Limit mortgage-backed/asset-backed fund positions to 10% to 20%. You can also invest in zero coupon bond funds and intermediate bond funds to reduce reinvestment risks.

10. Strategies for Managing Liquidity

It is important to make sure that there is sufficient liquidity in a portfolio by owning an adequate amount of short-term high quality bonds. During times of economic uncertainty, investors demand a greater liquidity. In addition, investors that hold long-term bonds demand a liquidity premium. It is best to choose bonds funds that are liquid, and avoid funds that only allow quarterly redemptions. Prime rate funds are an example of the latter.

Is it prudent to diversify by investing in a single state tax-exempt bond fund and a nationally diversified tax-exempt bond fund?

A nationally diversified portfolio of municipal bonds has potentially less risk than a single state municipal bond fund. If the bonds of a single state are downgraded the value of a single state tax-exempt bond fund could decline by a significant amount.

A nationally diversified portfolio allows the portfolio manager to invest in a large pool of high quality, state, city, and local municipal bonds. This added flexibility allows a manager to avoid states in which bonds are being downgraded and invest in states that offer higher yields. In most cases, single state funds yield no more than fifty basis points more, on average, than a nationally diversified tax-exempt bond fund. There is also a federal income tax offset on any state taxes paid on out of state bonds, reducing the yield advantage. At the same time, investors are buying into more risk. At some point the risk of concentrating outweighs the higher yield benefit.

How-to of Cash-equivalent Management

Why actively use cash-equivalents with investment management?

Cash-equivalents are an excellent way to build up liquidity in a portfolio, offset equity risk, and lower fluctuation in the overall value of a portfolio. But be sure to never use it for market timing purposes. Cash-equivalents act as a liquidity vehicle that can be tapped into when needed during emergencies or when the market corrects.

Money market funds serve as a "safe haven" for money which investors plan to spend within a couple of years. They are ideal to use as an emergency fund. These are "Lazy Assets" because money invested in cash-equivalents for the long term usually does not works as hard as money invested in equities. Returns have historically been higher in equities than cash-equivalents over long periods of time.

Therefore, only park enough money in cash equivalents to meet an investor's short-term obligations; perhaps a year's worth or so, of expenses depending upon someone's financial condition, plus enough to lower downside risk enough so the client can sleep soundly at night.

> **Insider Tip:** Instead of a money market fund, consider parking short-term assets in an ultra short bond fund. They can invest in fixed-income securities with maturities slightly greater than one year. Consequently, while the duration of an ultra short bond fund tends to be greater than a money market fund, the yield tends to be higher, too. Moreover, they have not had a one down year since Morningstar started tracking them in 1983. In addition, their return and yield has been consistently higher than money market funds. But only select ultra short bond funds that are investment grade! (Investments in mutual funds involve risk. Past performance is no guarantee of future performance. Mutual funds incur fees and expenses (including investment management and administrative fees). Investment returns and the principal value of a mutual fund will fluctuate, so that shares, when redeemed, may be worth more or less than their original cost. Obtain a prospectus for more complete information about the fund, including all fees and expenses. Carefully read the prospectus before you invest. Past performance is no guarantee of future performance).

Exhibit 10.20 illustrates how cash-equivalents can turn a riskier portfolio into the always better Northwest quadrant portfolio by lowering the overall portfolio's risk (standard deviation).

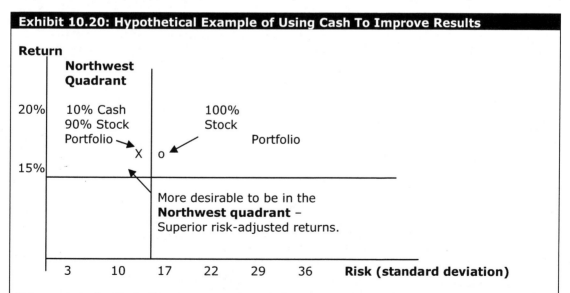

Exhibit 10.20: Hypothetical Example of Using Cash To Improve Results

This graph is for illustrative purposes only and does not predict or depict the performance of any investment. Standard deviation is an indicator of the portfolio's total return volatility. The larger the portfolio's standard deviation, the greater the portfolio's volatility.

What makes cash-equivalents an excellent investment tool to use with portfolio management?

Cash-equivalents is an asset class that has a low covariance with equities and, thus, is a true diversifying investment. Even a long-term investor who owns a broadly diversified portfolio of large-cap, and mid-to-small-cap equities is not well diversified. Why? When the market corrects, the value of the portfolio will drop because all of the investments belong to the same asset class -- equities.

To properly diversify, it is best to combine asset classes that have a low covariance with one another.

Exhibit 10.21: Correlation Matrix 1950-2002 Period.

	S&P 500 Index
Three-month T-Bill:	-0.016

Source: The Federal Reserve, Standard & Poor's. The three month Treasury Bill Index is derived from secondary market Treasury bill rates published by The Federal Reserve Bank or the 91-day Treasury bills data. The S&P 500 is a total return index widely regarded as the standard for measuring large-cap U.S. stock market performance and includes a representative sample of 500 leading companies based on industry representation, liquidity, and stability. Historically the index includes 400 industrial stocks, 40 financial stocks, 40 public utility stocks, and 20 transportation stocks. Indices include reinvested income, but not transaction costs or taxes, are unmanaged and cannot be purchased directly by investors. This chart is for illustrative purposes only and does not predict or depict the performance of any investment. Past performance is no guarantee of future performance. An investor cannot invest directly in an index, and its results are not indicative of any specific investment.

Should cash-equivalents be part of a portfolio even when the market is advancing and fundamentals look terrific?

In a word -- yes! You should always own cash-equivalents in a portfolio, even if a small percentage of assets are invested there. The benefits are greater liquidity and lower volatility, without significantly lowering long-term returns. Take a look at exhibit 10.22 and 10.23 to see what I mean.

Exhibit 10.22: A Fifty-fifty Mix of Treasury Bills and Stocks Captured 70% of the Equity Market Return with Approximately Half the Volatility

Portfolio	Mix	10-yr. return	Standard Deviation
S&P 500 Index	100%	11.17%	20.74
S&P/T-bill	50%/50%	7.78%	11.03

Source: The Federal Reserve, Standard & Poor's. Data is for the period ending 2002. Standard deviation is an indicator of the portfolio's total return volatility. The larger the portfolio's standard deviation, the greater the portfolio's volatility. The S&P 500 index is comprised of 500 U.S. stocks and is an indicator of the performance of the overall U.S. stock market. T-bill or cash is represented by three month Treasury Bill Index derived from secondary market Treasury bill rates published by The Federal Reserve Bank or the 91-day Treasury bills data. No fees or expenses are reflected in the performance of the index. An investor cannot invest directly in an index, and its results are not indicative of any specific investment.

What is the cheapest, simplest form of portfolio insurance?

Cash-equivalents are the easiest and cheapest way to partially hedge a portfolio. It will not offset losses due to a declining market, but it could dampen those losses.

Exhibit 10.23: A 10% Cash Position Lowered Downside Risk Without Sacrificing Long-term Returns.

Portfolio	Mix	10 yr. return	Max. Decline
S&P 500 Index	100%	11.17%	-37.61
S&P 500 Index/T-bill	90%/10%	10.05%	-29.46

Source: The Federal Reserve, Standard & Poor's. Data is for the period ending 2002. The S&P 500 index is comprised of 500 U.S. stocks and is an indicator of the performance of the overall U.S. stock market. T-bill or cash is represented by the three month Treasury Bill Index as derived from secondary market Treasury bill rates published by The Federal Reserve Bank or the 91-day Treasury bills data. Investment returns and principal value of a mutual fund will fluctuate, so that shares, when redeemed, may be worth more or less than their original cost. No fees or expenses are reflected in the performance of the index. An investor cannot invest directly in an index, and its results are not indicative of any specific investment.

When do cash-equivalents become even more attractive as an investment alternative?

When interest rate hikes begin, cash eventually becomes king!

Cash is a good alternative investment when inflation is persistently trending upward towards five percent. This has occurred in a period of rising rates. If you believe that the Fed will make a preemptive strike on inflation before inflationary pressures exist in the economy, then raising cash in the portfolio may be a smart tactical move.

A classic example of when to increase cash was in 1993 when the Fed comments alluded to a rate hike. In 1994, rates were increased six times, bonds had one of their most dreadful years on record, and stocks went nowhere. In addition, as the market cycle matures you can move to a neutral position.

Exhibit 10.24: Cash Has Been a Good Short-term Inflation Hedge

Year	Inflation	Stocks	Bonds	Cash-equivalents
1970	5.49%	+ 4.00%	+12.11%	+ 6.52%
1973	8.80%	-14.66%	- 1.11%	+ 6.93%
1977	6.77%	- 7.19%	- 0.69%	+ 5.12%
1981	8.94%	- 4.91%	+ 1.86%	+14.71%
1990	6.11%	- 3.17%	+ 6.18%	+ 7.81%

Source: Standard & Poor's, Lehman Brothers, The Federal Reserve, National Bureau of Economic Research. Data is for the 1970-2002 period. Stocks are represented by the S&P 500 index. The S&P 500 index is comprised of 500 U.S. stocks and is an indicator of the performance of the overall U.S. stock market. Bonds are represented by Lehman Brother Aggregate Bond Index. The Lehman Brothers Aggregate Bond Index is a market-capitalization weighted index of investment-grade fixed-rate debt issues, including government, corporate, asset-backed, and mortgage-backed securities, with maturities of at least one year. Cash is represented by the three month Treasury Bill Index derived from secondary market Treasury bill rates published by the Federal Reserve Bank or the 91-day Treasury bills data. Inflation figures obtained from National Bureau of Economic Research. Investment returns and principal value of a mutual fund will fluctuate, so that shares, when redeemed, may be worth more or less than their original cost. No fees or expenses are reflected in the performance of the index. An investor cannot invest directly in an index, and its results are not indicative of any specific investment. Past performance is no guarantee of future results.

During certain years, investors will be pleasantly surprised to learn that cash has outperformed other asset classes in a portfolio. Historically, cash-equivalents have outperformed stocks and bonds about 11% of the time from 1926-2003. Moreover, cash-equivalents were the second best performing asset class approximately 30% of the time from 1983 through 2003!

Exhibit 10.25: Cash-equivalents Is Sometimes a Top Performer

of Years Top Performer

Stocks	33
Bonds	12
Cash-equivalents	10

Source: Standard & Poor's, Lehman Brothers, The Federal Reserve. Data is for 1950-2004 period. U.S. stocks are represented by the S&P 500 index. The S&P 500 index is comprised of 500 U.S. stocks and is an indicator of the performance of the overall U.S. stock market. Bonds are represented by Lehman Brothers Aggregate Bond Index. The Lehman Brothers Aggregate Bond Index is a market-capitalization weighted index of investment-grade fixed-rate debt issues, including government, corporate, asset-backed, and mortgage-backed securities, with maturities of at least one year. Cash-equivalents are represented by the three month Treasury Bill Index as derived from secondary market Treasury bill rates published by The Federal Reserve Bank or the 91-day Treasury bills data. No fees or expenses are reflected in the performance of the index. An investor cannot invest directly in an index, and its results are not indicative of any specific investment. Past performance is no guarantee of future results.

About the Author

Patrick T. Byrne has more than twenty years experience in the investment management and advisory business. In his present position he serves as Chief Investment Officer for Aspetuck Financial Management LLC, a Registered Investment Advisor. Before founding Aspetuck Financial Management LLC, he served as Chief Investment Officer for Reby Advisory Services, a sizeable independent Registered Investment Adviser. While at Reby Advisory Services, the mutual fund portfolios he managed beat their respective benchmarks. While employed at USAA Investment Management Company he was responsible for sales distribution of mutual funds, fund wrap, and separate account investments. At USAA Investment Management Co. he developed a capital markets research program used to advise clients. Prior to joining USAA Investment Management Co., Mr. Byrne headed Neuberger Berman Management's business that manages portfolios of mutual fund holdings for institutions and retail investors. He helped launch the business and managed the fund wrap portfolios from 1996 through 2001. The institutional mutual fund portfolios he managed beat their respective benchmarks from inception on July 1, 1999 through 2001. He served as a member of the Advisory Services Investment Policy committee chaired by the firm's Chief Investment Officer. Mr. Byrne designed Neuberger Berman Management's fund wrap asset allocation program that established portfolio guidelines for construction and recommended tactical investment strategies. He also wrote the quarterly market commentary report.

Mr. Byrne has been a guest speaker on investing at numerous investor seminars and conferences. He has appeared on local TV shows, channels 23, 12, and 8, and on radio shows, Money Talk, and Your Money, speaking about the economy, markets, and investing. Mr. Byrne served as a practicing editor for the College for Financial Planning's Chartered Mutual Fund Counselor program and has been quoted for articles written in Smart Money, Money magazine, CBS market watch, Ticker, Fortune magazine, and the Wall Street journal.

Mr. Byrne studied economics at the University of New Hampshire, and graduated with honors from Baruch College with a B.B.A. degree in finance. He earned an M.B.A. from the University of Connecticut. He is a Certified Financial Planner™, and passed his Level I Chartered Financial Analyst exam.

He is married, has three children, Mark, Connor, and Brooke, and lives in Fairfield, Connecticut.

ISBN 1-41204311-5

9 781412 043113